Corporate Trust
Administration and Management

Corporate Trust

Administration and Management

FOURTH EDITION

Robert I. Landau

COLUMBIA UNIVERSITY PRESS

NEW YORK

Columbia University Press
New York   Oxford

Copyright © 1961, 1974 New York University Press
Copyright © 1985, 1992 Columbia University Press
All rights reserved

Library of Congress Cataloging-in-Publication Data
Landau, Robert I.
    Corporate trust administration and management / Robert I. Landau.
    —4th ed.
        p.   cm.
    Includes bibliographical references and index.
    ISBN 0-231-07670-3 (acid-free)
        1. Trust indentures—United States.   I. Title.
    KF1457.L36   1992
    346.73'0666—dc20
    [347.306666]   91–35147
                                                                         CIP

Casebound editions of Columbia University Press books are
Smyth-sewn and printed on permanent
and durable acid-free paper.

Printed in the United States of America

c 10 9 8 7 6 5 4 3 2 1

Contents

Preface

Thirty years ago the definitive work on corporate trust administration was written by the late Joseph C. Kennedy to fulfill the need for a teaching vehicle that would provide administrators in the emerging corporate trust industry with a systematic approach for learning the fundamentals of identure trustee administration.

In both the second and third editions, published in 1975 and 1985 respectively, I attempted to keep to the original concept of a teaching vehicle for a new generation of account managers, administrators, and operations specialists. In the latter revision I began the process of enlarging the scope of the book's coverage so that it would be useful also as an ongoing reference work for anyone who might be involved in or with the corporate trust industry. This necessitated the inclusion of a completely new section addressing the issues involved in the management of the corporate trust function and its relevance to the training and development of both managers and the technical/professional staff, a compendium of sample forms and checklists, a bibliography for those seeking to broaden their knowledge of the subjects covered, and an extensive glossary of securities industry terms.

In the current edition, I have continued the pattern I used earlier; older corporate trust managers (and there are a few left!) will recognize the same fundamental musical score, but with extensive changes in most of the lyrics. These revisions reflect the momentous events which have occurred in the capital markets and securities industry during the past six years, and the significant changes resulting from the enactment of the Trust Indenture Reform Act of 1990. In addition I have included discussion about the increased use of asset-backed collateral transactions, the impact of "event risk", the potential effect of significantly increased secondary market disclosure on trustees, the ongoing problems surrounding the payment of trustee's fees and expenses, the potential for environmental liability, and the increasing trend toward immobilization of securities certificates. Much greater emphasis has been placed on the administration of municipal trusteeships and operations/ product delivery activities of the corporate trust function.

In addition to updating and expanding the Exhibits, Bibliography, and Glossary, I have also included (at long last) the complete text of the Trust Indenture Act, as amended by the 1990 Reform Act. Now none of my colleagues in our industry can claim they don't have access to the basic legislation governing the administration of corporate trusteeships!

It is very evident that the changes I have indicated coupled with the fundamental shifts that have occurred in both the corporate trust function and the entire securities industry must be carefully considered, understood, and applied by every participant in this business to his or her activities. The players are clearly not limited to indenture account managers, administrators, and operations specialists, but include all those persons engaged in the drafting of debt financing instruments and documents and the marketing of bond issues, as well as those who are accountable for the establishment and implementation of statutes, rules, regulations, and other standards of performance applicable to the corporate trust industry.

Many of the problems present today are not necessarily caused by the participants in the corporate trust industry, but it is quite evident that those in the industry will have to function in an environment which is significantly and dramatically influenced by events, transactions, and general economic conditions occurring in *all* the capital markets, both domestic and international. The future demands not only an acute sense of alertness to the changing and very volatile financial environment but also the flexibility to meet the requirements of changing patterns of both debt financing and the processing of securities, funds, and information. To become a successful corporate trust professional as this industry moves into the last part of this century still requires a sound understanding of the basic concepts and principles together with a great deal of imagination, plain old savvy, and a deep commitment to acceptance of responsibility.

As with the earlier editions, I owe a debt of gratitude to literally hundreds of people with whom I have worked, studied, and taught over the past thirty years, including my former associates at Bankers Trust Company (many of whom have made me proud of their accomplishments and success in other organizations as well), individuals in other corporate trust organizations throughout the country, and scores of investment bankers, lawyers, members of federal regulatory agencies, and members of banking and securities industry associations—all of whom contributed to my education and understanding of this dynamic and changing industry.

I wish to acknowledge, with my deepest appreciation and thanks, the very important and meaningful contributions the following people made to this edition: Margaret "Meg" Allan, Anne R. Boer, William H. Berls, James F. Conlan, Robert I. Halpern, Linda L. Patterson, Jeffrey J. Powell, Ralph W. Renninghoff, John W. Rupley, and Donald M. Wilkinson. Any errors, minor or major, are mine alone.

And, for her unbridled spirit and constant encouragement during the past months of personal and professional changes, my eternal thanks to my wife, Valerie.

Robert I. Landau

I

Administration

A trustee is held to something stricter than the morals of the marketplace. Not honesty alone, but the punctilio of an honor the most sensitive, is then the standard of behavior.   —Justice Benjamin N. Cardozo
Meinhard v. Salmon
249 N.Y. 458, 464 (1928)

[A]n indenture trustee is not subject to the ordinary trustee's duty of undivided loyalty. Unlike the ordinary trustee, who has historic common-law duties imposed beyond those in the trust agreement, an indenture trustee is more like a stakeholder whose duties and obligations are exclusively defined by the terms of the indenture agreement.

Judge Richard J. Cardamone
Meckel v. Continental Resources
758 F.2d 811 (2d Cir. 1985)

Introduction

The study of corporate trust and the administration of the provisions of indenture contracts, including the servicing of debt obligations issued under indentures, bond resolutions, or other agreements is difficult, time consuming, and complex. It requires a basic understanding of the principles of corporate finance and fiduciary law, as well as detailed knowledge of relevant federal legislation and regulation governing the rights, duties, and liabilities of the debt issuer, the corporate trustee, and the security holders.

The ensuing chapters in part one are designed to thoroughly familiarize the corporate trust administrator and account officer, operations supervisor, and manager with such legislation and regulation and with the appropriate principles, policies, and procedures that together constitute the fundamentals of "doing the work." Explanatory and supplementary footnotes have been included to provide additional clarity and references to appropriate books, articles, statutes, regulations, and judicial decisions.

The whole spectrum of activities and responsibilities involved in administering the trust indenture contract and its related agency services has been undergoing an evolutionary process for almost a century. Many of the statutory and regulatory changes have, however, been most evident during the past ten years. Given the rapidly changing and volatile nature of the securities market, there is every reason to believe that this evolutionary process will not only continue but do so at an accelerated rate. Nevertheless, a sound understanding of the "basics" is essential to provide the corporate trust practitioner with the knowledge competencies to properly discharge his or her duties as a corporate trust professional.

ONE

Some General Principles of Corporate Finance

The corporate trust indenture is undoubtedly one of the most involved financial documents that has been devised. Even though development of a simplified or plain language form of indenture provided for a wider and easier comprehension of indenture provisions,[1] the administration of any indenture requires highly skilled and experienced personnel.

While a full discussion of the problems of corporate organization and finance is beyond the scope of this book, a basic knowledge and understanding of their essential features are important even to the beginner in the field. As a preliminary, therefore, this chapter considers some of the essential concepts involved in the corporate form of business enterprise and the financing thereof.

THE CORPORATE FORM OF BUSINESS ENTERPRISE

The most common form of business enterprise is the individual proprietorship in which is invested only the individual's own capital. The owner operates the business alone or with one or more employees and is entitled to all the profits realized or, conversely, suffers the losses. If the business should fail, not only the assets of the business but also all the personal assets of the proprietor are liable for payment of business creditors. The partnership is similar in nature and, in effect, simply

[1] Model Simplified Indenture, 38 *Bus. Law.* 741 (Feb. 1983)

involves the association of two or more individual proprietors in a common business undertaking. Essential features of both these forms are the direct participation of the owners in the operation of the business and their unlimited liability for debts of the business.[2]

The corporate form of business enterprise is a different matter. A creature of the industrial revolution, it has been essential to the growth and development of the industrialized economies with which we are familiar from the time of the British mercantile companies that were organized for colonial development.

A corporation is a creature of the state and exists only by reason of a charter granted by the state. In the early days of the United States a corporation could be created only by special legislative enactment. Such a special charter was granted after careful consideration and usually was for a very special and limited purpose. Some corporations still exist with charters so granted. Today, however, all states have general incorporation laws, and the creation of a corporation is relatively simple.

Because a corporation is a creature of the state it can exercise only such powers as are specifically granted it by the state. These powers are enumerated in the corporate charter that is a basic document of every corporation. Incorporators may include in a proposed charter any power not prohibited by law or contrary to public policy. It is therefore the general practice for every charter to include a very broad grant of powers. From the viewpoint of corporate indenture financing, essential powers that must be set forth are the right to borrow money and the right to mortgage and pledge assets of the corporation as security therefor. If a corporation performs or purports to perform an act for which it does not have authority in its charter, such an act is said to be *ultra vires,* and as such may constitute a defense in a suit against the corporation arising from the act so performed.

A corporation is subject not only to the limitations contained in its charter but also to all laws and regulations promulgated by the legislature or a regulatory authority of the state of incorporation in addition to those of any federal agency having jurisdiction over the corporation or its business activities.

Another important corporate document is the corporate bylaws. By-laws are essentially rules of procedure adopted by the stockholders and they can be amended at any time by a vote of the stockholders. They set

---

[2] Most states provide for the creation of limited partnerships, which limit the liability of the limited partners (as opposed to the general, or managing, partners) to the amount of money each has invested in the business.

forth such things as the form of the certificates of stock; the frequency, locations, and dates of stockholder meetings; procedures for calling special meetings; the scope and functions of the board of directors and the various committees; the powers and duties of the principal officers; and such other basic rules as may be necessary for or pertinent to the continued functioning of the corporate entity.

Stockholders are the owners of the business and as such are entitled to a vote in the management of its affairs in proportion to their ownership of the outstanding stock. They are also entitled to share in the profits of the corporation—but only through such dividends as may be declared from time to time by the corporate directors. Such rights of ownership, however, differ markedly from those involved in other forms of business enterprises. Stockholders, as such, do not participate directly in the management of the corporate business. They are also protected by the limited liability involved in the corporate form of business. If a venture fails, the stockholder's investment in the business is likely to be lost, but his/her personal assets are not liable for the payment of corporate debts.

The purchase of stock in a particular corporation usually results from a desire to make a profitable investment of savings or excess funds rather than from a desire to participate in a particular type of business venture. It is generally recognized that such investments are for the purpose of receiving income through receipt of dividend payments or profits from the eventual sale of the stock at a higher price, or both. The concept of the pooling of funds of many individuals to make possible the conduct of business on the vast scale we know today was the great contribution of the corporate form of business enterprise.

Management of a corporation is vested in a board of directors elected by the stockholders. In some cases this board is made up entirely of people who are active officers of the corporation, but it is more common in publicly held corporations for some of the directors to be drawn from prominent members of the community who are engaged primarily in other professions. The diversity of interests and viewpoints thus brought together is often helpful to the enterprise. Regardless of the composition of the board, the directors are primarily responsible for the affairs of the corporation and may become individually liable and accountable in other ways for unwarranted acts of the corporation.

Active management of corporate affairs is delegated to a corporate staff whose members devote their entire time to the enterprise. These officers are appointed by the board and their functions are set forth in the bylaws or are prescribed by resolutions of the board. An officer has only such authority as is specifically granted or necessarily implied, and anyone dealing with a corporation should be certain of the authority of the officials with whom he or she deals and of what constitutes proper authorization of any contract or undertaking.

CORPORATE FINANCIAL STATEMENTS

The activities of a corporation are summarized in the records that the corporate officers are required to maintain. These records show the results of operations for designated periods and are forwarded periodically to stockholders, creditors, and others. It is customary to have these records audited at least annually by a firm of independent public accountants which furnishes a certificate of examination. Whenever a corporation issues securities publicly it must file certified financial statements with the Securities and Exchange Commission ("SEC") and with each corporate trustee of its public debt securities.

Regulated industries, such as railroads, public utilities, banks, and similar corporations, are required to maintain their records in a uniform manner as prescribed by the particular regulatory authority having jurisdiction over them. Other corporations are not so restricted, so there may be some differences in the details required from various types of companies. In general, however, the development of modern accounting techniques and procedures and the requirements of federal tax regulations ensure substantial uniformity in the form and content of financial statements.

It is essential for the corporate trust practitioner to be familiar with financial statements and to be able to review and analyze them intelligently. A discussion of the financial statements ordinarily prepared follows.

Balance Sheet

The balance sheet presents the condition of a corporation as of a particular moment in its history. It also may be said to reflect the cumulative results of the company's operations from its inception to the date when the statement is rendered.

Assets represent the things that the corporation owns or is owed, together with the investment or other use of funds that have heretofore come into its hands. Assets are customarily classified as "current" or "fixed." Current assets include cash and such items as will be converted into cash in the normal operations of the business. Among such items are temporary investments, receivables (amounts owed by the company's customers), and inventories (either raw materials awaiting processing or finished goods available for sale). Fixed assets include whatever buildings and real property that the company owns and uses in the conduct of its business; permanent investments that the company may have in other companies; and other types of property that may be necessary or incidental to its operations, but that are normally not held for resale. Such things as goodwill, patents, trademarks, and franchise rights are intangibles and may be included as assets if they have a real value. Another term frequently employed is "tangible assets," which include all assets other than goodwill, patents, and other such intangibles which would have little, if any, value upon the liquidation of the business.

Assets are "balanced" against an equal amount of liabilities plus capital, which represent the source of funds by which the corporate assets were acquired. Current liabilities are the amounts due and payable within a specified period of time—usually a year—and incurred primarily in connection with normal business operations. The current asset and current liability accounts are considered the company's working capital accounts, and the excess of current assets over current liabilities is usually referred to as "working capital" or "net current assets." Money borrowed for a period longer than one year is usually referred to as "funded debt" and is shown on the balance sheet as a noncurrent liability, although any portion of funded debt due within one year, either by reason of maturity or of a sinking fund obligation, is customarily included as a current liability.

At this point it is appropriate to distinguish between various forms of borrowing. The ordinary bank loan, usually used to provide additional working capital, matures within a relatively short time, although in recent years, such loans have been for longer than the traditional one to three years. Since many businesses operate on a cyclical basis during the year, there may be periods of heavy inventory accumulation, including the purchase of raw materials for fabrication or processing. These periods often require heavy bank borrowing to provide funds for the purchase of these raw materials. During the ensuing period of heavy sales the finished goods are disposed of, inventory decreases, and the resulting surplus of cash is used to pay off the bank borrowing. (It is much less expensive to have temporary heavy cash requirements met by bank credit than to provide permanent capital sufficient to meet the company's peak cash demands.) All these transactions, as they occur, are reflected in the company's working capital accounts. Funds needed for capital or fixed property purposes are borrowed for longer periods of time. It is this type of borrowing with which we will be concerned in our consideration of the trust indenture.

Another type of permanent capital is that supplied by the owners of the business, *i.e.*, the stockholders. The net amount invested by the owners, comprising the amounts paid in for purchase of stock plus undistributed earnings that have been reinvested in the business, accounts for the rest of the liability side of the balance sheet.

Income and Retained Earnings Statements

The principal source of the company's income is the sale of its products, and the first item on the income statement is the amount of the net sales for the year together with other earned income. This may include interest on temporary investments, income from investments in other companies, the excess of proceeds over book value realized from the sale of fixed assets no longer required in the business, and other similar items.

From this is deducted the cost of the goods sold, including the cost of the raw materials and the costs directly chargeable to manufacturing operations. These costs will tend to vary in almost direct proportion to the volume of goods produced. Costs that are more or less "fixed" without regard to fluctuations in the volume of business are the expenses of the sales force, of advertising, general office expense, and other similar charges. These are usually shown separately on the income statement and in such detail as may be appropriate for proper presentation and understanding. Deduction of manufacturing and general expenses from net sales will give the net income resulting from the year's operations.

The charge for "depreciation" is a noncash expense. While certain assets represent permanent investments, they will in time become worn out as they are used in the manufacturing process and have to be replaced. It is therefore necessary to charge against each year's income an appropriate amount to represent the deterioration or decrease in value of such fixed assets. This is the depreciation charge. There are a number of ways in which depreciation may be computed, but it is sufficient to understand that the charge theoretically represents the portion of the total value of the fixed assets that were used up in the year's operations.

Other expense items that might be included would be losses on sales of investments or fixed assets, amortization of discounts on funded debt obligations sold below par, and so on. The final deduction is the amount of income taxes incurred for the year, and the resulting balance is the net income of the corporation from all activities during the period.

Retained earnings are the earnings of the company that have been reinvested in the business rather than distributed to the stockholders.

Changes in Financial Position Statement

The final example of a common type of financial statement is a "Statement of Changes in Financial Position," also sometimes called a Sources and Uses of Funds statement.

This type of statement is helpful in considering the financial transactions of a corporation. All corporate transactions are expressed in terms of dollars, but many transactions take place each day without a concurrent transfer of dollars. Goods are bought to be paid for at a later date; wages, taxes, and other items of expense accrue that require cash outlays in the future; similarly, sales are made on credit or services are performed to be paid for over a period of time.

Financial officers must plan to provide the cash, when required, to meet the payments called for by the corporate operations. Similarly, the primary concern of anyone extending credit to the company is that funds will be available to meet the service payments on the debt as they become due.

The Sources and Uses of Funds statement reflects the flow of cash through a company's operations for a stated period. Such an analysis can be extrapolated from the statements previously considered. Of more importance to financial officers is the use of the statement's projections as a part of budget preparation to ensure that the company's financial obligations will be met promptly.

A single balance sheet provides little information other than the financial condition of the company as of a particular moment. It does not reflect the trend of the business. However, by a comparative analysis of balance sheets for the beginning and the end of a designated period, a great deal of information may be gleaned concerning the activities of the corporation during the period. These records, combined with the income and retained earnings statements, provide sufficient information to construct a cash flow statement for the period.

Assets represent uses of funds; liabilities, sources of funds. An increase in assets or a decrease in liabilities during a period reflects the net use of corporate funds during that period. Similarly, the sum of the decrease in assets and increase in liabilities reflects the net source of corporate funds for the period. Another type of Sources and Uses of Funds statement can thus be constructed by rearranging the net increase and decrease in assets and liabilities reflected in the change in the balance sheet for the period in question. Of course, there are actually many thousands of sources and uses for any particular accounting period. For an adequate picture of the company's transactions, however, it is usually sufficient to summarize the net effect of all these transactions. While analysis of balance sheets alone would provide such a picture, it would not be as nearly complete as can be obtained by considering also the income accounts for the period. It is also common to regard the working capital accounts (current assets and current liabilities) as an entity in any such analysis. Thus, a net increase in working capital represents a use of funds and a net decrease, a source.

Financial Ratios

It is not intended to present all the factors that are important in a complete and thorough financial statement analysis, but the administrator should be familiar with the more commonly used financial ratios, which are referred to below.

Current ratio.   One of the more frequently used ratios, it indicates the proportion of current assets to current liabilities and is a measure of liquidity.

Interest coverage.   Strictly speaking this is not actually a ratio, but it is an important consideration in the extension of credit—particularly long-term credit—to a corporation. The purpose of this measure is to determine the relationship between the company's earnings and its annual interest charges, and it is computed by taking net earnings before interest and income taxes paid. If extension of new credit is being contemplated, interest charges on the new debt should also be included. It is customary to take average earnings over a period of years and, if the industry is a cyclical one, to consider earnings during the poorest year.

Of importance in connection with extension of long-term credit is the company's history of ample coverage of all fixed charges.

Cash income to total debt.   This ratio is related to the preceding computation, and its purpose is to determine what relationship the annual cash flow of the corporation bears to the total debt—both current and funded. On the assumption that all cash were applied to liquidating debt, this ratio would give a rough indication of the number of years' operations required for complete liquidation. Cash income is determined by adding depreciation charges to net income.

Working capital to funded debt.   Another measure of current liquidity, this is the ratio of net current assets to total funded debt.

Current assets to total debt.   A ratio similar to the preceding one, but a more accurate measure of liquidity, it is computed by adding current liabilities to funded debt and determining the amount of coverage represented by total current assets.

Tangible assets to debt.   This is the ratio of total tangible assets (all assets, less intangibles such as good will) to the sum of current liabilities and funded debt. Another variation is the ratio of net tangible assets (tangible assets less current liabilities) to funded debt.

Inventory turnover.   This is a measure of the liquidity of the inventory account and is computed by dividing the gross inventory into annual sales. It is intended to give a rough indication of the number of times inventory is turned over in the course of a year.

Debt ratio.   This is the ratio of funded debt to total capitalization, indicating the percentage of corporate capital supplied by creditors as related to the amount supplied by the owners of the business.

Ratios are useful tools in analyzing financial statements or determining the investment value of a company's securities. There is no magic formula for solving every type of financial problem, however, and these, as all other tools, must be used with judgment and discretion. Obviously ratios will vary among industries and different types of businesses, and a ratio indicative of a stable condition in one instance may be a signal of a weak position in another. Finally, ratios are at best no more than imperfect measures, and care should always be taken to see that the particular measure used is appropriate to the assessment desired.

FINANCING CAPITAL NEEDS

Corporate financial officers are continually faced with the problem of how to finance the money needs of the business. This is not a problem that will directly concern the corporate trust administrator under normal circumstances, and it is therefore unnecessary to deal with it in detail. Some understanding of the basic principles involved will, however, be helpful in understanding the reasons for some of the negotiations involved in the drafting of particular indenture provisions.

We have noted that short-term working capital needs are customarily financed by short-term bank loans. An additional and important source of short-term funds for companies of strong credit standing is the sale of commercial paper. This refers to short-term promissory notes, usually unsecured, which are typically written in multiples of $5,000 with maturities of from three days to nine months.[3] These notes do not bear interest, as such. Instead, an effective interest rate is established by the sale of the notes at a discount from face amount.

Medium-term needs (e.g., the purchase of equipment that can be paid for in four to five years) might be financed through a bank term loan or an equipment lease transaction.[4] Fixed capital requirements are normally supplied from the capital markets or through the medium of retained earnings. Since this is the type of financing with which the corporate trustee is concerned, discussion will be confined to an analysis of its elements.

Capital requirements can be financed in any one of four principal ways: through some form of borrowing—the issuance of debt securities; through the issuance of preferred stock (while this is a form of equity or ownership security, the holder is entitled only to a fixed return from the earnings of the company—as opposed to a possibly larger return to owners of common shares—but has a claim prior to common stockholders in the event of liquidation); through the sale of additional common stock; or, finally, through retained earnings. While every conservative management normally retains a portion of earnings for use in the business (and this might be said not to be financing in the true sense),

---

[3] Where the issuer needs additional security to obtain a top credit rating for its commercial paper, a bank will issue its irrevocable letter of credit, either on a standby or direct draw basis. In such instances, a bank is normally appointed as Trustee and Depositary for the letter of credit.

[4] For a discussion of this type of financing and the role of the trustee bank, see chapter 14.

retention of earnings is in effect a forced investment by existing stockholders, and many of the considerations applicable to other types of capital financing are pertinent to the question of what portion of earnings should be retained, particularly if thought is being given to a change in dividend policy.[5]

Many factors affect a decision on the type of financing to be used for a particular project. Among the more important are the following: (1) the nature of the project or expansion to be financed, the extent to which it is speculative, and its relationship in size, cost, and profitability to the existing business of the company; (2) the prospective earnings from the proposed investment and the precision with which it is possible to forecast such earnings; (3) the quality and durability of the existing earnings of the company and the extent to which they are affected by cyclical changes in the general economy; (4) the existing capital structure of the company and the effect that alternative financing methods would have on such structure; and (5) the cost of alternative methods of raising the needed capital.

These factors reduce themselves generally to a consideration of the risks involved in relation to the cost. It is assumed that the different types of capital are available at a price. If a particular method of financing is not available by reason of a prohibition in an existing contract, the quality of the company's credit, or for other reasons, choices are either more limited or nonexistent.

It is axiomatic that—from the point of view of the borrower—the less expensive the method of financing, the more risk is involved. Debt is usually the cheapest form of capital, but there is some risk inherent in every type of debt financing since they involve fixed commitments that must be met regardless of the earnings of the company at the particular time. From the viewpoint of the common stockholders the issuance of preferred stock involves more risk than selling additional common stock does, for it creates a class of holders with claims ranking prior to their own.

The cost of debt is the rate of interest that must be paid, but since interest paid is deductible under present tax laws in computing income tax, the actual cost of debt financing is less than half the nominal interest

___

[5]On the assumption that the company is viable, such decision is not whether to pay a dividend but when and how much to pay. Such companies usually increase dividend payments some time after an improvement in their internal cash generation becomes apparent, and the payment is raised only to an amount that the management believes they can reasonably and safely maintain.

rate under present tax laws. The cost of using preferred stock is the fixed dividend rate. Because of lower priority in case of insolvency, this rate will usually be higher than the rate on debt for the same company. In addition, and possibly of greater significance, preferred dividends are not, with some exceptions, deductible for income tax purposes.

Another factor that is sometimes of considerable importance is the effect[6] on existing capital structure that the proposed financing may have. The maintenance of a proper debt ratio is important not only because of the safety factor inherent in a sound equity base but also because of the adverse effect that excessive debt may have on the credit standing of the company. There is no approved ratio that should exist, and each analyst uses a different measurement for every class of industry. A fairly high debt ratio might be appropriate for a particular industry, whereas the same ratio in another would be cause for serious concern. Historically few companies could justify a debt ratio in excess of 50 percent, and for most a maximum of 35 percent was considered advisable.[7] When the ratio begins to exceed the theoretical ceiling the company's security rating is affected, and this makes additional debt financing more difficult and more expensive. Thus it is important that a proper proportion of equity to debt be maintained at all times, and it is advisable to include a certain amount of equity financing while a degree of flexibility remains, so that proper advantage can be taken of changing market conditions.

Corporate finance is a volatile and constantly changing field, innovation and "creative financing" being the hallmark of aggressive investment bankers. The expert of a decade ago emerging from a time capsule would find a strange world today. A number of factors introduced into the economy during the past ten years have contributed to these changes. One, of course, is the tremendous expansion that has taken place in the economy and that has created an unprecedented demand for investment funds, including the vast sums borrowed by states and municipalities. Another factor of equal or greater importance is the consideration that every corporation must give to the impact of the tax laws and regulations on its everyday activities. Big government and, particularly, big taxes

6A common assessment of the creditworthiness of an obligor with respect to any debt issue is based on: (1) the likelihood of the obligor paying the interest and repaying the principal, (2) the nature of and provisions of the obligation, and (3) the protection afforded by the relative position of the obligation in the event of a bankruptcy or reorganization.

7From 1985 through 1989, the average of total debt as a percent of total capitalization for "AAA" rated obligors was 20.3, for "AA" rated obligors, 25.9, and for "A" rated obligors, 34.2.

are ever-present specters, and it is no longer possible to make important decisions based on the economics of the situation alone.

One of the most important trends that has taken place in the area of debt financing is the growth in the number and volume of direct or private placement contracts. Originally this was the direct result of the concentration of funds in the hands of institutions that provided a major pool of available investment dollars—not only in savings bank and life insurance assets but also in both private and public pension funds, including the very significant growth in individual retirement plans, such as IRAs and Keoghs.

While avoidance of the uncertainties and expense of a public offering and compliance with the registration requirements of the Securities Act of 1933 ("33 Act") are frequently cited as the motivating factors, important considerations are the ability to achieve greater flexibility—to tailor each financing to fit the particular circumstances—and the greater ease in securing amendments to the contract necessitated by changing conditions. Some institutional investors prefer this type of investment. They not only may be able to secure a somewhat better return but also can plan investment operations more accurately by making commitments for fixed amounts at negotiated rates.

The private placement, which accounted for an insignificant percentage of total debt financing before 1960, assumed major importance during the 1960s and early 1970s when these placements accounted for approximately 50 percent of total capital debt financing of corporations. While statistics showed a similar percentage in the latter 1980s, by 1991 the market had shrunk significantly.

The adoption of certain initiatives by the SEC in April 1990 should however set the stage for another renaissance in the use of this financing sector. New Rule 144A permits institutional investors having a minimum of $100 million invested in securities to trade privately placed securities—eliminating the requirement that such securities be registered with the SEC as "public" securities under the 33 Act.[8] The effect of this new Rule and the amendment to Rule 144, permitting the required holding period (usually two years) for private placements to commence upon the original issuance of the securities, in effect sets the stage for the creation of a secondary market in such securities.

These actions constitute the first step in the liberalization of the private placement market and will significantly increase its liquidity,

[8] SEC Release 33–6862 and 34–27928 (Apr. 1990).

making it more attractive to investors and reducing the cost to issuers of such financings. It is also expected to increase the number of foreign issuers into this market—issuers which have been reluctant to subject themselves to the full registration requirements of the 33 Act.

Direct placement financing falls into three broad categories:

1. Issues that are secured by the traditional form of corporate indenture—either an existing mortgage or a new bond or debenture issue. Except for the number of holders and the likelihood of a home office payment agreement,[9] such an issue is almost the same as a publicly offered issue.

2. Special-purpose and third-party corporation financing. The variations are legion, and the security is more likely to involve leases, charter hires, throughput agreements, government–guaranteed home mortgages, or some form of contractual arrangement other than the traditional corporate mortgage. In this type of financing, the credit of the obligor issuer is seldom important, for in most cases it will be a corporation specifically created for the purpose of issuing the debt obligation. The loan is made on the credit of the lessee or other contract party and its agreement to perform under its contract with the obligor issuer.

3. Note issue involving a direct unsecured loan without a trustee. Initially these loans were very similar to bank credit agreements, except they were for longer terms and normally for capital purposes. The borrowers were corporations with high credit ratings and usually little or no other funded debt. Frequently, only one institutional lender was involved, and it was exceptional to have more than four or five. The loan agreements were uncomplicated, with few, if any, security covenants.

Inevitably, there was an increase not only in the number of borrowers using this device but also in the variety and purpose of the loans. Credit agreements have become more complicated, and there is wider participation in individual loans. Eight to ten investors are fairly common, and there have been many issues with twenty-five to fifty participants. In private placement financing these note agreements in many instances replaced debenture financing, but without the flexibility, marketability, and uniformity of administration provided by the traditional debenture agreement with a competent and experienced corporate trustee.

---

[9] Such an agreement provides that in consideration of payments of principal being mailed to the holder without requiring the presentation of the obligation for notation of payment, the holder, before disposing of the note, will surrender it to the obligor (or its agent) for such notation or issuance of a new note for the unpaid balance.

It might be helpful to note, without extensive discussion, several other significant trends of recent years:

1. The volatility and changing character of the market. In an environment of economic uncertainties, wide swings in interest rates have prevailed with innovative factors built into the particular financing vehicle. These, together with the issuance of short- and mixed-term maturities, have been essential to ensure the continued interest of investors in providing funds to both corporate and public sector borrowers. Thus such "new" type financings have included floating rate notes, deep discount and zero coupon issues, auction rate securities, equity notes (debt security with a commitment to buy the issuer's stock in the future), variable rate demand obligations, pay-in-kind ("PIK") securities,[10] put/demand options, medium term notes and mortgage pass-through and mortgage-backed bonds. The variations are almost endless, limited only by the imagination of investment bankers and the perceived appetite of the investing public.

2. Shelf registration under SEC Rule 415. This rule, permanently adopted as of December 31, 1983, permits top tier corporations to register the offering or sale of their securities on a delayed or continuous basis in the future.[11] The effect of this rule is to allow such issuers almost instant access to the marketplace—whenever a "window" is available.

3. The very significant increase in Eurobond financings by domestic U.S. corporations. The ease of entry in this market, with lower costs, and potential financial incentives when issuing in other currencies or with special features such as warrants or equity conversion option has proven to be very attractive to corporate finance officers. This trend has accelerated in recent years as major corporations and banks have extended their operations outside the United States and as foreign investors have increased their investments in top tier U.S. corporate debt obligations.

4. The increased popularity and rapid growth of Medium Term Notes, an instrument modeled after commercial paper issued by corporations to obtain short term operating funds. MTN's are not sold through the traditional underwriting process, but under a continuous offering proce-

---

[10] PIK's typically allow the issuer to choose between making interest payments in cash or securities and to pay cash-in-lieu for securities under a set principal amount. Usually the payment-in-kind is only for a limited period of time or until the occurrence of certain events. Many PIK issues have floating rates, adding to their flexibility and complexity.

[11] SEC Release 33-6499 (Nov. 1983).

dure in which the issuer, acting through an investment bank(s) as sales agent(s), makes securities available to investors desiring specific maturities ranging from nine months to as long as fifteen years. The most important feature of an MTN program (i.e., issue) is the sales agent's ability to tailor the maturity date to satisfy the issuer's need for funds to the investor's need for a specific investment period. Most MTN programs will provide for fixed semi-annual interest payments, although some issues have used a variable rate feature with interest being paid monthly.

5. The tremendous volume of public financing, including not only the continuous financing by the federal government involved in the management of the public debt but also the enormous amount of tax-exempt securities issued by states, state and local authorities, and municipalities. In addition to the increase in revenue bond financings, the broad-scale use of industrial development bonds (IDBs) has had a major impact on the market during the 1980s. The primary purpose of IDBs was to attract financing of new plants and/or the construction of pollution control facilities through use of the tax exempt privilege.

TWO

The Trust Indenture

The trust indenture is a device by which a corporation borrows money from the holders of savings—either the general public or the large institutional investors. The indenture provides the terms and conditions on which credit is extended; places restrictions on the activities of the issuing company so long as the indenture securities are outstanding; sets forth remedies available to the security holders if there should be a default in payments on the debt or in the terms of the indenture contract; and otherwise defines the rights, duties, and obligations of the obligor company, the security holders, and the trustee or trustees named in the instrument. If the indenture obligations are to be secured, the indenture creates or pledges the security and sets forth the terms and conditions for dealing with such security.

The principle of a mortgage to secure the repayment of money is an ancient one. Likewise, the concept of a "use" or "trust" was developed at an early period in the common law. However, the development of the corporate mortgage, or trust indenture, is of fairly recent origin. It was introduced for the first time around 1830 but until the latter part of the nineteenth century was used infrequently. The reasons for this are many. In the first place, early corporate financing was chiefly by stock rather than by bonds. Also, the earlier corporations were generally created for special purposes and by special charter and their power to incur debt or mortgage their properties was strictly limited.

The growth and development of trust indentures parallel closely the growth of the corporate form of business enterprise. With the passage of general incorporation laws in most states, organization of corporations became relatively simple and, as a result, use of this form of business organization became a common practice. The latter part of the nineteenth century was also a period of tremendous expansion and growth in the United States. Accordingly, there was a phenomenal increase in both the number and size of business corporations and the amount of capital required for their development.

The transaction of business by these vast enterprises came to involve not only large stock financing but also heavy borrowing. It became impractical to secure this financing through one bank, or even a group of banks, so there was developed a system of borrowing from the public at large through a multitude of small loans, each evidenced by the issuance of bonds of the corporation, and all secured by the same mortgage to one individual or a small group of individuals. The corporate mortgage was at first used almost exclusively by railroad corporations, but with the growth of the corporate form of business enterprise and the development of large corporate systems, the practice was extended until now there are corporations and corporate bond issues for almost every type of business undertaking.

Although the corporate indenture has become a necessary and most important factor in the economic life of the country, there is still a great deal of confusion about its essential nature. Whereas there have been a great many court decisions construing particular provisions and defining the rights of the parties with respect to particular problems that have arisen, there is a lack of uniformity among the courts concerning the overall significance of the contract. Because the indenture device is little more than a century old, and its real development achieved during the past forty years, there has been no opportunity for a slow and gradual development of legal precedents. Courts have looked for guidance to cases that had only a superficial similarity to the problems at hand, although the legal relationships appeared to be the same.

The trust indenture is an instrument sui generis, combining elements of several other legal relationships but being identical with none. Although most courts now agree that the indenture does not create a trust relationship in the customarily accepted sense, some cases have indicated that the full extent of fiduciary responsibility may be imposed upon the trustee. Indeed, it has been suggested that such measure of responsibility should be imposed by statute, even at the risk of seriously impairing its effective use.

Although every form of indenture has elements of similarity, there are various types, designed for the different kinds of obligations to be issued, each with peculiarities of its own. The title of the indenture usually describes the type of obligations to be issued thereunder and the nature of the security, if any. For example, a mortgage indenture indicates that the security consists primarily of a mortgage on the obligor's fixed property and that the obligations outstanding are mortgage bonds. A first mortgage indicates that the bonds are intended to be a first lien on such properties, a second mortgage a second lien, and so on. Normally, an indenture securing junior lien obligations will contain provisions for refunding the prior lien bonds, and in that event the indenture and the obligations issued thereunder will be called respectively a "refunding mortgage" and "refunding mortgage bonds," terms that sound more attractive than second or third mortgage. If the obligations have a first or prior lien on any property at all, the title "first and refunding mortgage" is frequently used. In some jurisdictions the term "trust deed" is preferred to mortgage, although in most cases this is simply a variation in title. A collateral trust agreement usually denotes an indenture under which the obligations have a collateral rather than a direct lien. A debenture agreement usually, although not necessarily, indicates unsecured obligations. There are many other variations, combinations, and different forms of designation depending on the type of obligation, the type of security, and other considerations. Although for most purposes these distinctions do not affect the fundamental nature of the indenture or of the rights and obligations of the parties, they do involve different types of provisions and covenants and undoubtedly account to some extent for the confusion and contradictions existing in the law relating to the subject matter.

The legal relationships of features of which the trust indenture most frequently partakes are mortgage, trust, and contract. It might be well to compare the ways in which they are similar and dissimilar to the commonly accepted meanings of these terms in order to get a better understanding of the true nature of the relationships created.

THE INDENTURE AS A MORTGAGE

Most secured indentures under which bonds are issued involve a mortgage of some kind. The nature and extent of the mortgage security will depend on the particular circumstances of the issue, but it usually involves a mortgage on the fixed property and equipment used by the issuer in its business. The property is usually described in detail by metes and bounds in the instrument; great care is exercised in the execution of the document to ensure that it conforms to the laws and customs of the jurisdictions where the property is located; it is then properly filed and recorded. All things are done to ensure that the indenture creates the lien that it purports to do. The net effect of all this effort, however, is usually quite different from that which the investor would expect when told that he or she has a first mortgage security.

In the customary mortgage transaction borrower and lender are dealing in terms of a security whose value both understand. In the absence of extraordinary developments, the property usually has an intrinsic and realizable value more than adequate to cover the amount of the loan, and if there is a default the lender can proceed to foreclose and realize on such security the full amount of the loan.

A transaction such as this is entirely different from a mortgage on the property of a large business enterprise. The average investor who purchases bonds has no conception of the value of a large railroad system, for example, although a "mortgage" thereon may constitute the security. Even if an examination of each separate parcel could be made, the investor would still be unable to ascertain its value, for in this case the value of the whole may be greater or less than the sum of the values of all its parts. As real estate, a railroad right-of-way one mile long and thirty feet wide may have little value, although the railroad may have issued "mortgage" bonds to the extent of $300,000 or more per mile. The real value of the property of a business enterprise is the "going concern" value of the enterprise. Considered separate and apart from its use for the purposes of the business, its inadequacy as security is readily apparent. In determining the value of securities, analysts concern themselves with balance sheets, profit and loss statements, competitive conditions, economic trends, and other factors that may influence the business as a "going concern," and only infrequently is the intrinsic value of the security, considered separate and apart, of substantial importance. A proper mortgage position is important, not only for the value that may be realized on a possible future foreclosure and sale, but also for the prior claim on earnings or preferred position in the event of default, bankruptcy, or reorganization.

THE INDENTURE AS A TRUST

There is another important distinction between the trust indenture and the ordinary mortgage. In the latter, the mortgagee is usually the real party in interest, holding the mortgage as security for credit it has extended. In the indenture, or corporate mortgage, immediately following the granting and *habendum* clauses, is a paragraph beginning with the words ''In Trust, Nevertheless,'' which converts the mortgage into a trust deed and defines the terms and purposes for which the conveyance was made.

The trust so created, however, differs substantially from the usual inter-vivos or testamentary trust with which courts and practitioners are more familiar. The fundamental characteristic of the ordinary personal trust is possession by the trustee of a specific trust *res* that he or she holds and administers for the benefit of designated and usually well-known beneficiaries.

The trustee under a corporate indenture, however, has no possession, or right to possession, of the mortgaged property until after a default occurs, and its rights even then are usually circumscribed and limited. It has no control of the business of the obligor (and if it did, it would be disqualified from acting) nor, except for infrequent and unusual circumstances, any voice in the management of its affairs. Efforts to subject it under these conditions to the same degree of care with respect to the security as is required of an ordinary trustee with respect to a specific trust *res* would make the position of the indenture trustee untenable and render financing of this type almost impossible. It would be unwise indeed, even if practicable, to endeavor to substitute the judgment of the indenture trustee for that of the management of the issuing corporation.

In the case of an ordinary trust there is usually a close and intimate relationship between the trustee and the beneficiaries. The trustee is normally acquainted with their needs, and necessary actions can be patterned accordingly. Substantial discretionary powers are normally given to the trustee by the trust instrument with the resultant duties arising as much from the relationship with the beneficiaries as from the specific provisions of the trust document. In an extreme or doubtful case the trustee can usually secure the directions of a court—or obtain the consent or waiver of all parties in interest—before proceeding in a given transaction. It is also possible for periodic accountings to be submitted so that administration can be kept more or less current.

An indenture trustee,[1] on the other hand, is in the position of both a stakeholder and trustee. Its administration covers a long period of time, and it is frequently called upon to make important and far-reaching

---

[1] See Sklar, *The Corporate Indenture Trustee: Genuine Fiduciary or Mere Stakeholder?* 106 *Banking L. Journal* 1 (1989).

decisions without the possibility of consulting the bondholders or seeking instructions of a court. In the ordinary case the beneficial owners of the indenture securities may be unknown to it and are changing frequently, so that an effort to secure their unanimous consent to a particular action is extremely difficult.[2] In addition, the indenture trustee normally has no pre-default discretionary power and only limited authority. It is entirely without authority to deal with or compromise the debt itself no matter how desirable such a compromise might appear to be.

The trustee of a personal trust is responsible only to the beneficiaries, such duty being to administer the trust solely in their interests. While the indenture trustee's primary fiduciary responsibility runs to the indenture security holders, it also owes to the obligor important practical and fiduciary duties, and in the interest of all parties it must be able to work cooperatively with the obligor.

A final and important distinction lies in the amount of compensation received by the two types of trustee. The fees of the trustee of an ordinary trust are measured by the amount of the trust *res* or the income therefrom. While the trustee is liable to be surcharged for a wrongful act or failure to exercise due care, the possible consequences of any particular course of action can normally be estimated with reasonable accuracy. The fees received by the indenture trustee are nominal in relation to the amount of indenture securities outstanding or the value of the trust estate. If it were to be held accountable for the full measure of discretion and fiduciary responsibility common to the ordinary trust, the amount for which it might be potentially liable would be out of all proportion to the compensation the obligor company could possibly pay.

THE INDENTURE AS A CONTRACT

While it partakes of the essence of other legal relationships, the trust indenture is most of all a contract, and courts have been in almost unanimous agreement in applying contractual principles to the relationship.

The parties to the contract, or the indenture, are the obligor company and the trustee, and it is these only who execute the instrument. However, there is another party, or class of parties, whose participation is

[2] Even with securities in fully registered form, such registration may be in nominee or street name. This is especially true of securities held in a depository or by bank custodians, brokerage firms, and trust fund accounts.

essential to make the contract operative, and that is the indenture security holders. Three distinct and separate sets of contractual rights and obligations are created by each indenture: those between the obligor and the trustee; those between the obligor and the indenture security holders; and those between the trustee and the indenture security holders.

It is important to distinguish between the contractual rights, duties, and obligations relating primarily to the debt itself and those relating principally to the security for the debt. The indenture provisions that define the principal rights, duties, and obligations of the trustee and its relationship with the obligor company relate primarily to the security for the obligations issued or to be issued, whether it be the specific security conveyed or pledged by the indenture or the "negative" security determined and defined by the indenture covenants. These provisions contain the trustee's authority for dealing with this security and define the limitations and restrictions on such authority. They also place restrictions on the issuing company in dealing with its property or in the conduct of its business. Since both the obligor company and the trustee have an opportunity to read and examine the indenture before it becomes effective, and both are signatory parties, some of the features of a true contract may be said to be present. Many are lacking, however, and it is of particular importance to bear in mind that until the contract is executed, the trustee is acting not as a principal but only as a *prospective* fiduciary. The trustee does not negotiate the substantive terms of the contract, and if it objects to particular provisions, it can only suggest and not demand that they be deleted or amended. Its only recourse is to refuse to act, for it does not and cannot become an active participating party until the contract is actually signed and delivered.

The obligations issued under the indenture run directly to the security holders and not to the trustee and are looked to primarily to define the relationship between the obligor and the security holders. It is therefore of paramount importance that any provisions of the indenture that modify or affect this relationship, or place limitations on the rights of the holders of these obligations, be also set forth or sufficiently described in the bond or debenture that runs to the holder. If there is any conflict or discrepancy between the indenture and the bond or debenture, the terms of the latter will be controlling in any suit by the holder thereof. Since the indenture sets forth in detail the rights, duties, and obligations of the parties (including the security holders) and the limitations on those rights, it is important that the security itself embody those provisions by adequate reference. It is obvious that the whole indenture cannot be fully set forth in the bond, debenture, or note, and it is usually sufficient to make specific reference to the indenture in general terms. This is done by including in the bond (or other obligation) language substantially as follows: "This bond is one of a duly authorized issue of bonds, issued and to be issued under, and all equally secured by a Mortgage and Deed of Trust dated as of_____, executed by_____Company to the_____Trust Company as Trustee, to which Indenture reference is hereby made for a description of the properties and franchises mortgaged, the nature and extent of the security, the rights of the holders of said bonds and of the trustee in respect of such security, and the terms and conditions under which the bonds are issued and secured."[3] While language such as this is usually adequate to put the security holder on notice about the existence of the indenture and to make its provisions binding on such holder, it is desirable to make specific reference to such provisions as directly affect the rights of the holder of the obligation itself. Such provisions would include redemption provisions, sinking fund, transfer and exchange of securities, any provisions permitting substantial modification of the indenture by less than all security holders, waiver of default, and similar matters.

The substantive provisions of the indenture that must be referred to in the bond are printed on the reverse of the certificate as a continuation of the bond form. An alternative procedure that has been used, made possible by the flexibility provided by Article 8 of the Uniform Commercial Code ("UCC") has been the printing of summaries of the pertinent indenture provisions in less formal and more easily understood language.

While holders of the indenture securities are parties to the indenture contract and bound by its terms, it is more difficult in their case to find all the essential elements of a true contractual relationship. Because they cannot exist as such until after the contract has been executed and delivered, it is obvious that they can have had no part in negotiating the terms contained therein, although it might be said that the counsel for underwriting houses that acted for the "purchasers" did so in their behalf. It might also be said that, in respect of the security holders, the indenture is in the nature of a unilateral contract to which they become parties by purchasing their security. Here too, however the analogy is somewhat strained, for the indenture is seldom read by the investor before the purchase of the securities. As a matter of fact,

---

[3] For a plain language version, *see* para. 4, 38 *Bus. Law. op. cit. supra,* at 776.

except for the institutional or professional class of investors, the indenture is almost never read by the security holders and, if it were, many would not understand it. Nevertheless, for the proper functioning of these financing arrangements, it is essential that contractual principles be applied and that the indenture provisions be binding on the security holders as parties. This is despite the fact that in dealing with the obligor the individual holder is at a distinct disadvantage if there should be a default in payment of the principal or interest on the obligation held.

These considerations have led many courts not only to construe indenture provisions strictly against the obligor but also to try to find some other legal theory or precedent with which to protect the interests of the security holders. Such decisions have contributed to much of the confusion that exists in the law, particularly as it relates to the third set of contractual relationships—those existing between the trustee and security holders. The existence of a "trust" is necessary to create and define the trustee's interest in and relation to the security and the contract, but its relationship thereto and to the security holders is essentially contractual rather than fiduciary. Its principal function is to administer the contract in accordance with its terms. It has only the authority and powers granted by the indenture and is subject to all the restrictions and limitations therein. Except to the limited extent specified, the trustee has no right or authority to represent or act for the security holders or to substitute its judgment for theirs. The trustee should be held accountable for failure to carry out its duties properly, but there is no basis for holding, as some courts have endeavored to do, that the trustee owes to each individual holder duties or obligations not specifically undertaken by it in the contract[4], or required of it by statute or regulation.

Where the trustee's obligation with respect to a particular subject matter is spelled out in the contract, no particular difficulty is encountered if the obligation has been carried out. There is danger, however, that where the indenture is silent on a particular point, effort will be made to find an implied obligation either from other indenture provisions or from legal precedents evolved under entirely different circumstances. It is therefore important from the viewpoint of the trustee that the indenture clearly indicate its responsibilities in regard to all significant matters relating to the security or to the obligations, even if it merely recites that no responsibility exists. For example, in a mortgage inden-

---

[4] See page 71, chapter 3, *infra*.

ture it is important that the trustee's obligations, or lack of thereof, with respect to maintenance, insurance, payment of taxes, and the like be clearly set forth to prevent the possibility of a finding of substantial responsibility in the absence of any provision at all.[5]

USUAL PROVISIONS OF A TYPICAL INDENTURE

Although the more important provisions of the indenture will be discussed in later chapters in detail in order to present a composite picture of the usual scope of a typical indenture, the customary articles contained therein are summarized briefly below. These examples have been taken from a mortgage indenture of an industrial corporation. Provisions of other indentures may differ in various respects, depending on the nature of the company, whether the obligations are secured or unsecured, the structure of the financing, and whether the indenture is qualified under the Trust Indenture Act of 1939 ("TIA").[6]

Recitals

Each indenture opens by naming the parties and usually contains a recital of the various factors that led to its creation. These recitals declare the purpose of the issue and state that all legal requirements and authorizations have been fulfilled or obtained. It is important that such recitals be included because they may constitute an estoppel against a later assertion by the obligor that the mortgage or debt was not properly authorized.

The form of bond, interest coupon (if a bearer bond,[7] and trustee's (and authenticating agent's if any) certificate of authentication are also customarily set forth in full therein. As stated above, it is important that the form of bond contain all the essentials of the contract, either specifically or by appropriate reference to the indenture. Only obligations

[5]For a discussion of the expanding scope of the trustee's potential liability, see chapter 3, and discussion covering secondary market disclosure in chapter 11.

[6]15 U.S.C. sec. 77aaa *et seq.* (1990), as amended by the Trust Indenture Reform Act of 1990, P.L. 101–550 ("TIRA"). References hereinafter are to TIA section numbers, 301 through 328. For complete text of the amended act, *see* the appendices.

[7]The Tax Equity and Fiscal Responsibility Act of 1982, Pub. L. 97–248, 96 Stat. 324, 576., effectively eliminated the issuance of corporate bearer bonds (as of January 1, 1983) and tax-exempt bearer bonds (as of July 1, 1983) by imposing adverse tax consequences on both issuer and investor.

conforming substantially to the form prescribed in the indenture should be authenticated by the trustee.

Granting Clauses

Following the recitals come the granting clauses that set forth the specific security for the obligations to be issued. These clauses include a recital of the consideration, a specific grant to the trustee, and a description of the property to be mortgaged in sufficient detail to enable the indenture to be properly recorded as a mortgage. If any securities or other properties are to be pledged, they are fully described. The specific property descriptions are usually followed by descriptions of other properties intended to be included in the conveyance in general terms, such as appurtenances, franchises, fixtures, and so on. The indenture should also set forth in detail the extent to which it is intended to become a lien on after-acquired property. It is also customary to enumerate the types or classes of property excepted from the conveyance and any other provisions that might aid in defining the exact nature and scope of the security intended to be granted. The granting clauses conclude with the *habendum* and trust clauses, which create the trust relationship and specify the purposes and conditions on which the grant is made.

Definitions

All the important terms used in the indenture are customarily defined, clearly and carefully, in a separate article. Not only is this a convenience for those who will later work with the indenture but it also makes the job of drafting much easier.

Amount, Form, Execution, Delivery, Registration, and Exchange of Bonds

Whether under this or a similar heading, these sections contain important mechanical provisions for dealing with the obligations themselves and deserve careful attention at the time of drafting, particularly by representatives of the trustee who will administer them. Included here are limitations, if any, on the principal amount of bonds that may be issued or that may be outstanding at any one time under the indenture; the form of the bonds (if not included in the recitals), or authority for the board of directors to determine the form, and other provisions with respect to any subsequent series; provisions with respect to the manner in which the bonds are to be executed; a statement of who may sign; authorization of the use of facsimile seal or facsimile signatures, if permitted by the law of the particular jurisdiction; authorization of temporary bonds in appropriate cases and provisions for their exchange for definitive bonds; appointment of a registrar and authorization of the issuance of bonds in registered form; provisions establishing the various denominations in which bonds may be issued and prescribing the conditions on which bonds of one denomination may be exchanged for a bond or bonds of other denominations; provisions with respect to the issuance of bonds in replacement of mutilated, destroyed, lost, or stolen bonds and the evidence and indemnity required; provisions with respect to treasury bonds or bonds reacquired by the obligor; language establishing and providing for the negotiability of the bonds; and similar provisions that may be deemed desirable to authorize and facilitate the efficient servicing of the obligations as long as they remain outstanding.[8]

Because most modern indentures, particularly open-end indentures, will remain in existence for a long period of time, it is important that these provisions be made as broad and as flexible as possible so that both the obligor and the trustee can take advantage of changing and more efficient methods for processing and handling the indenture securities.

Issuance of Bonds

Included in this section are the terms and conditions on which bonds may be issued under the indenture and the documents that must be furnished to the trustee on the basis of which it is authorized to authenticate and deliver the bonds.

Redemption of Bonds

If the obligor desires to reserve the right to retire the obligations, in whole or in part, before their stated maturity, this right must be reserved in the indenture. These provisions are included in a special article and set forth conditions on which bonds may be prepaid; the premium

---

[8] If the issue provides for book-entry–only certificates, the authorization for such should be included in this section. For specific sample provisions, *see* Article Two, Sample Uncertificated Debt Indenture, American Bar Assoc., Business Law Section, draft dated May 17, 1991. *See also* Report of the Ad Hoc Comm. on Uncertificated Debt Securities, 46 *Bus. Law.* 909 (May 1991).

required, if any; the method of giving notice to the holders; and other pertinent requirements.

Sinking Fund

If the obligor is required to provide a sinking fund for retirement of a portion of the outstanding bonds from time to time, this article will set forth the amount of such sinking fund, how it is to be paid, and the manner in which it must be applied by the trustee.

Particular Covenants

Covenants are an important part of each indenture contract and are normally set apart in a separate article. Most indentures, whether secured or unsecured, include covenants of some kind. They are both affirmative, requiring performance of certain things by the obligor company, either continuously or at specified times, and negative, placing restrictions on particular activities of the obligor, such as the incurring of additional debt. These covenants provide additional security to the holders of the indenture securities, and the trustee has particular duties with respect to their enforcement.

Provisions in Regard to Pledged Collateral

If the indenture is in the nature of a collateral trust, where the security consists in whole or in part of securities or similar collateral pledged with the trustee, the indenture must set forth in sufficient detail just how this collateral is to be administered. Matters such as the following should be covered: the form in which the collateral is to be held (whether bearer or registered and, if registered, in what name or names); collection and disposition of income; voting of stock; disposition of principal collected; enforcement of rights as a holder; action to be taken on default in payment or under the indenture securing bonds or debentures held; release, substitution, replacement, etc.; and any other matters that may be deemed to be pertinent to proper administration to accomplish the purposes for which the pledge was made.[9]

Remedies of Trustee and Bondholders

This article will include the default and remedial provisions. Events that will constitute a default under the indenture must be spelled out in

[9] For discussion of collateral represented by pools of assets, *see* chapter 14.

detail, including periods of grace, if any. Since the trustee has only the powers specifically granted by the contract, there must always be included the alternative remedies available on default, with a grant of sufficient authority to pursue such remedies. There will also be included a statement of the rights of security holders under the indenture, individually or collectively, and particularly, any limitation on rights of security holders.

Immunity of Incorporators, Stockholders, Officers, and Directors

Since the obligations are a corporate obligation, a provision is almost always included that specifically grants immunity to the stockholders, directors, officers, etc., with respect to the indenture or the securities to be issued thereunder. A similar provision is usually included in the form of the bond or debenture. While such immunity is now fairly well established as a matter of general law, the provision is intended as a protection against the possible application of some remote statutory or implied liability in a particular jurisdiction. It is doubtful that the protection would be applicable if fraudulent misrepresentations were involved. As a matter of fact, the 33 Act[10] includes specific penalties for misrepresentations or misleading statements in a registration statement or prospectus.

Consolidation, Merger, and Sale

This article will set forth the conditions under which the obligor company may sell or lease all or substantially all of its properties or may merge into or with another corporation. If the company has subsidiary companies, the latter should also be specifically covered in these provisions, for the conditions affecting subsidiaries may be quite different from those applicable to the parent company. In many indentures, particularly debenture agreements, this article is an additional negative covenant.

Releases

If the indenture is a secured indenture, and particularly if the security is a mortgage or collateral is held by the trustee, the obligor must be permitted to dispose of or substitute particular segments of the property

---

[10] 15 U.S.C. sec. 77a (1990).

as may be required or desirable from time to time. The indenture will set forth the conditions under which such disposition or substitution may be made and the documents and consideration that must be furnished to the trustee.

Possession Until Default—Defeasance

Since the trustee's interest in the property is simply a security interest the obligor is entitled to remain in possession, at least until default, and this article confirms such right. It is also important to provide for a reconveyance to the obligor, and the terms and conditions on which it will be made, if the obligor performs all the terms and conditions of the indenture.

Concerning the Trustee

This is a most important article and will be discussed in detail in the succeeding chapter. The specific duties, responsibilities, and liabilities of the trustee will be set forth in detail, as will an examination of the necessary and appropriate exculpatory and protective provisions.

Requirements in Regard to Evidence of Compliance with Indenture Provisions and Certificates

The TIA requires that certain statements or reports must be furnished the trustee as evidence of compliance with particular types of provisions and the contents of certificates and opinions with respect to compliance with conditions and covenants.[11]

Supplemental Indentures, Bondholders' Meetings, Bondholders'Acts, Holdings, and Apparent Authority

These provisions set forth the manner in which the indenture contract may be supplemented or amended. Some amendments may be made by the obligor and trustee without reference to the security holders, and these are usually enumerated. In general, any provision that does not affect a substantive right of the security holders may be added without their consent. Other provisions may be changed with the consent of a specified percentage of the holders, while others require 100 percent consent. If the consent of the holders is required, the manner in which

---

[11] TIA, secs. 314(c), (d), (e), and (f).

such consent is to be evidenced will be spelled out, as will the nature of evidence on which the trustee may rely in establishing ownership of particular obligations.

Various miscellaneous provisions will be embodied in a final article.

THE TRUST INDENTURE ACT OF 1939

The idea of regulation—particularly by the federal government—is a fixed and accepted principle in everyday business life and is assuming greater significance each year. Despite this fact, there are still wide differences of opinion about the proper scope and purpose of such regulation and the limits to which it may properly be extended. In certain areas of activity it undoubtedly performs an important and essential function. This function, however, should normally be limited to the establishment of minimum standards or modes of conduct deemed essential to the public interest to which all engaged in the particular activity are required to adhere. Its value is directly proportional to the uniformity of standards that exist, or are capable of existing, in the particular activity.

With respect to trust indentures the scope and value of government regulation are necessarily limited. Trust indentures do not in themselves constitute a "business"; they are simply the instruments by which all types of businesses secure financing necessary to their functioning. And each type of financing produces its own type of indenture.

The trust indenture was developed with few restrictions imposed by governmental authorities. Legislation concerning the sale or distribution of securities was initially limited to the blue-sky laws enacted by various states that focused on fraudulent devices in the sale of securities.

Following the financial collapse of the 1930s, defaults under indentures became numerous, and the savings of many individuals were seriously depleted and, in some cases, wiped out. The concurrence of the drop in security values with the Great Depression brought the whole security structure before the public attention. The result was the enactment by Congress of a series of securities acts designed for the protection of investors.

The first legislation was the 33 Act, sometimes called the "truth in securities" act. With certain exceptions, this act requires the filing of a registration statement covering each public issue of securities and the use of a prospectus in connection with their sale and distribution. Stringent penalties are imposed for misrepresentations or misleading statements in either of these documents. The Securities and Exchange Act of 1934 ("34 Act")[12] was designed for the regulation of national securities exchanges, the listing of securities thereon, and the purchase and a sale of securities through the facilities of such exchanges. This act also created the SEC to administer both this and the 33 Act. Section 211 of the 34 Act directed the Commission to "make a study and investigation of the work, activities, personnel, and functions of protective and reorganization committees in connection with the reorganization, readjustment, rehabilitation, liquidation, or consolidation of persons and properties and to report the result of its studies and investigations and its recommendations to the Congress." As a part of this study, the Commission included a report on the activities of trustees under indentures.

Because of this report the so-called Barkley bill was introduced in the Senate in 1937 and was referred to a subcommittee of the Committee on Banking and Currency. Although the measure was favorably reported by the committee, the Senate did not vote on it during that session. A similar bill was introduced in the House of Representatives in 1938, and in both the House and the Senate in 1939. The latter bill was enacted by Congress as the "Trust Indenture Act of 1939" and became effective on February 3, 1940.

The TIA was the first attempt by the federal government to regulate the indentures under which securities are issued. In its report the SEC recommended extremely stringent provisions, including continuous supervisory administration by it, and the initial bill introduced embodied these provisions. The legislation enacted was worked out by the SEC and a special committee of the American Bankers Association after extended hearings before the committees of the House and Senate. The TIA, as enacted, differed substantially from the bill originally recommended and did not do violence to the basic concept of the trust indenture as a special financing contract among the parties.

The TIA was enacted as Title III to the 33 Act, and its administrative provisions were drafted to dovetail with the SEC's administration of the securities act. In general, it required that all indentures, with specified exceptions, be submitted to the SEC for "qualification" along with the issuer's registration statement under the securities act.[13] The actual "regulation" provided by the TIA consisted solely of the qualification

[12]Codified in scattered sections of 15 U.S.C. sec. 77 and 78 (1990).
[13]TIA, sec. 305(b). See section 304 for securities that are exempted from the Act.

of the indenture. Once the indenture was qualified, the SEC, with one minor exception, had no further jurisdiction over the indenture or over the obligor, the trustee, or the security holders. The essential purpose of the act and the qualification of indentures thereunder was to ensure that every indenture contained the minimum standards imposed by the act and conformed to the requirements of the TIA.

In general, the legislation accomplished three basic purposes: (1) the establishment of certain minimum standards with respect to specified acts and duties of the obligor and trustee to which all indentures must conform (accomplished by requiring the inclusion, or incorporation by reference, in each qualified indenture, of specified provisions that became an essential part of the contract); (2) the inclusion of minimum standards of responsibility and accountability for trustees under indentures, and the elimination of the very broad exculpatory provisions formerly included; and (3) the elimination of conflicting relationships between the trustee and the obligor and between the trustee and underwriters for the obligor.

Although the original TIA did not eliminate the occurrence of defaults or losses to investors, it did not prove to be the burden that many trust companies had feared. It went into effect in 1940 and became accepted as part of the normal routine of indenture administration. Whereas the prescribed provisions were required only in indentures qualified under the act, most of them came to be accepted as reasonable standards for all indenture administration and came to be included in practically all indentures, whether or not qualification was required.

Before the enactment of the original TIA, the enforcement of any rights under the indenture contract was clearly governed by the common law of contracts and fiduciary obligations with appropriate remedies for breach of the contract available in state courts. The legislative history of the act itself suggested that Congress intended that this approach be continued, instead of having the enforcement of the TIA a matter of federal law, enforceable in federal courts.[14] In 1975, however, a federal district court in *Morris v. Cantor*[15] held that the TIA created substantiative liabilities for violations of the provisions of qualified indentures and that indenture security holders could enforce such liabilities as a

[14] See Dropkin, *Implied Civil Liability Under the Trust Indenture Act: Trends and Prospects,* 52 *Tul. L. Rev.* 299, 322–24 (1978).
[15] 390 F. Supp. 817 (S.D.N.Y. 1975).

matter of federal law in a federal court.[16] The judge concluded that the TIA "must be viewed as an indirect method of imposing nationally uniform and clearly defined obligations upon those associated with the issuance of corporate debt," and held that the act "created liability" as though it had directly mandated the same actions of trustees and issuers, and consequently, conferred jurisdiction upon district courts over lawsuits to enforce that liability.[17] Thus the existence of a private right of action was held to follow. The Third Circuit Court of Appeals reached the same conclusion[18] stating that "the interpretation of the indenture provisions mandated by the Act does not depend on ordinary contract principles—the intent of the parties—but depends on an interpretation of the legislation."[19]

THE TRUST INDENTURE REFORM ACT OF 1990

Following a five year effort by an ad hoc group of seven major corporate trustee banks, the first comprehensive revision of the TIA became effective November 15, 1990. Originally discussed and reviewed with the staff of the SEC in 1985, a proposed reform bill was approved by the Commission in 1987.[20] The bill was introduced in the 100th Congress in 1988, but no action was taken. It was reintroduced in the 101st Congress in 1989 as part of the Securities Acts Amendments of 1989. Despite passage by the Senate in November 1989 and no opposition to its enactment, the House failed to vote on the measure. Following passage by the House in the second session of the 101st Congress, the Trust Indenture Reform Act of 1990 ("TIRA"), designated as Title IV of the Securities Acts Amendments of 1990, was reconciled with the Senate version by Conference Committee and was passed on October 26, 1990. It was signed into law by President Bush on November 15, 1990, and took effect immediately.

16This result was recognized as a possibility in a footnote of Caplin v. Marine Midland Grace Trust Co., 406 U.S. 416, 426n.17 (1971).

17390 F.Supp. at 822.

18Zeffiro v. First Pennsylvania Banking and Trust Co., 623 F.2d 290 (3d Cir. 1980), cert. denied, 456 U.S. 1005 (1982), affirming 473 F.Supp. 301 (E.D. Pa. 1979).

19Id. at 299.

20See Memorandum of the SEC in Support of the Proposed Trust Indenture Reform Act of 1987, Fed. Sec. L. Rep. (CCH) ¶ 84,205 et seq. (November 19, 1987).

The prinicpal purpose for this major revision was to modernize the fifty-year-old TIA. As articulated in the Senate Committee report accompanying the reform bill in 1989,[21] "During this period, however, the public market for debt securities has undergone significant changes. Innovations in the forms of debt instruments have produced securities, such as collateralized mortgage obligations, [which] were not contemplated in 1939. Technological developments and regulatory changes have resulted in new distribution methods including shelf offerings, direct placements and 'dutch auctions.' In addition, public securities markets have been profoundly changed by the increasing internationalization of the securities markets. Thus, current market practices conflict with many of the assumptions underlying the Act, which were based on financial customs prevailing in 1939. . . . Enactment of Title IV would conform the Act to the present realities of the market and make it adaptable to future developments, while easing the administration of the Act."[22]

The following features of the TIRA, discussed in detail in other chapters, are the most significant:

1. The postponement of the resignation of the trustee for a conflict of interest until there is a default under the indenture. Except in certain limited instances, a creditor relationship with the obligor has been added as a conflicting interest.[23] There is, however, one conflict that is operative at all times; that is the absolute prohibition that the obligor and its affiliates cannot serve as trustee for its own securities.[24] To obviate the need to resign as the result of a "technical" default, the trustee's resignation is automatically stayed, except in the case of a payment default, pending its application to the SEC that such default may be soon cured or that its continuing on as trustee will not be inconsistent with the interests of the bondholders.

2. The elimination of the need to set out all the provisions of TIA sections 310 through 317 in the indenture. The TIRA now mandates such provisions as a matter of federal law, with the optional provisions now deemed to be *included* unless they are expressly excluded.

3. The trustee's "annual" report need only be prepared and sent

[21] Report 101–155, Senate Comm. on Banking, Housing & Urban Affairs (October 2, 1989).
[22] *Id.* at 29.
[23] TIA, sec. 310(b).
[24] *Id.* sec. 310(a)(5).

out to the security holders if there has been: (a) any change to its eligibility and qualifications under section 310(b); (b) the creation of or any material change in the relationships specified in section 310(b) (1) through (10); (c) any change in any loans owed by the obligor to it or in any property or funds in its possession; or (d) the happening of any of the transactions spelled out in section 313(a) (3), (6), (7), or (8).[25]

4. The obligor is required to furnish the trustee with an annual no-default certificate, a requirement which already exists in most corporate indentures. The major difference is that the TIRA requires that it be signed by the obligor's principal executive officer, principal financial officer, or principal accounting officer.[26]

5. The authority for, but not the requirement of, the obligor to establish a record date for determining those holders entitled to vote on or consent to any change in the indenture.[27]

6. The appointment of any successor trustee will become effective only upon the appointment of and acceptance by a successor. This provision, which is found in many indentures to prevent the orphaning of trusts, will apply in all situations, including the voluntary resignation of the trustee in anticipation of an obligor's default.[28]

7. The shortening—from four to three months preceding the filing of a proceeding under the Bankruptcy Reform Act of 1978—of the so-called clawback period, during which any payments made to the trustee bank would have to be shared with the security holders. This change merely conforms the requirement to the preferential claim period in the Bankruptcy Act.[29]

8. The application of the TIRA provisions to all outstanding indentures and the superseding of any inconsistent provision of any outstanding indenture. The only exception to the latter would be the *optional* provisions not contained in pre-November 15, 1990 indentures.

9. Indentures can now be qualified with a trustee to be appointed after the registration statement is effective (under a Rule 415 shelf registration filing), provided that the issuer files an application simultaneously with the trustee's statement of eligibility. The application will be effective

---

25*Id*. sec. 313(a). *See also* footnote 6, chapter 12, *infra*.
26*Id*. sec. 314(a)(4).
27*Id*. sec. 316(c).
28*Id*. sec. 310(b), last sentence.
29*Id*. sec. 311.

automatically after ten days, unless the SEC issues an order finding the trustee ineligible.[30]

10. Provision that a foreign bank can, under certain circumstances, act as a trustee.[31]

11. The granting to the SEC of sweeping and open-ended exemptive authority to act by rule, regulation, or order to exempt any person, indenture, security, or transaction from any one or more of the provisions of the Act, if such is necessary or appropriate in the public interest.[32]

12. The potential use of criminal sanctions for the violation of the TIA's provisions, which together with the SEC's new enforcement powers[33] and the retroactive effect of the TIRA, could be used against an issuer or trustee that fails to perform any of the specified duties. While this may cause some deep concern to corporate trustees, it should also be noted that TIA section 309(e), which was not affected by the TIRA, provides that the SEC is not empowered to conduct an investigation for the purpose of determining compliance with its provisions or to enforce such provisions. It is fairly obvious however, that both issuers and trustees should ensure that they have timely and comprehensive procedures in place to avoid any failure to comply with any of the provisions of this federal law.

For the purpose of maintaining some historical perspective with regard to this legislation, it is interesting to note that some of the concepts embodied in the TIRA had their origins in the proposed Federal Securities Code, a project begun in 1972 by the American Law Institute to review and codify the laws relating to securities distribution and markets, investment advisors, trust indentures, investment companies, and utility holding companies.[34] The Code included provisions that the duties and responsibilities of trustees and others be interpreted, approved, and enforced exclusively as a matter of federal law, that certain enumerated provisions would be required to be included in every qualified indenture (e.g., notice of "payment" default), and the expansion of the SEC's enforcement authority to a level comparable with that provided in other areas of securities law. The final Official Draft of the

---

[30] *Id.* sec. 305(b)(2).

[31] *Id.* sec. 310(a)(1).

[32] *Id.* sec. 304(d).

[33] *See* Securities Enforcement Remedies and Penny Stock Act of 1990, P.L. 101–249.

[34] *See generally,* Stark *The Trust Indenture Act of 1939* in the *Proposed Federal Securities Code,* 32 Vand. L. Rev. 527 (Mar. 1979); SEC Release No. 33–6242 (20 SEC Docket No. 19 at 1483, Sept. 18, 1980).

Code, which was completed and approved by the American Law Institute in 1978, received the support of the SEC, but legislation to enact it was never introduced in Congress.

THE UNIFORM COMMERCIAL CODE

The UCC has been adopted in forty-nine states, the District of Columbia, and the Virgin Islands. The only exception is Louisiana, which adopted only Articles 1,3,4,5,7, and 8. Although the UCC deals with all facets of commercial practice, Articles 8 and 9 are of particular importance in the corporate trust field.[35]

Article 8 deals with investment securities and conforms or establishes certain basic principles:

1. It makes all investment securities negotiable. This makes possible increased flexibility in the form of these instruments without fear of creating problems of negotiability.

2. It broadens the application of the rules relating to fiduciary transfers, placing responsibility on the fiduciary rather than the transfer agent, and in effect penalizing the transfer agent that requires excessive documentation.

3. It defines the responsibilities of an authenticating trustee, transfer agent, and registrar.

4. It imposes direct and independent responsibility and liability on the transfer agent or registrar for their acts. It is no defense to show that such action was strictly in accord with a principal's direction.

5. It establishes guides for issuers and transfer agents in dealing with adverse claims.

Under the 1977 Amendments to Article 8, provision has been made for the use of uncertificated securities, i.e., a share, participation, or other interest in property or an enterprise of the issuer or an obligation of the issuer that is not represented by an instrument, and whose transfer is registered on the issuer's books without a resultant issuance of a certificate.[36]

Article 9 deals with secured transactions and its impact on commer-

---

[35] For a detailed analysis of Article 8, *see* Egon Gutman, *Modern Securities Transfers* (Rev. Ed. 1989).

[36] U.C.C. 1978 Official Text (9th Ed., West, 1978). The 1978 version has been adopted in forty-four states.

cial transactions is probably more extensive than that of any other UCC article. Unlike Article 8, which deals specifically with investment securities, Article 9 was not drafted with corporate indentures primarily in mind. It is nevertheless of importance in this area since it establishes uniform rules relating to all security transactions involving personal property, regardless of the form of the particular transaction or the security documents. The present trend toward more special-purpose secured financing, where contract rights, equipment leases, receivables, other debt obligations, and the like constitute the principal security, makes an understanding of the basic purposes and principles of the Article particularly desirable.

In addition to providing a single body of law for security transactions affecting personal property, the UCC made significant changes or clarifications in four important areas:

1. It provides statutory authority and rules for accounts receivable financing.

2. It specifically authorizes and makes effective both arrangements for subjecting after-acquired property to a security agreement, and arrangements for the making of future advances under the agreement without the necessity of preparing, signing, and recording or filing of supplemental agreements. This greatly facilitates security arrangements involving property that is constantly being disposed of and replaced, such as inventory.

3. It repeals the troublesome rule enunciated in *Benedict v. Ratner*[37] and permits the debtor to mortgage its inventory, stock-in-trade, or similar property and continue to operate the business in a normal manner and in accordance with the understanding and agreement of the parties, without the necessity of cumbersome provisions for the flow of proceeds. A necessary corollary is the protection of those who deal with the debtor in the normal course of business.

4. It recognizes and provides for the special status of the purchase money security interest.

Most corporate mortgages secure obligations that will be outstanding for many years. Some railroad bonds have maturities extending for a hundred years or more, and many corporate mortgages, particularly those of public utilities and railroads, are open-end indentures, designed to serve as permanent financing media. As security, the obligor customarily mortgages all land, plants, equipment, machinery, fixtures, fran-

[37] 268 U.S. 353 (1925).

chises, and all other items of property, real, personal or mixed, then owned or thereafter acquired, which generally constitute its fixed plant and property account, permanent investments, and other classes of property exclusive of cash, receivables, merchandise, and the like.

While in the normal commercial financing arrangement the intrinsic value of the collateral is readily measureable and adequate to secure the loan, the real security underlying a corporate mortgage is the "going concern" value of the business itself rather than the special value of the individual items of property. The importance of the security interest is the priority claim against the capital assets of the business that are necessary to its continuance as a going concern. Because the specific items of property are constantly being replaced or otherwise changing, the effectiveness of the after-acquired property clause is of paramount importance.

Before enactment of the UCC the law in most jurisdictions had evolved so that no particular problems were encountered in entering into those long term security arrangements and in making effective the security interests intended. Public utility and railroad mortgages in particular had been accorded a special status. In many jurisdictions recording the indenture as a real estate mortgage was all that was required to perfect the security interest with respect to both the real estate and chattels. The effectiveness of the lien in regard to after-acquired property was recognized without the necessity of rerecording or refiling. In other states, often in relation to other types of obligors, an equitable lien on after-acquired property was recognized, so long as it was periodically perfected by recording a supplemental indenture, frequently in connection with additional financing under the indenture. Only rarely were obligors or corporate trustees concerned with statutes dealing with interests in personal property only. Property descriptions, in the case of public utility, railroad obligors, and, less frequently, industrial companies, were necessarily general, although no particular problems were encountered.

While the UCC excludes real property and interests flowing from real property from its scope, it does cover all security interests in personal property and in fixtures. Since every corporate mortgage involves security interests in fixtures and various types of personal property, Article 9 cast some doubt on the effectiveness of the pre-code financing arrangements and created problems of compliance, particularly in states that had no provision for central filing for this type of security interest.

Most railroads and utilities operate in a great many jurisdictions. The requirement for the filing of the security interest with respect to fixtures in each jurisdiction where real estate was located presented a dual problem: filing and refiling of financing statements in each such jurisdiction, and providing an adequate description of the real estate involved.

A special problem in the case of railroad rolling stock was involved. While the customary equipment trust is filed under Section 20(c) of the Interstate Commerce Act and is exempt from the UCC filing requirements because of the existence of the Federal statute, all railroad general mortgages also cover rolling stock. It had never been the practice to record general railroad mortgages with the Interstate Commerce Commission, although it indicated that it would accept corporate railroad mortgages for filing under section 20(c). The obligor could state that the mortgage covered any rolling stock then owned or thereafter acquired, subject to equipment trust obligations, although technically such filing did not comply with the regulations relating thereto.[38]

The problems referred to above have been dealt with to some extent by several of the states. In New York, a mortgage covering both real and personal property recorded as a real estate mortgage after the effective date of the UCC required only the filing of a financing statement in the department of state with respect to the fixtures and personal property, and it was unnecessary to include a description of the real estate in such financing statement.

Special efforts have been made to secure adoption of appropriate amendments to the UCC in all states. The alternatives suggested have been either (1) to exempt all public utility and railroad mortgages—and possibly all corporate mortgages—from the filing requirements of the UCC, or (2) to provide for central filing as under the New York statute and as recommended by the Association of American Railroads. It would also be desirable to eliminate the necessity of refiling a financing statement every five years. Since the corporate mortgage secures obligations that will be outstanding for many years, and since the date of maturity can be shown on the statement, no real purpose is served by the requirement for periodic refiling.

Although no further action is required to continue the perfected status of the security interest in personal property covered by a corporate mortgage of real and personal property recorded before the effective date of the UCC, it is not clear what action, if any, should be taken with respect to personal property acquired after the effective date. If a supple-

[38] 49 CFR secs. 57.1 to 57.5 (1963).

mental mortgage is executed and filed, or if there is additional financing under the mortgage, the requisite financing statement should be filed in the department of state.

If the obligor has outstanding more than one mortgage covering its property, and there is additional financing under a junior or refunding mortgage, financing statements under all mortgages have proper order of priority because of the "first to file" rule.

Where partial releases of personal property are executed under a corporate mortgage, it would seem unnecessary to make any filing with respect to such partial release unless it involves the release of all such property in the jurisdiction. If necessary to protect the purchaser of the property released, execution of the release on the bill of sale should be all that is required.

Despite repeal of the *Benedict v. Ratner* rule, drafters of corporate indentures should avoid the temptation to extend the scope of security coverage of the corporate indenture unnecessarily. Little will be added to the value of the security in the usual case and a great many problems may be created, particularly with respect to an indenture qualified under the TIA. A different question is presented, of course, if a principal purpose of the transaction is the financing of working capital. In such a situation the security must be tailored to the requirements of the particular arrangement.

Whereas a few ambiguities still exist and some problems have been created, the UCC on the whole represented a very significant contribution to our body of commercial law, but realization of the full potential offered still requires intelligent and realistic implementation by both attorneys and judges. The basic purposes and policies should always be kept in mind, as well as the express admonitions that the UCC is to be liberally construed and applied to promote these purposes and policies.

MODEL INDENTURES

Since the indenture was first used approximately 160 years ago, it has developed into the largest and, in many respects, the most complex of legal documents. Language was added through the years in response to frequent court decisions interpreting particular provisions, but until 1962 little effort had been made to reduce the excess verbiage or standardize its provisions.

In that year the American Bar Foundation announced the adoption of a "Corporate Debt Financing Project—A Project To Develop a Model Form of Corporate Debenture Indenture and Mortgage with Annotations and Comments."[39] The basic format adopted in 1965, after extended discussions by the Project committees, comprises two documents. One document called "Model Provisions" consists solely of the traditional boilerplate provisions common to most corporate debt indentures. The second document, sometimes called the "Incorporating Indenture," incorporates by reference the Model Provisions, or as many thereof as are agreed to by the parties to the particular financing. It also contains the negotiated provisions, which usually include the principal amount, the interest rate, the stated maturity and the terms of redemption of the debenture issue, certain particular covenants, and other special provisions, all as negotiated by the parties. These documents were the result of many meetings and discussions participated in by counsel who had frequently represented issuers or investors or investment bankers, a representative group of corporate trust officers, the SEC (with particular reference to conformity with the TIA), the New York Stock Exchange, and an Ad Hoc Consultative Committee of the American Institute of Certified Public Accountants. The final product inevitably represented many compromises. Nevertheless, it represented an important contribution by simplifying those provisions that were generally subject to negotiation in the drafting of indentures and providing standardized boilerplate for nonnegotiated provisions.[40]

The use of the 1965 Model Provisions (which provided for both bearer and fully registered debentures) was limited by the fact that by the time of publication a majority of new issues were being offered in registered form only. In the latter part of 1964, while the 1965 Model Provisions were still in the drafting stage, the corporate trust group urged the Project Directorate to undertake the preparation of Model Debenture Indenture Provisions for "all-registered" issues. This corporate trust group undertook the task of securing general agreement on the basic procedures that should be incorporated in such model provisions, and early in 1966 the group published its recommendations.[41] The result of this cooperative effort was the publication of a companion

[39]For a detailed discussion of the background of the project, *see* Rodgers, *The Corporate Trust Indenture Project,* 20 Bus. Law. 551 (1965).

[40]American Bar Foundation, Sample Incorporating Indenture—Model Debenture Indenture Provisions—1965.

[41]Corporate Trust Activities Committee, American Bankers Association, *Recommended Procedures For Registered Bond Issues* (1966). *See also* Kennedy and Landau, *Recent Developments in Debt Financing and Corporate Trust Admininstration,* 22 Bus. Law. 353 (1967).

Sample Incorporating Indenture and companion Model Provisions tailored to all-registered issues of debentures, but whose text was otherwise substantially the same as the two 1965 documents.[42]

The Model Provisions do not constitute an instrument but are intended as an exhibit to be attached to an indenture in the form recommended by the Sample Incorporating Indenture. It is, therefore, possible in the incorporating indenture to express specific deviations from the Model Provisions or to omit certain provisions entirely by not incorporating them in the Indenture.

The practice recommended by the Project of incorporating the Model Provisions in the indenture by reference has rarely been used in practice because of its complexities, but the substantive provisions of the Sample Incorporating Indenture and the Model Provisions are very often used as part of the modern indenture and are seldom modified or changed.

The publication of the "Commentaries on Indentures"[43] marked the third major step in accomplishing the Project's objective. The Commentaries were intended to accomplish a number of things: to outline the Model Provisions and how they were to be used; to explain why the particular form used was adopted and why certain traditional but outmoded provisions could be safely eliminated; to deal with the theories underlying the negotiable provisions of the indenture; and to offer sample alternative provisions that might be suited to particular requirements.

With the publication in 1981 of the Model Mortgage Bond Indenture Form, the Project completed its objectives established nineteen years earlier.[44]

The Model Mortgage Form is structured as an integrated mortgage indenture, instead of following the two-part technique used in the earlier models. It contains standardized model provisions and the negotiable provisions and includes many footnotes referring to the Debenture Commentaries, providing illustrations of alternative texts.

The next effort to streamline the trust indenture was the publication of a Model Simplified Indenture.[45] The model developed by the American Bar Association's Committee on Developments in Business Financing, is relatively short—some thirty-one pages—and written in "plain

[42] American Bar Foundation, Model Debenture Indenture Provisions—All Registered Issues—1967.

[43] American Bar Foundation, Commentaries on Indentures, 1972.

[44] American Bar Foundation, Model Mortgage Bond Indenture, 1981. *See also* Brown, *Review of Mortgage Bond Indenture Forms*, 36 *Bus. Law.* 1917 (1981).

[45] *See* note 1, chapter 1, *supra*.

English.'' The simplified model proceeds on the assumption "that (except for provisions specifically required by the TIA) nearly all portions of an indenture are subject to negotiation in varying degrees, but seek to prescribe the language of frequently encountered provisions in such a way as to achieve a consensus generally acceptable to counsel accustomed to analyzing indenture terms from the points of view of debenture holders, corporate borrowers, lending institutions, investment bankers and indenture trustees.''[46] The extensive notes to the model are often explained with a comparison to the American Bar Foundation's model indentures and commentaries or with reference to stock exchange listing requirements or prevailing administrative practice.

The most recent endeavor is the Sample Uncertificated Debt Indenture, which provides for the issuance of corporate debt securities in *either* certificated or noncertificated form at the holder's option.[47] Developed under the aegis of the Business Law Section of the American Bar Association by a group of distinguished securities lawyers with advice from several corporate trust professionals, the proposed indenture is an attempt to provide for the issuance of corporate debt instruments in pure uncertificated (i.e., dematerialized) form—as contemplated by the 1977 UCC Article 8 revisions, and the recommendations of the U.S. Working Committee of the Group of Thirty that "it is both desirable and achievable to eliminate use of the physical certificate by 1995 for the settlement of securities transactions".[48] In its report, the Ad Hoc Committee of the Business Law Section recognized that the application of this approach to municipal securities might be a problem, since "many state laws require that municipal securities receive approval from local or state agencies other than the issuer thereof. Even when such statutes contemplate uncertificated securities, there may be a problem in the approving agency delegating its certification responsibility to the indenture trustee. Certain of such statutes could be construed to require approving agency signatures (albeit facsimiles) on each transaction statement'' sent by the trustee to the seller and buyer involved.

The sum total of these efforts has produced important and valuable additions in the field of corporate finance and particularly in the simplification and standardization of the corporate trust indenture.

46 *Id.* at 742.
47 *See* note 8, *supra.*
48 *See, Status Report and Request For Comment,* U.S. Working Committee, Group of Thirty, Clearance and Settlement Project, at 8 (August 1990).

THREE

The Corporate Trustee

DEVELOPMENT OF THE TRUSTEE CONCEPT

The development of a firm concept of the duties and responsibilities of
the indenture trustee has closely paralleled the growth and development
of the trust indenture itself. In the very early history of corporate
mortgages there are cases where the mortgage ran directly to the bondholders themselves, without a trustee being named. The difficulties
presented by such an arrangement became apparent when the first default under such a mortgage occurred. The court ruled that in order for
the mortgage to be foreclosed, all bondholders had to join in the petition. Consequently, the practice of using a trustee to whom the mortgage
would run for the benefit of all the bondholders was developed at an
early date.

In the early years of this development, the trustee was usually a
single individual and was frequently an officer of the issuing corporation. Although such an individual's interests were obviously adverse to
those of the bondholders, it made little practical difference, for the
trustee at that time was simply a convenience for the mortgagor and had
few, if any, actual duties to perform. The trustee was in almost every
sense a mere stakeholder.

With the growth in the number of indentures and the gradually
increasing intricacies of corporate borrowing, criticism began to be
directed at this officer-trustee device and it soon became impractical.
The next step was the designation of an independent individual as

trustee. To give added status to the issue, individuals selected were usually outstanding citizens in the community.

The first instance of a bank being designated as an indenture trustee occurred in 1839, but the use of the institutional, as opposed to the individual, trustee did not become general practice until the latter part of the nineteenth century. The initial reason for the change was undoubtedly to avoid the problems presented by the death or incapacity of an individual trustee. After initial authentication of the bonds, there were still few duties to be performed, and responsibilities were not onerous.

As the use of the corporate indenture became more common and numerous problems were presented as a result of defaults, it was inevitable that greater powers should be placed in the hands of the corporate trustee. As corporations grew and the size of their bond issues increased and became more complex, it became difficult for bondholders themselves, either individually or collectively, to enforce their security in the event of default. Consequently, more and more restrictions were placed on suits by individual holders, and most rights of action were concentrated in the trustee. It was much easier to create an appearance of protection, however, than it was to provide remedies adequate in fact. Several factors operated to impede an orderly growth and development of the trustee's duties and responsibilities.

Corporate trusteeships were regarded by many banks as being in the nature of escrows and were accepted, usually without compensation, as a service to corporate banking customers. Laissez-faire was the guiding economic theory of the day, and it was not surprising that in this, as in other areas of corporate practice, a real sense of responsibility was slow in developing.

The growth in the trustee's duties was accompanied by an equivalent growth in the number and scope of exculpatory clauses. Early efforts to improve fees for trustee services met with stubborn resistance, and the resulting reluctance of the trustee to undertake lengthy, expensive, and time-consuming legal proceedings was understandable.

As has been indicated previously, there were no clearcut legal precedents and considerable confusion in the minds of courts about the exact nature of the indenture and the legal responsibility of the trustee for preserving and enforcing the security. Reliance by courts on different precedents and concepts led to many conflicting opinions and to the introduction of new and unusual provisions into each indenture. After each court decision, indenture drafters devised new language for the protection of the obligor and the trustee. As a result, the corporate indenture developed rapidly into one of the most complex of all legal documents, without offering a real solution to the basic problem of how to provide reasonable protection to security holders without exposing the trustee to undue and unwarranted liability.[1]

A start had been made, however. Many of the more responsible banks began to evince concern over the losses suffered by bondholders and the apparent ineffectiveness of remedies after default. The volume of corporate trust business was now sufficient to warrant the establishment of separate corporate trust units in the larger institutions, and this led to a reexamination of policies and practices. The sense of responsibility grew, and more attention was paid to all phases of corporate trust activity. Even among the older indentures, which contained little more than the basic mortgage provisions, advantage was taken of the "further assurance" clauses to secure continuing up-to-date information on the status of the security and the condition of the obligor's affairs. In newly drafted indentures, trustees began to insist on the inclusion of additional protective provisions and covenants. A new pattern of responsibility rapidly emerged, and by the late 1920s the corporate trustee had begun to be recognized as an important party to these financial transactions.

The pattern thus established by the more responsible institutions was not universal, however, and the practices still followed in a number of cases brought continued criticism by courts and recognized authorities in the field. The financial collapse of 1929 and the ensuing Great Depression resulted in an increasing number of defaults and led to a critical examination of all phases of security practice. Although the broad generalities embodied in the conclusions and recommendations of the SEC report[2] were neither impartial nor fair, no serious student of the subject could question the desirability of the establishment of minimum standards to which the trust indentures and the conduct of corporate trustees should conform. The TIA, in effect, codified the more important practices that had been developed and were already being followed by the leading corporate trust departments. As has been indicated, the essential provisions of this act are now fairly standard for all corporate indentures whether required to be qualified under the act or not, although private placement agreements usually do not impose the "prudent man" standard upon the occurrence of a default.

---

[1] Not entirely whimsically, the corporate indenture has been defined as "the crystalized fears of five generations of lawyers."

[2] See SEC, *Report on the Study and Investigation of the Work, Activities, Personnel and Functions of Protective and Reorganization Committees*, Part VI (1936).

Whereas by 1940 the practice of using an individual as opposed to institutional trustees was practically obsolete, the act required the designation of an institutional corporate trustee meeting certain minimum standards of eligibility under all indentures to be qualified under the act.

ESSENTIAL FUNCTION OF THE CORPORATE TRUSTEE

In succeeding chapters consideration will be given to the duties of the trustee with reference to typical specific indenture provisions and the issuance and servicing of the indenture securities. It might facilitate an understanding of the trustee function, however, to consider briefly the principal areas of the trustee's responsibility.

As indicated in the preceding chapter, the essential function of a trustee is the administration of the security provisions of a contract between the issuing corporation and the holders of the indenture securities. There are three principal areas of responsibility.

In the first place, if the issue is secured in any way, the trustee holds and deals with the security. If the security consists in whole or in part of a mortgage on corporate real property, the trustees is the mortgagee and must concern itself with problems related to maintenance, insurance, taxes, release, and replacement and, within the scope of the powers granted, must see that the security is maintained in the agreed manner. If the security for the bond issue is personal property, such as equipment, the trustee will normally "perfect" its security interest in the property by filing a financing statement pursuant to the Uniform Commercial Code of the applicable state.

Second, as administrator of the contract, the trustee has the responsibility of making sure that the convenants and other indenture provisions are performed in the agreed manner. This it does in large part through examining reports and certificates it receives from the obligor corporation or independent accountants, engineers, or other experts.

Finally, in the event of a default, the trustee has a primary responsibility for enforcing the remedial provisions of the contract. As will be discussed in greater detail in a later chapter, the nature of this responsibility has been substantially changed by the enactment of federal and state laws dealing with bankruptcy and creditors' rights.

In addition to the performance of specifically enumerated duties, the modern corporate trustee contributes a great deal more to the relationship. Most of the larger institutions have a trained staff experienced in handling many types of indentures and the innumerable problems concerning them that have arisen over the years. By virtue of this experience, corporate trust officers are able to make substantial contributions during the indenture drafting process and frequently can suggest an appropriate course of action whenever difficulties arise. These professionals are also continually devising new and more efficient methods of handling the many operational details involved in the processing and servicing of securities, thus accomplishing substantial savings to both issuers and holders.

In many instances an issuer will sell long-term debt obligations to a limited number of institutional investors under a "direct placement" contract. This practice eliminates the necessity of registering such securities under the 33 Act or of qualifying an indenture. Occasionally such securities are issued under purchase contracts with the separate investors, and no indenture or trustee is involved. Such a procedure is quite proper in the appropriate case. Where security is involved, however, or where more than a few investors purchase a single issue, or where complicated sinking fund or similar provisions are involved, or, again, where the terms of the contract are unusual and require frequent checking, the use of a trustee is recommended. From the point of view of the investor the activities of the trustee supplement rather than supersede those of the investor institution. From the point of view of the obligor the convenience and service obtained usually outweight the fairly nominal fees involved.

The terms of these issues are usually set in consultation with an investment banker and after discussion with one or more of the principal prospective purchasers. Special counsel appointed by the issuer to represent the purchaser traditionally drafts the financing documents. Although the flexibility available as a result of direct negotiations between issuer and purchaser is regarded as a major advantage of private placements, patterns of inflexibility developed as the major institutional investors established their own set of required convenants, sometimes without regard to the needs of a particular case. As a result many of the existing note purchase agreements follow a more or less rigid pattern, which is not always in the best interests of either issuer or investor. For public and many private issues an experienced corporate trustee, familiar with all types of financing arrangements, is an important addition to the team of experts who work out the details of the financing document.

A similar contribution can be made in the case of privately placed note issues.

The use of a corporate trustee for such issues also contributes to the solution of problems encountered in the past and, on the positive side, provides numerous benefits, such as:

1. Uniform administration of the security provisions of the contract.

2. Identification provided by the trustee's authentication of the notes issued, of holders of notes entitled to the benefits of the contract.

3. Improved marketability of the obligations. To qualify for exemption from the registration requirements of the 33 Act the notes must be purchased for investment and not for distribution. However it is essential from the point of view of an institutional investor that any obligation purchased be marketable: indeed an increasing volume of obligations originally placed privately is being sold by the original investors. This trend can be expected to burgeon with the development of the secondary market for private placements which SEC Rule 144A is intended to facilitate. Obvious problems are thus created, not only in consummating these transactions but also in determining rights of the transferees in the absence of an indenture and uniform provisions governing transfers or assignments.

4. Improved marketability should also reduce the interest cost to obligors. Institutional investors usually insist, because of limited marketability, on a premium of ten to twenty basis points in the rate of interest paid on notes acquired in a private placement. Anything that would tend to improve marketability should reduce this spread.

5. Efficient servicing of the debt obligations. Application of the amortization formula assures continuation of the relative interests of the investors vis-à-vis the total debt. Many issuers now employ a bank as agent to render these services.

6. More efficient communication. Each investor usually recieves a complete set of all documents delivered at each note closing, although it is difficult to understand what real purpose is served by the dissemination of this volume of paper. If a complete set of documents were provided the trustee acting on behalf of all investors, all that any investor should require would be the note itself, a copy of the purchase agreement, and opinion of its special counsel. This should represent a considerable saving to most institutional investors, as well as to issuers.

ELIGIBILITY REQUIREMENTS

Section 310 of the TIA sets forth the requirements that an institution must meet in order to be eligible to serve as indenture trustee. The act requires that there be at all times one or more trustees at least one of which must be a corporation organized and doing business under the laws of the United States or of any state or territory or the District of Columbia. Such trustee must be authorized under such laws to exercise corporate trust powers and be subject to supervision or examination by federal, state, territorial, or District of Columbia authority. It must have at all times a combined capital and surplus of not less than $150,000. Foreign institutions are now permitted to serve as corporate trustees under certain circumstances.[3] The act absolutely prohibits any obligor on the indenture securities or any person directly or indirectly controlling, controlled by, or under the common control with such obligor, from acting as trustee on the indenture securities.[4]

These minimum requirements are very light and enable almost any banking institution normally exercising trust powers to act. Many qualified indentures impose much more stringent requirements. For example a customary minimum capital and surplus requirement is $5,000,000.[5] It is also frequently required that the corporate trustee have its principal office in one of the large financial centers, such as New York City. This requirement is no longer of major importance, for many institutions throughout the country are now fully qualified to act under most indentures, although the actual experience and qualifications of the prospective trustee are important factors that should always be considered carefully. On some types of issues, investment bankers insist, quite properly, on limiting the area from which a trustee may be chosen. A typical example of this would be a large issue of a quasi-public corporation, the proceeds of which are to be used for construction of a major project. Selection of a trustee from outside the area of the project avoids the possibility of a conflict of interest or of the use of political pressures in connection with administration of the trusts. Administration of such an indenture also involves many technical problems of major importance with which most of the smaller institutions are not familiar.

3 TIA, sec. 310 (a)(1).
4 TIA, sec. 310 (a)(5).
5 Many major corporate issuers insist on a potential trustee bank's having at least $25 million of combined capital and surplus.

Inasmuch as the trustee will have been selected and will be acting at the time of the execution and delivery of the indenture, the purpose of the eligibility provision is to govern the selection of a successor trustee in the event the original trustee resigns or becomes incapable of acting. Because this is a substantive provision, a successor trustee that does not meet the specified standards cannot be named without the consent of all the security holders or a specified percentage thereof. In the unlikely event that no other trustee meeting the requirements of the indenture and willing to act can be found, it has been held that a trustee not meeting such requirements can be appointed and can exercise all the rights and powers granted by the indenture. If such a situation should develop, however, it is recommended that judicial sanction for such an appointment first be obtained.

PROHIBITION OF CONFLICTING INTERESTS— QUALIFICATION OF THE TRUSTEE

The problem of conflicting interests is a troublesome one and one of which the trustee should always be conscious.[6] Under normal circumstances an issuing corporation will select one of its principal banks to act as indenture trustee. The familiarity such an institution has with the corporation's affairs and the close continuing relationship, as a practical matter, will enable such an institution to do a more thorough job for the security holders, as well as for the issuing corporation. The administrative officers should familiarize themselves thoroughly with all relationships between their bank and the obligor corporation and ensure that no possibility arises for the fairness and impartiality of the trustee's acts to be questioned.

One of the innovations introduced by the TIA in 1939 was the setting down of certain "rules of thumb" that would disqualify an institution from acting as trustee under a qualified indenture. In recognition of the fact that prior to default the duties of the trustee are essentially administrative and ministerial in nature, the TIRA suspended the requirement of resignation for conflict of interest until a default occurs. These provisions are set forth in Section 310(b) and are now incorporated by force of law in all qualified indentures. This section does not, however, cover the whole field of conflicts or prohibit any interest that might possibly

---

[6]Even if the issue is exempt from the TIA, this does not necessarily mean that the trustee is completely exculpated from adherence to conduct that would be prohibited if the issue were qualified.

be a conflict. The trustee is deemed to have a potential conflicting interest if it has one or more of ten different relationships. For discussion, these relationships are considered from the viewpoint of prohibited general interests or affiliations.

Trusteeship Under More Than One Indenture

Section 310(b)(1) identifies as a potential conflicting interest the same trustee acting under more than one indenture of the same obligor "or is trustee for more than one outstanding series of securities . . . under a single indenture of an obligor". The latter provision, which was unfortunately included in the TIRA, appears to mandate that there be separate trustees for each series of defaulted bonds issued under secured indentures, e.g., utility and railroad mortgages. Hopefully the SEC's broad exemptive powers, as well as the stay of resignation provisions absent a payment default will ameliorate this problem. Two situations are excepted. The first occurs where the qualified indenture is a collateral indenture, the only collateral consisting of obligations issued under the other indenture. The second exception is where both issues are unsecured and confer upon the holders substantially the same rights. It is required, however, that the qualified indenture specifically refer to the obligations under the other (prior) indenture. Exception is allowed where the second indenture is subsequently qualified under the act. Upon application, the SEC may permit trusteeship under more than one indenture subsequent to a default if it finds that such trusteeship is not likely to involve a material conflict of interest.

The significance of the same trustee acting under separate indentures is apparent. Although before default the trustee might act under two indentures of the same obligor without encountering difficulty, the happening of an event of default will usually create a conflict and prevent the trustee from adequately representing holders under both indentures, for their interests are quite likely to be adverse. The importance of having independent representation in proceedings after default was recognized in an 1895 decision of the federal court in New York, which permitted intervention of individual bondholders in a foreclosure suit where the trustee was acting under several indentures. Also, it was suggested that the trustee should be subjected to a higher standard of care where it was acting under more than one indenture.

The term "obligor" is defined in the TIA as every person (including a guarantor) who is liable on the indenture securities.[7] Trusteeship under

[7] TIA, sec. 303 (12).

indentures of affiliated companies is permissible provided the same company is not liable on the indenture securities issued under more than one of such indentures.

A difficult question is presented where no guaranty in fact exists but where the credit of one corporation is the primary security for obligations issued by another. Such a situation would arise, for example, if corporation A issued securities for the construction of certain facilities to be leased to corporation B, the rental payments being sufficient to service the securities and the lease, and the right to receive the rents being pledged under the indenture. These facts alone are not sufficient to constitute corporation B an "obligor" on the securities, but greater care should be exercised in such a situation, and all the facts surrounding the proposed transaction should be considered to determine if an actual, as distinguished from a technical, conflict is likely to arise.

Ownership of Securities

Subdivisions (5) to (9) of Section 310(b) set down certain rules for the disqualification of the trustee based on affiliations through security ownership. Disqualification under these subdivisions does not depend on the existence of actual control of or any conflicting interest in fact, but beneficial ownership of the specified percentage of securities is required to be made a conflicting interest as a part of the contract between the parties. A potential conflicting interest is deemed to exist, and the trustee upon default will be disqualified from acting as such, if any of the following situations exist:

1. Ten percent or more of the voting securities of the trustee is beneficially owned either by an obligor or by any director, partner, or executive officer of an obligor; 20 percent or more of such voting securities is owned, collectively, by any two or more of such persons; or 10 percent or more of such voting securities is beneficially owned by either an underwriter for any such obligor or by any director, partner, or executive officer thereof, or is beneficially owned, collectively, by any two or more such persons.

2. Beneficial ownership by the trustee or the holding by the trustee as collateral security for an obligation that is in default as to principal for thirty days or more of:

    a. 5 percent or more of the voting securities of the obligor;

    b. 10 percent or more of any other class of security of the obligor, excluding all securities issued under an indenture for which the trustee is acting as trustee;

c. 5 percent or more of the voting securities of a person who, to the knowledge of the trustee, owns 10 percent or more of the voting securities of, or controls directly or indirectly, or is under direct or indirect common control with, an obligor;

d. 10 percent or more of any class of security of a person who, to the knowledge of the trustee, owns 50 percent or more of the voting securities of an obligor; or

e. 10 percent or more of any class of security of an underwriter for an obligor.

Since a conflicting interest by reason of the trustee's ownership of the above percentage of securities is predicated on the existence of an adverse interest in the trustee, ownership of securities issued under the particular indenture in question, or under any other indenture for which the trustee also acts as trustee, has been excluded.

3. Ownership by the trustee of securities in a fiduciary capacity. The trustee is required to make a check of its holdings promptly after the date of a default on the indenture securities, and annually as long as the default continues, of the types of securities enumerated above in its capacity as executor, administrator, testamentary or intervivos trustee, guardian, committee, conservator, or any similar capacity. A potential conflicting interest is deemed to exist if, on such date, the trustee holds in such capacities an aggregate of 25 percent or more or any class of security, the beneficial ownership of a specified percentage of which would constitute a conflict. In order to eliminate the possibility of an inadvertent conflict arising by reason of acquisition of securities in new estates, the act provides that the conflict provisions will not apply, for a period not to exceed two years from the date of such acquisition, to the extent that such securities do not exceed 25 percent or more of the particular class outstanding.

In the event that there is a default in the payment of principal or interest under an indenture that continues for thirty days, the trustee is required to make a prompt check of its fiduciary holdings, and thereafter any ownership in such capacity of securities over which it has sole or joint control is to be deemed beneficial ownership for the purpose of determining whether a potential conflict exists.

Excluded from the operation of subdivisions (6) to (9) of Section 310(b) is any security held by the trustee as collateral security for an obligation not in default; held as collateral security under the indenture, irrespective of any default thereunder; or held by it in the capacity of custodian, escrow agent, depositary, agent for collection, or any similar representative capacity.

Other Affiliations Between Trustee and Obligor or Underwriters

Four other situations are specified in Section 310(b), the existence of any one of which will constitute a potential conflict of interest.

First, if the trustee or any of its directors or executive officers is an underwriter for an obligor. The TIRA defines an underwriter as any person who, within one year prior to the time the determination is made, was an underwriter of any security of an obligor.

Second, if the trustee or any of its directors or executive officers is a director, officer, partner, employee, appointee, or representative of an obligor or of any underwriter (other than the trustee itself) for an obligor. One individual may be a director and/or executive officer of the trustee and a director and/or executive officer of an obligor, provided such individual is not at the same time an executive officer of both. Also, if, and so long as, the number of directors of the trustee in office is more than nine, one additional individual may be a director and/or executive officer of the trustee and a director of such obligor.[8]

Third, if the trustee directly or indirectly controls, is directly or indirectly controlled by, or is under direct or indirect common control with an underwriter for an obligor. The control referred to here is actual control, whether or not it involves ownership of a prohibited percentage of the securities referred to above. The question of whether or not actual control exists must be determined by the circumstances of each case.

Finally, a potential conflict of interest arises if the trustee is or becomes a creditor of the obligor. This new potential conflict codifies the existing practice of most major corporate trustees to resign a trusteeship for a financially troubled obligor when it is also a creditor.

---

[8] The SEC has indicated that "it is now our view that the term "director" as defined in Section 303(5) of the (Trust Indenture) Act would not include emeritus, honorary or advisory directors who are appointed rather than elected and who serve merely as advisors without any other customary responsibilities or duties, including the right to vote, of directors." SEC letter, dated June 22, 1981, to James D. McLaughlin Government Relations Counsel, American Bankers Association.

ADMINISTRATIVE RESPONSIBILITY UNDER CONFLICT PROVISIONS

Under a qualified indenture, if a conflict of interest as outlined above exists or develops, the trustee, within ninety days after default must either eliminate such conflict or resign (subject to the "stay" provisions of TIA, section 310(b)). The trustee should therefore establish procedures and checks that will bring to light any conflict that may develop. No established routine is required but the trustee should be in a position to show that it has exercised reasonable care, and it must report annually any change to its eligibility and qualifications to serve as trustee, and the creation of or any material change in any of the potential conflict of interest relationships set forth in TIA section 310(b)(1) through (10). Material change can be any change that would cause the trustee to resign (if a default occurred), or would permit the bank to remain as trustee if there were a existing default under the indenture. It is recommended that an annual report be obtained from the obligor: as to the latter's holding of trustee's securities, if any; as to the outstanding securities of such obligor; and as to firms that have acted as underwriters for such obligor within the preceding year. Procedures within the trustee's office should be established to ensure the prompt reporting of such security holdings as might constitute a potential conflict.

PROBLEMS OF QUALIFICATION IN FOREIGN STATES

A corporation is a creature of the state in which it is incorporated but is a foreign entity insofar as other states are concerned. Although it is regarded as a "person" for many purposes of the law, it is not entitled to the protection of the "privileges and immunities" clause of the United States Constitution. Accordingly, with certain exceptions relating to interstate or foreign commerce, a state may exclude a corporation of another state from doing business within its borders and from suing in its courts with respect to any prohibited transactions or otherwise engaging in activities over which the state has jurisdiction. It may also impose such terms and conditions as it deems proper for the granting of permission to do business within its borders. Most states have general statutes, whether on a basis of reciprocity or otherwise, relating to the conduct of business by foreign corporations. Although exceptions are growing each year, banking corporations are generally not permitted to do general banking business in other states, but the exercise of trust powers may, or may not, be permitted. Some states permit the exercise of such powers under specified conditions; a few have specific prohibitions; but most have no statute at all relating to the matter.

This presents a special problem for the corporate trustee. Most of the larger corporations do business and own property in a number of different states. When such a corporation wishes to execute a mortgage on its fixed properties to secure a bond issue, the question arises of whether the designated trustee may properly hold a security interest in property in all of the states in which such property is located. It is impossible to set down a general rule as a guide in these situations because the law differs from state to state. The following may be taken as a basic guide: (1) where there is a specific statute prescribing conditions for the exercise of trust powers by foreign banking corporations, the trustee should qualify under such a statute before accepting a mortgage or security interest in fixed property within that state; (2) where there is no statutory provision, the trustee may normally hold such a security interest unless such act contravenes the general "doing of business" statutes; (3) where there is a specific prohibition against the exercise of trust powers by a foreign bank, the trustee should not undertake to hold a security interest in property in such a state. These are suggested as general guides only, however, because the statutes, and judicial interpretation of statutes, vary from state to state. Counsel should therefore be certain of the proper authority of the corporate trustee in each such situation.

If a corporate trustee undertakes to act without authority, it may not only subject itself to heavy penalties but, from the viewpoint of its fiduciary resonsibility, it may also be denied access to the courts of the state for enforcement of the security if such becomes necessary.

The usual solution to this problem is the designation of an individual to act as a cotrustee under the indenture. Where only one state is in question, it would also be appropriate to designate a banking corporation in that state as a cotrustee. Under the federal constitution, an individual citizen of a state is entitled to all the privileges and immunities of citizens of other states and cannot be excluded from holding property or doing business as can a foreign corporation. In any situation in which there is a question about the authority of the corporate trustee, an individual cotrustee should be named.

Care must be exercised in drafting the appropriate indenture provisions. The usual provision, and a requirement of the TIA for qualified indentures, is that all rights, powers, duties, and obligations conferred or imposed upon the trustees shall be conferred or imposed upon and exercised by the institutional corporate trustee, or the institutional trustee and the cotrustee jointly, except to the extent that under any law of any jurisdiction in which any act or acts are to be performed, such institutional trustee is incompetent or unqualified to perform such act or acts, in which event such rights, powers, duties, and obligations shall be exercised and performed by the cotrustee.

Since all rights, powers, and duties are to be performed by the corporate trustee, except only such functions as it is incapable of performing, the corporate trustee is usually given the right, either alone or jointly with the obligor, to remove the designated individual trustee at any time and to appoint another individual to act. It is also a common practice to reserve to the corporate trustee and obligor the right to designate a cotrustee or an additional cotrustee at any time in the event such designation is necessary or desirable for the carrying out of any specific duty. This is done even though in the first instance a cotrustee may not be required, for it avoids the possibility of a situation arising where the corporate trustee cannot act and no mechanism is available for resolving the difficulty.

Although any individual citizen may be designated as cotrustee, the usual practice is for an officer of the corporate trustee to be designated as the individual cotrustee. This facilitates the exercise of powers or the performance of duties, such as the execution of releases of supplemental indentures, that the trustees are required to perform jointly.

Two states (Florida and Missouri) prohibit the exercise of trust powers by other than a corporation or individual citizen of such state. Although such statutes probably do not exclude an individual citizen of another state from holding or enforcing a security interest in property, it is advisable to comply with the letter of the law and designate an individual or a bank in such a state as the cotrustee.

The problems outlined above do not arise in the case of an unsecured debenture or note agreement, or in other indentures where no property is mortgaged or pledged, for the trustee normally performs no acts outside its principal office.

Special Provisions Relating to Trustee

In addition to the matters previously discussed, there are certain general provisions relating to the trustee that should be incorporated in all indentures. These are usually found in the separate "Trustee" article.

First is the acceptance by the trustee of the trusts and obligations imposed upon it by the indenture. Although the act of execution would undoubtedly constitute a sufficient acceptance, it is customary to include an affirmative statement to this effect in the indenture.

Second, a provision should be included relating to the compensation and expenses of the trustee. Rather than setting specific rates of compensation, the common practice is to provide that the trustee shall be entitled to reasonable compensation that shall not be limited by any statutory provision governing compensation of trustees. The latter is to avoid the possibility that statutes that exist in many states fixing maximum compensation for executors and trustees of testamentary or intervivos trusts would be held applicable to these agreements. It is also desirable for the trustee to include a provision under which the obligor agrees to indemnify it with respect to any liability incurred or damage suffered by it resulting from other than its own negligence. The trustee should also be permitted, but not required, to make advances to preserve the mortgaged property, pay taxes, or for other purposes. All these items, including all expenses and disbursements made by the trustee, should be payable by the obligor on demand (with interest in the case of any funds advanced by the trustee). If the indenture is a secured indenture, the trustee is usually given a lien on the security (prior to that of the indenture securities) to assure payment of its compensation, expenses, advances, and liabilities. This is desirable, although one would be hard pressed to find a case in which the full implications of such priority of lien has been upheld.

Third, the trustee should be given authority to act through agents or attorneys in carrying out its duties, and it is customarily provided that the trustee will not be liable for the acts of such agents or attorneys if reasonable care is exercised in their selection.

Finally, the indenture should contain appropriate provisions relative to the resignation or removal of the trustee. As has been indicated, a conflict of interest may develop requiring the trustee's resignation. The trustee should also be permitted to submit its resignation at any time for any reason it deems sufficient, or for no reason if it no longer wishes to act. The indenture should provide appropriate procedures for such resignation and for the appointment of a successor, which must be eligible and qualified to act. A majority in principal amount of the holders of the indenture securities are usually given the absolute right to designate the successor trustee, but until such right is exercised, any successor appointed by the obligor has full authority and power to act. As a practical matter, a successor trustee is usually appointed by the obligor and seldom by the bondholders. If the trustee is involved in a merger or consolidation with another institution, it is usually provided that the surviving corporation will automatically succeed to the trusteeship without further act, if it is eligible and qualified.

A majority in principal amount of the indenture security holders are customarily given the absolute right, at any time and with or without cause, to remove the trustee. Because the latter is supposed to serve their interests, it is quite appropriate that they have the power, by majority action, to remove the trustee and substitute another if for any reason they believe their interests are not being served properly. The obligor, however, should never be given the right by unilateral action to remove the trustee.

If the trustee submits its resignation and no successor is appointed within a reasonable time, the trustee or any security holder may petition a court for appointment of a successor, and an institution so appointed will be qualified to act.

EXCULPATORY PROVISIONS

Among the provisions that were the subject of a great amount of comment, criticism, and controversy in pre-TIA days were the "exculpatory clauses," which had come to be more or less standard in all indentures. The general legal effect of these provisions was to exempt the trustee from liability for any act or failure to act, short of willful misconduct or gross negligence. Much could be written pro and con on this matter, for these clauses were enlarged and expanded over a lengthy period. This was due in no small part to the misunderstandings on the part of security holders and courts concerning the essential nature of the trustee function and to attempt to hold the trustee accountable in some way for every unfortunate and unwise investment. Under these conditions it was essential for even conscientious trustees and their counsel to endeavor to protect themselves. Notwithstanding the validity of arguments that could be, and were, made in favor of these provisions, they had two unfortunate results. They provided protection even to a trustee indifferent to its fiduciary responsibility, and they subjected all trustees to criticism, even those who were diligent and conscientious in the performance of their duties, these latter comprising the great majority of trustees.

One result of the enactment of the TIA was the prohibition of such broad immunity provisions.[9] A qualified indenture may not contain provisions relieving the trustee of liability for its own negligent action, its own negligent failure to act, or its own willful misconduct, although the trustee shall be protected from liability for any error of judgment made in good faith by a responsible officer, where the trustee was not negligent in ascertaining the pertinent facts. This has become the accepted practice for almost all modern indentures, whether or not qualified.

Certain exculpatory provisions are still perfectly proper and permissible if they do not contravene the foregoing prohibition. Trustees should endeavor to have them included to prevent a court reading into an indenture an implied covenant or duty on the part of the trustee where none was intended. Several cases make it apparent, however, that trustees can no longer be absolutely assured that such exculpatory provisions will provide the protection intended. These cases seem to fall into two categories: those holding that only a trial can determine whether the trustee's duties extended beyond the provisions of the indenture,[10] and those that question the trustee's protection in relying on information and advice given it by the obligor, bond counsel, and even by its own legal counsel.[11]

Despite these cases, trustee's counsel should ensure that in the absence of any express duty in the indenture, or only to the extent of any duty specifically imposed, the following provisions be included:

1. The trustee has no obligation or duty to record the indenture.
2. The trustee has no responsibility for the truth or accuracy of the recitals in the indenture.
3. The trustee has no responsibility in regard to the application of the proceeds of any bonds, or with respect to the use or application of

[9] TIA, sec. 315(d).

[10] Cronin v. Midwestern Oklahoma Development Authority, 619 F.2d 856 (10th Cir. 1980); Nelson v. Quimby Island Reclamation District Facilities Corporation, 491 F. Supp. 1364 (N.D. Cal. 1980).

[11] Mathews v. Fischer, 1979–80 Fed. Sec. L. Rptr. para 97,336 (S.D. Ohio 1978); Woods v. Holmes & Structures of Pittsburgh, Kansas, 489 F. Supp. 1270 (Kan. 1980).

any property or monies released or paid out in accordance with indenture provisions.

4. The trustee may consult with counsel and shall be held harmless for anything done, in good faith, in accordance with the opinion of such counsel.
5. The trustee is not responsible for the validity of the indenture or of any securities issued thereunder, or for the obligor's title to, or the value of, the security held.
6. In the absence of bad faith, the trustee may rely on any certificates, opinions, documents, or other papers furnished to it and believed by it to be genuine and to be signed by the proper party or parties; the trustee is under a duty, however, to examine any such instruments furnished to it in accordance with an indenture provision to make sure that they comply with such provision.
7. The trustee shall not be liable for any action taken at the request or direction of holders of a majority in principal amount of the indenture securities.

PRESCRIBED STANDARDS OF CONDUCT

What should be the prescribed standard of conduct for an indenture trustee?[12] A clear distinction should be made between the duties before a default and those existing after a default occurs, when the security holder's investment is in jeopardy. In the normal case the obligor will perform its obligations and covenants, and the investor's principal concern is in receiving interest and principal when due. Under these circumstances the duties of the trustee are largely administrative. It is important, however, that the interests of the security holders be protected at all times, no matter how solvent or secure the obligor may appear. An active and vigilant administration by the trustee is necessary at all times to ensure, if possible, that there is no default, or, if default occurs, that the bondholders will have the security for which they bargained from which to recover.

In this connection, corporate trust administrative officers may wish to

[12] It is the board of directors which is ultimately responsible for the proper exercise of fiduciary powers by every national bank. All matters pertinent thereto, including the determination of policies, the investment and disposition of property held in a fiduciary capacity, and the direction and review of all officers, employees, and committees utilized by the bank in the exercise of its fiduciary powers, are the responsibility of the board. See 12 CFR sec. 9.7(a)(1) (1989).

review *Exhibit 2, Discharge of Fiduciary Obligations,* which sets forth recommended policies and procedures governing the conduct and performance of the bank acting as a corporate trustee.

The nature and extent of the duties of the trustee will vary with each indenture, depending on its terms. Because it constitutes a contract between the obligor and trustee, it not only prescribes rules of conduct for the former but also defines the limits of the trustee's authority, and the latter may do only what the indenture either in express terms or by necessary implication authorizes it to do.

As authorized by the TIA before default: (1) the trustee shall be liable only for the performance of such duties as are specifically set forth in the indenture; (2) the extent of such duties shall be determined solely by the express provisions of the indenture; and (3) no implied duties or covenants on the part of the trustee shall be read into the indenture.[13]

Most early court decisions dealing with the issue of fiduciary responsibilities relate to indentures that did not contain this language, and many courts found implied duties not expressly set forth, frequently basing their decision on the nature of the agreement itself. The majority of indentures still contain language from which it might be possible to infer such duties. For example, it is usually provided that a trustee may on its own initiative make independent investigations or require further evidence of the performance by the obligor of its covenants. Such a provision is highly desirable, but it is recommended that an express qualification be inserted to the effect that the trustee is under no duty to do so. Some courts have indicated that the trustee is under an implied duty to do whatever may be necessary to preserve the trust estate and that to this extent such duty cannot be abridged even by agreement.[14]

A real problem exists whenever the trustee deems it necessary to act beyond the scope of its express duties and powers. It is quite possible that an even higher standard of care may be imposed with respect to any such action, and the trustee may lose the benefit of the exculpatory clauses. Although situations sometimes arise where it is imperative that action be taken, every effort should be made to find an indenture provision on which to base such action.

The TIA requires that upon the occurrence of an event of default, the trustee shall exercise such of the rights and powers vested in it by the indenture and shall use the same degree of care and skill in their

---

[13] TIA, sec. 315(a).

[14] *See generally,* Schreiber and Wood, *Caveat Indenture Trustees: Avoiding the Expanding Scope of Sutton's Law,* 121/1 *Trusts and Estate* 48 (Jan. 1982).

exercise, as a prudent man would exercise or use under the circumstances in the conduct of his own affairs.[15]

Despite some earlier court cases that held that trustees may have pre-default obligations beyond those set forth in the indenture,[16] it is now well established that prior to a default under an indenture the trustee's responsibilities are defined and determined solely by the terms of the indenture.[17] In *Meckel v. Continental Resources Co.*, the court concluded that "unlike the ordinary trustee, who has historic common-law duties imposed beyond those in the trust agreement, an indenture trustee is more like a stakeholder whose duties and obligations are exclusively defined by the terms of the indenture agreement."[18] Further reinforcing this doctrine, the court in *Elliott Associates v. J. Henry Schroder Bank & Trust Co* stated that "we therefore conclude that, so long as the trustee fulfills its obligations under the express terms of the indenture, it owes the debenture holders no additional, implicit pre-default duties or obligations except to avoid conflicts of interest".[19]

OTHER RELATIONS BETWEEN TRUSTEE AND OBLIGOR

A trustee is generally selected from among the banks with which the obligor has a banking relationship. This is perfectly proper, and the indenture usually contains provisions specifically permitting all other normal and customary relationships. The trustee, in its individual capacity, may own indenture securities and, as such holder, has the same

---

[15] When the TIA was initially introduced in the Senate, it required inclusion of a provision in every qualified indenture that the trustee had to discharge its pre-default duties and obligations in a manner consistent with that which a "prudent man" would assume and perform [S.2065, 76th Cong., 1st Sess., sec. 315(a) (1939)]. The version of the Act introduced in the House of Representatives excluded the imposition of a pre-default "prudent man" duty on the trustee [H.R. 5220, 76th Cong., 1st Sess., sec. 315 (1939)], which was ultimately the version enacted as Section 315(c).

[16] *Dabney v. Chase National Bank*, 196 F.2d 668 (2d Cir. 1952), *appeal dismissed*, 346 U.S. 863 (1953), *Van Gemert v. Boeing Co.*, 520 F.2d 1373 (2d Cir. 1975), *cert. denied*, 423 U.S. 947 (1975).

[17] *Meckel v. Continental Resources Co.*, 758 F.2d 811 (2d Cir. 1985), *Elliott Associates v. J. Henry Schroder Bank & Trust Co.*, 838 F.2d 66 (2d Cir. 1988). In *Lorenz v. CSX*, 736 F. Supp. 650 (W.D.Pa 1990), involving a non-TIA indenture, the court reached the same conclusion.

[18] 758 F.2d at 816.

[19] 838 F.2d at 71.

rights and privileges as other holders. It may act as depositary, custodian, transfer agent, registrar, paying agent, fiscal agent, escrow agent, or in any similar capacity.[20] Subject to the qualification provisions of the indenture, it may also act as trustee for the obligor, whether under an indenture or otherwise.

Although the existence of a creditor relationship between the obligor and the trustee had not been a conflict of interest under the TIA as originally enacted, the TIRA added such a relationship as a potential conflict of interest. This was a logical step in view of the suspension of the conflict of interest provisions until default since it is obvious that the bank as creditor of an obligor may be in a position adverse to the bank as trustee for security holders of the obligor whenever the obligor is in a difficult financial position or faces insolvency.

Section 311 of the TIA as originally enacted, represented an effort to address the creditor relationship in a different way, and, in view of the TIRA, it remains as something of an anachronism, although presumably it will serve to govern the contractual rights of a trustee that has received payment on debt of the obligor within three months of an indenture default, or those of a former trustee/creditor that has resigned upon an indenture default. This section provides that if the trustee shall be, or shall become, a creditor, directly or indirectly, of an obligor upon the indenture securities within three months before a default in the payment of principal or interest on the indenture securities, it may not enforce any preferential collection of its claim against the obligor except on the conditions therein specified. The trustee bank under these circumstances must set aside, in a special account, for the benefit of itself and the indenture security holders: (1) an amount equal to any and all reductions in the amount due and owing upon any claim as such creditor with respect to principal and interest effected after the beginning of such three months' period and (2) all property received in respect of any claim as such creditor, either as security therefor or in satisfaction or composition thereof, after the beginning of such three months' period, or an amount equal to the proceeds of such property if it shall have been disposed of.

The trustee bank is entitled: (1) to exercise any right of setoff it could have exercised if a petition in bankruptcy had been filed by or against such obligor upon the date of the default; (2) to retain for its own account payments made on account of its claim by a third person, and/

20TIA, sec. 310(b)(4)(C).

or distributions made in cash, securities, or other property in respect of claims filed against such obligor in bankruptcy or receivership or in proceedings for reorganization pursuant to a bankruptcy act or applicable state laws; (3) to realize for its own account on any property held as collateral security for such claim before the beginning of the three months' period; (4) to realize for its own account on any property received as security simultaneously with the creation of such claim if the trustee bank became a creditor after the beginning of such three months' period and had no reasonable cause to believe that a default would occur; and (5) to receive payment on any claim against the release of any property held as security therefor to the extent of the fair value of such property. Property substituted after the beginning of the three months' period has the same status as property released to the extent of the fair value of the latter, and any renewal effected after the beginning of such period has the same status as the preexisting claim.

The language in Section 311 relative to the disposition of any funds or property segregated in such a special account is somewhat laborious. It appears that the property in the account cannot be apportioned until the obligor has gone through bankruptcy, receivership, or reorganization proceedings. The court having jurisdiction of such proceedings is given the right to apportion the property in accordance with TIA Section 311(a) or, in lieu of such apportionment, to give due consideration to such provisions in determining the fairness of the distributions to be made to the security holders and the trustee bank in such proceedings.

The formula according to which the property in the account is to be distributed is quite simple. Secured portions of the claims of both the security holders and the trustee bank are to be disregarded, and the respective claims are to be reduced to the extent of distributions with respect to such portions. The funds in the special account are then to be allocated so that the security holders and the trustee bank will receive the same proportion of the unsecured portions of their claims from such account and from dividends paid from the obligor's estate with respect to such unsecured portions. The problem will be one of applying the formula. Anyone familiar with reorganization proceedings will appreciate the difficulty of even approximating the value of any particular lien position or of the securities and interests distributed in reorganization. The ascertainment of such values to the extent necessary to permit an allocation of a fund according to an exact mathematical formula is all but impossible.

If the trustee resigns or is removed after the beginning of the three months' period, it is still subject to these provisions. If the resignation or removal was prior to such period, the trustee bank is subject to such provisions only if the receipt of property or reduction of claim occurred after the beginning of such three months' period, and within three months after such resignation or removal.

Certain creditor relationships may be excluded from the operation of this section. These consist of creditor relationships arising from: (1) the ownership or acquisition of securities issued under an indenture, or any security having a maturity of one year or more at the time of its acquisition by the trustee; (2) advances for the purpose of preserving the trust estate, or discharging taxes, prior liens, etc. authorized by the indenture, or by a bankruptcy or receivership court, if notice of such advance is given as provided in the indenture; (3) disbursements made in the ordinary course of business as trustee under an indenture, transfer agent, registrar, custodian, paying agent, fiscal agent, depositary, or similar capacity; (4) indebtedness created as a result of services rendered or premises rented, or as a result of goods or securities sold in a cash transaction; (5) the ownership of stock or of other securities of a corporation organized under the provisions of Section 25(a) of the Federal Reserve Act, as amended, that is directly or indirectly a creditor of the obligor; or (6) the acquisition, ownership, acceptance, or negotiation of any drafts, bills of exchange, acceptances, or obligations that fall within the classification of self-liquidating paper.

The increased use of the subordinated debenture issue raises special problems for a bank that is also a creditor of the issuer. In addition to prior funded indebtedness, these issues are usually made subordinate to all existing bank indebtedness and all future bank indebtedness up to specified amounts.

What is the status of a trustee bank that is or becomes the holder of preferred indebtedness to which the debentures issued under the indenture are specifically subordinated? The intent is clear, but an ambiguity is created by the provisions of TIA Section 311, unless there is specifically excepted from its operation the preferred indebtedness to which the debentures are subordinate. Indebtedness to the bank with a maturity in excess of one year at the time of its creation is undoubtedly exempt from this section, for a note is a "security" within the meaning of the TIA, and securities having a maturity in excess of one year are exempt from the provisions of Section 311. As to shorter term indebtedness, a court might well take into consideration the expressed intent of the parties in making an allocation in a bankruptcy or reorganization proceeding, although there is no assurance that this would be done.

Although the SEC has not conceded that the Section is not operative, historically they have permitted the inclusion of a provision qualifying the preferential collection of claims provisions to the extent that the trustee is entitled to all of the rights (in the indenture) with respect to any senior indebtedness at any time held by it to the same extent as any other holder of senior indebtedness and that no other section of the indenture should be construed to deprive the trustee of any of its rights as such holder. Now that the TIA provisions are deemed incorporated into every qualified indenture and will no longer be set forth, trustees should specifically include such a qualifying provision in the subordination provisions.

Despite the inequity of the possibility of treatment on a basis different from that accorded other holders of the same indebtedness, until this question has been clarified by statutory amendment or judicial decision, trustees should be well advised to assume that they will be required to account in accordance with Section 311 even though they hold an obligation that by its terms is superior to the indenture securities. If they are unwilling to continue on the basis of such an assumption, the alternative is to refuse an appointment as trustee under a subordinated indenture.

FOUR

Preparation, Execution, and Recording of Indenture

SELECTION OF METHOD OF FINANCING

It is the prime responsibility of corporate financial officers to secure the necessary funds for the expansion and operation of the corporate enterprise, in the amounts and at the times they are required. To the extent that such funds are not generated from operations of the business itself, they must be obtained in the highly competitive and often volatile financial markets. Efforts must be made to secure the most favorable terms with the fewest possible restrictions placed on the company's freedom of action.

There are many reasons why capital financing has to be undertaken. The most common is the providing of new facilities in the form of plant and equipment for the expanded needs of the business. It may be desired to construct a new office building to house the executive and administrative staffs. Additional working capital may be required. Conditions may be appropriate for refunding existing indebtedness on more favorable terms, or funds may be needed to meet an existing maturity. During the late 1980s, much of the corporate debt financing was fueled by the rapid growth and widespread use of leveraged buyouts and mergers. Because capital financing is an expensive operation even for major corporations with a high credit rating, careful planning is required so that there will be no necessity for too frequent recourse to the capital markets. Many companies resort to their commercial banks for interim financing, with the understanding that at periodic intervals or within an agreed period funded debt will be issued and the bank loans paid off.

Many factors enter into determination of the form and method of financing, including the purpose of the loan, the credit standing of the issuer, existing capital structure, availability of investment funds, market conditions, and so on. While the exact terms will be determined by negotiation, the corporate officials, usually with the assistance of qualified financial advisers, will normally make a preliminary determination of the amount of the issue, whether it will be secured or unsecured, the approximate amount that can be repaid annually by way of a sinking fund, the restrictive provisions that will be permitted, and the ultimate maturity date. Decision must then be made on how the issue will be marketed or distributed. Although there are a myriad of investment bankers with innovative and creative financing ideas in the financial marketplace, there are essentially three methods by which financing needs are met: negotiated transactions, public bids, and direct placements.

In a negotiated transaction, an investment banking firm is selected to underwrite the issue, and the substantive terms of the issue are negotiated with this firm. Where this method of marketing is used, the investment bankers usually, although not necessarily, act for all issues of the particular company and are thoroughly familiar with the corporation's financial affairs and programs. In addition to underwriting the company's public offerings, the firm may be retained as a general financial consultant and is able to render substantial valuable collateral services to the corporate officials. The investment bankers usually participate in discussions from the earliest date; their familiarity with security markets, as well as the company's affairs, will enable them to tailor the issue to meet the company's requirements and current market conditions. Compensation of the underwriters is provided by the "spread" between the wholesale price they pay for the entire issue and the retail price at which the securities are sold to the investors (often referred to as "underwriters' discount"). Usually the principal or lead underwriter will bring together a number of other firms (called a syndicate) to market the issue, with each firm being responsible for, and assuming the risk involved in, a percentage of the total issue. The amount of the underwriter's "spread" will vary, but it is calculated to provide a reasonable profit based on the work involved and the risk assumed in the particular financing.

Another method for marketing debt securities issues is through a public invitation for bids. All companies subject to the jurisdiction of the SEC under the Public Utility Holding Company Act are required to sell their securities in this manner unless specifically exempted. Other public bodies having jurisdiction over regulated industries may or may not prescribe or influence the manner in which securities are offered, but they must approve the method selected and the terms of sale. Under the method of public bidding, the issuing corporation will engage an independent firm of counsel, experienced in the field, to represent the prospective purchasers of the securities, and the terms and details of the offering will be negotiated between the company and such firm, except for the price, which will be determined by the public bids. Occasionally the company will retain investment bankers as advisers who work for a fee and who will not participate in the bidding. Usually the company and counsel will know the investment houses that head the various syndicates likely to participate in the bidding, and these firms may be consulted in advance about some of the proposed terms of the issue. Since market conditions determine the price at which securities can be offered successfully, most bids are very close to one another, and competition revolves around the amount of the underwriter's commission. There are certain advantages and disadvantages to the use of public bids as opposed to the negotiated method. Some regulatory bodies feel that the corporation obtains a better price through public bids, although experts differ on this matter. This advantage can be weighed against the value placed on a continuing relationship with, and the advisory service received from, selected investment bankers in a negotiated transaction.

A third method of marketing that is frequently used by the more mature companies with a high credit rating is direct placement (i.e., private placement). Under this method the issue is not underwritten at all, but negotiations are conducted with a group of institutional investors who are the actual purchasers of the securities. The corporation usually retains an investment house or the corporate finance department of a major bank as an agent to find interested purchasers and negotiate the terms, although it may elect to do this itself. Such an issue does not have to be registered under the securities acts, and the indenture is not qualified. In some instances where the issue is unsecured only a few purchasers are involved, the terms are not complicated, and an indenture and trustee are not used. The company will execute separate but identical agreements with each purchaser, embodying all the terms of the contract.

While the three methods outlined are the principal ones used in distributing debt securities, others are sometimes used. Mention has been made of the offering of convertible debentures, which may or may not be underwritten, to existing stockholders. Mergers, acquisitions, recapitalizations, reorganizations, and similar transactions usually involve the offering of securities to existing security holders of either the issuing or a different corporation. The corporation itself may elect to market its securities publicly without the assistance of an underwriting firm, although this practice is rare. Moreover, with the adoption of SEC Rule 415 permitting shelf registrations to be filed, a corporation gains tremendous flexibility in its issuance of debt securities as well as almost instant access to the capital markets.

PREPARATION OF THE INDENTURE

Because the indenture, when executed, becomes a contract binding on the security holders, the corporation (as obligor), and the trustee, establishing the obligations and rights of the parties, and setting limitations on the rights of all, it follows that the preparation of the indenture is one of the most important steps in the whole process. It is here that the security holders stand in the greatest need of protection, and it is here that they frequently lack adequate representation. The substantive terms are established by agreement between the issuer and the underwriter, or counsel appointed to represent the underwriter. While some protection is afforded by this process—for the leading investment houses feel some moral responsibility for issues they sponsor—the underwriter's primary concern is in securing terms that will make the issue readily marketable and not necessarily terms that a security holder, in retrospect, might have considered desirable.

Over the years a number of developments have substantially resolved this problem, with the result that the typical indenture is a fairly sound financial document with reasonably adequate safeguards designed to protect the investor. Among such developments are the following:

1. The increasing influence of the institutional investor. Whereas the direct placement contract is the only situation in which the investors actually negotiate the terms of an issue, the institutional purchaser is also important in publicly distributed issues, and both issuers and underwriters endeavor to style the issue and the terms of the contract so as to attract the professional investor.

2. The minimum standards set forth in the TIA. They are now applicable, *as a matter of law*, to every qualified indenture, and should not be written into the indenture itself. It may be helpful however to

include a TIA section reference page at the beginning of each indenture; an example of which is set forth in Exhibit 17.

3. The disclosure provisions of the 33 Act. Most public issues of securities are required to be registered under this act, which requires full disclosure not only of the history and current financial condition of the issuer but also of all important terms and provisions of the indenture and the securities to be issued. This information, or appropriate summaries thereof, is required to be set forth in a prospectus, preliminary offering statement, or offering memorandum that must be furnished to all prospective investors. Thus, the investor has available all pertinent information, necessary to make an informed investment decision. If the investor fails to use or comprehend the information so furnished (assuming it is accurate), he or she has no one else to blame.

4. The regulatory powers of the SEC and other regulatory agencies. These agencies have set certain minimum standards required in cases where they have the authority to approve or prescribe the terms and conditions of proposed financing.

5. The patterns for typical indentures that have become established among investment houses, institutional investors, and bond counsel.

6. The influence of the more experienced corporate trustees and their counsel.

Once the essential terms of the indenture have been agreed upon, the process of drafting is relatively simple. A prior indenture, frequently of the same obligor, is selected as a model. Many of the provisions will remain exactly the same. Clauses that are not appropriate to the current transaction or that experience has shown to be troublesome will be eliminated; the new provisions that embody the terms of the contract will be added, as well as any new clauses that the evolutionary process has revealed as beneficial or desirable. Once an initial draft of the new indenture is ready, copies are distributed to all interested parties, and the document is modified until all parties are reasonably satisfied.

FUNCTION OF THE TRUSTEE

At some point the corporate trustee must be selected, usually by the issuer itself, but in many instances upon the advice and recommendation of its investment banker, underwriter, or attorneys. This should be done at the earliest possible moment, for the trustee can make important contributions to the process of finalizing the terms of the indenture.

Although it has no responsibility for the substantive provisions of the contract and, under normal circumstances, should never undertake to alter the terms of the basic contract, it is the party that will have to administer the agreement and is therefore entitled to participate fully in all discussions relative to translating the contract into indenture language.

Given the importance of all phases of the indenture preparation process, the trustee should always be represented by experienced legal counsel and should work closely with such counsel until the indenture has been executed and the initial bonds delivered. Some corporate trustees follow the practice of relinquishing to counsel the conduct of all matters during this preliminary process. This is inadvisable. A number of business, as well as legal, considerations are involved, and the trustee cannot delegate, nor should it permit counsel to usurp the trustee's responsibility for making decisions. The corporate trustee, however, should consult with counsel on all legal questions.

It would be difficult to set down in detail the exact procedure the trustee should follow in its examination and review of the terms of the proposed indenture.[1] A number of general principles may be suggested:

1. Since the recitals constitute no part of the substantive contract and the trustee has no responsibility with respect thereto, there is a tendency to skip over these clauses. It is important, however, that the due authorization by the obligor of all acts relating to creation of the indenture, issuance of the securities, and mortgaging or pledging of property be stated. Whereas appropriate evidence of such authorization should be obtained and examined, the recitals may constitute an estoppel against the company if it should subsequently claim lack of proper authorization.

2. The form of bond as set forth in the indenture should be examined closely. Since the bonds, when executed, become separate instruments and constitute separate contracts and obligations running directly to the holders thereof, the bond form should contain specific reference to the indenture and should also set forth in sufficient detail any provision of the indenture that modifies or affects the obligation contained in the bond or imposes any limitations upon the rights of the holder. In any suit by a bondholder, if the provisions of the indenture conflict with the provisions of the bond itself, the latter are controlling.

---

[1] To facilitate this effort it is useful to prepare check lists as a guide. Exhibit 3 is a comprehensive guide for use in reviewing new and additional securities issues under indentures.

3. The adequacy of the granting clauses to convey the property and create the lien (or "perfect" the security interest) intended is a legal matter and should be a concern primarily for counsel. The trustee should secure appropriate legal opinions covering these points. A detailed examination of the property descriptions would serve no purpose, for the trustee usually has nothing against which to check or compare such descriptions and must rely on the company and its counsel, although the use of a title company can be helpful. The trustee should make sure, however, that it is qualified to hold property as mortgagee in the various jurisdictions in which the property is located. If there is any question consideration should be given to appointment of a cotrustee so qualified. Where the ownership of franchises, rights, or permits is essential to the carrying on of the obligor's business, the trustee should make certain that these are included among the mortgaged property. The same care should be taken with regard to any important leases, easements, contracts, rights of way, etc., the purpose being to ensure that the lien covers the obligor's property as a "going concern." If any important franchises, leases, contracts, etc. expire before the maturity date of the securities to be issued, any renewal privileges or the securing of alternative rights should be investigated to avoid the possibility of a substantial diminution of security or of a default. If an after-acquired property clause is included, the trustee should ensure that it expresses clearly the intent as to what subsequently acquired property is to be covered. If any property is to be assigned or pledged, proper record should be made so that an executed assignment or physical delivery of such property is obtained at the closing. If any part of such property is in the possession of another trustee, proper notification should be given to the other trustee and a tickler record prepared to obtain possession of such property on satisfaction of the other lien. If any leasehold estate is mortgaged, the last day of the term of each such lease should be specifically excluded. This avoids the creation for the trustee of an estate identical with that of the obligor-lessee, and the possibility of a claim that the trustee is liable for performance of the lessee's obligations under the lease. Finally, consideration should be given to the possible applicability of any special laws or regulations in the jurisdictions in which the property is located, or the mortgage contract executed and delivered, or where a financing statement is to be filed.

4. Although the trustee has no responsibility for the substantive provisions of the contract or for the covenants that may be included, it

should review these provisions carefully to make certain that they are clear and unambiguous and adequately set forth the intent of the parties.

5. The trustee should examine carefully the evidence it is to receive of compliance by the obligor with the various indenture covenants to ensure its adequacy. It should be noted that section 314(a)(4) of the TIA requires the obligor to furnish the trustee annually, a certificate "from the principal executive officer, principal financial officer or principal accounting officer as to his or her knowledge of such obligor's compliance with all conditions and covenants under the indenture" (i.e., a "no-default" certificate). This should be in addition to specific evidence on the more important covenants.

6. It is the obligor's and not the trustee's responsibility to see that an indenture to be qualified does not contain provisions contrary to the TIA. A diligent trustee, however, will carefully review the indenture language and advise the obligor (or its counsel) of any inconsistent language.

7. The trustee has a particular responsibility for the operational provisions that relate to the servicing of the indenture securities. It should verify that they are workable and not in conflict with its established practices and procedures as well as applicable state law (e.g., escheatment). The greatest degree of flexibility consistent with clarity should be retained. Whenever possible the manner in which a particular operation is to be conducted should be left to the discretion of the trustee rather than set forth in detail. This permits a change in procedure to conform with evolving and more efficient methods and systems' developments and is not only proper but also desirable so long as substantive rights are not affected.

8. Particular attention should be given to the remedial provisions and to the trustee article. The rights, powers, duties, and responsibilities of the trustee, and any limitation on its rights and powers, will be governed by the general provisions of these articles. The trustee should ascertain that it has all requisite power and authority to carry out its duties. It should also be careful to see that appropriate exculpatory and protective provisions are included, for the potential liability is substantial.

9. Finally, after appropriate attention has been given to each separate section, the contract should be considered as an entity. It is important that the various provisions and covenants be consistent, for the indenture must be considered and construed as a single document. The trustee should have a clear understanding of the essential purpose and intent of

the transaction, and the provisions of the indenture, considered together, should clearly express and carry out this purpose and intent.

THE REGISTRATION STATEMENT AND QUALIFICATION OF THE INDENTURE

Issuance of securities is not only a delicate marketing operation but also a matter of careful planning and timing. The many different transactions that together constitute a unified operation must be initiated at the appropriate time so that everything will be completed on the date set for delivery of the securities. Time is usually of the essence, and the customary procedure is to select a date for sale of the securities and to relate all other activities to this date.

Where securities are to be distributed publicly, they must be registered under the 33 Act. Unless the issuer has filed an SEC Rule 415 shelf registration[2] it can take five to eight weeks for a registration to be cleared and to become effective. A copy of the indenture has to be filed as an exhibit to the registration statement, and the indenture should be in as complete and final form as possible in order to minimize the number of amendments that have to be filed.

The contents of the registration statement and the prospectus are the responsibility of the obligor and not the trustee. It is advisable for the latter to review copies of these documents, however, to ensure that no information is disclosed therein that might affect its rights or obligations or that might be contrary to its understanding of the transaction. In particular, the sections summarizing indenture provisions should be carefully reviewed.

The TIA requires the filing with each registration statement of such information and documents as the Commission may prescribe to enable it to determine whether any person designated to act as trustee is eligible and qualified. The SEC has prescribed the form in which this information is to be furnished. Form T-1 is required for domestic institutional trustees, Form T-2 for individual trustees, and T-6 for foreign trustees. Form T-1 requires the filing, among other documents, of the trustee's most recent report of condition, a copy of its articles of association or incorporation, a certificate of authority to commence business, a copy of its bylaws, and the consent of the trustee that copies of reports of

2 See note 11, chapter 1, *supra.*

examination by federal, state, territorial, or district authorities may be furnished to the Commission. Forms T-1, T-2, and T-6 require information sufficient to enable the Commission to determine whether the proposed trustee is qualified to act under section 310(a) of the TIA.[3]

EXECUTION, DELIVERY, AND RECORDING OF THE INDENTURE

As soon as the registration statement has become effective and all other authorizations and approvals have been obtained, the indenture may be executed and the securities delivered (often referred to as the "bond closing"). The trustee should make certain that the officers of the obligor company who execute the indenture have been authorized to do so. The trustee is also usually requested to furnish an appropriate certificate of the authority of its officers who join in the execution of the indenture (i.e., trustee's certificate of incumbency).

The indenture customarily contains an express statement that the laws of a particular state will apply with respect to all questions that may arise in its interpretation. This is important, for the laws of different states may vary substantially in important respects. It is desirable, although not essential, that the state specified be that in which the office of the trustee is located, for its laws are the ones with which it is presumably most familiar. In the absence of an express provision the law applied will be that of the state in which the contract is executed and delivered. If delivery takes place at the office of the trustee, there is no problem. Where the laws that are to govern are those of another state a problem may be presented, since the trustee may not be qualified to do business in that state. More important the trustee may be barred from bringing an action in that state against the obligor if this should be necessary. If it is impossible to negotiate a change in the language of the "governing law" provision, the trustee should make every effort to have additional language inserted stating that the rights, duties, liabilities, and obligations of the trustee be governed and construed in accordance with the laws of its state of incorporation or principal place of business. Provision should also be made that the parties to the indenture

[3] The text and instructions for Forms T-1, T-2, and T-6 are set forth in 17 CFR 269.1, 269.2, and 269.9, respectively. *See also* "Rules and Forms to Implement the Trust Indenture Reform Act of 1990." SEC Release Numbers 33–6892 and 39–2263 (May 8, 1991).

agree that any action by the obligor against the trustee be brought in the district or state courts in the state where the trustee is located, and that the parties consent to such forum.

At the time of the delivery of the indenture the trustee should receive documents sufficient to establish the due authorization of all proceedings in connection with the indenture and the securities. Counsel should be consulted about the documents required and the form and content thereof. (*See Exhibit 5, Requirements For Appointment as Trustee Under Corporate Indentures.*)

If the indenture grants a mortgage or lien on any property, one of the first steps to be taken after it has been executed is to have it recorded in all jurisdictions in which the property is located. Sometimes this is done before or simultaneously with delivery of the securities, but it is usually sufficient if done promptly thereafter. Whereas the contract is binding on the obligor when delivered, the importance of recording is to give public notice of the lien and prevent a third party from obtaining a lien prior to that of the trustee. Recording is the responsibility of counsel to the issuing corporation. If a number of jurisdictions are involved, local counsel familiar with the laws of each jurisdiction are used to ensure strict adherence to recording requirements.

If the indenture creates a security interest in real estate, including a lease or rents thereunder, *and* in any personal property or fixtures, the filing provisions of Article 9 of the UCC will be applicable to "perfect" the security interest in the personal property. The appropriate filing must be done even though the mortgage or supplemental mortgage creating the lien on real and personal property is properly recorded as a real estate mortgage. (If, however, the mortgage or supplement creating such lien was properly recorded as a mortgage of real property *prior* to the effective date of the UCC, no filing is necessary.)

If all the collateral under an indenture is in the possession of the trustee, that alone will "perfect" the security interest, and no filing is necessary. In the usual collateral trust indenture, this will consist of negotiable instruments or securities such as stock and bonds.

Where filing is necessary, the UCC prescribes the formal requisites for the financing statement; most states have adopted a standard form for this purpose. Completion is merely a matter of filling in the blank spaces and having it signed by the obligor company (the debtor) and the trustee (the secured party). Although the indenture itself may be filed if it meets the particular state's requirements, as a practical matter it is simpler to use the prescribed form of this purpose.

The trustee should obtain appropriate evidence of such recording and/ or filing. The recorded counterparts of the indenture and/or a filing counterpart of each financing statement showing the recording or filing data are usually returned to and retained by the trustee.

In addition, the obligor must furnish the trustee with a legal opinion or opinions on the sufficiency of such recording and/or filing. This requirement provides that the obligor will furnish the trustee (1) promptly after the execution and delivery of the indenture and of each indenture supplemental thereto, an opinion of counsel either stating that in the opinion of such counsel the indenture has been properly recorded and/or filed so as to make effective the lien or security interest intended to be created thereby, and reciting the details of such action, or stating that, in the opinion of such counsel, no action is necessary to make such lien or security interest effective; and (2) at least annually thereafter an opinion of counsel either stating that in the opinion of such counsel such action has been taken with respect to the recording, filing, re-recording, and refiling of the indenture and of each supplement as is necessary to maintain the lien or security interest of such indenture, and reciting the details of such action, or stating that in the opinion of such counsel no such action is necessary to maintain such lien or security interest.[4]

Although a mortgage of real property usually need not be recorded to maintain the lien, a financing statement perfecting a security interest in personal property will lapse after five years from the filing date unless a continuation statement is filed within six months prior to the expiration of the five-year period. Upon timely filing of continuation statements, the effectiveness of the original statement can be continued for successive five-year periods.

One of the first actions that should be taken by the trustee after execution and delivery of the indenture is to make a complete review of the indenture provisions and establish an appropriate tickler record in relation to all actions that the obligor or trustee has to take in connection with administration of the indenture. These would include such things as dates on which the sinking fund is to operate, the date when certificates and opinions are required to be filed, and so on. No particular form of record is required, provided the form used is adequate to ensure that appropriate timely reminders will be brought to the attention of the administrative officers and that monitoring of uncompleted items can be followed up.

[4]TIA, sec. 314(b)(1) and (2).

SUPPLEMENTAL INDENTURES

In addition to the original indenture, supplemental indentures may be executed from time to time for various purposes. They may provide the terms of additional series of securities to be issued under the indenture; they may convey additional property or pledge additional security; they may modify or amend provisions of the original contract; they may impose additional restrictions on the obligor; or they may be executed for other reasons that require that the original contract be supplemented or amended.

The same care in regard to the proper authorization, execution, delivery, recording, and filing of these instruments should be exercised as in the case of the original indenture. The trustee should also ensure that each such supplement is consistent with and is authorized, either explicitly or by necessary implication, by the original indenture.

Once the supplement has been executed and delivered, it constitutes a part of the contract and the original indenture, and all supplemental indentures must be read together to determine the rights, duties, and obligations of the parties.

Since the effect of many provisions in the TIRA is to relax restrictions previously imposed on the trustee, and since the act does not preclude the trustee from "agreeing" to more rigorous contractual provisions, it would be wise to include in any supplemental indenture to a pre-November 15, 1990 qualified indenture, language substantially as follows: "Except to the extent specifically provided therein, no provision of this supplemental indenture or any future supplemental indenture is intended to modify, and the parties do hereby adopt and confirm, the provisions of section 318(c) of the Trust Indenture Act which amend and supersede the provisions of the [Indenture] in effect prior to November 15, 1990."

FIVE

Issuance of Indenture Securities

TRUSTEE'S RESPONSIBILITIES

Since the whole purpose of the indenture is to provide security for the outstanding securities and to set forth the terms and conditions upon which they can be issued, the proceedings surrounding the authentication and delivery of the indenture securities are among the more important responsibilities of the trustee. The issuance of securities in certificated form and, as is increasingly likely in the future, in uncertificated form is governed by the indenture provisions, and it is the trustee's responsibility to see that the necessary conditions precedent have been fulfilled.[1] Where the trustee receives the documents called for by the indenture, it is entitled to rely thereon and is not required to make an independent examination of the facts certified. If it acts in good faith it will be protected even if it develops that such certificates were false. Where the requisite conditions precedent do not exist and the trustee fails to receive the requisite documents, or where the documents are not in the required form, or where they disclose facts that put the trustee on notice that the requisite conditions precedent do not exist, the trustee

[1] See note 36, chapter 2, *supra*. The distinction between a pure "book-entry" system in which *no* physical securities certificates are issued and all transfers of ownership are made through entries on the issuer's books of record and an "immobilized clearance" system should be understood. In the latter case, a large portion of an outstanding issue is held in a depository facility represented by one or more jumbo certificates with record ownership changes effected by entry on the depository's books. The balance of the issue is held in certificate form by investors with certificates flowing in and out of the depository as the public's need for actual securities certificates fluctuates.

may be held liable by the security holders. The measure of liability has been held to be that which would be required to put the security holders in the same position as they would be if the requisite conditions had been performed.

All securities physically issued under the indenture are required to be authenticated by the trustee. This is accomplished by application of the trustee's signature to a certificate imprinted on each separate bond or debenture. The form of this certificate seldom varies from standard phraseology, which is substantially as follows: "This bond is one of the bones, of the series designated therein, described in the within mentioned indenture." The bond should provide that it will not become valid for any purpose until this certificate has been executed by the trustee.

The basic purpose of the authentication certificate is to enable the trustee to control the amount of the issue and to prevent an overissuance. It ensures that the obligor corporation cannot sell bonds in excess of the amount authorized. The authentication certificate is not a guaranty nor is it an implied warranty of the sufficiency of the security or the regularity of the obligor's conduct in issuing bonds. The trustee should be careful that the certificate contains no representation, lest it be held to be under a duty to ascertain the accuracy of the facts represented. For example, a certificate stating that this is a "Convertible Subordinated Sinking Fund Debenture" may be held to be a representation by the trustee. Although a diligent trustee will to the best of its ability ascertain that all representations made by the obligor are accurate, it is seldom in a position to make an absolute check of all facts, and a representation that it has done so is neither required nor advisable.[2]

FORM AND CONTENT OF SECURITIES

Because the trustee is authorized to authenticate only the securities provided for in the indenture, it is under a duty to see that the securities do conform with the indenture provisions. The indenture will set forth the form and text of the securities authorized, and the trustee should carefully compare the text of the security itself with the text set forth in the indenture. Minor variations in detail are permissible, but each such variation should be noted and reviewed. To avoid possible embarrassment, the trustee should arrange to examine proofs of all securities

[2] For potential liability regarding additional representations, *see* Nelson v. Quimby, note 10, chapter 3, *supra* at 1371.

before they are prepared in final form. As a practical matter, bank note companies that prepare these securities generally require approval by the trustee before they will prepare the final securities. Despite this preliminary check, a final examination should be made of one bond of each denomination before the securities are released.

Not only should the text be compared, but the securities must also be in the form required by the indenture. The various requirements for form will be set forth in substantial detail and will be designed to comply with stock exchange regulations or with general usage. The New York Stock Exchange has probably the most detailed regulations of any national exchange for the form of securities, the purpose of which is to guard against duplication, alteration, or forgery. These regulations require that the border, vignette, denomination or "money" boxes, the promise to pay clause, and certain other standard provisions of the bond be engraved. Variable parts of the text, including those that appear on the reverse side, may be lithographed or printed.

Before 1964 most corporate debt securities were issued in bearer form, for they were the only ones that constituted a good delivery when sold. Municipal debt issues, on the other hand, were issued primarily in bearer form until July 1, 1983.[3] The indenture usually provided that the holder could have the bond registered as to principal, in which case, it could be transferred only by assignment of the registered holder. It was also customarily provided that bonds could be issued in fully registered form, without coupons, whereby both principal and interest were payable only to a registered holder. As the institutional investors became more important, a number of corporate trustees urged issuers to liberalize exchange provisions to encourage increased holding of large registered pieces by these investors. As the result of such efforts and the cooperation of the underwriters and dealers, as well as the increased awareness on the part of the investing public of the advantages involved, the number of corporate issues sold only in fully registered form grew steadily each year until, by the end of 1982, 99 percent of the new corporate issues marketed were in such form. The major exception to this change has involved the sale of debt securities by domestic corporations to nonresident alien investors, the so-called "Eurobond" issues. Because of the reluctance of such investors to hold these debt obligations in registered form, almost all of these issues have been sold in bearer form with coupons.[4]

[3] See note 7, chapter 2, *supra.*

[4] The sale of such bearer bonds of issues sold after July 18, 1984 to off-shore investors has been affected by the repeal of the 30 percent withholding tax on interest paid. (*See* sec. 127,

The indenture will set forth the denominations in which the securities may be issued, and no other denominations are authorized or should be authenticated by the trustee. The customary and recommended practice for corporate issues is to authorize these in $1,000 denominations and any denomination that is a multiple of $1,000. Municipal issues, however, customarily, are issued in minimum denominations of $5,000, and multiples of $5,000.

The huge volume of all registered issues, the greater use of automated equipment to process the certificates, and the ever-present storage problem, have dictated the need for the use of the uniform "stock certificate size" (8" by 12"). As discussed before, the substantive provisions of the indenture or summaries of the pertinent provisions are printed on the reverse of the certificates as a continuation of the bond form. The use of certificates with preprinted denominations is also very desirable, as well as "blank" or unspecified denomination certificates. In addition to the standard $1,000 denomination certificate, both $5,000 and $10,000 certificates probably should be prepared for corporate issues in excess of $100 million. However, for those bond registrars using computer-generated certificates, the use of only "blank" denominated certificates may be especially attractive.

For a "good delivery" of certificates of issues listed on the New York Stock Exchange, the denomination amount should be engraved in both upper corners of the face of the certificate, the bond number being printed directly below. "Blank" denomination certificates up to $100,000 are also acceptable, provided the numeric amount is macerated or "matrixed" on the certificate. Such blank certificates need only have the numeric dollar amount recorded in the upper right corner, the upper left corner being used for the bond number. For unlisted issues, the same requirements are also recommended.[5]

The indenture will also specify the manner in which the bonds are to be executed by the obligor, and the trustee should see that this provision is adhered to strictly. All signatures should appear on the face of the certificate and, whenever possible, those of the obligor should be fac-

---

Tax Reform Act of 1984, P.L. 98–369, 98 Stat. 552.) To qualify for the exemption, certain procedures are prescribed by the Internal Revenue Service. (*See* IRC sec. 163 (f)(2)(B) and IRS Regulations, sec. 1.163–65(c)T.

[5]For specific recommendations on certificate format and paper quality standards *see: Recommended Certificate Standards For Registered Bond Issues,* Corporate Trust Activities Committee, American Bankers Association (1974); *Specifications For Fully Registered Municipal Securities,* American National Standards Institute, X9.12–1983.

simile. The trustee's authentication should, however, never be other than a manual signature. The corporate seal on the bond is usually a facsimile, but this also should be specifically authorized by the indenture.

Not only should the trustee compare the text of the bonds of each denomination with that set forth in the indenture, but each individual bond should also be examined by the trustee to see that it is properly signed and sealed; that the text on both face and reverse is complete (to guard against a mechanical printing failure); that the bonds are numbered consecutively; and that the aggregate amount of bonds so executed is the amount authorized to be authenticated.

It is the trustee's responsibility to control the total principal amount of bonds authenticated and delivered, and appropriate records should be set up so that this can be done. A proper notation should be made of each bond received, authenticated, delivered, canceled, or otherwise dealt with by the trustee so that it will be in a position to certify the bonds outstanding at any time.

UNCERTIFICATED SECURITIES

As the result of the back-office paper crisis that occurred on Wall Street in the late 1960s, several far-reaching innovations took place, their aim being to make the entire transfer process for securities more efficient. Among the most significant was the effort to eliminate the use of the physical certificate as evidence of ownership in a corporation, and as evidence of indebtedness of both public and private corporations.

The U.S. Treasury was the first to eliminate paper certificates and in 1967 began the process of eliminating physical Treasury Bill securities. By 1986 all marketable U.S. Treasury obligations were in book-entry form, as presently are all securities issued by the Federal National Mortgage Association, the Student Loan Marketing Association, and the Federal Home Loan Mortgage Association.

By 1977 comprehensive revisions to Article 8 of the UCC were completed and promulgated; included are provisions that permit the issuance of pure uncertificated securities and govern the legal relationships and liabilities of the parties dealing with such.

Despite these efforts over the past twenty-five years, the most visible real progress toward the eventual elimination of the security certificate has been the very successful development of the "immobilized clearance'' system by the Depository Trust Company, which by 1990 accounted for almost 65 percent of the outstanding shares and public debt securities of companies listed on the New York Stock Exchange. In most cases, DTC holds the physical certificates that are registered by the issuer's transfer agent/bond registrar in the name of ''Cede & Co.,'' their nominee. However, for a significant percentage of municipal issues and a growing number of corporate issues, a so-called book-entry–only process for debt securities has been implemented—the difference between it and a pure book-entry system is that in this case one jumbo certificate is prepared and registered by the bond registrar in the name of Cede & Co. To avoid the necessity of issuing a new jumbo certificate each time securities move in or out of DTC's position, many bond registrars indicate on the certificate itself that the face amount of the certificate is ''such amount as shall be shown on the securities' register from time to time as the amount payable to Cede & Co.''

The trend of the future is clearly in the direction of the complete elimination of the paper certificate. The movement has received reinforcement from the recommendations of the U.S. Working Committee of the Group of Thirty (an independent, nonpartisan, non-profit organization established in 1978 to address public policy issues around the world). In its August 1990 interim report, the U.S. Working Committee reached the preliminary conclusion/recommendation that ''it is both desirable and achievable to eliminate the use of the physical certificate by 1995 for the settlement of securities transactions and transfers.''

Despite the slow progress over the past twenty-five years, it is evident that by the end of this century paper certificates may very well be found only in attics and antique shops![6]

DISPOSITION OF BOND PROCEEDS

In the absence of express provisions in the indenture, the trustee is under no duty to see to the application of the proceeds of bonds, and the indenture will usually so provide. There have been a few cases where courts have found an implied duty even in the face of an express provision to the contrary but these cases have all involved situations where a specific use was set forth and the facts indicated that the trustee had actual knowledge of misapplication.

[6]*See also* discussion on municipal securities and the depository, chapter 15.

Generally, where the indenture provides for proceeds of bonds to be applied to a specific purpose, it should require the furnishing of appropriate evidence to the trustee of such application. In such cases the trustee should be authorized to retain possession of the bond proceeds and disburse them as required upon receipt of proper certificates. A typical example would be where the bond issue is authorized for construction of a specific project. In the case of a newly formed corporation that has no substantial property, or where the proposed expenditure is substantial in relation to the net worth of the company, such protective provisions are essential, and a trustee should not accept an appointment unless they are included. In the normal case, however, where all conditions precedent to the authentication and delivery of bonds have been fulfilled, the trustee should not concern itself about the actual use made of the specific proceeds.

TYPICAL PROVISIONS GOVERNING THE ISSUANCE OF BONDS

The indenture must set forth specifically the terms and conditions pursuant to which the indenture securities may be issued. The usual debenture or note agreement will provide for issuance of all authorized securities initially, so that each issue of such obligations will be covered by a separate agreement or indenture. This is not always the case, however, and it is perfectly proper for such an indenture to provide for the creation and issuance of additional series of obligations, provided that such obligations are of the same class. The conditions precedent to the issuance of additional obligations under such an agreement will usually be the existence of no default, and if the indenture requires maintenance of specified financial ratios, such required ratios must exist after the additional obligations have been issued.

As distinguished from the usual debenture or note agreement, a typical mortgage bond indenture is open ended and is designed to provide not only for the current financing but also for all future bond financing of the corporation. The reasons for this are obvious. Not only would the creation of a separate indenture for each financing be expensive, but also use of a single mortgage indenture is the only way in which secured obligations, ranking *pari passu,* can be issued from time to time over a period of years. Because a first mortgage obligation will normally command a better price and be more readily marketable than one having a junior lien position, it is desirable to provide a vehicle under which senior securities can continue to be issued.

Such an indenture will set forth the detailed provisions of the first series of bonds to be issued and will stipulate the manner in which the terms and provisions of later series are to be established. This is done either by a resolution of the board of directors of the corporation or by a supplemental indenture, or usually by both, for such supplement must be approved by the board. It is recommended that a supplemental indenture always be used. Recording of the original indenture will give public notice only of the initial series of bonds. While the lien created will probably be effective until specifically discharged, it is desirable that public notice be given of additional debt secured, particularly if the maturity date of the later series extends beyond that of the initial series. Such notice will be given by the proper execution and recording of a supplemental indenture.

The indenture will authorize the authentication and delivery of a specified principal amount of bonds initially. These bonds will usually be authorized to be authenticated and delivered upon request of specified officers of the corporation, without compliance by the corporation with any conditions other than execution and delivery of the indenture and the furnishing of the requisite documents and authorities to support such execution and delivery.

Additional issuance can be secured, however, only after specified conditions have been met. Bondholders contract for specific security coverage for their obligations as a condition to the extension of credit. Each additional creation of debt, ranking equally with that outstanding, will automatically deplete the security interest of each bondholder in the property existing at that time. The purpose of the detailed provisions governing the creation of additional indebtedness is to ensure that such security interest is not reduced proportionately (as related to the aggregate value of the property) below the minimum contracted for in the indenture. This is the basic concept that the trustee should have in mind in reviewing these sections of every proposed secured indenture.

No attempt will be made to describe every purpose for which additional bonds might be authorized. The more common and customary purposes will be described briefly.

1. To provide funds for the construction of property additions or to reimburse the company for expenditures made in such construction.

Property additions should always be specifically defined, but they normally include any type of property that is properly includable in the company's fixed property accounts in accordance with accepted accounting practices. All property owned by the corporation at the date of the indenture (or frequently as of the end of the fiscal period next preceding or next succeeding such date) is regarded as "funded" and is not available for use as a basis for the issuance of additional bonds or for any other purpose under the indenture. Property acquired after such date can be so used. Under an after-acquired property clause, such property becomes subject to the lien of the indenture as acquired but remains "unfunded" until it has been used for a specific purpose under the indenture, at which time its character changes to that of being funded.

An active corporation is almost continuously adding property and retiring property that has become worn out or obsolete. In order that the proper security may be maintained, only "net property additions" should be taken into account when considering the amount of property that can be "bonded" (*i.e.,* used to support the issuance of additional bonds). At times the computations to determine this become quite involved, for frequently other indenture provisions and the use of property thereunder have to be taken into account. The general purport, however, is to take the gross amount of all unfunded property additions and deduct those from the book value of all property retired to determine net property additions. The value at which the gross property additions may be taken into account is the lesser of the cost to the company, or the fair market value as of the date of the certification.

When the net value of property additions has been determined, it is then necessary to compute the amount of bonds that can be issued on the basis thereof. Rarely are companies permitted to issue bonds to the full value of such property. The importance of the debt ratio has been previously mentioned, and bondholders should always insist on a reasonable margin of security. A frequent percentage found in utility mortgages, for example, is 60 percent, which means that for each one thousand dollars of net value added to the fixed property account, a maximum of six hundred dollars of additional secured indebtedness is permitted.

2. To retire prior lien obligations.

Where prior liens exist on all or any part of the property mortgaged, provisions should always be made for their retirement. Even though no such liens exist at the time of the creation of the indenture, consideration should be given to this problem, for additional property is often acquired that is subject to a lien at the time of acquisition. If such additional property is used as a basis for the issuance of bonds, the amount of the prior lien should first be deducted from the bondable value of the property. It is then appropriate to permit refunding of the prior lien by the issuance of additional bonds under the indenture.

This is one of the situations in which the trustee is responsible for the proper application of bond proceeds. A frequent requirement is the surrender to the trustee of the prior lien obligations as a condition for the issuance of the bonds. Such is usually the case where the prior lien is only partially retired, and quite often the prior lien obligations are required to be held alive by the trustee. The desirability of such a provision is questionable, for it is unlikely that the trustee could claim a position *pari passu* with the remaining holders of prior lien obligations to the extent of such obligations held by it. A certificate of the prior lien trustee with respect to cancellation of a specified amount of prior lien obligations would seem to afford the same protection as the delivery thereof to the trustee, and an indenture provision to this effect should be acceptable.

Where the prior lien is to be retired in whole, the trustee should be protected in paying over the proceeds to the prior lien trustee or to the company if it receives a duly executed and recorded counterpart of the satisfaction of the prior lien obligation.

3. Refunding of outstanding indenture securities.

This is obviously a proper purpose, for it results merely in the substitution of one indenture obligation for another. Where bonds are acquired by the obligor company by purchase or otherwise, their surrender to the trustee for cancellation is a sufficient basis for the authentication and delivery of an equivalent amount of bonds of another series. Where a preceding series is to be redeemed in whole or in part, it is sufficient if the trustee holds, in trust, funds sufficient to effect such redemption and is authorized to take the necessary steps required. Any premium or interest payable on the redemption must be supplied separately by the obligor.

Frequently previously issued bonds will be retired or redeemed without the concurrent issuance of additional bonds, but the obligor will wish to reserve the right to issue bonds on the basis of such retirement. This is perfectly proper, and it is unnecessary to require that such previously issued bonds be held alive in the company's treasury to preserve this right.

Bonds retired through operation of a sinking fund or similar provisions normally should not be permitted to be made the basis for the issuance of additional bonds under the indenture. This would result in an indirect depletion of the bondholders' security.

4. Issuance of bonds against deposit of cash.

A common indenture provision permits the issuance of bonds against the deposit with the trustee of an equivalent amount of cash. The cash so deposited is subject to withdrawal upon the company's establishing its right to the authentication and delivery of an equivalent amount of bonds under other provisions of the indenture. Each separate bond financing is expensive. Where a company contemplates a substantial expansion program or where such a program and a refunding may be under consideration, it may take down its estimated total requirements through one issue against deposit of cash with the trustee. As property additions are completed, it makes the necessary certifications to the trustee and withdraws cash in an amount equal to the principal amount of bonds it could issue on the basis of such property. The net result is the same. This was once a frequently used provision, although it is more common now for corporations to resort to interim bank financing to finance construction programs, deferring permanent bond financing until the program is substantially completed. This practice tends to reduce interests costs. But bond financing rather than interim bank credit might be more advantageous during a period of a favorable bond market with low interest rates.

One final point should be noted. If a default should occur after bonds have been issued under such a provision and before the cash is withdrawn, such cash is part of the general trust estate securing all bonds outstanding and cannot be set apart for the benefit of the holders of the specific series issued against its deposit. In the absence of express and specific provisions to the contrary, all indenture securities are on a parity in regard to their claims against the trust estate and the obligor.

EVIDENCE REQUIRED BY TRUSTEE AS TO COMPLIANCE WITH CONDITIONS PRECEDENT

The indenture will specify the particular documents to be delivered to the trustee to establish the company's right to the authentication and delivery of the bonds requested. The trustee is under a duty to examine all such documents carefully to see that they establish compliance with all conditions precedent, and it must also make sure that the documents are in the form required by the indenture. Because of the importance of these transactions, the trustee should always have such documents reviewed by counsel.

The documents received will be determined by the particular purpose for which the bonds are to be issued. (*See Exhibit 5.*) Three documents should be received in all cases, however. These include a resolution of the board of directors of the company (or in the case of tax-exempt bonds, of the directors or governing body of the tax-exempt entity) authorizing the issuance of the bonds, setting forth the purpose for which they are to be issued, directing the execution of the bonds by specified officers, providing for execution and delivery of necessary documents to the trustee, and requesting authentication and delivery of the bonds by the trustee. The trustee should also receive a certificate executed by authorized officers of the company to the effect that there is no default under the indenture and that all conditions precedent to the authentication and delivery of the bonds requested have been performed. This should be accompanied by an opinion of counsel that all such conditions precedent have been fulfilled.

Where authentication and delivery of bonds is on the basis of property additions, these property additions should be certified to the trustee by authorized officers in sufficient detail to permit their identification. The certification should also include an appropriate computation of the net bondable value of such property to establish the company's right to the issuance of the bonds requested. This certificate should be accompanied by a separate certificate from an engineer, appraiser, or other expert setting forth the value of the property additions. Under certain circumstances such engineer's certificate must be executed by an independent engineer or appraiser not under the obligor's control.

Frequently an earnings requirement is included as a condition precedent. The customary form of such a condition is that for a specified period, the net earnings of the company available for interest (or the average earnings if the period is in excess of a year) must be so many times the interest charges on all indebtedness including the bonds to be issued. Compliance with this condition should be established by an accountant's certificate, which under certain conditions must be a certificate of an independent public accountant.

Where property additions are made the basis for the issuance of bonds, the trustee should receive an opinion of counsel on the instruments of conveyance required to subject such property to the lien of the indenture, or assurance that no such instruments are necessary. As previously indicated, if the bonds to be issued are a new series, a supplemental indenture is desirable. A specific conveyance of the property is customarily included in the same supplement.

In the event that authorization of any regulatory agency or public body is required, evidence of such authorization should be secured.[7] If the bonds are to be issued publicly, registration requirements under the 33 Act must be completed, including the filing of a new Form T-1.

In addition to the documents specifically required by the pertinent indenture provisions, the trustee should receive all the documents outlined in *Exhibit 5* or have such documents brought up to date.

For the convenience of the administrator, it is helpful to use a guide sheet for each new issue of securities, as outlined in *Exhibit 3*. This guide sheet calls attention to the various matters that should be considered, or the actions to be taken, and when completed can be added to the bond issue documents for historical reference.

[7] For a discussion of problems relating to public utilities bonding of nuclear generating facilities, *see* Corporate Trust Activities Committee, American Bankers Association, *The Bondability of Nuclear Facilities* (1977).

SIX

Sinking Fund and Maintenance Provisions

A common type of covenant found in indentures is the sinking fund provision. This is a device for amortization of the debt, or a part thereof, over the life of the issue and, being essentially a security provision, is most important. It is almost always found in an unsecured debenture or note agreement but is also quite common to bond indentures. If an issue is created for the construction or purchase of certain fixed property or facilities, the holders' security will tend to be depleted unless the amount of the debt is reduced proportionately to the depreciation or loss in value of the property as it is used in the business. One of the frequent uses for cash generated by the depreciation charge is reduction of debt incurred to purchase the property. Even though unrelated to specific property or security, a sinking fund is a convenient device for reducing corporate funded debt.

In mortgage indentures, particularly those of utility and railroad corporations, a maintenance covenant is frequently included in lieu of, and sometimes in addition to, a sinking fund provision. The type of covenant referred to is not the simple maintenance covenant that constitutes an undertaking by the obligor to keep the mortgaged property in good working order and condition, which should be in all mortgage indentures, but is more in the nature of an undertaking to expend a stated amount of money for renewal and replacement of the property. The theory of such a covenant is that, in lieu of retiring debt as the value of the property depreciates, the company will maintain the value of the security by expending an equivalent amount for the construction or acquisition of additional property.

The operation and purpose of these covenants can be illustrated by a simple example. Let us suppose that a corporation acquires a new plant for $100,000,000 with an estimated productive economic life of twenty-five years. For convenience it will be assumed that the value will depreciate on a level basis, or at the rate of $4,000,000 per year. The plant is financed with $40,000,000 of equity money and $60,000,000 of bonds, secured by a mortgage on the property. It is obvious that for the bondholders to maintain their margin of security, $2,400,000 in bonds would have to be retired each year. This would be done through operation of a sinking fund. An alternative method would be for the company to maintain the security at $100,000,000. This could be done by mortgaging entirely new facilities, by additions to the existing plant, or by the replacement of portions of the plant as they become old or worn out. Such an alternate undertaking would be set forth in a maintenance or a renewal and replacement covenant.

THE SINKING FUND COVENANT

A sinking fund covenant may take any of a different number of forms, and the exact terms included will result from the negotiations leading up to the issue. Some indentures will not contain a sinking fund, although investors usually insist upon the inclusion of an orderly procedure for retirement of debt. This is particularly true in the case of the unsecured debenture or note issue, and it is now very rare for an agreement of this kind not to include a sinking fund. An alternate method would be to provide for the securities issued to mature serially—that is, so many each year—rather than have all come due at the same time. Serial issues are very common in the case of state and municipal bonds. Purchasers of corporate bonds, however, prefer term bonds with a sinking fund rather than serial maturities, and consequently the latter are not often found in issues of industrial companies.

The trustee has substantial duties and responsibilities for the proper operation of the sinking fund. The indenture provisions should receive its careful attention during the drafting of the indenture and in connection with each sinking fund operation since, if the trustee misapplies the funds it may incur substantial liability. This may be true even though the funds are applied to retirement of indenture securities if they are used otherwise than is required by the indenture.

Method of Computation

A sinking fund may be required to operate annually, semiannually, or even at more frequent intervals. Because each separate operation may be quite expensive, it is inadvisable to provide for an operation more frequently than is required to carry out the basic purpose of the contract. There are many different ways in which computation of each sinking fund payment may be made, and there is no particular preference or advantage for one method over another, the one selected being the one best suited to obtain the desired result.

The more commonly used methods are: (1) payment of a fixed dollar amount; (2) payment of an amount calculated as a percentage of the maximum amount of securities that have been at any time authenticated and outstanding; or (3) payment of an amount sufficient to retire a fixed percentage of such bonds. The last might be the preferred method in any case where a redemption premium on a declining scale is involved in any sinking fund operation, for it ensures retirement of a level rather than a variable amount of bonds.

While most sinking funds are fixed in some definite amount or according to a specified formula, a variable sinking fund is often used. Such a sinking fund might be measured by a percentage of net earnings, either of the total net earnings of the company or from a specified source. There might also be a combination of several factors; for example, a minimum fixed sinking fund might be provided, to which is added a percentage of net earnings over a specified amount. This type might be particularly desirable in the case of a company whose earnings tend to fluctuate substantially with cyclical changes in the economy, ensuring greater retirement of debt during good years and providing some measure of protection in other years.

It is also common for the amount of the fixed sinking fund payment to vary from year to year. Provision might be made for retirement of a smaller percentage of bonds during the earlier years and an increasing percentage during later years. This method is almost always used where the principal security is a lease or contract obligation. Level amortization payments are provided to cover both interest and sinking fund. The amount required for interest decreases with each payment, leaving a greater amount available for retirement of principal.

Where several series of bonds are outstanding under the same indenture, different procedures may be followed. A separate sinking fund may be created for each series and a number of separate payments will be made, either at the same or different times, and each will involve an entirely separate operation related to the securities of the particular series involved. On the other hand, a single sinking fund may be set up that can be applied to the bonds of any or all series. The only change that takes place when a new series is created is that the amount of each such sinking fund is usually increased.

Where a single sinking fund payment is made for bonds of different series having different interest rates and maturity dates, the trustee should exercise special care in the application of such monies and should always endeavor to see that the indenture spells out the exact procedure to be followed. The usual provision requires the retirement of bonds that, computed on the basis of the price to be paid, provide the highest yield to maturity. Such application is the most advantageous to the obligor company, results in the greatest reduction in annual fixed charges, and in that way might be said to be the most beneficial to the trust estate. Whereas the usual effect is to eliminate certain series of bonds from any participation in the sinking fund and thus might be said to be unfair in this respect, it should be borne in mind that it is part of their contract, and theoretically at least, the holders of such series could have bargained for a separate sinking fund allocable to their series of bonds if they had so desired.

The trustee should make certain that the indenture is clear about how the interest and premium (if any) required to be paid in connection with any sinking fund retirement are to be provided. It may be evident from the manner in which the sinking fund is computed, but if such is not the case, language should be included specifying whether the company is to provide these amounts separately or whether they are chargeable against the sinking fund.

Inasmuch as bonds can usually be retired through operation of a sinking fund without premium, or at a lower premium than for optional redemption, the obligor company has no right to increase the amount of a sinking fund or to anticipate sinking fund payments unless such right is specially reserved. If the indenture includes such reservation, there should also be no doubt about whether the obligor is entitled to a credit against subsequent sinking fund payments for any amounts so anticipated or paid beyond normal requirements.

Method of Application of Sinking Fund Monies

The trustee should ensure that the method for application of sinking fund monies is clearly set forth in the indenture and, if alternate methods are provided, that the indenture is specific as to the order in which such alternate methods are to be used or the conditions that determine selection of the particular method.

Once specific bonds have been selected for purchase or redemption by the sinking fund and all steps necessary to effect the purchase or redemption taken except the actual surrender of the bonds, the funds in the hands of the trustee cease to be general trust estate funds and become specifically allocated to the particular bond or bonds so selected. In the event of a subsequent default, the holder is entitled to payment upon surrender of his or her bond, regardless of what may be realized by other indenture security holders.

A more difficult problem is presented, however, when a default occurs before there has been any application of such monies or before all steps necessary for the retirement of specific bonds have been concluded. The problem is complicated further if the sinking fund payment was made with respect to a particular series of bonds or if the trustee has selected specific bonds for retirement but has not mailed the notice of redemption.

The law applicable to such a situation is not clear, and the trustee's action should be guided by counsel. As a general rule it is suggested that all further action be suspended, any preliminary steps that may have been taken be revoked, and the funds be retained by the trustee without application until the default has been cured or waived or until the trustee receives judicial direction on disposition of the funds. Even where only one series of bonds is involved, application of funds to retirement of specific bonds with knowledge of a default might involve participation by the trustee in an unlawful preference for which it might be held liable. Aside from the question of the trustee's liability, such an application would be obviously unfair if, as a result of the default, the remaining security holders received less than their full claim.

The obligor company is frequently given the right to receive credit against its sinking fund obligation for any bonds it surrenders to the trustee for cancellation. (Such right may, in the case of a convertible debenture issue, also include the principal amount of debentures already converted.) This enables the obligor company to acquire bonds throughout the year in the open market, taking advantage of favorable market conditions, and some companies continuously satisfy their entire sinking fund obligations in this manner. The amount of the credit the company receives for bonds so surrendered may be the par value of the bonds, or the actual cost of the bonds to the company not in excess of the par value, or the current sinking fund redemption price if more than par.

In the absence of a specific right of the obligor to surrender bonds against credit or in lieu of a sinking fund payment, a question arises about the trustee's right to acquire or purchase bonds held by the obligor company in its treasury in applying sinking fund monies. It is preferable to have such right specifically set forth, although such actions are a more or less accepted practice and, in the absence of an express prohibition, would seem to be entirely in order. Care should be used, however, that any such acquisition is at or below the price at which equivalent bonds could be obtained by purchase from other holders.

The trustee may be directed to apply sinking fund monies to the purchase of bonds in the open market at a price not in excess of the current redemption price. If the bonds are noncallable a more or less arbitrary price is fixed by the indenture. Interest and commission paid on such purchases are usually, although not necessarily, separately reimbursed by the obligor. If not, then such amounts should be added in when computing the maximum price that can be offered. A time limit is customarily set for this method of operation, and if the funds cannot be exhausted within such time, a different method must be followed for the remaining funds.

Another method of operation is for the trustee to invite tenders of bonds. This is regarded by some as a fairer method of operation, although it usually results in payment of a higher average price than would be the case in an open-market operation. When the current market price is in excess of the maximum price at which tenders can be accepted (usually the sinking fund redemption price), an invitation for tenders is essentially an idle gesture, and where the trustee has discretion about the method to be followed, this fact should be considered.

The procedure to be followed in the case of an invitation of tenders is relatively simple but it still requires the exercise of care. A date is selected for the submission of tenders, with both the hour and the day specified. The invitation is then mailed in accordance with indenture provisions to all registered holders of securities. (If bearer bonds are outstanding the notice must be published, and copies mailed to all holders who may have filed their names with the trustee for the purpose of receiving reports and notices.) It is desirable to request submission of sealed tenders, and all other conditions should be clearly set forth in the notice. The right to reject tenders in whole or in part should always be specifically reserved. To avoid error it is recommended that some form of dual control be established for all tenders received. As they are received a record of receipt should be made and the tenders deposited in a locked container. If any are received unsealed, they should be examined to see that all necessary information is included and then immediately sealed and deposited. No record of prices should be made, and until the tenders have been opened and examined at the appointed time, no information should be disclosed to anyone, including the obligor company.

When the hour set has arrived the tenders should be opened, examined, and listed and a recapitulation made in the order of the prices at which bonds are offered. In the case of different issues with different interest rates and maturity dates, price should be computed on the basis of yield to maturity, the higher the yield the lower the price. Sufficient bonds should then be accepted at the lowest prices offered to exhaust the monies available. Mailing of notice of acceptance completes the contract.

A final method of operation is through selection of bonds for redemption through operation of the redemption provisions of the indenture. Bonds are usually redeemable at par for the purpose of the sinking fund, or at prices less than would be required in the case of an optional redemption. The particular bonds to be redeemed will be selected as set forth in the indenture, and it is customary for such selection to be made by the trustee. In drafting such provisions it is desirable for the trustee to retain flexibility. It is therefore much better to have a provision allowing for the selection to be made in such manner as the trustee shall deem equitable, rather than have the mechanics spelled out in detail. Once the particular bonds to be redeemed have been selected, the trustee arranges to mail an appropriate notice in the manner prescribed by the indenture.[1] Once the notice has been mailed, the designated bonds become due and payable on the date specified, and the necessary funds should be segregated by the trustee and held in an account specifically allocated to their payment.

In the case of direct placements where all securities are held by institutional investors it is customary to provide that in lieu of applica-

---

[1] If bonds are outstanding in bearer form, an appropriate notice must also be published.

tion by lot, sinking fund monies proportionate to their holdings must be allocated among the owners. Care must be exercised both in drafting and administering the provision, the objective being for each holder to retain its proportional percentage of the debt obligations as nearly as possible. Normally, bonds must be retired in even multiples of $1,000, and no problem is presented where application of the sinking fund percentage to each separate holding would result in an even multiple of $1,000. This seldom happens, however, and it is necessary for the trustee to devise an appropriate formula for each operation. No particular formula is required so long as the same formula is applied consistently year after year and produces the desired allocation. *Exhibit 7* describes a typical formula and illustrates the application thereof.

Bonds retired through the sinking fund are usually canceled by the trustee and cannot be reissued or used by the obligor as a credit under any other indenture provision.

MAINTENANCE AND REPLACEMENT COVENANTS

As indicated previously, a maintenance and replacement covenant is sometimes used in lieu of, or in addition to, a sinking fund. This is more common in the case of a regulated company, such as an electric utility, which requires a more or less continuous supply of funds for capital purposes and for which a somewhat higher debt ratio is permissible. The fund established pursuant to such a covenant is more properly a renewal and replacement than a maintenance fund. Every corporation is expected to provide funds for normal maintenance of its properties, and these constitute expenses chargeable to its income account. The fund under consideration here is a capital fund and the expenditures therefrom are normally chargeable to fixed property accounts.

There is no fixed formula by which the amount of such fund is to be computed, and it will tend to vary with the type of company involved, the nature of its properties, and other considerations. In the case of regulated companies, the regulatory authority may require application of a particular formula, or it may otherwise be determined as part of the negotiations relating to the drafting of the indenture. Ordinarily, it should be closely related to the amount of the company's annual depreciation charges and in any event should be designed to provide such amount as will enable the company to preserve the value of the property securing its outstanding bonds.

As an illustration, a more or less arbitrary rule of thumb was at one time applied to electric utility operating companies. It was developed that, as a general average, the investment of four dollars in fixed plant was required to produce one dollar of gross annual revenue. Also, as a general average, application to the entire property account of the amounts resulting from the application of required depreciation percentages to specified classes of property indicated an annual average depreciation charge of 3¾ percent. By use of these figures, a covenant to expend 15 percent of annual gross revenues from operations for maintenance and replacement purposes was frequently used in indentures of these companies. This percentage might be varied in particular cases where the character of a company's property differed substantially from the norm. More recent indentures have tended to pattern the covenant to fit the circumstances of the particular company rather than to follow a preestablished pattern, but this illustrates the manner in which these percentages may be computed and the purpose of the provision.

The indenture will require annual filing with the trustee of a certificate in sufficient detail to show compliance with the covenant. All computations should be shown, and the trustee should check them carefully. To the extent possible, it should also check the data included against the financial statements and other information it may receive.

All property acquired by the company and certified to the trustee in compliance with this covenant becomes funded property and cannot be used as a basis for the issuance of bonds or for other purposes. Accordingly, the trustee should receive all the supplemental documents with respect to such property as it would receive if the property were being used as a basis for the issuance of bonds. Such documents would include engineer's certificates of value, an opinion of counsel as to the company's title to the property and as to the lien of the indenture thereon, and such instruments of specific conveyance as might be required.

As distinguished from the case of the issuance of bonds, property additions can be taken under this covenant at 100 percent rather than at the bondable percentage of their value. On the other hand, if any of such property is subject to a prior lien, it is necessary to deduct an amount equivalent to the bondable property value of such prior lien. For example, if the bondable percentage of property additions under the indenture were 60 percent, in such a computation 166⅔ percent of any prior lien bonds would be deducted.

It is customary to combine the normal maintenance covenant with such a renewal and replacement covenant and to allow the obligor to take expenditures for normal repairs and maintenance as a credit. It is also necessary, as in the case of the issuance of bonds, to deduct the book value of property retirements from the gross property expenditures to determine the net credit to be allowed.

One of the difficult administrative problems is in dealing with property certificates under a number of different indenture provisions.[2] Although the value of a particular addition can be used only once, the value of the addition may be in excess of the amount certified for a particular purpose and the excess can be used for another purpose. Similarly, it is necessary that deduction for property retirements or prior liens be made only once. The certificates should be so drawn as to enable the trustee to check these facts.

Where during any particular year the obligor expends more than the required percentage for maintenance and replacement, it is normally allowed a credit for such excess against the requirement of subsequent years. This credit may be unlimited in that it can be taken at any time, or it may be required to be used within a specified time. If the latter is the case, a further word of caution is necessary. If, for example, the use of such a credit is limited to the three succeeding years and the company has excess expenditures for four successive years, the amount of the credit for the first of the four years is no longer available. This would seem to be obvious, except that the certificates may be so drawn as to indicate that in each year the company first uses the credit for the preceding year and that the resulting larger credit for the current year is allocable to that year and not to both years. The result may be to carry forward indefinitely a substantial credit that would otherwise have lapsed.

If the computation indicates that the company has not expended the required percentage during the year, a deficit for the year is indicated. This deficit may be offset by the amount of any credit the company was entitled to carry forward from previous years. To the extent not so offset, the obligor must deposit cash or bonds with the trustee. These may be subsequently withdrawn against certification of property additions or on the basis of a credit shown in a subsequent maintenance certificate. If the company desires, any bonds so deposited may be canceled as a credit against the maintenance requirements. The bonds so canceled have the same status as sinking fund bonds and cannot be reissued or used as a basis for any other action under the indenture.

[2] See note 7, chapter 5, *supra*.

SEVEN

Release and Substitution of Property

Another major segment of the indenture contract dealing with maintenance and preservation of the bondholders' security is the section dealing with the release and substitution of property. These provisions are not, of course, pertinent to the unsecured debenture or note agreement, but in almost every case where specific property is mortgaged to or pledged with the trustee, the indenture contains detailed provisions for how the obligor may deal with its properties and prescribes conditions for the release and substitution of specific properties on which the indenture is a lien.

The necessity for and importance of such provisions become clear when one considers that in the usual case the real security is the business of the obligor company as a going concern and not the aggregate of the individual parcels of property. It is customary for mortgage indentures to continue for an indefinite period, and the needs of the mortgagor company will be likely to change considerably over the yields. Also, many parts of the original property will become worn out and unfit for use in the company's business. The primary purpose of the release provisions is to enable the obligor to dispose of such obsolete and unproductive properties, free from the lien of the indenture, and to use the proceeds to acquire additional properties or improvements necessary or useful in its business operations. Because it is desirable to provide as carefully as possible for almost every contingency, the release provisions cannot be limited to mere disposition of worn out or obsolete properties and usually cover any property that the obligor may sell or otherwise dispose of.

Inasmuch as the trustee's primary responsibilities revolve around the preservation of the bondholders' security, the duties discussed in this and the two preceeding chapters might be regarded as the tripartite base on which most of the predefault administrative provisions of a secured indenture are founded. The sections dealing with the issuance of bonds limit the creation of additional debt to a prescribed percentage of the additional value added to the security and are designed to insure that the requisite equity is maintained. The sinking fund and maintenance provisions have as their purpose the continuation of the predetermined minimum ratio of security value to debt through insuring the retirement of debt in proportion to the effect of depreciation and obsolescence factors on the obligor's properties. Finally, the release provisions enable the company to deal with its properties efficiently and expeditiously, provided that equivalent value is substituted for properties sold or otherwise disposed of. Once this basic concept is thoroughly understood, a proper foundation is laid for the intelligent consideration of applications or certificates filed under any of the various sections. While the entire indenture constitutes, and must be considered as, a single contract, it is of particular importance that these three major segments be complementary. In reviewing the terms of a proposed new mortgage indenture, the trustee should make sufficient analysis to assure itself that the various provisions are entirely consistent and designed to carry out the essential purposes outlined above.

From the viewpoint of both the obligor and the trustee, the release provisions are of the greatest importance, and some of the most intricate problems involved in indenture administration have to do with the release of property. It is simple enough to state the basic proposition that the trustee's duty is discharged if equivalent value is received for value surrendered, but how is "value" in such an instance to be determined? If a piece of property is sold as a result of arm's length bargaining, isn't the sale price fairly conclusive in relation to the "value" involved? But this means that we are dealing solely with intrinsic values. What happens to the concept that the important consideration is the maintaining of the value of the business as a going concern and not the intrinsic value of the individual pieces of property? Given the "going concern" theory, is it ever proper for the trustee to accept less than the intrinsic value of the specific property being disposed of? In particular situations, should it insist on receiving a great deal more?

The problem is further complicated by the dual fiduciary responsibilities of the trustee. Preservation of the security is the most fundamental responsibility of the trustee, and to this end its fiduciary duty to the bondholders is absolute. Conversely, before default the obligor has the right within the terms of its contract to deal with its property in such manner as seems to be in the best interest of all parties, and is in a much better position than the trustee to make such a determination. The release provisions constitute a part of the contract between the obligor and the trustee, and if the necessary conditions precedent are fulfilled, the trustee is under a duty to assent to a requested release and may be liable if it refuses to do so.

This essential problem may be illustrated by considering a specific situation. Assume that two extensive railway systems—Railroad A and Railroad B—serve exactly the same territory between two points on their lines approximately two hundred miles apart and that for this distance their lines roughly parallel each other. The property of each is heavily mortgaged. As a result of detailed studies and with approval of the Interstate Commerce Commission, the companies agree that Railroad A will grant to Railroad B the right in perpetuity to use A's tracks between the points in question and that the latter will abandon its trackage and right-of-way. The remaining single line is capable of handling all traffic and no revenue loss will be occasioned. Actually, a saving of several million dollars annually will result from reductions in property taxes, maintenance, and terminal expenses. Railroad B makes application to its mortgage trustee for release of its entire two-hundred-mile line, the consideration being the mortgaging of the trackage right from Railroad A and the deposit of all proceeds of salvage, the latter to be used for the enlargement and improvement of certain facilities on the new joint line to facilitate the handling of the increased traffic. What should be the attitude of the mortgage trustee? Despite the economic desirability of effectuating the agreement, isn't the value of the trust estate being diminished? Does the trust estate benefit at all by the savings realized, unless they are set aside and used to reduce outstanding indebtedness? It is doubtful that the trustee could successfully impose this as a condition to the release, if it receives an engineer's certification to the effect that the value of the trackage rights is at least equal to the value of the right-of-way to be abandoned.

The Railroad A trustee also has a problem, although possibly not so great as that of the Railroad B trustee. The latter would have to insist that the rights granted be superior to all mortgages on the Railroad A property, although this would result in a substantial encumbrance ranking ahead of the lien of the Railroad A mortgage, requiring a consent or release by the trustee thereof. Again, the consideration could only be the savings in expense, which might or might not directly benefit the trust estate.

In administering the release provisions the trustee must always insist upon receiving the certificates and other documents required and must examine them to see that the proper statements and certifications are made. (*See Exhibit 8 Release Check Sheet.*) The question is the extent, if any, to which the trustee should examine the practical aspects and possible consequences of the proposed transaction and interpose its independent judgment. The matter is further complicated when the action requested is unusual, and there is uncertainty about whether it is specifically authorized by the indenture provisions. The trustee is confronted with a difficult decision in these cases, even though the contemplated action appears to be clearly in the interest of the bondholders. If it assents to the proposed release without requisite authority and loss results, it may be liable for acting beyond the scope of its powers. Conversely, if it refuses to execute a release and loss results, it may be liable both to security holders and to the obligor if in fact the transaction was within the scope of the indenture. All too frequently time is of the essence, and it is impossible in these situations to obtain a judicial construction of the indenture language.

The whole problem of releases has been the subject of considerable comment over the years, both in judicial decisions and by writers on the subject. Unfortunately, no consistent pattern has been established that might serve as a guide to the trustee. The cases considered have for the most part involved situations where substantial losses resulted, and the trustees involved were subjected to severe criticism even though the facts indicated that the terms of the indenture had been followed strictly. In other cases where trustees departed from indenture restrictions and logically might be subject to criticism, their actions were upheld. A striking example of the latter situation is presented by the numerous cases involving the substitution of buses for municipal railway systems. Few of the railway system indentures provided for the release of lines of railway, and in fact, many contained an express prohibition against it. Most companies, however, would have faced serious financial trouble and possible loss of franchises if a way had not been found to effect a change in the method of transportation. The courts almost without exception were able to find implied authority in the indenture sufficient to permit the transactions. One court held that bondholders acquired their obligations with implied knowledge of a possible change in methods of conducting business and that this was implicit in the agreement.[1] Another found the requisite authority in the provisions reserving to the company, before default, the right to possess, manage, and operate the mortgaged properties.[2]

The extent to which a trustee may go in refusing to execute a release where it appears that the bondholders' security will be impaired, even though the necessary conditions precedent exist, is problematic. Two cases on this point, both decided by New York courts, illustrate the problem.

The first case involved a collateral trust indenture where the collateral consisted largely of bonds secured by real estate mortgages. The indenture provided that such bonds could be accepted as collateral only when accompanied by appraisals showing that the unpaid balance was not in excess of 75 percent of the value of the real estate. The indenture further provided that whenever the principal amount of bonds outstanding under the indenture was less than 83⅓ percent of the par value of collateral pledged, excess collateral could be withdrawn until such percentage was reached. The case involved application for withdrawal of eight million dollars excess collateral computed on this basis. The trustee refused to comply, arguing that, despite the fact that the collateral bonds were adequately secured at the time of deposit, depreciation in real estate values had wiped out the 25 percent margin and that in many cases the value of the underlying real estate was less than the face amount of the bonds. The trustee's position was upheld by the court, which ruled that the release provisions were qualified by an implied intent that a 25 percent margin in security for all collateral be maintained.[3]

The second case involved a mortgage indenture that contained a rather unusual provision permitting releases upon deposit with the trustee of a stated proportion of the consideration for which the property was sold, the percentage varying with the gross sales price of the property. On December 18, the obligor notified the trustee that it would default on the interest installment due on the succeeding January 1. On December 30 it applied for the release of certain property, tendering 20 percent of the sales price, which was the required percentage under the applica-

1 Mayor *et al* of City of Baltimore v. United Railways and Electric Company of Baltimore City, 108 Md. 64, 69 Atl. 436 (1908).

2 New York State Railways v. Security Trust Company of Rochester, 135 Misc. 456, 238 N.Y.S. 354 (1929).

3 Prudence Company Inc. v. Central Hanover Bank and Trust Company, 261 N.Y. 420, 184 N.E. 687 (1933).

ble indenture clause. The trustee refused to release the property, but the courts upheld the company's suit for specific performance, holding that, since a default did not exist on the date of application, the trustee had no right to refuse.[4]

Under the TIA the trustee is afforded protection if it relies in good faith on certificates furnished to it pursuant to the indenture provisions, but it must examine the certificates to ensure that they do conform to such provisions.[5] In most situations, no problem will be encountered if the trustee follows this rule. No hard-and-fast rule can be established to guide the trustee in the unusual or special situation however. The requirement of good faith means that it cannot free itself from considering the practical aspects and potential consequences of the proposed transaction.

In considering the usual and customary provision of the indenture relating to these matters, the mortgage indenture and the collateral indenture will be dealt with separately. Although the essential purpose is the same in both, different problems are presented.

DEALING WITH PROPERTY UNDER MORTGAGE INDENTURES

Before default, the mortgagor corporation has the absolute right to possess, manage, and operate its properties free from restriction or interference, provided only that it complies with the convenants and provisions of the indenture. It is customary for this right to be specifically affirmed in general terms by the indenture. The first sections of the release article will then proceed to enumerate specific rights retained by the mortgagor in furtherance of this general affirmation.

The first such provision deals with the company's right to remove and dispose of property and equipment that has become obsolete or unserviceable or is no longer useful in the company's business activities. This can be done without the necessity of release or other action by the trustee. The only condition is that the property so disposed of be replaced by other property of at least equal value or that, to the extent of any deficiency, cash be deposited with the trustee. Mechanically, the most feasible method of ensuring compliance is to require the filing with

[4] Indian River Islands Corporation v. Manufacturers Trust Company *et al.*, 253 App. Div. 549, 2 N.Y.S. 2d 860 (1938).
[5] TIA, sec. 315(a)(2).

the trustee of an annual certificate of the aggregate value of property so retired, the value of property substituted, and the amount of the cash deficiency, if any.

A second section gives the obligor the right to relocate machinery or equipment; to move any of the property from one location to another; to alter, remodel, or change the location of any building or structure; or to make any similar change or alteration so long as the aggregate value of the mortgaged property is not diminished. Because these rights do not affect the lien of the indenture, no accounting to the trustee is necessary.

Finally, the mortgagor is given the right to alter or amend any lease, contract, easement, license, franchise, or similar right, or to enter into any such agreements. This right is usually conditioned on a finding by the company's board of directors that the alteration or amendment will not prejudice the company's activities or the trust estate or that it will be in the best interests of the company and its bondholders. Such other conditions may be imposed as may be appropriate to the circumstances of the particular company. For example, if the company is given the right to grant leases or other interests in its property, it is usually provided that these must be made expressly subject to the prior rights of the trustee as mortgagee.

This reservation of rights in the company is a necessary and integral part of its right to possession and use of the property and is to be exercised without reference to or action by the trustee. It is normally provided, however, that upon request by the company the trustee will execute such release or other documents that may be necessary or desirable to confirm the company's action in any particular situation.

Because the trustee retains no control over such dealing with its security, it follows that these sections should be carefully examined by it to ensure that the security will not be prejudiced by any such action. Of equal importance, the restrictions and qualifications on the company's unilateral action under these sections should not be so broad as to prejudice the action the company can take with the concurrence of the trustee, under the general release provisions. In a recent situation, a provision prohibiting the granting of leases, except subject to the prior lien of the indenture, raised a serious question when a trustee was presented with an application for the release of a leasehold estate to enable the separate financing of substantial improvements to a particular property, in the absence of a clear right to execute such a release. It would have been simple to make the restriction applicable only to unilateral action by the company, carrying out the obvious intent of the parties.

Whereas the sections permitting unilateral action by an obligor should be fairly restrictive, a great deal of flexibility is desirable with respect to the action that may be taken with the consent and concurrence of the trustee. As long as the essential character of the security is preserved, the company should be given the right to obtain the release of any property it wishes to dispose of, upon the substitution of property of equivalent value or upon an appropriate reduction in the amount of the secured indebtedness.

The conditions precedent to the company's right to secure a release of property and the documents required to substantiate compliance with such conditions are set forth in Section 314(d) of the TIA.

Many indentures provide that property cannot be released unless the company has sold or contracted to sell the specific property in question. Although this would appear to present no problem, a number of situations have arisen where this has proved to be too restrictive. Occasionally it may be desirable to effect a change in the terms of a lease, contract, easement, or other property right where no actual sale is involved and under circumstances requiring the consent or participation of the trustee. Any such general limitation or restriction should be questioned.

One of the basic documents to be required is a resolution of the company's board of directors reciting the essential facts surrounding the transaction, containing an adequate description of the property, and requesting execution of a release by the trustee. While seldom specifically required, it is desirable also to have the resolution specifically state that the company is not in default and that the requested release will not impair the security of the indenture in contravention of the provisions thereof. These are required conditions and must be covered in other certificates. The basic purpose in requiring a resolution, in addition to seeing that requisite authority is given the company officers, is to ensure that the transaction has been referred to and authorized by the senior responsible body of the corporation, and it is desirable to require affirmative consideration of all aspects of the transaction.

The value of the property to be released is determined by the certificate of an engineer, appraiser, or other expert. This certification must also state affirmatively that the proposed release will not impair the security of the indenture. Under certain circumstances, where the value of the property to be released is in excess of a specified amount, this certification must be made by an independent engineer, appraiser, or expert having no affiliation with the company. The certificate must recite in sufficient detail the scope of the examination and investigation that formed the basis of the opinion certified. Normally the company is given the right to select the engineer or appraiser, but such selection should be made subject to the trustee's approval. In view of the importance of this certificate, the trustee should insist upon receiving an adequate statement of the expert's qualifications and should make an evaluation of such qualifications.

Two additional documents are always required—a certificate of designated officers of the company and an opinion of counsel, each of which must state that all conditions precedent to the requested release exist or have been performed, and recite in sufficient detail the examination and investigation made by the signers to ascertain the necessary facts. In addition to this general statement, it is customary to require the officers to certify affirmatively to all pertinent facts—that there is no default, that the property has been sold or that a release is necessary for the reasons set forth, that the release is desirable in the conduct of the company's business and will not impair the security of the indenture, and such other facts as may be appropriate to the particular situation.

Finally, consideration for the release must be furnished. This should equal the greater of the fair value of the property released or the consideration received by the company on the sale thereof. Such consideration is normally in the form of cash or other real or personal property, but occasionally it may take the form of purchase money obligations secured by the property released. If the latter, it should be limited to a fixed percentage (usually 66⅔ percent) of the value of the property. It is also desirable to limit strictly the aggregate amount of such obligations that may be held. While they may constitute perfectly good security, they diminish the working capital of any corporation that is not in the business of investing in mortgages.

Any cash received is deposited with the trustee and may be withdrawn by the company to reimburse itself for any additional property acquired and subjected to the lien of the indenture, in an amount equal to the lesser of the cost or the fair value of such property to the company. Whenever any property is subjected to the lien of the indenture, either as the basis for the release of other property or for the withdrawal of cash, substantially the same documents must be filed as in the case of the issuance of bonds on the basis of property additions. These must include an engineer's or appraiser's certificate of the fair value of such property to the company; an opinion of counsel that all conditions precedent to the withdrawal have been complied with and that such property is subject to the lien of the indenture; and an officers' certificate that such property is useful and desirable in the conduct of the company's business and that all conditions precedent to the transaction have been complied with. If counsel indicates that instruments of conveyance are necessary or desirable to perfect the lien of the indenture on such property, such instruments must be executed and recorded and become supplements to the indenture.

Some confusion is frequently created in the mind of the inexperienced administrator by complex provisions, often included in open-ended mortgages, that endeavor to classify properties used as a basis for releases and to permit their reuse at a later date under other provisions of the indenture. The reason for this becomes clear if the distinction between funded and unfunded property is borne in mind. "Funded" property is that which has been bonded or used as a basis for credit under a sinking fund, maintenance, or similar provision. "Unfunded" property, while subject to the lien of the indenture, is excess property available for use by the company in certifying compliance with the pertinent indenture sections. Property substituted for other property released should retain the latter status, and when this is unfunded, the new property still remains available for use for other purposes, even though certified to the trustee as a basis for release of other unfunded property.

It is desirable also to include a provision that, although used infrequently, permits the trustee to apply any cash deposited to the purchase or redemption of bonds. In the normal situation, such application should be at the option of the obligor company.

Miscellaneous Provisions

In furtherance of the general purposes of the release clauses, and to provide for special situations or contingencies that may arise, it is customary to include a number of general sections in the release article, most of which become operative only on the happening of particular events.

Where it is contemplated that frequent sales of property will be made, it is desirable to include a provision permitting the company, without application to or release by the trustee, to consummate sales up to a specified aggregate amount each year. Preparation of individual release applications is time-consuming and expensive, and such a provision results in substantial savings in time and expense. The company is required to provide a single annual accounting to the trustee. Although it is seldom required, it would be desirable to have a single release covering all such properties executed annually. The conveyance of property without a specific release of a mortgage lien will create a possible cloud on title that may require expensive proceedings to remove at a later date. Sometimes it is difficult to identify a particular parcel as one that was properly sold under such a general section, and the trustee is placed in an embarrassing position when it is requested, years later, to join in a confirmatory release.

There should always be included a statement to the effect that the purchaser of any property released by the trustee is protected and under no duty to inquire into the particular circumstances or the propriety of any such release. Where the trustee executes a release improperly or without the requisite authority, it is not clear what the effect on the title of the purchaser may be. Some cases have held that a release so executed is invalid, and the purchaser does not acquire good title. Courts have held, however, that where the indenture contains such a provision protecting the purchaser, the provision is controlling and the purchaser is protected even though the trustee's action was *ultra vires*. No one should question the desirability or equity of such a rule.

There should always be included provisions dealing with the disposition of property taken through the exercise of the power of eminent domain, or by the exercise of any right of any government, bureau, or agency, or any public or quasi-public body to condemn or take possession or title to any property or interest therein. Usually, the award granted for any such taking will be paid to the trustee. It is desirable to include a greater degree of flexibility, however, and the procedure will be simplified if the company is given the right to compromise or settle its claim in such a situation. The practice usually followed is to proceed under the general release section, but sometimes the conditions precedent are not completely satisfied, and because it is a special situation, not subject to the company's control, it is better to deal with it as such. An appropriate certificate of the fairness of the proposed settlement would serve as a basis for the release of the property. This would enable the company to use the proceeds promptly in acquisition of substitute property and avoid the delay and expense of pursuing the condemnation route.

The normal release provisions are operative only on condition that no default exists under the indenture. Some thought should be given to the problem that will be presented if a default should occur. It is customary to provide that the rights of the company under the release article may be exercised by a trustee appointed in bankruptcy or reorganization proceedings. As a practical matter such an official will operate under orders of the court having jurisdiction, which may direct the sale of particular property whether or not there is indenture authorization, but it is desirable nevertheless to provide for this contingency.

Of more significance is the situation that exists when no formal proceedings have been instituted. Here the trustee is required to exercise more discretion and judgment, and the release sections are usually made permissive. If in the judgment of the trustee the proposed transaction seems desirable, it is granted authority to execute a release but is permitted to refuse to do so. The trustee should receive the same certifications and documents as in the case of a predefault release and may require such additional evidence as seems indicated to enable it to reach an appropriate conclusion.

Finally, provisions should be inserted to deal with any special situation or special properties that may be significant in the case of the particular company involved. The nature of such provisions, if any, will depend on the special circumstances existing. Certain property or classes of property may be of such significance in the financing arrangement as to warrant a prohibition against their disposal or a provision that the proceeds can be applied only to retirement of the debt. Acquisition of particular classes of property with trust monies may be forbidden or may be limited to a fixed aggregate amount or to a percentage of the indenture securities outstanding. There may be any number of variations, and the trustee should ensure that it understands the purpose intended and that the provisions inserted are designed properly to effectuate such purpose.

PROVISIONS AS TO PLEDGED COLLATERAL

The traditional collateral trust indenture does not now occupy the importance in corporate financing that it did during the period of the 1920s and 1930s.[6] This was the era of the growth and influence of the large holding company systems, particularly in the public utility industry. The parent companies in these systems, and quite frequently the companies on the second and even third tiers of the intracorporate structure, owned no physical operating properties at all but merely held securities of subsidiary and affiliated companies in the system. Capital debt financing

[6]For discussion of various types of collateral used in asset-backed transactions, *see* chapter 14.

by these corporations was arranged through the collateral trust device, under which securities of affiliated companies constituted the sole security for the outstanding obligations. The rapid expansion of these systems and the numerous recapitalizations resulted in substantial pyramiding of the debt and frequent withdrawals and substitutions of collateral under the various indentures.

A number of events occurred that greatly lessened the relative significance of these arrangements. Of the greatest importance was the enactment of the Public Utility Holding Company Act under which the giant systems have either disappeared or been substantially curtailed. In the process the old indentures were satisfied through the exchange of securities during the reorganization process. The capital structures of the companies have been simplified and valuation has been placed on a more realistic basis. Debt securities of the system are not usually issued by the subsidiary operating companies where operating properties rather than collateral constitute the security. Public financing by the parent holding company is normally done through sale of equity; where debt securities are issued, it is done on an unsecured basis.

Where securities are held as part of the trust estate, requirements governing their release are now substantially the same as those relating to real property. Of particular importance is the requirement of certificates of value, both of collateral being released and of collateral being substituted for other property. These certificates must be made by experts who are required to set forth the criteria that form the basis of their appraisal and that can be subjected to objective scrutiny. In particular situations, these certificates must be furnished by independent appraisers.

Despite the decline in importance of the traditional collateral trust indenture as such, the handling of collateral security is a significant factor in many mortgage indentures and asset-backed financing vehicles. Numerous companies still conduct a portion of their business through subsidiary or affiliated companies, and to provide security on the complete business operation it is necessary to create a combined mortgage and collateral trust indenture. The significance of the pledge of securities, however, lies not in their current market value but in the granting of a collateral lien on the parent company's allied or subsidiary operations conducted through the companies whose securities are pledged. The pertinent indenture provisions should therefore be designed to carry out this essential purpose.

It is important that all securities of such affiliates or subsidiaries owned by the obligor company be included in the pledge. This need not necessarily cover open-book advances, although these too are frequently included through a requirement for execution and pledging of an unsecured note. In the case of a real property mortgage, creation of a prior lien is effectively prevented by recording requirements. A collateral lien can, however, be impaired by the issuance of senior securities ranking ahead of those pledged. In the absence of a specific requirement for the pledging of any such securities, protection should be obtained in the form of negative covenants controlling the amount of such securities that can be issued.

Before default no particular action is required of the trustee other than the custody of the securities pledged. The obligor company is entitled to all income thereof and should be permitted to exercise all voting rights except on matters that might affect the value of the collateral lien. Enforcement of the principal of any debt obligations so pledged is not important, and the trustee may properly be freed from any duty in this connection. Despite the lien nature of the pledge, however, any payments made on account of principal or received on retirement of equity securities should be received by the trustee. Such a requirement is roughly equivalent to the maintenance requirement relating to mortgaged property.

Adequate provisions should be included to facilitate any exchange, recapitalization, merger, or other type of intracompany transactions that may occur from time to time. These should authorize the trustee, upon receipt of appropriate resolutions and certificates establishing the desirability of the proposed arrangement, to execute such documents or give such consents as may be required.

By reason of the special purpose of this collateral pledge, normally no part of the securities of any particular company held (except on payment, exchange, or for a similar reason) should be released unless all the securities of the particular company involved are disposed of simultaneously.

As in the case of real property, any special situations should be dealt with specially, and appropriate authority should be included in the indenture for the trustee's guidance.

After default the trustee should have all rights of ownership with respect to pledged securities, including the right to receive and retain income, the right of sale or other disposition, and the right to exercise full voting control.

EIGHT

Indenture Covenants

In addition to provisions that relate specifically to the trust estate or to the debt and the rights of the parties with respect thereto, most indentures contain a number of covenants designed to place restrictions on the activities of the obligor. The number and nature of the covenants included result from negotiations between the obligor and the person or persons representing the prospective purchasers of the securities (in a public issue, normally counsel to the underwriters). The type of covenants included depends to a large extent on the nature of the business of the obligor, the term of the loan, the purpose for which it is being made, whether it is secured or unsecured, the extent and nature of other outstanding obligations, and other, similar considerations.[1]

The trustee has, of course, no responsibility for what covenants are or are not included in a particular indenture, for this is essentially a part of the substantive contract between borrower and lender. While the trustee does not draft the covenants, it should carefully review all of them and insist on language that gives it the options to exercise its duties and responsibilities in a timely and flexible manner to protect the bondholders' interests. Once the contract is executed, however, the trustee will have the primary duty of enforcing it and therefore must be concerned with all provisions included. A more effective job can be done if there is a clear understanding, not only of what the language means but

[1] See TIA, sec. 314. The TIRA converted several frequently used covenants, designed to afford the continuing supply of information to the trustee about the company's affairs, into legislatively mandated obligations.

also of the purpose it is intended to accomplish and why the provision was included in a particular indenture. Unfortunately, some drafters have special provisions they like and sometimes insert them without regard to their relevance to the essential purpose of the contract. An astute trustee will examine these provisions closely and make sure their relevance and purpose are clearly understood by the parties to the contract. Once the indenture is executed and delivered, it is difficult and expensive, sometimes even impossible, to have it modified. It is unfortunate when a particular covenant, designed to enhance the credit and protect the investor, actually threatens the security primarily relied on and places the obligor in a difficult situation. When faced with such a development the trustee finds itself in an unenviable position that might have been avoided by the exercise of greater care when the contract was still in draft form.

Of paramount importance, of course, is the cardinal rule applicable to all indenture language—that its meaning be clear and unambiguous. One of the most difficult tasks a trustee has is in the interpretation and application of a particular provision to a situation not contemplated at the time it was drafted and that the covenant was not designed to address. No matter how sincere and honest corporate financial officers may be, they tend to interpret provisions in light of the particular problem with which they may be faced from time to time, the language taking on different shades of meaning as the circumstances of a particular company undergo change. Since many covenants require only unilateral action on the part of the obligor, it is possible for a default to occur unintentionally because of an incorrect or slightly distorted interpretation on the part of the company officials.

Of equal importance is the necessity that the covenant be so drafted that its violation is easily detected. Where the existence of particular facts or prohibited acts or situations is solely within the knowledge of the obligor, and not likely to be readily disclosed by the financial statements or other information furnished by the trustee, every effort should be made to obtain periodic certification of compliance with the covenant, either as part of a general certification or with adequate detail about the facts indicating compliance or noncompliance with the specific provision.

In general, covenants should be related to and designed to faciliate the carrying out of the purpose of each particular loan contract. It is impossible to detail or recite all covenants that might be desirable in a particular case. The enumeration set forth below is intended to present only the covenants more commonly used. Many of those listed would not be applicable to particular indentures, but a thorough understanding of the uses and purposes of these will provide a basic background that should be adequate for indenture administrators in most situations.

Covenants may be classified in a number of ways, but probably the simplest classification is to distinguish between *affirmative* covenants, which require specific action on the part of the obligor, either continuously or at specified periods, and *negative* covenants, which are prohibitive or restrictive and require, not the taking of action, but the refraining from certain actions.

AFFIRMATIVE COVENANTS

As the name implies, an affirmative covenant requires some positive or definite action on the part of the obligor. It requires the taking of specific action, either continuously, from time to time, or at specified times. A sinking fund covenant is, of course, of this type, although it is almost always covered in a separate action of the indenture and is not included in the enumeration below. Many affirmative covenants are pertinent only to mortgage indentures and relate to the mortgage security, while others are equally applicable whether the issue is secured or unsecured.

Some provisions are frequently included in the covenant section as such, although they are more in the nature of warranties. Typical of such provisions are the following:

1. Covenant that the company has complied with all legal requirements and is duly authorized to execute and deliver the indenture and to issue the indenture securities and that the indenture securities in the hands of the holders thereof will be valid and enforceable obligations.
2. Covenant that the company is lawfully possessed of the mortgaged and pledged property and has good right and lawful authority to mortgage and pledge the same.
3. Covenant that the company will warrant and defend the title to the property and the trustee's security interest therein against all claims and demands.

These provisions may be included as recitals in the indenture instead of, or in addition to, being included as specific covenants. It probably makes little difference where they appear, for the conditions recited go so obviously to the essence of the contract that a violation would provide a basis for immediately prematuring the debt and bringing the remedial provisions into play. Their inclusion as specific covenants provides a direct relationship with the default and remedial section and is to be preferred for that reason. Whether included as covenants or recitals, or both, they serve as an estoppel against the corporation and prevent its questioning the validity of its acts, even though there may have been some technical failure to secure due and proper authorization of the indenture, the indenture securities, or the mortgage. Such estoppel would not be effective against third parties who obtained rights for value and in good faith. Its inclusion in the indenture, therefore, does not mean that the trustee and its counsel should be less diligent in assuring themselves about the due and proper authorization of the indenture and the obligations issued thereunder.

Other types of affirmative covenants are applicable only to secured indentures and are usually to be found—in one form or another—in most mortgage indentures. Some of these may be included as parts of other covenants or undertakings, but are listed separately for clarity.

4. Covenant to maintain and preserve the lien of the indenture.
5. Covenant to give further assurances.
6. Covenant to subject to the lien of the indenture, by supplement, if necessary, all property acquired after the date of the indenture and intended to be covered thereby.

All these covenants are undertakings to give further assurances and provide a basis for a trustee's demand that additional documents be executed or things be done that will better ensure maintenance of the security the indenture purported to create, and extend the lien thereon to additionally acquired property should any question exist about the effectiveness of an after-acquired property clause in any jurisdiction. For example, the further assurances covenant has been used as a basis for a request, in a nonqualified indenture, for an annual certificate of after-acquired property and an annual opinion on the timely recording and filing of the indenture and the necessity for any periodic re-recording or refiling.

7. Covenant to record the indenture and all supplements, and to furnish opinions of counsel, after each such recording and an-

nually, as to the due recording thereof and the necessity for any re-recording or refiling to preserve the lien thereof.

Section 314(b)(1) of the TIA imposes such a requirement for all indentures qualified thereunder that include a mortgage or pledge of property. The matter of recording is of such obvious importance that this is a more-or-less standard provision in all mortgage indentures even if not qualified under the act. Because of the multiplicity of jurisdictions frequently involved and the diversity of recording statutes, reliance must be placed on counsel who are familiar with the laws of the various states where the property is located.

8. Covenants with respect to prior lien bonds.

Where prior lien bonds are outstanding, it is customary to include provisions with respect to such prior liens. These provisions are designed to prevent a default under the prior lien and its extension or refunding thereafter with other prior lien obligations. The indenture will therefore usually contain covenants to the effect that the obligor will comply with all provisions of prior lien indentures; that it will pay the obligations when due and will not consent to the extension of the maturity thereof (the indenture will usually contain provisions for the refunding thereunder of prior lien obligations); and that upon satisfaction of any prior lien indenture, it will cause such trustee to surrender to the trustee all specific property pledged with such prior lien trustee. Where prior lien obligations are retired in part or acquired by the obligor, the indenture often provides that they will be held alive and pledged with the trustee. The theory of such a provision is that, to the extent of the obligations so held, the trustee will acquire rights *pari passu* with the other holders of such prior lien obligations. The validity of this theory is doubtful, however, except to the extent of value actually paid by the trustee for such obligations.

There are many other affirmative covenants applicable equally to secured or unsecured indentures, although their context or purpose may differ, depending on the nature of the company and the indenture. Some of the more common covenants of this type are set forth below.

9. Covenant that the company will duly and punctually pay the principal of and interest and premium, if any, on all of the indenture securities outstanding according to the terms thereof.

Inasmuch as the obligations themselves contain an absolute promise to pay, inclusion of such a provision in the indenture might seem unnecessary and redundant. The obligation in the securities, however, runs directly to the holders thereof and not to the trustee. The indenture covenant runs to the trustee and enables it to enforce the obligation for the benefit of the security holders if there should be a default in the payment of any installment of principal or interest.

10. Covenant to maintain an office or agency where the bonds may be presented for payment and where notices and demands may be served on the company.

It is customary to provide that such an office or agency will be maintained in one or more specified cities and that, if the company should fail to keep or provide such office, presentation may be made and such notices and demands served at the principal office of the trustee. As a practical matter the office of the trustee is almost always designated as such an office or agency, and in any event demands and inquiries by security holders are customarily directed to the trustee.

11. Covenant to pay all taxes, assessments, and other charges or claims imposed upon the company's property, or upon the income or profits thereof, or upon the lien or interest of the trustee in respect of such property or such income.

It is usually also provided that the obligor may delay payment of any such claim so long as it is, in good faith, contesting the validity thereof by appropriate legal proceedings. The purpose of such a covenant is to prevent the creation of any lien or claim that might be given preference by operation of law to the indenture securities.

12. Covenant to maintain its corporate existence and maintain, preserve, and renew all rights, powers, privileges, and franchises owned by it.

The purpose of this undertaking is obvious. Because the loan is based on the credit of the corporation as a "going concern," all rights essential to its continuing as such must be preserved. This covenant is usually made subject to the merger clause and occasionally to the release and other provisions of the indenture.

13. Covenant to maintain, preserve, and keep its properties in good repair, working order, and condition.

14. Covenant to set aside from earnings each year proper reserves for renewals and replacements, obsolescence, depletion, exhaustion, and depreciation.

These are customary covenants in most indentures, whether secured or unsecured, and emphasize further the importance of the "going concern" concept of the business and to maintenance of the security for the debt. In some types of mortgage indentures—particularly those of regulated companies, such as public utilities and railroads—the covenants are combined and enlarged into an elaborate maintenance covenant as outlined and discussed in chapter 6.

15. Covenant to maintain insurance.

Some indentures require maintenance of specific types of insurance; for example, in some businesses, public liability insurance may be of great importance, and failure to provide it in proper amounts might result in a severe loss to the company and prejudice to the security holders' claims. Needs and requirements tend to change over the years, however, and as a general rule it is unwise to try to be too specific. The customary and more desirable form is to provide that insurance of such kinds and amounts will be maintained as is customary in the industry or as is customarily maintained by other companies operating similar business. As long as the covenant requires maintenance of adequate insurance, it is desirable to permit as much flexibility as possible. The obligor should be permitted to select the insurance companies, to participate in an insurance pool, or if desired, to provide its own system of self-insurance. Where properties are widely scattered with no great percentage of the total value concentrated at one point, this last may be a very desirable arrangement. Other innovations may also be appropriate in particular cases, such as inclusion of a deductible clause of a substantial amount to avoid a multiplicity of small claims and correspondingly heavier premium charges. In any system of self-insurance, the trustee should insist that the indenture contain requirements for appropriate certification to it of the adequacy of such a system and the reserves maintained.

In many of the old type of indentures, the insurance policies were required to be deposited with the trustee. The modern practice is to provide instead for a periodic certificate to be furnished, usually on an annual basis. This certificate should set forth proper details about the kinds and amounts of insurance and the names of the companies and contain a statement of the adequacy of the insurance coverage. Although such a detailed statement is not as essential in an unsecured indenture, it is frequently provided for, or the trustee is given the right to request it. If the certificate indicates that policies expire before the next certificate is to be furnished, an appropriate tickler should be set up and a follow-up made to see that the insurance is renewed.

When the indenture constitutes a lien on the company's properties the trustee should be named in the policies as an assured, so that any proceeds of insurance will be received by it. It is usually provided that any such proceeds up to a specified amount may be turned over immediately to the obligor, but amounts in excess thereof should be retained by the trustee until receipt of appropriate evidence that the property has been restored or replaced.

16. Covenant to honor obligations as lessee.

If an important part of the company's property consists of leaseholds or ground rent estates, it is advisable to include a covenant that the company will perform all covenants and obligations as lessee, will see that the lessor observes all its covenants and obligations in the leases, and will renew the terms of any leases that expire before the maturity date of the indenture obligations.

17. Covenant to continue to engage in a particular business or in the business in which the company is presently engaged.

This is an example of the type of covenant that should be examined carefully and used only if particular circumstances would seem to make it appropriate. If the indenture is to run for a long period of time, there is danger in such an undertaking, as any harness maker could verify. In a majority of indentures, it is obviously unnecessary. It might be appropriate to a situation where the loan is of relatively short duration and the principal security is a special inventory or special purpose machinery and equipment suitable only for a particular business.

18. Covenant to keep true books of record and account.
19. Covenant to file with the trustee balance sheets, income and surplus statements, and other pertinent financial statements.
20. Covenant to furnish copies of all reports forwarded to stockholders or filed with the SEC and such other information as may

be prescribed from time to time by regulations of the Commission.[2]

21. Covenant to permit a representative of the trustee at all reasonable times, upon request, to inspect the books and properties of the company.

22. Covenant to furnish such other data and information pertaining to the affairs of the company as the trustee may reasonably request.

These covenants all relate to the keeping of proper financial and accounting records and the filing with the trustee of periodic reports relative to the company's financial affairs. Section 314(a)(1) of the TIA requires that the obligor file with the trustee copies of the reports required to be filed with the SEC pursuant to Sections 13 or 15(d) of the 34 Act. These sections require the filing of periodic financial reports and supplementary reports to keep current various data filed with the original registration statement. In addition, copies of the annual audited statements certified by independent public accountants are required to be filed within a specified period after the close of the company's fiscal year.[3] Interim statements may also be required in particular cases, and it is usually sufficient to have these certified by one of the company's financial officers. In a situation where the condition of the business may be subject to rapid change and where the maintenance of certain ratios or a minimum amount of working capital is important, a more frequent check on the company's condition than is provided by the annual audited statements may be desirable.

The extent to which the trustee should make a detailed examination and analysis of the financial statements is not prescribed. Some corporate trust departments follow the practice of having all such statements reviewed by outside accountants. This seems extreme and, except in a most unusual situation, should not be necessary. Finance is a bank's business, and a trust company that purports to act as a corporate trustee should have personnel sufficiently qualified to make whatever analysis would seem to be indicated. The trustee is charged with the knowledge of any facts that would be revealed by a reasonable examination, and the minimum required would seem to be a sufficient check to see that no violation of any indenture provision is disclosed. The experienced administrator or account officer will also review the pertinent footnotes

[2] *See* TIA, sec. 314(a)(2). The annual report of the obligor should be accompanied by a certificate or opinion of independent public accountants, as to the obligor's compliance with those conditions or covenants in the indenture which are subject to verification by accountants.

[3] TIA, sec. 314(a)(2).

and commentary, the latter often called "Management's Discussion and Analysis" or similar heading. Any unfavorable trend or situation that might warrant a more careful follow-up should be noted. The nature of the business, the financial standing of the obligor, the purpose of the loan, specific responsibilities of the trustee, and other similar considerations will serve as a guide to the degree of care and attention that should be devoted to the examination beyond the limits indicated.

23. Covenant to furnish to the trustee annually a certificate signed by "the principal executive officer, principal financial officer or principal accounting officer as to his or her knowledge of such obligor's compliance with all conditions and covenants under the indenture."[4]

In pre-TIRA indentures which require a different certification or are required to be signed by different officers, it is recommended that both the requirements of the indenture and the section be complied with. In most cases, this can be satisfied by a certification reciting what the TIA requires and any other indenture requirement, to be signed by two "officers" (as defined in the indenture) one of whom is the principal executive, financial, or accounting officer.

Recognizing the importance of this certification, the TIRA converted what was a commonly used affirmative undertaking into a new legislatively mandated covenant. Not only does it give the trustee appropriate evidence on which it is entitled to rely, but more importantly by making such certification a Federal law requirement for all qualified indentures, criminal sanctions and civil suits are possible in the event of late, missed, or untrue certificates.

NEGATIVE COVENANTS

The distinction between negative and affirmative covenants is not so much in the form of phraseology used, for almost any covenant can be expressed in the positive, as well as the negative. The distinction lies rather in the fact that the so-called negative covenants, as a general rule, place restrictions on the activities of the obligor for the purpose of protecting the interests of the investor or lender. While certain of these

[4]See TIA, sec. 314(a)(4). This certification need not include the four compliance statements set forth in sec. 314(e).

covenants are common to both bond and debenture agreements, the negative type of covenant is most commonly associated with the debenture indenture, or unsecured financing. Their essential purpose is to insure, to the extent possible, that the investor for whose benefit they are made will remain in essentially the same relative position (in regard to other creditors) as exists at the time of the extension of credit.

Their use has been severely criticized from time to time, particularly in an early report of the SEC.[5] The argument was made that these covenants tended to lead the investor into a sense of false security and were of limited value because of the ease with which they could be violated and the lack of any effective legal remedy to prevent such violation. These conclusions stemmed from a number of early court decisions that seemed to indicate that security holders did lack an effective remedy. Two will suffice for illustration.

In 1932 Paramount-Publix Corporation had outstanding an issue of debentures under an indenture that provided that, so long as the debentures should be outstanding, the company would not create any lien on any assets directly owned by it. The company needed additional cash and was also faced with the maturity of large bank loans. Its banks agreed to renew the loans and provide the additional cash if all the loans were secured. The company had on hand a large supply of unfinished negatives. A subsidiary company was created, and these assets were transferred to it. Notes of the subsidiary in payment of these assets were pledged with the banks. In suits brought by individual security holders, the courts refused to enjoin the transfer to the subsidiary[6] or set it aside after it had been effected.[7] These decisions may have been influenced by the technical fact that the suits were brought by the security holders and not the trustee and that no demand on the trustee for action, as prescribed in the indenture, had been made.

The other case involved Insull Utilities Investments, Inc., which had outstanding two issues of debentures totaling sixty-six million dollars under indentures that provided that the company would not mortgage or pledge any of its property without securing the debentures pro rata, except for loans in the ordinary course of business with maturities not exceeding one year. In 1931 the company borrowed seventeen million dollars from banks, secured by the pledge of various stocks. The loans

5 See note 2, chapter 3, *supra.*

6 Relmar Holding Company v. Paramount-Publix Corporation, 147 Misc. 824, 263 N.Y.S. 776 (1932), *affirmed* 237 App. Div. 870, 261 N.Y.S. 959 (1933).

7 Ernst *et al.* v. Fisher Production Corporation, 148 Misc. 62, 264 N.Y.S. 227 (1933).

were for less than one year but were renewed. Debenture holders sued to have the pledge set aside or to be ratably secured thereby. The court dismissed the suit, holding that the negative pledge clause referred only to long-term funded debt and would not prevent bank loans, even though not in the ordinary course of business.[8] On appeal from this decision, however, the U.S. Circuit Court indicated that the holders might be able to succeed in their suit if they could establish: (1) that the loans were not in the ordinary course of business and (2) that the leading banks had knowledge of the negative pledge clause.[9] In line with this dictum, the courts in New York have indicated that if the trustee bank itself, in its individual capacity, advances money to an obligor in violation of such a clause, the holders might be able to set a pledge aside and that this would be so if the total term of the loan, including renewals, ran for more than a year, even though each note was for a shorter period.

The results in the two cases cited appear to have followed from a basic ineffectiveness of the clauses themselves. The problem in the Paramount-Publix case is now generally resolved by including the principal obligor and all its subsidiaries within the scope of the restrictive provisions and prohibiting transfer of substantial properties from the company or a restricted subsidiary to an unrestricted subsidiary (i.e., one to which the covenant does not apply) or other company. Quite frequently, also, covenants against the incurring of additional debt extend to current, as well as funded debt, or place very specific conditions and limitations on either or both.

The statement that no effective remedy exists to prevent the violation of these clauses is also subject to question. Theoretically, in an appropriate case, an action for specific performance or for injunctive relief should be possible, although it is likely that these remedies will offer little protection in the usual case because the trustee will probably not know of the violation until the transfer or pledge of assets or the obtaining of a prohibited loan or advance is an accomplished fact. To have such a transaction set aside would require proof not only of the violation but also of knowledge on the part of the pledger or transferee. There is one remedy, however, that can be most effective. This is the right to declare a default under the indenture and premature the indenture obligations. While this may not result in placing the security holders in as good a position as formerly, and therefore cannot be said to constitute full protection, it does stand as a potent weapon that should

[8] Kelly v. Central Hanover Bank & Trust Company 11 F. Supp. 497 (S.D.N.Y. 1935).
[9] 85 F. 2d 61 (2d Cir. 1936).

deter all but the most callous. Faced with such a threat, the company is more likely to endeavor to resolve a difficult situation through frank disclosure and negotiation rather than through intentional violation of a restrictive covenant.

In many cases an unsecured obligation under a carefully drawn indenture will provide as much protection and security to the investor as a mortgage bond will. The principal considerations in either case are the credit of the obligor as a going concern and the caliber of its management. In some cases the unsecured credit of the borrower is so good that few restrictions or covenants are necessary. Where the investors are obtaining a senior creditor position, all that is reasonably required are provisions in the agreement that under normal conditions will assure the retention of such a position. It is impossible to protect against every possible contingency, and an effort to do so by placing overly restrictive conditions on the continued operation of the business is as likely to prejudice as to improve the security holders' position.

It is quite possible, however, that the lack of strong restrictive covenants can imperil the value of bondholders' investments. This became strikingly evident during the 1980s when the growth of complex and diverse financial instruments, coupled with the explosion of novel and debt-laden corporate capital structures, had a major impact on the holders of bonds issued during the preceding twenty years. During this past decade there has been a widespread trend by major corporate issuers to reduce the number of restrictive covenants applicable to their new issues, particularly those which restricted the payment of dividends or the incurring of additional debt.[10]

The losses incurred by bondholders who had purchased high grade debt instruments and ended up with so-called junk bonds can be expected to reinforce a reversal of that trend. Institutional investors, in particular, are likely to demand much greater protection against recapitalization transactions, commonly called "event risk," which can have such a devastating adverse impact on the value of their investments. It is evident that "the tension between restrictive financial covenants and business flexibility for the issuer has led the marketplace away from covenants which measure the 'symptoms' of a worsening financial condition to covenants designed to identify the events which cause the condition and provide an immediate bailout opportunity for the holder upon the occurrence of those events."[11]

10 McDaniel, *Bondholders and Corporate Governance*, 41 *Bus. Law.* 413, 425–427 (1986).

11 Vlahakis, *Old Indentures—New Transactions*, 929 *Law Journal* (Seminars-Press) 19 (1989).

The original "poison put" provision was designed to ward off unfriendly takeovers and did not normally operate in the event of a friendly takeover (e.g., a management buyout). But the latter event can be just as disastrous to the bondholders as any hostile acquisition, with the result that institutional investors have increased their insistence on the inclusion of "super poison put" covenants, which eliminate the distinction between friendly and hostile transactions. Such covenants can include change of control tests and others directed at the obligor creditworthiness such as:

1. Net worth call. This provides for the acceleration of a sinking fund in the event that the obligor's net worth falls below a specified level.
2. Poison Puts. An immediate tender can be made back to the obligor if there is an increase in the debt to equity ratio over a specified amount, or if there is a downgrade in the obligor's credit rating.
3. Interest Rate Reset. This provides for a set increase in the interest rate if certain specified ratios are not maintained.
4. Automatic redemption. This covenant mandates an automatic redemption with a premium, either fixed or based on a spread over long-term U.S. Treasury bonds.[12]

Because it is impossible to foresee every contingency that is likely to arise over the extended period that the obligations are to be outstanding, it is desirable to provide for some degree of flexibility. This is a difficult problem. Where the notes or debentures are purchased directly by informed institutional investors, such a situation can be resolved by an agreement among such holders to amend the indenture or to modify or waive a particular provision either permanently or during a temporary period of stress. A different problem is presented where an issue is sold publicly. The first principle to be observed is to include only such restrictive covenants as under reasonably foreseeable conditions are not likely to cause undue hardship or seriously impede the normal conduct of the company's business. If the credit is not good enough under those conditions, it is best avoided. It is also desirable to include a provision permitting modification of the indenture by the holders of a specified percentage of the indenture securities. The customary percentage used is 66⅔ percent. Although it may be almost impossible to contact all holders of a publicly held issue, consent of a reasonable percentage can

---

[12]*See also* Vlahakis, *Deleveraging: A Search for Rules in a Financial Free-for-All*, M & A and Corporate Governance Law Reptr., vol. 2, no. 2 at 290 (October 1990); Clemens, *Poison Debt: The New Takeover Defense*, 42 *Bus. Law.* 747 (May 1987).

normally be obtained if the modification proposed is reasonable and desirable and if adequate foresight and preparation are exercised.[13]

The trustee is frequently asked to consent to a temporary waiver or modification of a particular provision or at least to consent to take no action for some period of time after a breach. Under the circumstances in which it is presented, the proposed action by the obligor usually appears reasonable and, frequently, highly desirable from the viewpoint of the security holders. Whereas a good argument can be made for granting such discretionary powers to a trustee, under the usual indenture it has no such power and no authority or right to give any such consent or waiver.

Once a breach has occurred and matured into a default under the indenture, the trustee's conduct is subject to the prudent man standard of judgment. It is unfortunate that relatively few judicial precedents exist for the trustee's guidance in such situations, since, in their absence, the trustee may quite logically be inclined to take immediate action under the remedial provisions to avoid subjecting itself to substantial potential liability. In a great number of cases the exercise of patience and a reasonable degree of judgment and discretion would enable the situation to be worked out without subjecting the company and the security holders to the substantial expense and virtually inevitable losses incurred in a reorganization proceeding. To avoid this some indentures provide that a default will not occur for breach of an indenture covenant of this type unless and until the trustee has received notice thereof from a specified percentage of the security holders. This type of provision is generally undesirable because it tends to restrict too greatly the trustee's right to take action. A more desirable provision, and one that is common in most indentures, permits a majority in principal amount of the security holders to waive a default or to direct the trustee's course of conduct in the event of a default.[14]

As in the case of affirmative covenants, the types of negative clauses are many and varied. It is desirable, therefore, to include restrictive provisions to fit the circumstances of each particular case rather than to endeavor to apply a set pattern or formula to each and every situation. The provisions discussed below are some of the more common covenants used and are set forth to illustrate the types of clauses under discussion and the purposes they are designed to accomplish. It is important to bear in mind that where the company conducts part of its

13 *See* TIA sec. 316(a)(1)(B) and 316(c).
14 *Id.*

operations through subsidiaries, or may subsequently do so, the covenants should be so phrased as to apply to subsidiaries, as well as to the obligor itself.

1. Covenants relating to the maintenance of working capital.

Covenants of this type relate to maintenance of working capital (sometimes called "Net Current Assets" and representing excess of current assets over current liabilities) at a certain minimum level. The covenant takes different forms. Sometimes the company is required to maintain working capital of a certain stated amount; sometimes the current ratio (current assets divided by current liabilities) cannot fall below a prescribed minimum; frequently the covenant requires maintenance of working capital as a stated percentage of funded debt; occasionally there will be a combination of several requirements of this type. It is common practice to combine this requirement with other negative covenants. For example, the company may be permitted to borrow additional funds so long as the net working capital is maintained at the required percentage of total funded debt.

This type of covenant is of particular importance and is almost always included where the principal purpose of the credit being arranged is for working capital, for such purposes as expansion of inventory. Regardless of the proposed use of funds, if the nature of the business requires a large amount of working capital, this is one indicator that should be monitored closely in examining the company's statements, and it is desirable to provide some basis for action if there are signs that the company's position may be deteriorating.

2. Covenant against creation of additional debt.

This is a covenant that is commonly found in most debenture agreements. Because the obligations to be issued are unsecured, it is obvious that continued unrestricted borrowing might seriously prejudice the security holders' position or impair the equity on the basis of which they undertook to extend credit.

The basic prohibition is against creation of additional funded debt (usually defined as that having a maturity in excess of one year at the time incurred), but it is sometimes extended to include current debt or current borrowings above a stated amount.

There are normally a number of permitted exceptions to this restriction that can be expressed in several ways. Always exempt from its operation are liabilities (other than for borrowed money) incurred in the ordinary course of business, accrual of taxes, claims for labor, and other similar accruals that are an essential part of the orderly operation of the business.

As indicated above, the restriction is frequently made inoperative so long as certain ratios are maintained. The ratios most frequently used are working capital to total debt and net tangible assets to debt. The latter restriction is frequently expressed in another way: aggregate debt is limited to a certain percentage of the total capitalization of the company. These requirements are usually combined with an earnings requirement. An example of this would be a provision that the average profit before interest and taxes during the past five years, and for each of the two preceding years, available to pay interest, must have been at least nine times the total interest requirements on all debt, including that proposed to be issued.

Finally, the limitation of debt may be merely a total dollar limitation, expressed either with or without the exclusion of liabilities incurred in the ordinary course of business.

3. Covenant against sale and leaseback.

Under this type of financing, a company that owns substantial real estate, such as office buildings, warehouses, or retail stores, arranges for the sale of such property to one or more investors and takes back a noncancelable lease for a specified term at a rental aggregating the purchase price plus an amount equivalent to the going rate of interest on the unamortized purchase price. This not only provides a convenient method of raising funds but also enables the company to keep its capital invested in its primary business rather than in the ownership and operation of real estate.

The covenant is designed to prohibit or limit such arrangements during the terms of the loan. The limitation may be expressed in any number of ways, such as a dollar limitation on the gross value of property so transferred, a limitation on the aggregate annual rentals equal to a percentage of net earnings for a prescribed period, or, as in the case of the preceding covenant, a limitation in terms of maintenance of certain ratios of working capital or net tangible assets to debt, where the aggregate of all leaseback sales is added to debt.

The purpose of the covenant is twofold. The first consideration is substantially the same as the restriction against debt. Rentals under the leases become fixed obligations, and a limitation on the incurring of such obligations is usually important. A second consideration is related to the "negative pledge" clause and involves a prohibition against sale of productive facilities to which recourse might be had in event of a default. Thus, in some cases, sale of an office building or similar holding may be permitted while sale of factories, warehouses, or other essential productive property is restricted.

4. Covenant against execution of lease of real property or equipment.
5. Covenant against rental or lease of personal property sold by the company or acquired by an investor for rental or lease to the company.

These covenants are similar and serve the same purpose as the restriction on sale and leaseback arrangements. Here again the prohibition may be absolute or may be expressed in terms of certain limitations or exceptions. Such limitations may be expressed in terms of a maximum dollar amount of annual rentals or aggregate rentals as a percentage of net earnings, or such leases may be permitted if the terms thereof (including renewals) do not exceed a stated period, usually not more than five years.

6. Covenant against creation of prior liens (negative pledge clause).

This restriction is designed to prohibit the creation of claims or obligations paramount to those of the indenture securities so as to insure maintenance of the same priority position of the holders thereof as exists at the time of extension of credit. This essential purpose may be accomplished in either of two ways; the covenant is frequently expressed either in terms of absolutely restricting creation of liens on company property or of permitting their creation only on condition that the indenture obligations are equally secured at the same time.[15]

In order to permit the orderly conduct of the company's business, certain logical exceptions to the restriction are usually permitted. These include the following: (1) liens for taxes not yet due; (2) liens existing on property at the time of its acquisition by the company or purchase money mortgages created in connection with the acquisition of additional property (These liens may be limited to a certain percentage of the value of such property, and it is usually expressly provided that they

[15]For an excellent review of this topic, *see* McDaniel, *Are Negative Pledge Clauses in Public Debt Issues Obsolete?*, 38 *Bus. Law.* 867 (May 1983).

cannot extend to any other property of the company. It is customary to include a maximum dollar limitation on the aggregate of all such liens); (3) renewals or extension of liens referred to in (2), provided they are not increased and do not extend to other property; (4) liens incurred in the ordinary course of business not involving the borrowing of money; and (5) deposits of money or property to secure performance of a contract or obligation, such as deposits required by worker's compensation laws, under government contracts, in connection with self-insurance arrangements, and the like.

This covenant is frequently referred to as a "negative pledge" clause, which is actually a misnomer. The clause does not create a pledge of any assets nor does it give an equitable lien on any property that may be thereafter pledged or transferred in violation of the covenant.

7. Covenant against loans, advances, and guarantees.
8. Covenant against pledge or discount of receivables or their sale at less than par.
9. Covenant against mortgage of patents, copyrights, or similar property.
10. Covenant against ownership of securities, except stock or indebtedness of subsidiaries or obligations of the United States.

These covenants fall into the same general category as the preceding one and are intended to prevent the encumberance, dissipation, or use of company assets except in the orderly conduct of its business. The covenant against loans, advances, and guarantees usually includes an exemption of intrasystem transactions if a portion of the company's business is conducted through subsidiaries, and the restrictive covenants in the indenture apply to both company and subsidiaries. Transactions in the ordinary course of business may also be excepted if guarantees are normally granted as a part of the conduct of the business.

11. Covenant restricting payment of dividends or purchase or retirement of stock.

Equity capital, or the stockholders' investment in a business, is made up not only of the stated capital and surplus, which they have paid into the business as consideration for the issuance of their shares, but also of the amount of the earned surplus, which represents the aggregate of the earnings that have been retained by the company for use in the business. Generally speaking, earned surplus is not subject to any restrictions and could be paid out or distributed to stockholders at any time as dividends. Such distribution could be in cash or in property.

One of the principal concerns of an investor in extending credit is the amount of the stockholders' equity, particularly in relation to the amount of the debt that will be outstanding. Because debt represents a priority claim against the assets of the company, any excessive distribution to stockholders may be regarded as a preferential distribution to a subordinate claimant.

It is therefore quite common in all indentures, whether secured or unsecured, to include a provision that will prevent any unwarranted distribution. This is usually done by placing a substantial portion of the unrestricted earned surplus in a restricted category for the duration of the loan. A portion of such surplus is usually left in an unrestricted category available for dividends, the amount being a matter for negotiation, but quite frequently it represents a sum approximately equal to one year's dividends on the stock. In working out the other terms of the credit, the amount so unrestricted is usually disregarded by the investor and, to the extent it is thereafter retained, provides an additional cushion to bolster the credit extended.

The covenant usually provides that no dividends will be distributed to stockholders or any funds of the corporation applied to the purchase, redemption, or other retirement of shares of stock in excess of the sum of (1) the amount of the earned surplus left in an unrestricted category, (2) net earnings of the company after a stated date (usually the end of the next preceding fiscal year), and (3) the amount received by the company as proceeds of sale of additional shares of stock.

Payment of dividends or other distributions to stockholders is always made contingent on there being no default under the arrangement and, quite frequently, on the existence of certain minimum ratios at the time of declaration.

12. Covenants relating to subsidiaries, the most common being: *a.* against the sale of stock or debt of a subsidiary; *b.* against the issue of stock of a subsidiary except to the parent company or to another subsidiary; *c.* against permitting a subsidiary to issue preferred stock except to the company or to another subsidiary.

As indicated above, where subsidiary companies are important to a system operation, all general restrictive covenants, such as those against additional debt or against creation of liens, are made applicable alike to parent company and subsidiaries. Because the companies are viewed as an entity for the purpose of the credit, intrasystem transactions are customarily excluded from operation of these restrictions. It is therefore necessary to add other restrictions to prevent the weakening of the entity by reducing the system percentage ownership of any subsidiary company.

The first of the covenants prohibits disposal of the investment in a subsidiary. In order to permit flexibility, the restrictive provision usually states that no stock or indebtedness of a subsidiary may be sold except as an entirety and then only if: (1) the operations conducted by such subsidiary do not represent a significant part of system operations; (2) in the judgment of the obligor's board of directors, retention of the investment therein is no longer necessary for system operations; (3) the sale is for a cash consideration representing the full value of the system investment in such subsidiary; and (4) such subsidiary owns no stock or indebtedness of another subsidiary.

In the case of subsidiary companies that are less than 100 percent owned by the system, covenant *b.* above is usually qualified to prohibit any issuance of stock that would result in a decrease in the *pro rata* interest of the system.

The reason for prohibition of a public issue of preferred stock of a subsidiary follows the same theory as the prohibition against prior liens. As far as the obligor itself is concerned, the indenture securities have priority over any preferred stock issue. Stock of a subsidiary company is, however, an asset of the obligor, and permitting the issuance of another class of stock having priority would be equivalent to subjecting the property represented by such asset to a prior claim.

13. Covenant against merger of the obligor or sale or lease of all or substantially all of its assets.

The indenture usually contains a separate section dealing with mergers, consolidations, and so on. It is included here because it is, in effect, a restrictive covenant. There is usually no absolute prohibition against mergers or consolidations or sale of company assets, but such activities are permitted only under certain conditions, which should be carefully and explicitly stated. The following conditions are usually included:

a. Either the obligor must be the surviving corporation, or the obligations under the indenture must be expressly assumed in writing (usually by supplemental indenture) by the survivor.

    b. There must be no default under the indenture, and no default can exist after completion of the merger.

    c. If any other debt will become a lien on any properties of the obligor upon completion of the merger, the indenture securities must be secured by a mortgage or other lien on the obligor's properties prior to the merger.

    d. If the surviving corporation will have secured debt outstanding in excess of a given amount (whether or not the obligor's property will become subject to such lien), the indenture securities must be first secured by a lien on the obligor's properties.

    e. If the indenture requires the maintenance of a certain specified ratios (such as minimum working capital, working capital to debt, or net tangible assets to debt), it is usually provided that these ratios must exist in the prescribed minimum amount immediately following the merger.

In reviewing a draft of a proposed indenture contract, all the provisions should be read together as in the aggregate constituting a single entity. This is particularly true of all the covenants of the indenture. In addition, the administrator should ensure that none of them are inconsistent with any of the obligations/covenants mandated by the TIA. In order to administer a contract properly, the trustee must understand it. This means not only making sense out of the language of each provision considered separately but also understanding the meaning and purpose of the whole indenture as a single contract. The investor is willing to extend credit on certain terms and conditions that the borrower is willing to meet. The indenture contract should spell out those terms and conditions completely and unambiguously, and all the provisions thereof should fit together as a pattern. Once the concept of the entire contract is understood thoroughly, each separate covenant will take on its proper meaning, and the job of administration will be rendered much easier.

NINE

Payment and Redemption of Bonds

Although the "perpetual debenture" without a fixed maturity has been used with success in the United Kingdom and certain of the Commonwealth countries, this practice never developed in the United States. Such obligations are frequently regarded more as stock than debt, and certainly they have many of the aspects of permanent equity capital. Almost without exception, corporate debt obligations issued in this country under indentures have a fixed maturity. This is, of course, an essential condition to the negotiability of the securities.

The fixed obligation in the bonds and the corresponding indenture covenants to pay the principal and interest as they become due are the most important undertakings of the obligor. On or before the fixed maturity of the debt, funds must be provided to make payment thereof, although this is not always easy. As previously discussed, one device is the use of the sinking fund whereby a portion of the debt is retired each year over its life, thereby eliminating, or substantially reducing, the problem presented at final maturity. Another common device used in issues of states and municipalities is to provide for serial maturities, with a portion of the debt actually falling due by its terms each year. This practice has been seldom used in issues of business corporations, because of marketing problems.

It is unusual for a corporation to be able to pay off a large fixed principal maturity out of available cash. Even where a sinking fund covenant has been included, there is often a substantial portion of the obligations to be taken care of at final maturity. The corporate financial officer must therefore plan the cash flow sufficiently in advance of the maturity date to ensure that funds will be on hand to pay the obligations at that time. Some form of refunding that involves the issuance of other securities to provide the cash to pay off the maturing issue is usually necessary. As pointed out in chapter 5, among the purposes for which additional bonds are customarily authorized to be issued under open-end indentures is the refunding of prior lien bonds or other series of bonds outstanding under the indenture.

Where the obligor enjoys a good credit rating and where adequate thought has gone into the drafting of the contracts involved in the company's financial undertaking, no serious difficulty is presented by an approaching debt maturity date. An important question of timing and cost may, however, be involved. If a company is faced with the necessity of meeting a maturity during a period of relatively high interest rates, its annual fixed charges may be substantially increased. From the company's point of view, therefore, it is desirable that a considerable degree of flexibility be reserved in the indenture to facilitate its dealing with its debt obligations.

To provide such flexibility, the redemption provisions of the indenture are important. These provisions usually appear in a separate article of the indenture and constitute the reservation by the obligor of the privilege of prepaying its securities, or designated portions thereof, at its option, before their stated maturity. For the exercise of this privilege the obligor pays a price, in the form of a redemption premium, in addition to the principal and accrued interest to the date of prepayment. The right of redemption before maturity is a significant right and the terms on which it may be exercised, including the amount of premium that must be paid, are important elements in the original negotiations. It is fairly common, however, to set the initial redemption premium at an amount equivalent to one year's interest on the securities. This premium is then scaled down, in substantially equal amounts throughout the life of the issue, no premium being payable during the last year.

Because this is a substantive provision that affects the rights of the holders of securities, the redemption privilege must be set forth in the text of the securities themselves, as well as in the indenture. The language should be in sufficient detail to put the holder on notice about the essential terms and conditions on which the obligation may be called for prepayment.

During periods of relatively high interest rates, investors prefer to protect themselves against the possibility that the obligations they purchase will be refunded as soon as a change in market conditions makes it advantageous for the issuer to do so. When there is a rapid change in market conditions and a substantial decline in interest rates, obligors may seek to call their bonds, even if they have been outstanding less than a year. As a result investors may suffer substantial losses because of their having sold other securities (or passed up other investment opportunities) to purchase these obligations whose subsequent redemption necessitated reinvestment at much lower yields.

The protection against such a possibility takes the form of a noncallable or nonrefundable provision in the bond and indenture. A noncallable provision means merely that the obligor may not redeem its securities (except for sinking fund purposes) for a stated period of time. A nonrefundable provision permits redemption but specifies that this cannot be done with other funds borrowed at a rate of interest less than that borne by the indenture securities. These restrictions are usually limited to a specified period of time following the date of issue—commonly five or ten years.

A noncallable provision is easily administered. A nonrefundable provision may present difficulties, however. The trustee should insist that there be included in the indenture a provision for its receipt of a certificate from appropriate officials of the company to the effect that a proposed redemption does not violate the restriction, and it should be authorized to rely conclusively on such a certificate.

Some indentures provide that the obligor at its discretion may purchase bonds on the open market and submit them to the trustee in satisfaction of a mandatory sinking fund redemption and in lieu of calling bonds. Corporate obligors are particularly likely to do this during periods when current market prices for the securities are lower than the call price. Indentures permitting this alternative should clearly specify that the obligor must provide a certificate to the trustee, well in advance of the date specified for the trustee to select bonds to be called, stating exactly how a particular sinking fund will be satisfied.

Whether or not an indenture provides for a sinking fund, it may permit the obligor to purchase bonds on the open market and submit them to the trustee for cancellation. Many corporate obligors take advantage of this in periods of favorable market conditions in order to reduce the debt outstanding and related carrying costs. In this situation the trustee should receive an appropriate certification well in advance of the time when it would normally begin to select bonds for redemption.

Another alternative to a sinking fund call in some indentures, particularly municipal revenue issues, is the right of the obligor to instruct the trustee to use accumulated amounts in the sinking fund to conduct a tender offer for bonds, selecting sufficient bonds from among all bonds tendered to satisfy the sinking fund requirement. The indenture should clearly spell out the mechanics of such a procedure including the timing of and criteria for holder notification and bond certificate selection.

A different form of redemption giving the bondholder the right to sell the security back to the issuer, at par, has also been used. In issues with this provision, the holder gets a "put" or "demand" option, the distinction being that in the former case the security may be sold back *only* at a fixed date or dates, whereas in the latter case the right may be exercised at any time, usually on one to seven days' notice. In either situation the underlying agreement must carefully spell out the holder's option rights.

Put and demand options evolved during the late 1970s and 1980s in response to investors' desire for greater liquidity in periods of economic uncertainty and interest rate volatility. Obligors have utilized one-to-seven day put bond issues as alternatives to issuance of commercial paper. Although puts were initially associated primarily with municipal bonds, they have been utilized in many forms by corporate issuers. One such variety, developed as part of a corporate antitakeover strategy is the "poison put", in which holders may put their bonds back to the issuer, as for example in event of a significant change in ownership of management of the obligor (i.e., a hostile takeover).

Some bonds, although issued without put or demand features, have put options attached to them by investment bankers to improve the marketability in times of sharply rising interest rates. Certificates representing these "added on" options are totally separate from the bond itself, and the terms will be specified in a separate option agreement. Usually the bondholder pays a price, whether deducted from interest payments or otherwise paid, for the right to the put option in these situations.

Risk and Liability Concerns

Because of the great surge in number and amount of bond calls in the late 1980s and 1990s, trustees and paying agents have been subjected to ever increasing pressure from the investment community and the public to compensate holders for losses resulting from failure to present and redeem called bonds in a timely manner. In seeking such compensation, holders frequently claim that the trustee/paying agent was "unjustly enriched" as a result of the holder failing to submit a called bond until sometime after the redemption date. In such situations the holder may allege that he/she did not receive proper notification of the bond call. In an effort to establish industry guidance for the payment of such claims, the American Bankers Association (ABA), through its Fiduciary and Securities Operations Division, developed a set of Compensation Guidelines covering processing timeframes and conditions for payment of called debt securities, and seting parameters for payment of compensation in the event of error or noncompliance by the trustees and paying agents.[1]

These guidelines, which are expected to be approved and disseminated late in 1991, are intended to apply to all corporate and municipal debt securities, and to the presentation of called securities either through physical or book-entry delivery.

Uniform standards for redemption notices and compensation claims are particularly important in limiting risk to trustees/paying agents in processing calls of zero coupon bonds. Because these obligations do not pay periodic interest, a holder who misses a bond call may not become aware that his/her bond was called until presenting it for payment years later upon final maturity. At that time, upon finding that the bond can be redeemed for only the accreted value as of the call date many years earlier, a holder may attempt to lodge a claim or file a lawsuit against the trustee/paying agent.

Of related concern to the trustee/paying agent is liability which may result from the method of giving notice to bondholders. Although an indenture for a fully registered issue may require that notice be given by publication only, it is wise for the trustee also to mail notice to the registered holders to avoid claims and possible litigation.

For both partial and full redemptions an appropriate affidavit should be prepared by the trustee and filed as part of its records. This would be attached to the affidavit of mailing of the redemption notice to the registered holders by the trustee. In case of bearer bond issues, the list of the serial numbers arranged numerically by denomination should be included as part of the redemption notice as published and mailed. Appropriate affidavits of both publication and mailing should also be obtained by the trustee.

Another area of concern in risk management is redemption in struc-

---

[1] For recommended redemption notification guidelines, *see* note 2, *infra*.

tured financing transactions. The trustee/paying agent must be careful to execute redemptions in accordance with operative documents, because failure to do so may adversely affect cash flow coverage of future debt service, and could destroy the integrity of nonrecourse financing. In financings requiring a "strip call" or involving zero coupon bonds, failure to call the correct bonds on just one occasion may have an escalating negative effect over future years. Credit enhancement providers and rating agencies monitor trustee/paying agent performance in these areas, and the trustee/paying agent may be held liable for damage to cash flows arising out of errors in redemption processing. Examples of structured financings where these concerns are critical include those involving multifamily housing, single family housing, and collateralized mortgage obligations.

MECHANICAL PROVISIONS

Terms and Conditions

The terms and conditions on which the securities may be called for prepayment should be carefully spelled out in the indenture. Although it is the obligor that theoretically exercises the right, as a practical matter the trustee will usually be called upon to carry out all details. (*See Exhibit 9* for a *Full Redemption Procedure Guide* and *Exhibit 10* for a *Partial Redemption Procedure Guide.*) Therefore, these provisions should receive its careful attention as it reviews the prospective contract. Under an open-end indenture, providing for different series of bonds, the redemption terms (other than the amount of premium payable) are usually set forth in the original indenture and are made applicable to all series of bonds including those to be issued in the future. As an alternative, the terms of the original indenture may be made applicable only to the initial series of bonds, the terms and conditions for subsequent series being included in the supplemental indenture creating each such series. Although not frequently used, the latter practice is recommended as providing the greater degree of flexibility.

The first condition to which attention should be directed is the nature and extent of the right. Subject to any provisions for nonrefundability, this right should be as broadly based as possible. The right should be reserved to redeem all, or any part, of the indenture securities at any time or from time to time. Occasionally a partial redemption is restricted to a minimum principal amount, and such a restriction is proper both from the point of view of the obligor and the investor. Some indentures restrict the redemption to an interest payment date, although such a provision should be avoided unless the particular circumstances make it necessary.

The redemption premiums should be set forth explicitly. They are customarily expressed as a percentage of the principal amount. If a formula for a declining percentage is to be used, it should be worked out in advance and the actual prices (by dates) set forth in the indenture and in the bonds. This formula avoids any possibility of error or misunderstanding at a later date. When there is a sinking fund, the redemption premium for sinking funds redemption will normally be less than that for an optional retirement, or frequently, bonds may be callable for sinking fund purposes at par, without premium. If there are other circumstances under which the sinking fund redemption price rather than the optional price will be applicable, these should be carefully and specifically enumerated.

From the viewpoint of practical handling of redemptions, two provisions are desirable for the trustee: where registered securities are involved, no endorsement or assignment should be required if payment is to be made to the registered holder. When redemption is on an interest payment date, the interest check should be mailed to the registered holders as of the record date in the normal manner; in the case of bearer securities, the holders should be instructed to detach and present separately the interest coupon maturing on that date; otherwise a great deal of confusion may arise in subsequent accountings.

Notices

Notice of redemption must be given to the holders of the securities. The indenture must specify not only the method of giving notice but also the period of time before the redemption date when such notice must be given. A minimum of thirty days notice is ordinarily required, and it is also common for a maximum period to be specified. The usual provision is to require the first notice to be given not less than thirty, nor more than sixty, days before the date designated for the redemption.

The indenture should specify the information to be included in the notice. Such information would include a full description of the issue: including date of issue; maturity dates; interest rates; the date of redemption; the price payable; the CUSIP number; certificate numbers and called amounts for each certificate (for partial calls); the place or places of payment to which the called securities should be presented; the total principal amount called, if less than the entire issue is called, and whether a new bond will be issued for the unredeemed portion; and any other information that may be pertinent to the particular situation or required by law or regulation.

It is important that the notice state that on the designated redemption date, the called securities (or portions thereof) shall become due and payable, and that on and after such date all interest thereon will cease to accrue and the holders shall cease to be entitled to the benefits of the indenture, their rights being limited to receipt of the redemption price in the hands of the trustee, or paying agent, upon presentation of their securities for cancellation.

To assist in overcoming problems in the redemption notification process of municipal securities, the SEC in 1986 published a set of six guidelines based on a consensus of opinions expressed by major securities industry associations, the self-regulatory organizations, and federal regulatory agencies. The standards which the SEC endorsed were:

1. that notices of municipal bond redemptions should contain the information indicated above;
2. that all such notices should be sent in a secure fashion (e.g., certified mail or overnight express) to all registered securities depositories and to the national information services that disseminate such information;
3. that such notices provide for a thirty-day period between notice date and redemption date;
4. that such notices should be sent to the registered depositories in advance of the publication date (a guideline generally not acceptable to corporate trustees);
5. that second notices of advance refunding of municipal securities should be given thirty days prior to the redemption date; and
6. that the CUSIP number should be indicated on all redemption payments (checks and wires).[2]

These guidelines were further refined and disseminated as "Recommended Guidelines for Processing Bond Calls" by the ABA's Corporate Trust Committee in the summer of 1989. To further encourage industry-wide acceptance of these guidelines (with even greater specificity), the

[2] SEC Release 34–23856 (December 3, 1986), 51 Fed. Register 235 at 44398 (December 9, 1986).

American National Standards Institute, working through its X9D Committee, has developed a revised set of standards which is expected to be adopted and published by 1992. These will include: notice of redemption, publication of notice of redemption, follow-up notices, and suggested trust indenture language.

In the case of a partial call of a fully registered bond issue, use of the traditional form of notice listing all the bond numbers and applicable principal amounts called for redemption can be avoided by using a letter form of notice incorporating the required details of redemption. This notice should be accompanied by a special form addressed to each holder affected by the call setting forth the principal amount of holdings selected for redemption and the bond(s) against which the selection was allocated, to be presented for payment. Copies of this form can also be used for follow-up and posting operations. Such notice should be given by mail to the registered holders at their addresses as indicated in the bond register. The notice needs only to be sent to the holders of bonds selected for redemption. Notice by registered or certified mail should never be required. No requirement should be set forth in the indenture for any publication of the notice, for this is expensive and unnecessary where all bonds are registered. However, when an issue is actively traded, it is very desirable to have a list of the numbers of the called bonds made available to any securities exchange on which the bonds are listed, in addition to the securities depositories and information services specified in the guidelines described above.

When securities are outstanding in bearer form, notice is given by publication in an authorized newspaper. What constitutes an "authorized newspaper" should be carefully defined in the indenture. Because a number of papers are not published on Saturdays, Sundays, or legal holidays, this fact should be borne in mind if it is planned to use any such periodical. It is desirable to provide for a number of publications so that the information will be disseminated as widely as possible. Only the first of these notices needs to be within the prescribed time limits, and considerable flexibility about subsequent publication is desirable. Nor should publication be restricted to the same day of the week. Published notices should comply with the appropriate standards specified in the SEC guidelines. Copies should also be sent to any securities exchanges on which the securities are listed.

In addition to publication of the required notice, which should also indicate the specific serial numbers of the bearer bonds to be redeemed and the coupons that must be attached to them, a copy should be sent to each registered holder of called bonds. Although it is usually provided that if proper publication is made, mailing is not a required condition, the trustee should be most careful to see that such mailing is effected, and at the same time as the initial publication. Although not required, it is also recommended that a copy of the notice be mailed to each holder whose name has been filed with the trustee for the purpose of receiving reports (see chapter 12, *infra*).

If the redemption is for the sinking fund, or is achieved by use of special funds constituting a part of the trust estate, the particular notice should be mailed (or published) under the name of trustee (or sinking fund agent, if other than the trustee) unless the indenture specifies otherwise. If redemption is pursuant to an option right reserved to the obligor, it should be mailed (or published) under the name of the company, even though it was actually prepared and disseminated by the trustee.

Payment Provisions

Provision should be made for deposit with the trustee of the funds required to effect the redemption. It is not necessary that this be done before the selection and mailing (or publication) of notice, although it should be made on or before the date of payment and in the full amount. Such a deposit should be made in trust, and the funds held in a special account specifically allocated to payment of the securities to be redeemed.

If such deposit is made with a paying agent other than the trustee, it should be placed in a special trust account in the name of the trustee and should be under its control and not that of the company. An appropriate undertaking letter to this effect should also be obtained from the paying agent unless such an undertaking is included in a general letter at the time of execution of the indenture. If not so deposited, or if the company acts as its own paying agent and retains the redemption funds under its control, the called bonds should not be discharged from the trustee's records until they are actually received and canceled by it.

Where, by reason of a refunding or for other reasons, funds necessary to effect the redemption are deposited before the date of the mailing (or first publication) of notice, a prior payment offer is sometimes made. This is an offer to pay the full redemption price upon presentation of bonds at any time after mailing (or publication) of notice even if presentation is before the redemption date. The making of such an offer is an acceptable, although seldom used, practice, but it should be made at the discretion of the company, and must be made if the indenture so requires. The trustee should not undertake, by agreement with anyone other than the company, to effect such a prior payment, even though the funds may be in its possession.

When payment is made for redeemed bonds, the trustee/paying agent must ensure that proper procedures have been established in the operational area so that IRS Form 1099B will be issued for each payment made. Such forms should be issued as of the redemption date and for the year in which the redemption date occurs, regardless of when redeemed bonds are actually presented for payment. This, of course, applies to all securities redeemed, whether interest on such securities is taxable or tax-exempt. If the trustee/paying agent has not previously received a certified taxpayer identification number for a payee on IRS Form W-8 or W-9, it must obtain such a certification prior to disbursing redemption proceeds. As set forth in the Interest and Dividend Tax Compliance Act of 1983, the trustee may be required to withhold 20 percent of the total redemption proceeds for a payment in the event such payee fails to provide certain certifications, or if the trustee/paying agent is ordered to withhold by the IRS.

PARTIAL REDEMPTIONS

Where fewer than all of the bonds of an issue are to be redeemed, provision must be made for selection of the particular bonds. This should be done by the trustee, and the method followed is the same as in the case of selection of bonds for redemption by a sinking fund. As noted in chapter 6, it is very desirable that the indenture give to the trustee the utmost flexibility in determining the particular method to be used. Rather than set forth in detail the particular procedures to be employed, indenture drafters should leave this entirely to the trustee's discretion. The only requirement should be that the method adopted be fair and equitable to all holders. In this way the trustee is enabled to keep up with current practices rather than be bound by possibly antiquated procedures.

The traditional method of selection has been by bond number, with a basic unit of $1,000, bonds of larger denominations being assigned as many unit numbers as there are multiples of $1,000. Where all or a substantial portion of an issue is outstanding in registered form, this can become a cumbersome and expensive procedure, particularly if there has been substantial transfer activity. Other methods of selection are equally fair and may prove much more easily administered, depending on the circumstances of the particular case. In the case of an all registered issue it is frequently easier to make the selection by holder (either *pro rata* or by lot in terms of the number of "units" of the holding) and then allocate the portions selected against a particular bond or bonds. The significance of this method is that the selection is of a portion (or all) of a holding as of a particular date, and not of any one-specific bond by serial number. Accordingly, the validity of the call is not affected if the particular "allocation" is made against an incorrect serial number. This may be of particular importance where the entire issue, or a substantial portion, is held in book-entry form.

Frequently the holdings of a single registered holder are represented by more than one bond. Where it is clear that a single beneficial holding is involved, it is desirable that the portion of the holding affected by a call be allocated against a single bond. This practice is now fairly common. In the case of bank nominees, brokers, or depository nominees, where there is a reasonable presumption that different pieces represent different beneficial holdings, the preferred practice is to treat each separate bond as a separate holding. Here again a more nearly uniform practice would seem desirable. It is suggested that for the purpose of any selection: (1) each separate bond in the name of a nominee or broker be considered a separate holding; (2) the total holdings of all other registered holders be considered a single beneficial holding; and (3) any holder have the right to direct the trustee that the holdings be considered an entity or that separate bonds be regarded as separate beneficial holdings, such direction to be effective for all selections until rescinded.

Some structured financings with serial bonds require a partial call so that the aggregate annual debt service requirement will be reduced proportionately for each serial maturity. For this type of call, known as a "strip call," bonds must be selected across all maturities, including maturities comprised of zero coupon bonds, so that proportionate reduction is achieved. The proper execution of these calls in accordance with indenture provisions can be critical to the adequacy of future cash flows.

The necessity for closing the bond register during the selection period is obvious, and there is no way in which changes in the holders or numbers of outstanding registered bonds can be permitted. The indenture should provide that the privilege of transfer or exchange of bonds may be suspended for a period of fifteen days preceding the mailing of notice of redemption of a part of an issue. It is incumbent upon the trustee, however, to use its best efforts to keep the suspension to a minimum period of time, especially in an active bond issue, so that registration of transfers as a result of trading will not be unduly disrupted. Where the parties desire, an interim receipt could be issued for a bond presented for registration of transfer or in exchange during the period the bond register is closed. In such event, however, the registrar should place a legend on the receipt to the effect that the bond register is closed for purpose of partial selection of bonds for redemption at a designated price on a designated date; that the bond presented for registration of transfer or exchange is subject to selection for redemption in whole or in part; and that in the event of such selection, new bond(s) registered, as indicated on the receipt, for the uncalled portion will be delivered in exchange for the receipt, together with a redemption ticket redeemable on the redemption date, for the called portion of such bond.

Once the selection has been made and the notice mailed (or first published), the bonds selected become due and payable on the date designated. On such date they cease to be outstanding for any purpose of the indenture except to receive payment and should be removed from the classification of outstanding bonds by appropriate entry in the trustee's records. It is desirable to control them in a subsidiary redemption ledger, with appropriate entry being made as the bonds are actually surrendered and paid.

It is possible that some of the bonds will not be presented promptly. Care should be taken on the next record date for payment of interest that appropriate stop payments are noted on the registrar's records. In the case of bearer bonds, the stop payment should be noted against the coupons appurtenant to all such bonds that remain outstanding. This will not only prevent the making of an unauthorized payment but will also facilitate notice to such holders who have not surrendered their called bonds.

After the selection has been completed and the bond register re-opened, any bond not affected by the call may of course be transferred, exchanged, or otherwise dealt with. Where a portion of a bond has been selected for redemption and such bond is presented for transfer or exchange before the redemption date, it is perfectly proper to effect the requested transaction with respect to the uncalled portion of the bond. The original bond, now representing only the called portion, should be retained by the trustee (or forwarded by the registrar to the trustee or paying agent) for payment on the redemption date. It has been suggested that provision be made for registration of transfer of called bonds between the date of selection and the redemption date. It is difficult to understand why this should be desired, for the status of the obligation has now been changed. It represents only the right to receive payment of the redemption price on the redemption date and can no longer be used in settlement of a contract to deliver a "bond" of the issue.

If the entire issue has been called for redemption, it may be desirable to continue the registration of transfer process and permit the trading of "called" bonds. In such a situation any bonds delivered should be overstamped with an appropriate legend of the redemption.

CONVERTIBLE SECURITIES

Where debt securities are issued that by their terms may be converted, at the option of the holder, into other types of securities of the issuer, the trustee should see that this privilege is protected. The common practice where any securities are called for redemption is to continue the conversion privilege to and including the redemption date. The trustee should urge that such a provision be included. Some issues provide that a conversion privilege will terminate several days before the redemption date. No matter how carefully it is spelled out in the notice, many holders invariably miss the cutoff date and consequently sustain substantial loss.

In preparing the redemption notice, it is recommended that the conversion privilege, if of value, be stated separately so that the holder's attention is drawn to it. It is inevitable that some holders will lose their privilege through misunderstanding or carelessness, but every effort should be made to keep such loss to a minimum.[3]

For convertible issues, the trustee should insist that the indenture provisions contain specific time frames prior to a redemption date in which the obligor may notify the trustee of its election to redeem bonds. Discretion for the trustee to determine that a shorter notice period is

[3] See Van Gemert v. Boeing Co. 520 F. 2d 1373 (2d. Cir.), *cert. denied* 423 U.S. 947, (1975).

satisfactory may lead to claims or litigation by holders in the event that the economic return to the holders resulting from such conversion and redemption timing is affected.[4]

Funds held in the redemption account for payment of securities converted are usually returned free to the obligor. This is proper, for in effect payment for the securities has been made by the issuance of other securities (e.g., stock). The trustee should make certain that this is explicitly covered in the indenture.

[4]*See* Elliott Associates v. J. Henry Schroder Bk & Trust Company, 838 F.2d 66 (2d Cir. 1988).

TEN

Satisfaction and Defeasance

An important part of every indenture is the section pertaining to satisfaction and discharge, or defeasance. Defeasance relates to the "undoing" or release from the lien of the indenture or the mortgage of property originally pledged or mortgaged to secure the payment of principal and interest, and to ensure performance by the obligor of its covenants. For any type of secured issue, including a mortgage bond indenture, defeasance will entitle the obligor or mortgagor to receive its pledged or mortgaged property free and clear from the lien of the indenture.

Such defeasance should not be confused with "in-substance defeasance" (also referred to as "taxable defeasance," "de facto defeasance," and "effective defeasance"), which are transactions intended to satisfy debt obligations in substance although there is no legal discharge of the obligation. In effect, an issuer purchases U.S. government obligations at a discount and places them in a trust, pledging the future income and principal of the governments to pay off the interest and principal on its own outstanding bond issue. Such transaction may be advantageous to the issuer in that it can (1) enhance its financial statements, (2) upgrade its debt rating, and (3) result in effectively retiring an outstanding bond issue without having to repurchase the bonds.[1] Special concerns with these transactions are discussed in greater detail in the sections that follow.

[1] See Financial Accounting Standards Board, *Statement of Financial Accounting Standards No. 76, Extinguishment of Debt* (Nov. 1983); and SEC Interpretive Release Nos. 33–6501, 34–20509, 35–23176, FR-15 (Dec. 22, 1983).

In the usual case the indenture covenants are included as additional security provisions to guarantee performance of the basic covenant, namely, to pay the indenture obligations as they become due. Accordingly, if all such obligations have been paid, or satisfactory provision made therefor, the obligor is entitled to a satisfaction even though a default may have occurred or may at the time exist under a particular security covenant.

The obligor must, however, have discharged, or provided for the discharge of, all its obligations to the security holders. For example, if the securities contain a convertible provision, an option to purchase stock, or any other condition or provision that constitutes an additional consideration for purchase of the securities by the holders thereof, it is not sufficient merely to provide for payment of principal and interest on the indenture securities. All other conditions must be performed or their performance provided for before the obligor is entitled to a formal satisfaction and discharge of the indenture.

The obligor must also have discharged all obligations owing to the trustee and other agents. These include payment of all disbursements, repayment of all advances (with interest if properly chargeable), and payment of all fees and other compensation due, including reasonable fees for execution of a satisfaction and any other duties required to be performed subsequently.

If the trustee executes and delivers a satisfaction improperly, it will be liable for legal damages to anyone injured by its action. Conversely, if it improperly withholds a satisfaction, it may be liable to the obligor. The trustee must therefore exercise due care in all matters relating to the satisfaction and discharge of the indenture.

It would be impractical and unfair to require actual payment of all the outstanding bonds before the obligor could obtain a satisfaction. Over a long period of time some bonds become misplaced or lost, or holders are slow in presenting them for payment. Occasionally, a small percentage of the obligations are never presented, and in many instances several years may elapse before all the obligations are actually retired. On the other hand, the bondholders are entitled to their security until they receive payment for their bonds, and it is important that such payment be secured for them before the indenture is satisfied.

The usual provision is to require deposit with the trustee, in trust, of funds sufficient to pay all principal and interest on the bonds to maturity date, or to the redemption date, if the bonds have been called and for the indenture to provide that, upon such deposit, the obligor shall become entitled to a satisfaction of the indenture. Where any facts must be established or any conditions precedent performed, the indenture should provide that the trustee will be protected if it accepts and relies in good faith on an officers' certificate and opinion of counsel as to the existence of such facts or the performance of such conditions.

It is not essential that all steps be taken to effect the redemption before a satisfaction can be given. This fact may be important if the redemption funds are being provided through refunding under another indenture. In order that the obligor give a proper lien under the new indenture, which is essential to enable it to secure the necessary funds, it must at the same time be able to secure a legal discharge of the former lien. It is sufficient if the requisite funds are deposited with the trustee together with irrevocable instructions to perform all acts necessary to effect the redemption.

ACCOUNTING ANALYSIS

For the trustee to determine what funds are required, an appropriate accounting may have to be prepared. This may take any form as long as it is reasonably detailed and accurate and includes all obligations that have become due under the indenture and the provision made for their discharge. If the appropriate records have been accurately maintained throughout the life of the issue (especially if bearer obligations are involved), the analysis for a final maturity (or full redemption) will present no problem; if not done or if the records are out of proof, then a major task may be involved.

Exhibits 11 and *12* set forth a typical accounting analysis for a mixed (i.e., bearer and registered) issue.[2] However, these cover only a single series of bonds. If more than one series has been issued under the indenture, an analysis should be made for each series.

The analysis of principal requires accounting for the total principal amount authenticated by the trustee at any time under any provision of the indenture. As bonds will have been issued because of registration of transfer, exchange, or replacement or for other purposes, the aggregate of obligations to be accounted for will usually exceed the amount outstanding at any time under the indenture. Offsetting principal obliga-

---

[2] If a data base system captures certificate cancellation data and is able to produce a report of such covering specified time periods, it should not be necessary to detail the reason for the certificate cancellation in the final accounting. *See also* chapter 15, *infra*.

tions so authenticated will be the aggregate of all such obligations that have been canceled by the trustee. In a usual case, all such cancellations will be evidenced by executed destruction certificates in the trustee's possession. To the extent that the total bonds canceled are not evidenced by destruction certificates or canceled bonds in the trustee's possession, the trustee should satisfy itself that proper disposition has been made of the canceled obligations. If the trustee's records do not disclose cancellation of such obligations, it should insist on surrender thereof so that proper disposition may be ensured. Subtracting the principal amount of obligations canceled from the aggregate amount authenticated will give the principal remaining to be accounted for. This may be offset by funds on deposit with the trustee, by monies to be deposited, or by satisfactory indemnity bonds on file.

In preparing any interest accounting, the principal amount of obligations outstanding on each interest payment date should be ascertained and the interest calculated for each such date. The amount of registered interest paid, the aggregate amount of coupons canceled, and the coupons paid against bonds of indemnity for each period should be shown separately. The sum of these subtracted from the interest due leaves the balance due for each interest date represented by outstanding unpresented coupons. The aggregate of these amounts should represent the funds on deposit with the trustee or paying agent.

If the trustee is not the agent for paying registered interest, it should receive an appropriate certificate of a responsible disbursing agent. This should be examined and proved to the total of the registered interest due, and appropriate record should be made for use on the subsequent accounting.

Coupons paid are customarily destroyed by the trustee, and the destruction certificates provide the evidence necessary to support this phase of the accounting. Where there are paying agents other than the trustee, the latter should arrange to have all interest obligations surrendered to it periodically for verification and destruction. In lieu of such surrender, the trustee may accept a destruction certificate from a reliable agent, although good practice should prohibit acceptance of such a certificate of the obligor company without independent verification.

Most indentures permit replacement of lost, stolen, or destroyed obligations, or their payment, in lieu of replacement, upon furnishing of evidence of such loss, theft, or destruction and provision of satisfactory indemnity. Such replacement securities, however, constitute additional contractual obligations entitled to the security of the indenture. In connection with a final accounting, it is customary to give credit for all obligations covered by a satisfactory bond of indemnity, if an original counterpart is on file with the trustee and if the latter is named as an obligee. This is a matter for the trustee's discretion, however. If the security afforded by such bonds of indemnity is not in all respects satisfactory, the trustee is entitled to insist on the furnishing of adequate security or to the deposit of funds to cover such obligations.

DEPOSIT OF FUNDS

The trustee is entitled to, and should insist on, deposit with it of all funds due for all outstanding obligations before it executes a satisfaction. If funds to meet matured and unpresented obligations are on deposit with other agents, arrangements should be made for their transfer to the trustee. This is true even though deposit with such other agent is in trust. The fact that a statute of limitations may have run against particular interest obligations is immaterial unless the indenture contains a specific provision that no further claim may be asserted with respect thereto.

In the exceptional cases where deposit with the trustee is not feasible, either because the latter is not an authorized depositary or for other reasons, the depositary should be satisfactory to and approved by the trustee, and the deposit should be under the exclusive control of the trustee. In such a case the trustee will not be liable if reasonable care was used in the selection of the depositary, even if the funds are subsequently lost through failure of the depositary.

The issuer's obligation contained in its bonds runs directly to the holders thereof. Where requisite funds for their payment are deposited with the trustee, however, it has been held that this is equivalent to payment to the holders, and the issuer is not liable if the trustee misapplies the funds or becomes bankrupt. This is true, however, only from and after the date on which funds in the hands of the trustee become available to the bondholders upon surrender of their bonds.

DOCUMENTATION

When all requisite accountings have been prepared and checked and the trustee has satisfied itself that it has funds in its possession to pay all obligations shown to be still outstanding; when it has received an officers' certificate and an opinion of counsel on compliance by the obligor company with all conditions precedent; and when it has received from the obligor company irrevocable instructions to complete all conditions requisite to redemption of the securities not previously completed, it is then in a position to execute and deliver a satisfaction and discharge of the indenture.

The instruments of satisfaction will usually be prepared by counsel for the obligor, but they should be checked carefully by the trustee.

In the case of a debenture agreement or unsecured indenture, execution of a formal instrument of satisfaction is not absolutely necessary, for no property has to be reconveyed. It is good practice, however, to acknowledge formally the compliance by the obligor with its obligations, and this is almost always observed. Complete and final accountings should be prepared in any event, as in the case of a mortgage indenture.

Under a mortgage indenture, the instrument of satisfaction constitutes a reconveyance of all the trustee's interest in the mortgaged property.[3] It must, therefore, be in a form that can be recorded in the necessary jurisdictions to discharge the lien of the indenture of record. Care should be used to see that the instrument is in the form of a release or quitclaim deed and that no warranties are included. It is good practice to have included in the instrument an affirmative statement to the effect that the instrument is executed without covenant or warranty, express or implied, and without recourse against the trustee in any event. The instrument should always run to the obligor and never to a third party.

"IN SUBSTANCE" DEFEASANCE

For various economic and financial reasons, and particularly during periods where short term interest rates are lower than those born by an obligor's bonds, an obligor may elect to defease an indenture, with bonds to be redeemed at a future date or dates. Indentures for tax exempt issues frequently permit this type of defeasance, and tax exempt obligors often use refunding bonds to finance such a transaction. One factor leading to this type of defeasance may be that the bonds are "call protected," i.e., not subject to an optional redemption until a future date, if at all. Indentures may permit such a transaction, stating that cash or government securities be deposited with the trustee, pro-

---

[3] In the case of a collateral trust indenture, where the trustee had perfected its security interest by filing a financing statement under the UCC, the release of its security interest is effected by the filing of a termination statement.

vided that such securities and cash together with interest to be earned upon them will be sufficient to pay all principal, premium, if any, and interest upon the outstanding bonds as they become due by their term or through redemption. Some indentures however, require that an amount of cash sufficient to pay all future debt service be deposited to effect defeasance. The trustee should be careful to distinguish this type of defeasance (sometimes termed "gross defeasance") from the former type which allows future investment earnings to be factored into the equation ("net defeasance"). For either type of "in substance" defeasance, the trustee should request that the obligor obtain and provide an accounting from a recognized accounting firm clearly showing that the cash, securities, and investment income, if any, will cover all debt service in future years, up to and including final maturity or redemption.

For tax-exempt financings in most instances the trustee and obligor will enter into a separate escrow deposit agreement, setting forth the obligations and duties of both parties until all bonds are redeemed or mature by their terms. The escrow deposit agreement should include all of the provisions from the defeased indenture with regard to registration of transfer and payment of the bonds, as well as exculpation, indemnification, and protection for the trustee in its new capacity as escrow agent. Although structured as an escrow agreement, the funds are nevertheless held in trust by the escrow agent for the benefit of bondholders. The agreement also should clearly spell out the agent's responsibility for future investment and reinvestment of cash, securities, and investment income, and the disposition of any excess funds not required to pay principal and interest as they become due.

When an "in substance" defeasance is being done for a tax-exempt issue, the trustee would be wise also to request an opinion of nationally recognized municipal bond counsel to the effect that such defeasance will not adversely affect the tax-exempt status of the bonds. This should be in addition to any other opinions required by the indenture as a condition precedent to the defeasance.

DISPOSITION OF COLLATERAL FUNDS AND RECORDS

For all defeasances, arrangements should be made for return to the obligor of pledged collateral or other items of property that are physically in the possession of the trustee but not required to be held as part of an escrow or otherwise for future payments to bondholders. In this connection, the trustee should make sure that there is no junior lienor entitled to possession of such property. If such lien exists, arrangements should be made to surrender the property to the trustee of the junior lien against proper receipt. This may include the right to proceeds of any released property, insurance proceeds, or similar funds in the hands of the trustee.

It is desirable to provide in every indenture for return to the obligor company of all unclaimed funds deposited to pay the indenture obligations after a specified number of years have elapsed following satisfaction of the indenture. The most common period used is six years. The specific period is not material as long as some period is included. If no such provision is included, the trustee may be required to retain a small balance on its books permanently, for it is unlikely that each and every obligation will be presented to it. Conversely, securities have been discovered and surrendered for payment as long as sixty years after their stated maturity.

In the absence of appropriate indenture authority, the trustee runs a risk in returning any unclaimed funds to the company, no matter how many years may have elapsed, for the company has no legal right to such return. Similarly, the obligor is not entitled to have such funds invested for its benefit, and if such an investment is made, the trustee may be liable if loss results.

In recent years, most states have further complicated the problems of corporate financial officers and corporate trustees and paying agents by the enactment of sundry escheat or abandoned property laws. The general purport of these statutes is to require the transfer to the state of all funds and, in some states, securities held unclaimed for a stated period of time. Since theoretically a state can seize only property belonging to its residents, a difficult problem is presented where funds are held for the payment of bearer securities.[4] This is particularly true where no

---

[4] In Texas v. New Jersey 379 U.S. 674 (1965), the Supreme Court held that the right and power to escheat belongs to the state of the creditor's last known address as shown on the debtor's books and records. This was in direct conflict with the Uniform Disposition of Unclaimed Property Act of 1954, as revised, which had been adopted, in one form or another by thirty-one states and the District of Columbia. In order to provide for this decision and to update the administration of unclaimed property, the Commissioners on Uniform State Laws promulgated the Uniform Unclaimed Property Act in 1981, which has now been adopted by twenty-two states. For a state-by-state analysis, see Commerce Clearing House, Inc., STOCK TRANSFER GUIDE, ESCHEAT LAWS.

provision is made for subsequent payment to a rightful claimant and outright confiscation is involved.

The indenture provisions relating to disposition of unclaimed moneys should be drafted in relation to any applicable escheat or abandoned property law. Where an appropriate indenture provision is lacking, the trustee is presented with a difficult decision when called upon to execute a satisfaction. For example, let us assume that during the life of a particular issue the obligor has paid over several thousands of dollars pursuant to an escheat law requiring transfer of all interest moneys held unclaimed for six years. The issue matures and the obligor tenders, to the trustee, funds to pay the principal and all unclaimed interest due within the preceding six years and demands execution of an instrument of satisfaction. Should the trustee comply or should it insist upon deposit of an amount equivalent to the funds previously escheated? This is not an easy decision, but unless the escheat law was sufficient to discharge the trustee's obligation with respect to such unclaimed interest, it may act at its peril if it executes a satisfaction without adequately securing such unpaid interest, the coupons for which may be subsequently presented to it. Under such circumstances, the trustee would be well advised to secure at least an appropriate indemnity from the obligor.

One final problem remains. Now that the indenture has been satisfied and appropriate provision made for payment of all outstanding obligations, what disposition should be made of the mountain of documents and papers that the trustee has accumulated during the life of the indenture? Obviously the answer will depend to some extent on any laws or regulations that exist in the jurisdiction of the trustee relating to the disposition of fiduciary records. Most corporate trustees tend to follow a very conservative practice and to hold on to papers and documents for many years beyond the time when they can serve any conceivable purpose. This is an expensive folly, and it is urged that each trust company give consideration to establishing a reasonable schedule for the systematic disposition of obsolete records. (See Exhibit 13 for such a *Document Disposition Guide*).

Certain records accumulated by a corporate trustee should be retained permanently. These would include one original executed counterpart of the indenture and of the instrument of satisfaction; a copy of its final accounting with respect to all indenture securities; copies of all destruction certificates; originals of all bonds of indemnity or assumptions of liability of others with respect to any indenture securities or other obligations; and any document relating to an obligation or undertaking beyond the maturity of the indenture securities or essential to establishing the basic historical continuity of the trusteeship, such as an assumption agreement by a successor obligor.

Most other documents can be disposed of within a reasonable time after termination of the appointment or after the running of applicable statutes of limitation.

Once the indenture has been satisfied, the recorded counterparts of the indenture and all supplements are no longer of any value to the trustee. They may be returned to the obligor corporation if it desires them. Otherwise they should be destroyed.

The original counterparts of indentures executed prior to 1966 bear canceled federal documentary stamps evidencing payment of the original issue tax and should be dealt with carefully. Because this evidences payment of an obligation by the obligor, it may be returned to the obligor if the latter wishes. A receipt should be obtained that should recite the principal amount of canceled tax obligations affixed. If the obligor does not wish to have this document returned, which is usually the case, it may be destroyed by the trustee. The destruction certificates should include a statement of the face amount of such tax stamps so destroyed.

Exhibit 14 Maturity Procedure Guide may be helpful in completing the necessary actions upon the final maturity of an issue.

ELEVEN

Default and Remedial Provisions

Administration of indentures after default provides the greatest test of the corporate trust officer's skill and expertise. In addition to the requirements of the TIA most indentures provide that before default the trustee shall be charged with performance of only such duties as are specifically set forth in the indenture. The instrument itself serves as the guide for the action to be taken on each problem that arises. However, there are often no applicable precedents to follow and the trustee may find itself navigating in uncharted waters.

It is impossible to prescribe an exact course of conduct to be followed in the event of a default. The indenture is essentially a security instrument, and should reflect the premise that the primary objective of the trustee, both before and after default, is to protect the security position of the indenture security holders. If liquidation or reorganization should become necessary, the trustee should see that the security holders realize in full, or to the greatest extent possible, on their claims.

Except for the duties imposed by the TIA,[1] the rights and powers of the trustee after default are derived from the authority granted by the indenture, or are such as may be properly inferred from the authority expressly granted. Before discussing the general principles of default indenture administration, it might be well to consider the default and remedial provisions customarily included in trust indentures.

[1] Sec. 315(a) and (c) and 317(a).

EVENTS OF DEFAULT

The events that will constitute a default and give rise to the remedial provisions must be set forth clearly in the indenture.[2] Although there is occasional variance by reason of particular circumstances existing in a given case, the provisions in general are fairly uniform and consist of the following:

1. Default in the payment of the principal of any of the indenture securities when the same become due, whether at maturity, by call, by declaration, or otherwise. Because of the serious nature of this type of default, no period of grace is provided, for it is unlikely to happen by inadvertence. Also, prompt action on the part of the trustee may be indicated and it should not be hampered by having to wait for the running of a period of grace.
2. Default in the payment of any installment of interest on any of the indenture securities when the same becomes due. Most indentures provide a period of grace, usually thirty to sixty days, within which the obligor may cure such a default. The remedies provided in the indenture are stayed until this period of grace has expired.
3. If the indenture provides for any sinking fund or purchase fund, or similar payments to be made to the trustee, failure to make any such payments will constitute an Event of Default. It is desirable to allow a period of grace for the curing of such default and such a provision is customarily, although not always, included.
4. If there are prior lien bonds outstanding, or other obligations that constitute a lien prior to the lien of the indenture securities on the trust estate or some part thereof, a covenant to pay such prior liens and comply with all provisions of the indenture securing the same should be included in the indenture. Failure to discharge these prior lien obligations when due should be made a default under the indenture after a period of grace. There is a sound reason for this. Although failure to discharge the prior lien will normally constitute a default under the prior lien obligation, the holder thereof may take no action to enforce the obligation. Unless this also constituted an Event of Default under the indenture securing junior obligations, the holders of the latter might be unable to take steps

---

[2] It should be noted that a so-called lower-case default will ripen into an *Event of Default* when: there is no grace period; or the appropriate grace period in the indenture has expired; or upon the trustee's giving of notice as prescribed in the indenture. The remedial provisions of the indenture will become operative only upon the occurrence of an Event of Default.

to protect their equity in the property until it had been substantially dissipated.

5. It is an Event of Default if the obligor pursuant to or within the meaning of any federal or state bankruptcy law commences a voluntary case, consents to the entry of an order for relief against it in an involuntary case, consents to the appointment of a custodian of it or for all or substantially all of its property, or makes a general assignment for the benefit of its creditors; or a court of competent jurisdiction enters an order or decree under any bankruptcy law that is for relief against the obligor in an involuntary case, appoints a custodian of the obligor or for all or substantially all of its property, or orders the liquidation of the obligor and the order or decree remains unstayed and in effect for sixty days.[3]

6. Finally, the breach of any covenant or the failure of the obligor to perform any condition provided for in the indenture will in turn lead to a default. It is customarily provided that an Event of Default shall not occur for this reason until the expiration of a stated period of time after the trustee or a specified percentage of the indenture security holders shall have notified the obligor in writing of the breach of the convenant or condition.

Whereas both notice and a period of grace should be provided for in the event of a breach of most indenture covenants, circumstances may exist when either or both may be unwise. For example, in the case of certain negative covenants, such as those against the incurring of indebtedness, the creation of prior liens, the transfer of properties, or a declaration of dividends, time may be of the essence and the trustee should have the right to move promptly if such action seems warranted. This should include the obtaining of injunctive relief from an appropriate court. Although the trustee does not draft these provisions, it should insist on such flexibility during the indenture review and negotiation sessions with the issuer (or its counsel).

A situation may also arise where there is a dispute between the trustee and the obligor about whether in fact a default has occurred under the terms of the indenture. This may result from differing opinions of counsel (to the obligor and to the trustee) on the proper interpretation or application of a particular indenture covenant. In this case, the trustee

[3] Derived from the Federal Bankruptcy Code, 11 U.S.C.A. sections 301 and 303 (h) (2), Pub. L. No. 95–598, 92 Stat. 2549 (1978), and the Model Simplified Indenture, 38 *Bus. Law.* at 756. See also Committee on Developments in Business Financing, *Structuring and Documenting Business Financing Transactions Under the Federal Bankruptcy Code of 1978*, 35 *Bus. Law.* 1645 (1980).

should consider the possibility of instituting a declaratory judgment action against the obligor in federal court, seeking a judicial determination of whether a default has in fact occurred.[4] Thus, the trustee may be able to avoid future litigation, either by the obligor or the security holders, for it will have received judicial approval of its action or nonaction.

REMEDIAL PROVISIONS

The indenture contains various remedial provisions to which, theoretically, recourse may be had once an Event of Default has occurred. To the average security holder the powers of enforcement granted the trustee seem entirely adequate, and an investor may therefore be at a loss to understand why in many situations the repayment of bonds is less than bargained for. Unfortunately, remedial action normally requires judicial proceedings of some kind, and the remedies included are those with which courts and lawyers are familiar. Where the intrinsic value of the security is sufficient, these remedies might be adequate. In the case of the usual corporate obligor, however, such are often inadequate, unenforceable, or impractical.

The remedies found most frequently in secured indentures are the following:

1. The right to accelerate maturity of the indenture securities and to declare all principal due.
2. The right of the trustee to recover judgment in its own name and as trustee of an express trust.
3. The right to sue in equity or at law for specific performance of any covenant or agreement, or for enforcement of any rights of the trustee and security holders, or for the enforcement of any appropriate equitable or legal remedy.
4. The right of entry on and possession of the mortgaged property by a custodian, agents, or otherwise, such possession to continue until all defaults are cured.
5. The right to sell the trust estate at public auction, with or without entry.
6. In the case of a collateral indenture, the exercise of full rights of ownership with respect to any collateral held.

[4] Such action may be possible under the Declaratory Judgment Act, 28 U.S.C.A. sec. 2201.

7. The right to the appointment of a custodian or receiver of the mortgaged property and to foreclosure thereon by appropriate judicial action.

8. The right to file proofs of claim on behalf of all the security holders in any judicial proceedings.

In the case of an unsecured indenture, the same remedies will usually be included, except for numbers 4, 5, 6, and 7 above, which relate to specific action for realizing on the indenture security. The unsecured indenture customarily contains a general provision permitting the trustee to have a custodian or receiver of the obligor's property appointed and to bring suit to foreclose on the property to satisfy its judgment for the amounts owing on the indenture securities. The advantage of the mortgage indenture is that the lien on the properties is already established.

In aid of the trustee's powers of enforcement, the remedial sections usually contain three covenants on the part of the obligor:

1. In the event of a default in payment of principal or interest (whether at maturity, on redemption, or by declaration), to pay to the trustee promptly all amounts then due and owing. Because it is obvious that if the obligor could do this no default would have occurred, the provision may appear meaningless. It is intended as an aid to the trustee's obtaining a prompt judgment on the basis of which it may proceed to the enforcement of other remedies.

2. Upon the commencement of any action, suit, or proceeding by the trustee, to waive the issuance and service of process and to enter its voluntary appearance in such action, suit, or proceeding and to consent to the entry of judgment in favor of the trustee for all amounts owing under the indenture.

3. So far as it lawfully and effectively may, to waive and relinquish the benefit and advantage of any and all valuation, stay, appraisement, extension, or redemption laws then existing or thereafter enacted.

Rights and Duties of Trustee on Default

Nature of the Trustee's Responsibility

Before enactment of the TIA, most indentures provided that the trustee was under no duty to take action to enforce the remedial provisions of the indenture until it had received an official demand by a specified percentage of the indenture security holders, together with whatever indemnity might be required to protect it against expense and liability. This provision was accompanied by broad exculpatory clauses that relieved the trustee of liability except for acts amounting to willful misconduct or gross negligence.

Despite the great amount of criticism directed against these provisions, there was a sound and logical basis for their existence. Initially, as has been noted, the trustee was a mere stakeholder and its function was limited to that of holding the specific security for the benefit of the bondholders. Despite the grant of broad rights and powers to the trustee, this concept did not disappear entirely. Even though the trustee was given the right to proceed on its own to enforce the remedial provisions, in practice it continued to be regarded primarily as the instrumentality of the security holders in exercising the right. Accordingly, the customary procedure whenever a default occurred or seemed imminent was for the trustee: (1) to confer with the obligor to ascertain the essential facts and, if possible, to work out some tentative program or course of action; (2) to take such action, with the cooperation of the obligor, if possible, as might be necessary to preserve the status quo insofar as was possible; (3) to communicate the essential facts to the indenture security holders and, if indicated, to assist in the organization of a committee to represent the security holders; and (4) to work with the security holders and their committee and to take such action in the enforcement of the indenture remedial provisions as might be decided upon by the trustee and the committee. Whenever possible, an effort was made to work out a compromise solution without recourse to the drastic indenture remedies.

This process was, of course, time-consuming. The indenture provisions referred to above were included as a protection to the trustee to enable it to delay pursuit of the indenture remedies until opportunity was afforded for consultation with the security holders on its action.

Whereas the procedure outlined above was the one most frequently followed, at times the trustee initiated action without awaiting direction of the security holders. It is possible, though by no means certain, that if this had been done more often, some of the serious consequences that resulted might have been ameliorated. In any event, the security holders were regarded as having the inherent right to decide for themselves whether their interests would be served best by compromise or by strict enforcement of the indenture remedies.

The position of the trustee was rendered more difficult by incorporation in all qualified indentures, and in most other indentures since 1940, of certain provisions required by the TIA. Although no specific course of action was prescribed, the act established a new standard for trustees after default. Section 315 (c), required the inclusion in each qualified indenture executed prior to November 15, 1990, of a provision that the indenture trustee shall exercise, *in case of default,* such of the rights and powers vested in it by the indenture and shall use the same degree of care and skill in their exercise as a *prudent* man would exercise or use under similar circumstances in the conduct of his own affairs. The TIRA has made this duty a legislatively mandated standard of care.

The "prudent man" standard was not a novel concept. It existed in the law of numerous states as the fiduciary standard for executors, administrators, or inter-vivos trustees, and under early judicial decisions.[5] Precedent is a significant factor in determining compliance in a particular case and, in relation to the various types of "personal" trusts, precedent is not too difficult to establish. By reason of the generally high level of economic activity from 1950 to 1987, there were relatively few defaults under qualified indentures. As a result, the indenture act provisions were not fully tested and adjudicated. Even with the significant increase in the number of defaults during the past few years, there has not been a major acceleration in the development of legal principles related to the trustee's role in this area. Many of the "precedents" that still exist for the conduct of indenture trustees are those of pre-TIA days. These should not be relied upon in the future, for it must be assumed that the primary reason for changing the rules was dissatisfaction with these precedents.

Of more importance is the fact that the trustee still has only limited powers. It is axiomatic that imposition of responsibility should be accompanied by the grant of sufficient power and authority to discharge it properly. Yet what occurred was the establishment of a new standard of conduct for indenture trustees without any change in its limited authority. The prudent man in managing his own affairs can take *any* action that seems to be indicated by the circumstances. The same is generally true with reference to the classes of fiduciaries to which the rule has been applied heretofore. As applied to indenture trustees, it will be noted that the trustee is limited to the exercise of the rights and powers vested in it by the indenture. A review of the customary remedial provisions set forth earlier in this chapter will indicate clearly that they

[5] See Sturges v. Knapp, 31 Vt 1 (1858); Harvard College v. Amory, Pick. 446, 461 (Mass. 1831).

contemplate action to be taken only on the most serious type of default. What course of action should the trustee follow when prudence dictates remedies or procedures not included within the rights and powers vested in it by the indenture?

This question will arise many times, and for purpose of illustration, let us consider two possible "defaults." The first involves default in a covenant to maintain working capital in a specified amount. The obligor's financial condition remains basically sound, but because of circumstances beyond its control, its working capital falls below the minimum required. No judicial action will remedy the situation. What should the trustee do?

The second situation involves a sinking fund default. Owing to depressed business conditions the obligor is unable to meet its large principal payments. It appears, however, that a rearrangement of the maturity schedule through deferment of a portion of the current installments will resolve the difficulty. Can the trustee properly cooperate in securing the necessary adjustment, especially when it may require a substantial period of time to secure the requisite consents?

The answer to these and other questions must await the course of future court decisions. In the meantime, indenture trustees should consider the following possibilities:

1. Because the limitations of liability to performance of duties specifically set forth in the indenture is, by the terms of the indenture, related to predefault activities, courts may very well find implied discretionary powers to perform acts or take action not specifically embraced within the indenture language.
2. Despite this possibility, the taking of any action for which express authority is not included within the indenture may subject the trustee to the highest degree of care or to a stricter level of liability.
3. The right of the trustee to rely conclusively on certificates or opinions conforming to indenture requirements is limited to certificates with respect to predefault activities.[6] After a default occurs, these certificates and opinions may not constitute adequate protection if an independent investigation would have disclosed a different state of facts or resulted in a different conclusion.
4. In appropriate situations, full advantage should be taken of the indenture provisions permitting amendment of the indenture with the consent of a requisite percentage of security holders. The two hypothetical cases cited above would seem appropriate situations

6 TIA, sec. 315 (a) (2).

for recourse to this provision. As this would seem the prudent course, the trustee should be fully protected in cooperating with the obligor in presenting a proposal to the security holders and requesting their consent. Care must be exercised to see that no material adverse change in the situation occurs during the interim.

5. Where the default is merely technical, or seemingly temporary, or in the judgment of the trustee is capable of being cured or resolved through appropriate negotiation or adjustment with the obligor, the trustee undoubtedly has sufficient authority to take the necessary action without reference to the security holders or without recourse to the remedial sections. This authority is necessarily implicit in other provisions of the indenture.

6. Upon the occurrence of a serious default, the trustee is under an affirmative duty to take appropriate action. It is doubtful that the changes imposed by the TIA were intended to alter the basic concept of the trustee's responsibility. Accordingly, if the trustee acts reasonably and in a manner calculated to preserve the status quo until it has an opportunity to consult with the indenture security holders, this should be sufficient in the normal situation. The circumstances of each case will, however, determine the degree of care and course of action that should be followed. Although the trustee is responsible for taking prompt and decisive action, no specific course of action can be prescribed for every situation, but each must be carefully considered at the time. It is unfortunate, but the trustee's action or lack of action is almost always judged in hindsight.

Notice of Default

One of the first problems with which the trustee is confronted is whether or not to notify the indenture security holders of the occurrence of a default. In qualified indentures the trustee is under a duty to give security holders prompt notice of all defaults known to it. This notice must be given within ninety days after the occurrence of the default. This giving of notice is mandatory with respect to any default in the payment of the principal of, or interest on, any security, or in the payment of any sinking fund or purchase fund installment.[7] The trustee is protected in withholding notice of other defaults as long as its board of directors, executive committee, or trust committee determine in good

---

[7] TIA, sec. 315 (b). In actual practice, most trustees will give holders notice of such default within ten days of its occurrence or after the expiration of any applicable grace period.

faith that the withholding of notice is in the interest of the indenture security holders.

Under most indentures before the TIA, the trustee was under no express duty to notify the security holders of a default. Although such a general notice was sometimes given, it was the exception rather than the rule. Where action by security holders seemed indicated, the trustee frequently contacted institutional and other holders of substantial amounts of securities known to it and also consulted with any security holders who made inquiry. General circularization of security holders was usually deferred until it was determined that committee organization was desirable, and then notice was given by committee representatives rather than by the trustee. In other situations where some arrangement or adjustment appeared feasible, the trustee would work out an appropriate proposal with the obligor, which would then be submitted to security holders by the latter.

The absence of a specific indenture requirement did not, however, always serve as full protection to the trustee in withholding notice. In one case, an indenture contained a covenant that the obligor would not consolidate or merge with another corporation. With the knowledge of the trustee, the company merged into another corporation and the latter continued to pay interest. Subsequently, bankruptcy ensued. The court held that the trustee was guilty of gross negligence and bad faith in failing to give notice of the default despite the fact that the indenture provided that the trustee need take no notice of a default unless notified by a specified percentage of the bondholders.[8]

Another court held that a trustee, in a suit brought against it by bondholders, was under a duty to explain why it had permitted a default for several years without taking action to notify the bondholders or protect their interests.[9]

Where the trustee advances its own funds to meet interest payments and thus prevents the bondholders from learning of the obligor's default, it may be liable for any reduction in the value of the security that subsequently results. It has also been held in such a situation that the trustee is not entitled to assert a claim for reimbursement or share *pro rata* with the bondholders in a subsequent sale of the property. Similarly, it has been held that where the controlling stockholder of the obligor, engaged in marketing its bonds, personally advanced money to pay coupons to prevent notice of default, such coupons are paid and not

8 Seelig *et al*. v. First National Bank of Chicago, 20 F. Supp. 61, (D.C.N.D. Ill. 1936).
9 Bolyston v. Senate Apartment Building Corporation, 11 N.E. 2d 636 (1937).

purchased and are not entitled to either priority to or equality against the obligor's assets.

As has already been noted, where there is a paying agent for the obligor's securities other than the trustee, the paying agent is under a duty to notify the trustee in case the obligor defaults in any installment of principal or interest when it falls due.

Most indentures provide that the trustee may, at its sole discretion, advance moneys for the payment of taxes, insurance, rentals under leases, or other items for preserving the trust estate. It is also provided that to secure such advances the trustee shall be entitled to a lien on the trust estate prior to the lien of any bonds issued under the indenture. This type of advance is, however, exclusively for the purpose of preserving the trust estate or to prevent the creation of a prior lien thereon. It is to be distinguished from the type of advance referred to above, which prevents security holders from learning of a serious default.

In the case of advances by the trustee to preserve the trust estate, the trustee is required under the TIA to give notice within ninety days of the making of any such advance if the amount of advances remaining unpaid aggregates more than 10 percent of the principal amount of indenture securities outstanding.[10] The trustee must also include in an annual report to security holders a report of any advances made by it that remain unpaid on the date of the report, if the unpaid advances aggregate more than one-half of 1 percent of the principal amount of the indenture securities outstanding on such date.[11]

There is still some inconsistency in the TIA provisions in this regard. As noted, the report sections require notice of advances only when they aggregate certain specified minimum amounts. Section 311 appears, however, to protect the trustee's lien and right to prior repayment only with respect to advances that have been reported to security holders, regardless of amount. Except under special circumstances it is unlikely that the trustee would make advances unless the obligor had defaulted. Notice of such default would have to be reported, unless it were withheld for the reasons permitted by the indenture. If these reasons are sufficient for withholding notice, the trustee should not be penalized by losing its lien or right to prior repayment. It is likely that the omission in Section 311 is an inadvertence and the trustee would be protected if it complied with the specific requirements for reporting outlined in other sections of the act. If such a situation arises, however, these provisions should receive the careful attention of the trustee and its counsel.

10 TIA, sec. 313 (b) (2).
11 TIA, sec. 313 (a) (3).

It is very important that the trustee be given broad discretion in the matter of withholding notice of default and that it be protected in the exercise of such discretion. The security holders are entitled to prompt notice if their security or their investment is prejudiced, and the trustee should be prompt in notifying them of any serious default. As indicated, such notice is mandatory in the case of a default in payment of principal or interest. The primary objective of all parties should, however, be to prevent a default or to remedy the situation. If this is possible, then too hasty action in publicizing the default can cause irreparable damage. The trustee should always have sufficient time to explore the possibility of curing a default or of working out some arrangement to prevent a serious loss to security holders.

The duty to act with a high degree of care embraces responsibility for withholding, as well as giving, notice in appropriate situations. The trustee should consider that the withholding of notice of technical default may result in preventing the holders from exercising their rights (e.g., declaring an Event of Default) and therefore it may be held accountable for any resultant loss. In a doubtful or borderline case, notice should be given. All facts should be investigated promptly and weighed carefully. Whatever the conclusion of the administrative officer, it is recommended that the final decision in each case be made, with the advice of counsel, by the trust committee or, if there is none, by the executive committee or board of directors of the trustee.

The Trustee and the Indenture Remedial Provisions

Even though under modern practice, with certain special exceptions, recourse is seldom made to the specific remedial provisions set forth in the indenture, it is desirable to describe briefly the general principles applicable to their use.

1. Trustee's discretion toward remedy.   Subject to the right of a majority in principal amount of the indenture security holders to direct the time, method, and place of conducting any proceeding for any remedy available to the trustee—which exists under most indentures— the trustee has broad discretion with respect to the particular remedy to be pursued. As long as it acts in good faith and not in a wholly unreasonable and arbitrary manner, a court should not interfere with the trustee's exercise of discretion. This is true even though the trustee may have a conflicting interest. Likewise, the trustee will not be liable for any error of judgment made in good faith by a responsible officer, unless it can be shown that the trustee was negligent in ascertaining the pertinent facts.[12]

Although the trustee's powers are strictly limited by the indenture, a court may find implied powers or responsibilities or, in a particular situation, may authorize the trustee to perform acts it would otherwise have no power to perform. Thus, in a case where depressed economic conditions had rendered it impossible for the obligor to perform a covenant in an indenture secured by real estate bonds relating to the maintenance of certain value ratios, and where the only alternative was foreclosure, the trustee was permitted to enter into a working agreement with the obligor permitting the latter to retain possession.[13] In another case where the security consisted of various collateral, the court held that it had the power to authorize the trustee to secure a loan on the collateral and make a distribution to security holders rather than dispose of it at a forced sale.[14]

In pursuing a course of action not specifically authorized or permitted by the indenture, however, the trustee should obtain an outside legal opinion or expert opinion, and in appropriate cases the authority of a court or permission of a majority in principal amount of the security holders. If it endeavors to act on its own without authority, even though in good faith and in an honest effort to preserve the security for the bondholders, it may be liable for any loss resulting from its action.

2. Rights incident to other remedies.   The first two remedies enumerated above are included primarily for the purpose of enabling the more adequate enforcement of other remedies.

The first of these is the right of acceleration of the maturity of the indenture securities. This right is given to the trustee alone and, frequently, to a specified percentage of the indenture security holders acting without the trustee's concurrence. The purpose of the provision is to enable conversion of the company's obligation into a matured debt so that foreclosure or other proceedings may be undertaken to the same

---

[12] TIA, sec. 315 (d) (2). The act does not define "responsible officer." However the Model Provisions (*see* note 29, chapter 2, *supra*) define the term to include senior officers and designated junior officers of the trustee and any other officer of the trustee customarily performing functions similar to those performed by the two designated officers, and with respect to any particular corporate trust matter, any other officer to whom such matter is referred because of his (her) knowledge or any familiarity with the particular subject.

[13] N.J. National Bank & Trust Co. v. Lincoln Mortgage & Title Guaranty Company, *et al.*, 105 N.J. Eq. 557, 148 Atl. 713 (1930).

[14] Seigle, *et al.* v. First National Company, *et al.*, 338 Mo. 417, 90 S.W. 2d 776 (1936).

extent as if there had been a principal default. If the indenture does not contain such a provision, the trustee may not be able to foreclose, in the event of a default in interest, except to the extent of past due interest. This would necessitate successive actions until maturity of the principal debt. It is therefore important that every indenture contain an acceleration clause.

Another provision in all qualified indentures is that giving the trustee the right to recover judgment in its own name in the event of a default in the payment of principal or interest. Inasmuch as the trustee's duties relate primarily to enforcement of the security, and the security holders themselves own the debt, a serious question arose about the extent of the trustee's rights in the absence of this power. Some courts have held that on foreclosure the trustee could not recover a deficiency judgment in the absence of such a provision.

3. Rights of entry, sale, and foreclosure.   Some of the powers given the trustee in case of default are seldom exercised. One of these is the right of entry and possession until the default is cured. The theory underlying the right is prevention of mismanagement of the property and the diversion of the rents and profits therefrom to purposes other than the paying of interest and principal on the indenture securities. The theory is that the trustee should be able to take possession, receive the rents and profits until all defaults are cured, and then return the property in good condition to the mortgagor. Although such a procedure might be feasible in the case of a real estate mortgage, it is not practicable in the case of the usual industrial or utility mortgage where management is highly specialized. Where a trustee is in possession pursuant to such a provision, however, it has all the rights of a mortgagee-in-possession and is accountable to the mortgagor only after all payments required by the indenture have been made to the bondholders.

Another remedy seldom pursued any longer is that of sale without judicial proceedings. It is usually impossible for an outright sale of property to be made to an independent purchaser, and sale of the properties is therefore only an incident to some form of reorganization proceedings and actually is unnecessary under existing provisions of the bankruptcy statutes. This power has been used in particular situations, such as under a railroad equipment trust agreement. It may also be of value where the trustee holds marketable collateral securities. Except for such situations, however, the power of sale does not provide an effective usable remedy.

One of the important rights on default, which is incident to the concept of the indenture as a mortgage, is the right of foreclosure. Before enactment of Sections 77 and 77B of the old Bankruptcy Act, this was the most important remedy available and was used frequently to accomplish an effective reorganization. For this reason courts customarily found sufficient power vested in the trustee to initiate foreclosure proceedings, even where the indenture provisions were not clear or seemed to qualify the right. For example, when the only provision was an authorization for the trustee to foreclose on request of a specified percentage in principal amount of bondholders, it was held to have the right to do so on its own initiative.

As an incident to foreclosure proceedings or other remedies, an application should be made for appointment of a custodian for the benefit of the indenture trustee and the security holders. This is important in connection with provisions relating to assignment of rents and profits. The usual indenture is so drafted that the indenture trustee has no right to rents or profits until it takes possession. It has been held that a provision stating that an Event of Default would act as an automatic assignment of rents and profits is valid and enforceable. In any case, however, it is desirable to apply for appointment of a custodian and the segregation of rents and profits for the benefit of the trustee and bondholders.

One of the problems that arose in connection with foreclosure proceedings was the trustee's right to bid in the property. Where no such power was granted, the trustee's rights have been held to be limited to the taking of such steps as would lead to a cash distribution to bondholders, and therefore no right to purchase the property could exist. Other courts have held that such a power could be implied or, if not expressly given, could be authorized by the court. Unless expressly required by the indenture, the trustee cannot be compelled to bid in the property. Where the trustee does bid in the property, it has an implied power to resell it for the best price obtainable.

Within the past few years, concern over the indenture trustee's potential liability in dealing with potentially contaminated property has become increasingly evident. The basis of this concern is the application of the Comprehensive Environmental Response, Compensation, and Liability Act of 1980 ("CERCLA"), also known as the "Superfund Act," to bond issues which are secured by property on which there may be hazardous waste.[15]

Under CERCLA, an "owner" or "operator" of a facility on which

[15] 42 U.S.C. sec. 9601, et seq. (1980).

there are hazardous substances will be liable to reimburse the Environmental Protection Agency for any cleanup costs.[16] Excluced from this group are those persons who, without participating in the management of the facility, hold an indicia of ownership in the facility primarily to protect a security interest (i.e., "secured lenders").[17] Such secured lenders, presumably including bondholders and indenture trustees, should be protected so long as they don't participate in the management of the obligor's operations, or become "overly entangled" in the "day-to-day operational aspects of the site."[18] It is possible however, that if the indenture trustee forecloses on the property and/or takes legal title to it, it may be deemed to be an "owner."[19]

Until the application of CERCLA's provisions to secured lenders and, by implication, to bondholders and indenture trustees is settled, either through a court decision or appropriate legislation, any involvement of a trustee with an obligor of a secured bond issue that is in default (or on the trustee's "watch list") must be carefully analyzed and considered in light of this legislation, comparable state laws, and current case law. It is evident that trustees should consult also with counsel in these situations as to what actions it should or should not take to avoid any possible finding or even inference that it is participating in the "management of a hazardous waste site" or facility.[20]

Inherent Difficulties of Default Administration

Having considered the various indenture provisions relating to default, it might be well to summarize the essential problems that face the trustee on default and the difficulty in dealing with them effectively.

[16] Id., sec. 9067.

[17] Id., sec. 9601 (20) (A).

[18] United States v. Mirable, 15 Envtl. L. Rep. 20994 (E.D. Pa. 1985).

[19] United States v. Maryland Bank & Trust Co., 632 F. Supp. 573 (D. Md. 1986); Guidice v. BFG Electroplating and Manufacturing Co., Inc. 732 F. Supp. 556 (W.D. Pa. 1989).

[20] Consulting with knowledgeable counsel is essential in light of a U.S. Court of Appeals decision which held that "it is not necessary for the secured creditor to involve itself in the day-to-day operations of the facility in order to be liable . . . rather, a secured creditor will be liable if its involvement with the management of the facility is sufficiently broad to support the inference that it could effect hazardous waste disposal decisions if it so chose." United States v. Fleet Factors Corp., 901 F. 2d 1550 (11th Cir. 1990), *cert. denied,* No. 90–504 (Jan. 14, 1991).

While it is essential to include the broad remedial provisions in indentures, one of the unfortunate consequences is the false sense of security created in the minds of individual security holders. As has been emphasized, the real security for holders of securities is the "going concern" value of the obligor and the income and profits realized from operation of its business. The indenture convenants constitute a strong deterrent, and, if the business is profitable, the obligor is most concerned to see that no default occurs so that it may remain in the undisturbed possession and enjoyment of its properties. If the business becomes unprofitable, this "going concern" value, and hence the bondholders' real security, is depleted. The obligor is unable to meet its obligations, and the realizable value of the property, as distinguished from its value in the operation of the business for which it was intended, is usually insufficient to discharge these obligations. This is particularly true when the default occurs during a period of general economic recession or when the industry of which the obligor is a part is undergoing strain or depressed conditions. These are economic facts. They are the risks that each investor must personally evaluate, and no contract provisions can afford the investor complete protection against them. This scenario is especially true for unsecured issues, whereas in a collateralized bond issue, the real security will depend almost entirely on the value of the collateral itself, independent of the obligor as a "going concern."

A serious indenture default will usually be accompanied by a general inability of the obligor to meet its obligations or by insolvency. Where such a situation exists, the obligor can protect itself against the strict enforcement of indenture remedial provisions by seeking protection under the Federal Bankruptcy Code.[21] This in fact is what usually occurs. The trustee is than enjoined by the court from instituting or continuing any proceedings for enforcement of the indenture provisions.

Of even greater significance than the rights, powers, and remedies available to the trustee, are those it does not have, either by express limitation or by the absence of a grant. The provisions customarily included that have become more or less standard are derived from traditional common law remedies developed in relation to small, readily identifiable properties having inherent intrinsic values. They were not designed for large industrial properties devoted to corporate rather than

[21] See note 3, *supra.*

individual use. They contemplate some form of liquidation and sale, which in most cases is undesirable and impractical.

Even if it were possible to enforce the remedial provisions according to the letter of the contract, this is seldom desirable, at least during the initial phases of most defaults. What is called for is some form of cooperative working arrangement to enable the obligor alone, or in conjunction with its major creditors, to endeavor to resolve its financial problems outside of the Bankruptcy laws. It is in this area that the trustee can only act in a conciliatory mode, since it is almost without power or authority to act independently. It is true that action can be taken with the support and consent of certain percentages in principal amount of the indenture security holders, but the delay necessarily involved, as well as the occasional harassment by individual or minority groups of holders, is unfortunate. As a result, the trustee must frequently walk a rather tenuous path. As suggested previously, further obstacles may have been created by the imposition of a stricter standard without a concurrent grant of broader authority.

Whether an indenture trustee should be given additional or broader powers is debatable. It has been argued that it is important to have provisions in the default section which allow the trustee to take legal action even when no monetary or other default has occurred, but where the very security of the bond issue may be impaired (e.g., where there is an effort to transfer assets to another entity prior to a principal payment or redemption). In such situations the trustee should have the right to obtain judicial determination to prevent any such impairment of the rights or interests of the bondholders or the trustee under the indenture.[22] It is certain that such grant would be resisted by trustees themselves unless adequate provisions for their protection in the exercise of discretion were included, as well as assurance that their expenses and appropriate compensation would be paid. Most corporate trust organizations are not staffed to make the detailed studies and investigations called for, and employment of experts would be necessary in most cases.

Such a grant of power would also involve a delegation of authority that traditionally has been reserved to security holders themselves. Some authority for dealing with the situation during an interim period until security holders could be organized would be desirable, if accompanied by appropriate immunity, protective provisions, and compensation.

[22] See James Spiotto, *The Problems of Indenture Trustees and Bondholders,* Course Handbook Series Number 343 at 671, Practising Law Institute, New York (1990).

In general, the powers granted to the trustee relate solely to the strict enforcement of the contractual rights under the indenture. To the extent that the obligor can be compelled, through judicial proceedings or otherwise, to perform its convenants and obligations under the indenture, or to the extent that a sale or foreclosure under the indenture is indicated and can be effected, the trustee has requisite authority.

Because the usual corporate indenture involves important and necessary operating properties, liquidation such as is contemplated by sale or foreclosure is seldom feasible. Security holders will usually realize more through a reorganization or readjustment of the obligor's capital structure than through liquidation, even if the latter were permitted. Accordingly, where a major default occurs the object of most proceedings is the reorganization of the financial structure of the obligor.

While the authority of the trustee in these proceedings is usually sufficient to enable it to take all preliminary steps, there are strict limitations on its rights to represent the security holders. A reorganization can generally be effected only if the security holders are willing to accept other securities of the reorganized company in satisfaction of their claims. This normally involves some compromise of claims.

The trustee has no power or authority to make such a compromise on behalf of the indenture security holders or to accept anything but cash in satisfaction of their claim. The trustee has no title to, or interest in, the debt secured, except to the extent that it may recover judgment against the obligor as an incident to enforcement of the security. The debt secured cannot be compromised or discharged except by appropriate judicial decree or, if specifically provided for in the indenture, with the consent of the security holders themselves. Unusual circumstances may justify an exception to this general rule. In *United States v. Freeman*[23] the court held that indenture trustees had power and authority to consent to a compromise settlement binding on bondholders. The case involved a liquidation proceeding following a terminated unsuccessful effort to reorganize a railroad. One of the powers of the trustees was the right to take possession, operate the properties, and pay taxes and other proper charges superior to the lien of the mortgage. Although the trustees were not in possession and had been specifically enjoined from enforcing indenture remedies, the court found that since the amount realized on liquidation was less than the claims alleged to be prior to the indenture lien, the trustees had a right to enter into an agreement compromising

[23] D.C., S.D.N.Y. (1/25/60).

all claims and that "this right of the trustees to assent on behalf of the bondholders was unquestioned."

In view of the limitations on the rights and powers of the trustee, it is important to consider the rights and powers of indenture security holders, both individually and collectively. This will be done in the next chapter before the problems involved in bankruptcy and reorganization proceedings are discussed.

TWELVE

Rights of Security Holders

The primary purpose of the indenture is to afford protection to the holders of the securities issued thereunder. The covenants and remedial provisions are of no avail unless ample power of enforcing them is given. In the previous chapter we considered the rights and duties of protecting such security holders' interests as are placed in the trustee. It was indicated, however, that these rights are not all-inclusive but are limited to those expressly granted. Therefore it is important to consider the rights the security holders have with respect to the indenture, the enforcement of the provisions thereof, and the claims represented by the securities they hold.

These considerations present a difficult question, and one that still remains to be resolved adequately and satisfactorily. It is important to bear in mind always a distinction already made. The obligation of the company to pay principal and interest on the individual securities runs directly to the security holders themselves. The ownership of the debt represented by the obligation rests in each individually. As a general principle, no one should be permitted to amend, modify, prejudice, or deal with such debt without the consent of the owner thereof.

The difficulty arises when it is necessary to distinguish between the claim of an individual holder, which may be represented by only one of many thousands of obligations identical in terms, and claims under the indenture, which secures the entire debt represented by all such obligations outstanding. From the viewpoint of the obligor and the trustee, the debt secured by the indenture is a single obligation and is dealt with as such.

The rights, duties, and responsibilities of the trustee relate to enforcement of the security provisions of the indenture that secures this entire debt. Its right to sue and recover judgment for the debt is in furtherance of such enforcement. While it owes a duty to each individual holder, its primary responsibility is to security holders as a class, and it cannot permit the claim of an individual holder to prejudice the rights of the holders as a group. In addition, the trustee also has a duty to protect the interests of the minority holders. For example, if the obligor enters into a side agreement with several large holders to "take out" their bonds in exchange for their consent to changes in certain covenants, the trustee must be alert to ensure that such actions do not result in the unfair impairment of the minority holders' interests.

Also, during the life of a bond issue the obligor accounts to the trustee with respect to its duties and obligations under the indenture. One of the advantages to an obligor of the indenture-trustee device is that it has only one entity with which to deal on most problems that arise. Whereas most companies endeavor to provide any reasonable information requested by an individual holder, they cannot for practical reasons deal with many thousands of such holders individually.

A distinction should be made between holders of obligations issued publicly and holders who acquire obligations through "direct placement" negotiations. In the latter case, besides executing an indenture with the trustee, the obligor enters into a separate "purchase agreement" with each purchaser of a part of the debt. In these agreements the purchasers usually require filing of periodic financial and other information directly with them. These rights are, however, acquired under separate agreements with the obligor and not under the indenture. In such cases, these rights may also be "personal" in that they are not transferred on sale of the obligations to a subsequent purchaser.[1]

Whereas in relation to enforcement, many of the rules that would apply to holders of a publicly distributed issue would also apply to holders under direct placement contracts, in the following pages we will be concerned only with the former.

RIGHTS PRIOR TO DEFAULT

Information and Disclosure Provisions

Adequate protection of the investor's interest involves factors over and above enforcement and remedial provisions of the indenture. The inves-

---

[1] See discussion on issuance of private placements under SEC Rule 144A, page 17, *supra*.

tor is entitled to have complete information about the obligations offered for purchase. The investor is entitled to the opportunity to be kept reasonably informed of developments that may affect such investment so long as it is held. The investor is also entitled to have knowledge of the rights in the event that action is required to enforce the claim represented by such investment.

One of the basic purposes of the 33 Act was to require full disclosure of information relative to new securities being issued publicly. The provisions of this act were enlarged by the TIA, which requires filing of copies of the indenture in connection with registrations of new securities. Summaries of important provisions of the indenture must be included in the registration statement. Pertinent financial and other information contained in such statement, including summaries of the indenture provisions, must be incorporated in the prospectus pursuant to which sale of the securities is made. Each purchaser must be delivered a copy of the prospectus so that the investor now has available all pertinent information on which an intelligent decision can be made.

The security itself refers to important sections of the indenture, particularly any that impose limitations on the rights of the holder. If further information is desired, the trustee will always make a copy of the indenture available for the holder's inspection or advise the holder about the contents of particular sections that are of concern.

While not directly related to the individual security holder, the activities of the SEC under the 34 Act and the subsequently enacted federal securities acts are designed to afford protection to security holders generally. Rules and regulations of the Municipal Securities Rulemaking Board (MSRB), national securities exchanges, the National Association of Security Dealers, and other groups have the same purpose.

Secondary Market Disclosure

A great deal of attention has centered on the lack of sufficient secondary market information for investors in municipal bonds. This situation has become particularly acute since 1986 when industrial revenue bonds, housing bonds, and nursing and hospital bond issues have accounted for almost three-quarters of the total dollar amount of payment defaults of all municipal securities. Because municipal issues are excluded from the registration requirements of the 33 Act, and the disclosure regulations promulgated by the SEC for corporate issues, the patterns of information dissemination and disclosure that have developed over the years by issuers, underwriters, and trustees have been neither uniform nor consistent.

Since the corporate trustee is an essential party to the ongoing administration of the bond issue and may be in possession of information which is material to the financing transaction, it has been at the center of ongoing discussions by participants in the securities industry. Efforts to broaden the trustee's burden of disclosure of information beyond that permitted by the indenture have put the trustee in a very difficult position. While it is universally accepted that the trustee owes a post-default fiduciary duty to its bondholders, including disclosure of relevant information in its possession, it is not settled as to how extensive that duty is pre-default, including the issue of what is relevant or the timeliness of any such disclosure. Traditionally, indentures have provided very little guidance to trustees on what can or should be disclosed, other than that which is required by the TIA. Trustees quite properly have been reluctant to provide information which could be of financial benefit to those receiving the information, and have been deeply concerned over the potential liability they may have for any such disclosure.[2]

It is clearly the issuer (and in the case of a conduit financing, the obligor) that must have the primary responsibility for continuing market disclosure. The issuer has the most direct access to such information and is in the best position to evaluate its accuracy and materiality. Where however, the trustee has material information in its possession, the disclosure of such to the bondholders effectively puts it into the public domain, and the trustee can without violating any duty to its bondholders release that information to the marketplace.[3]

In order to assist participants in the securities industry, and those involved in the need to develop consistent and uniform guidelines for the ongoing disclosure of information, corporate trustees acting through the Corporate Trust Committee of the ABA have worked with other legal and securities organizations to establish workable practices and procedures, including draft provisions that can be incorporated into bond indentures providing for the public disclosure of material information on

[2] With the evolution taking place in the traditional role of the trustee, it is evident that legal "safe harbors" will need to be developed to protect trustees from risk and liability that it was never intended they assume, and for which the compensation they receive is grossly inadequate.

[3] It is expected that the MSRB will establish a central repository to which issuers and trustees will send information, for further dissemination by private sector organizations, sometimes referred to as "nationally recognized information reporting services."

a periodic or ongoing basis by the issuer or the trustee. In addition, such provisions can set forth the obligation of the trustee to furnish the issuer with information uniquely in its possession, the means of distributing such information, the compensation to the trustee for the additional responsibilities, and the indemnification of the trustee by the issuer for effecting disclosure at the issuer's direction.

Where information reporting arrangements cannot be provided for within the context of the indenture itself, as in the case of existing municipal bond issues, it is possible for the issuer (and, in the case of a conduit financing, the obligor) to enter into an agency contract whereby the trustee acts as an "information reporting agent" for the issuer. It must be understood, however, that any such agency arrangement must be subordinated to the obligation of the trustee to the bondholders; for example, information disclosed to the secondary market should not be more complete or different from that given to the bondholders, nor should it be given to the bondholders after being released to the marketplace.

The decision as to exactly what information should be released to the marketplace is clearly part of the financing transaction itself, and must be determined by the issuer (obligor), the underwriter and bond counsel, with advice by the trustee at the inception of the financing.[4]

Reports of the Obligor and the Trustee

Each obligor that has any security listed on any national securities exchange is required to file, with the SEC, with each such exchange on which any securities are listed, and with the trustee under any indentures of such obligor, periodic financial statements and other reports. All such reports are public information and are available for inspection by any security holder.[5]

Each qualified indenture must also contain a provision requiring the obligor to transmit to indenture security holders summaries of such reports and other information as the SEC may prescribe by rules and

[4] For a complete set of guidelines covering the dissemination of information and recommended disclosure standards *see, Disclosure Guidelines for State and Local Government Securities,* Government Finance Officers Association (1991).

[5] Arguing that bondholders do not receive sufficient information, a learned commentator suggests that such holders should have the same right to receive information and reports as shareholders of a publicly traded company do. McDaniel, *Disclosure for Corporate Debt Securities,* S & P Corporation, 16 Rev. of Sec. Reg., No. 9 at 907 (May 4, 1983).

regulations. No such rules or regulations have been issued; therefore, this provision is currently inoperative. Many companies, however, endeavor to forward, to known holders of their debt securities, copies of annual reports forwarded to stockholders. It is probable that almost every obligor would do so in response to a specific request by a security holder.

Section 313 of the TIA requires the trustee send an "annual" report to security holders under indentures qualified under the TIA if there has occurred within the previous twelve months: (1) any change in the continued eligibility and qualification of the trustee; (2) the creation of or any material change to one of the post-default "conflict of interest" relationships set forth in section 310(b)(1) through (10); (3) the character and amount of any advances made by it, as indenture trustee, that remain unpaid on the date of the report and for reimbursement of which it claims, or may claim, a lien or charge prior to that of the indenture securities, on the trust estate, or on property or funds held or collected by it, if such advances remaining unpaid aggregate more than one-half of 1 percent of the principal amount of the indenture securities outstanding; (4) any change to any indebtedness owing to the trustee in its individual capacity and the security therefor, if any;[6] (5) any change to the property and funds physically in possession of the indenture trustee; (6) any release, or release and substitution, of property under the indenture, and the consideration received therefor not previously reported; (7) any additional issue of indenture securities not previously reported; and (8) any other action taken by it in the performance of its duties under the indenture that in its opinion materially affects the indenture securities or the trust estate.[7]

Previously considered were the notices the trustee must give of Events of Default under the indenture. There may be omitted from the "annual" report, however, notice of any default being withheld pursuant to appropriate indenture provisions for the reasons previously discussed.

In addition to the "annual" report the trustee must also submit special interim reports of important transactions.[8] Other than reports of default, these include the following:

[6] A drafting error in the TIRA added the words "any change to" in subparagraph (6) rather than (4). The SEC has advised trustees to prepare their reports consistent with congressional intent, as indicated here. SEC Release 33–6892 (May 8, 1991).

[7] See TIA, sec. 313(a). In my opinion a similar report, as appropriate, should also be sent annually to holders of securities under non-TIA-qualified indentures, including municipal revenue bond issues (and particularly industrial development bonds).

[8] TIA, sec. 313(b).

1. A brief report of the release, or release and substitution, of any property subject to the lien of the indenture, and the consideration therefor, if any, if the fair value of such property is 10 percent or more of the principal amount of indenture securities outstanding on the date of the release. Such report must be transmitted to security holders within ninety days after execution and delivery of the release.

2. A report on the character and amount of any advances made by the trustee pursuant to the indenture, for which it claims or may claim a lien on the trust estate prior to that of the indenture security holders, if the amount of all advances remaining unpaid aggregates 10 percent or more of the principal amount of indenture securities outstanding. This report must also be transmitted within ninety days.

Bondholder Lists

Under the TIA the corporate obligor is required to furnish to the trustee, at intervals of not more than six months, all information coming into its possession, or that of its paying agents, about the names and addresses of security holders.[9] The trustee is also required to retain any such information it may receive in its capacity as paying agent. The indenture should provide that all such information will be preserved by the trustee until a new list is received and prepared (which is done in connection with payment of the next maturing interest installment) and that the previous list may then be destroyed. The purpose is to keep such information in as current a form as possible.

In the case of debt obligations outstanding in bearer form, the only way that current information can be obtained about the names of the holders is in connection with collection of the semiannual interest coupons. Under current law (i.e., effective January 1, 1984), presentors of corporate bearer coupons must indicate in their transmittal, their name, address, and taxpayer identification number.[10]

To deal with the situation where the issuer or the trustee desires to communicate with holders of bearer tax-exempt securities in connection with a specific matter, such as an amendment to the indenture or other

[9]Id. sec. 312.

[10]Interest and Dividend Tax Compliance Act of 1983, Pub. L.98–67, 97 Stat. 369, sections 104, 105, and 108.

special matter, a procedure was developed whereby substantial information can be obtained in connection with the collection of interest coupons. This is done through use of a special form of Memorandum Certificate of Ownership (see *Exhibit 16*). If notified at least thirty days in advance of an interest payment date, the paying agent can prepare and deliver to the collecting agents a supply of such certificates with the request that they be completed and submitted with the interest coupons. This is an effective procedure and can provide a fairly complete list of holders as of the particular date.

A major drawback to this method of obtaining information is that it can be done only when interest is being paid. Once a default in interest occurs, no further coupons are presented, and the trustee should consider the publication of a notice requesting the owners of the defaulted issue to send it their names and addresses.

The most accurate list of holders is that obtained from the registration records. Whether the security be fully registered, or registered as to principal only, the holder is assured of receiving all reports the trustee submits to security holders. Of more practical importance, the holder is promptly notified of any redemption call that affects his or her holdings.

Where the holder of an old corporate bearer instrument does not wish to have such security registered, another alternative is possible. The holder may advise the trustee of such holdings and request that his or her name be placed on file as the holder of particular securities. The trustee is required under the TIA to maintain the name on file for a period of two years.[11] In acknowledging any such request, the trustee should call attention to the two-year limitation and suggest filing of a renewal request on or before a particular date.

Although the trustee is required only to mail copies of reports to the holders on this special list, most trustees treat it in the same manner as lists of registered holders. This is good practice, and it is suggested that copies of all redemption notices or other material of special interest to security holders be sent to all holders on the two-year list maintained by the trustee.

Annual reports of the trustee and reports submitted by it on occurrence of Events of Default are required to be submitted to all known holders of indenture securities. This includes the list obtained from the obligor, the list maintained by it as paying agent, the list of registered holders, and the special two-year list. Interim reports on re-

11 TIA, sec. 313(c)(2).

leases or advances by the trustee are required to be submitted only to registered holders and holders on the special two-year list. As a practical matter, however, any such interim reports are usually submitted to all holders, regardless of the source from which information was derived.

Access to Confidential Information

Information about names and addresses of security holders is of importance to the obligor and to the trustee. On occasion it may also be of importance to security holders. Whereas this is particularly true in the event of a default or a threatened default, it may be important in relation to other proposed transactions. For example, certain holders may oppose a proposed amendment to the indenture and desire to organize other holders in opposition thereto. Where they feel that their rights may be prejudiced by any proposed action, they should be permitted to communicate their opposition and the reasons therefor to other holders. This right is recognized by the requirement that under any qualified indenture three or more holders of the indenture securities may petition the trustee and state their desire to communicate with other holders of indenture securities.[12] If such holders can establish by reasonable proof that they have been holders of indenture securities for six months or longer, the trustee must afford to such applicants all information in its possession about the names and addresses of security holders, or inform them about the number of holders on the list maintained by it and the approximate cost of mailing the proxy or other information desired to be mailed by the applicants. Upon request of the petitioning security holders and payment of such costs, the trustee is required to mail copies of the proxy or other information to all security holders known to it. If it determines that mailing of such information would not be in the best interests of security holders, it must, within five days after receiving the proxy or other material, file with the SEC and the applicants copies of the material submitted, together with its reasons for its belief that mailing of such material would not be in the interests of security holders. The act provides for a hearing by the Commission and for a finding either sustaining or rejecting the trustee's contention. If rejected, the trustee must mail copies of such material with reasonable promptness to all security holders known to it.

The trustee is protected with respect to disclosure of information or

12*Id.*, sec. 312(b).

mailing of any material in accordance with the provisions of the statute or the order of the Commission.

Amendments to Indenture[13]

Quite frequently it is necessary to amend the indenture by an appropriate supplement. Most amendments can be made by agreement between the obligor and the trustee without reference to or approval of the security holders. The most common amendments of this kind are the following:

1. To create and provide the terms of additional series of securities authorized by the indenture to be issued.
2. To mortgage or pledge under the indenture specific property or additional property as security and to provide the terms and conditions upon which such property may be dealt with by the trustee, consistent with other provisions of the indenture.
3. To modify, amend, or add to the provisions of the indenture in such manner as to permit the qualification thereof under the TIA.
4. To add to the covenants and agreements of the obligor.
5. To evidence the succession of another corporation to the obligor, and the assumption of the securities and the covenants and obligations of the obligor by such successor corporation.
6. To cure any ambiguity, or any defective or inconsistent provision of the indenture, so long as the rights of the security holders are not adversely affected.

Although amendments of the type described above do not adversely affect any substantive rights of security holders and so could be made without express authority therefor in the indenture, it is desirable and good practice to include such authority in every new indenture. This obviates the possibility of any objection being raised thereto.

At times it is considered necessary or desirable to make other changes or amendments to the indenture, or eliminate specific provisions thereof, that may affect a substantive right of the security holders. In the absence of indenture authority such changes cannot be made without the consent of all of the security holders or of all holders whose rights might be affected.

---

[13] In executing any supplemental indenture to an indenture entered into prior to November 15, 1990, the trustee must be exceedingly careful *not* to reaffirm the provisions of the original indenture that are now deemed included as the result of the TIRA. The unintended result could be to have a different (and higher) set of standards imposed on the trustee through a contractual agreement with the obligor. *See also* page 88, *supra.*

It is therefore of great importance to include in the indenture a section setting forth the manner in which such changes may be made and the authority required. It is customary to permit such modifications with the consent of the holders of two-thirds of the principal amount of the securities outstanding, excluding any securities held by or for the account of any obligor. The indenture should set forth in sufficient detail just how such consent is to be evidenced and the manner in which proof of security holdings is to be made.[14] Here again it is desirable not to spell out such requirements in detail, but rather to permit the trustee to make rules and regulations covering such administrative matters.

It is well to provide for delivery to the trustee of executed consents within a specified period or, in the alternative, to permit modification of the indenture by vote of security holders at a formal meeting called for such purpose. In the latter event, provision should be made for voting by proxy. Where securities are outstanding in bearer form, notice of the proposed meeting should be made by publication sufficiently in advance. In addition, whether or not required by the indenture—and except for registered holders it is proper for technical reasons for the indenture not to so require—the trustee should mail copies of the notice to all security holders on the list maintained by it.

Even though the obligor may be able to obtain the required consents without a formal meeting or approach to all security holders, the trustee should insist that notice of the proposed amendment be published or otherwise communicated to all holders. This will apprise everyone interested of the indicated change and afford them an opportunity to express their opinion thereon.

When the trustee has received the required consents, it is then authorized to join in the proposed amendment.

Certain provisions should not be subject to change or amendment without consent of all holders, or at least all of those who may be affected. Such matters would include extension of the time for payment of principal or interest on any securities; reduction in the rate of interest; modification of any sinking fund or purchase fund; alteration of the rights of holders of some securities without similar alteration of the rights of other holders; or reduction of the percentage of the holders required to consent to any future amendment, to waive any default, or to waive compliance with any provision of the indenture.

It should be noted that the trustee cannot be compelled to execute an

---

14 *See* TIA, sec. 316(c).

amendment, without its consent, which changes its own rights, duties, and liabilities under the indenture.

RIGHTS AFTER DEFAULT

Limitations on Rights of Individual Holders

Every indenture should contain limitations on the right of individual holders to institute an action to enforce the security provided in the indenture. One of the basic reasons for appointing a trustee is to make it the agent for the enforcement of the security holders' rights as a class. To permit individual security holders to bring suit for the enforcement of their individual security as soon as default occurred would prejudice the rights of the other security holders, as well as subject the obligor to an unnecessary multiplicity of suits.

The usual provision is that no individual holder can institute a suit to enforce the security provided in the indenture, or otherwise, unless after demand on the trustee by the holders of a specified percentage of the indenture securities and offer of indemnity, the trustee refuses or neglects to take action. The percentage of security holders usually required to make such a demand is 25 percent, although this may vary.[15] Holders purchase their securities subject to the provisions of the indenture, and such a provision restricting suits by individual holders has been enforced by the courts, even where it was established that it was impossible to secure the necessary percentage to make demands on the trustee. It has also been held that without showing compliance with the indenture provisions, a bondholder could not institute a suit for the foreclosure of the mortgage or for an accounting for breach of trust on the trustee's failure to foreclose; apply for the appointment of a receiver for the mortgaged property; accelerate the principal of the bonds; or institute suit for the breach of a sinking fund provision.

Such restrictions on a holder's rights of action are strictly construed, however, and must be clearly set forth in the bond or debenture itself. Accordingly, in one case where the only reference to the indenture in the bond was for the description and nature of the security, it was held that the bondholder's right of individual action could not be defeated by

---

[15] TIA sec. 316(b); Quirke v. San Francisco Railroad Company 277 F. 2d 705 (8th Cir. 1960); Friedman v. Chesapeake & O. Ry., 261 F. Supp. 728 (S.D.N.Y. 1966) *aff'd* 395 F.2d 663 (2nd Cir. 1968).

a restrictive provision in the indenture. Also, it has been indicated that such restrictions would be limited to suits for collection of the bonds or enforcement of the security and that a bondholder could maintain an action to restrain impairment of the property by waste, deterioration, or destruction. In an early case a corporation had an issue of bonds outstanding when all of its property was taken over by another corporation for cash, debenture shares, and stock. The cash and debenture shares were applied toward the reduction of the corporation's liabilities, including purchase and retirement of bonds. When all liabilities except $1,300,000 of bonds had been paid, and the corporation had $31,000,000 of cash and debenture shares remaining, it proposed to distribute $26,000,000 to its stockholders. A suit by bondholders for an injunction was sustained despite the fact that the corporation had $5,000,000 left for application to its bonds and that no demand had been made on the trustee. The court held that a bondholder had an inherent right to protect his security.[16]

When the necessary percentage of holders has made demand on the trustee and the latter has taken no action within the time required, suit may then be instituted by the holders themselves. If the indenture has been appropriately drafted, and the trustee has instituted action for foreclosure, or for enforcement of any of the other remedies, an individual holder cannot intervene in the proceedings as a matter of right.

Although the TIA neither requires nor prohibits restrictions on an individual holder's suits for enforcement, it includes a provision designed to prevent "strike suits" by individuals. This provision authorizes any court, in its discretion, in any suit for the enforcement of any right or remedy under the indenture, or in any suit against the trustee for any action taken or omitted by it as trustee, to require the filing by any party litigant of an undertaking to pay the cost of such suit. It also provides that the court may, in its discretion, assess reasonable costs, including reasonable attorneys' fees, against any party litigant in such suit, having due regard to the merits and good faith of the claims or defenses made by such party litigant. The provision is not applicable to any suit instituted by a holder or holders of more than 10 percent of the indenture securities outstanding or to any suit by any holder for principal of, or interest on, the security on or after the respective due dates expressed in the security.[17]

---

[16]Hoyt, et al. v. E. I. du Pont de Nemours Powder Company, et al., 88 N.J. Eq. 196, 102 Alt. 666 (1917).

[17]TIA, sec. 315(e).

Suit for Principal or Interest

Although provisions restraining suits by individual holders to enforce the indenture have been generally upheld, a different question is presented where the suit is for payment of the principal of, or interest on, the security.

Inasmuch as the right to sue for principal or interest is regarded as an inherent part of the contract, any restriction on such right must be clearly and unambiguously set forth. The restriction must not only be included in the indenture but must also clearly appear on the face of the bond. A provision on the face of a bond that all rights of action on the bond, except as otherwise provided in the indenture, were vested in the trustee was held sufficient to prevent an individual bondholder's suit for principal; on the other hand, a mere reference on the face of the bond to the indenture for a description of the property mortgaged and the nature and extent of the security was held insufficient to incorporate such a restrictive provision.

Where the trustee has brought suit to foreclose the mortgage and has recovered judgment for the entire debt, this is held to merge the bondholders' rights and bar subsequent individual suits. The provision giving the trustee or bondholders the right to accelerate maturity is a right incident to enforcement of the remedies and does not give an individual holder the right to sue for principal following such acceleration.

It is clear that the indenture provision requiring demand on the trustee relates only to enforcement of the remedies and does not restrain an individual's right to sue for principal at maturity of such bond. Even though a substantial majority of the holders have consented to an extension of maturity, a nonassenter may still bring suit at the regular maturity. It has been indicated, however, that in such a case judgment could not be enforced by levy against any of the property mortgaged.

The TIA expressly recognizes the right of an individual holder to sue for principal or interest as it matures.[18] In order to protect the holders as a class and facilitate temporary readjustments, there is permitted to be included a provision authorizing the holders of not less than 75 percent in principal amount of the indenture securities outstanding (or if specified in the indenture, of any series of securities) to consent to the postponement of any interest payment for a period not exceeding three

[18] TIA, sec. 316(b).

years from its due date.[19] This consent will bind all holders. With this one exception, however, the indenture must provide that the right of any holder to receive payment of the principal of, or interest on, his or her security on and after the respective due dates expressed in such security, or to institute suit for the enforcement of any such payment, cannot be impaired without the holder's consent.[20]

The only qualification on this absolute right is that the indenture may provide that the suit cannot be maintained if the institution or prosecution thereof, or the entry of judgment therein, would result in the surrender, impairment, waiver, or loss of the lien of the indenture upon any property subject to such lien.

Collective Action by Security Holders

1. Right to direct proceedings.   The restrictions customarily placed on actions by individual holders do not apply to action by security holders as a group and a demand by such percentage can compel the trustee to take action or will give the holders themselves the right to do so.

Under every qualified indenture the holders of a majority in principal amount of the indenture securities outstanding have the right to direct the time, method, and place of conducting any proceeding for any remedy available to the trustee or of exercising any trust or power conferred upon the trustee under the indenture.[21]

Although this provision may be expressly excluded, it is a desirable one, and should serve in most cases for the better protection of the security holders' interests. (If it is excluded, the trustee should insist on a proviso that it may refuse to follow directions unduly prejudicial to bondholders not joining in any direction to it, or involving the trustee in additional potential liability.) The right given to a majority to control the trustee's action should greatly assist the trustee in determining the proper remedy to be pursued. Because the trustee is subject to the "prudent man" standard after default, in a doubtful case it may well accelerate the principal and institute suit for foreclosure or file a petition under the Bankruptcy Code[22] to protect itself against a charge of negligence for failing to take action. In some cases it might be possible to prevent liquidation or reorganization by delaying such proceedings.

19 *Id.*, sec. 316(a)(2).
20 *Id.*, sec. 316(b).
21 *Id.*, sec. 316(a)(1).
22 See note 1, chapter 13, *infra*.

Because the trustee is protected in acting or refraining from acting in accordance with the direction of a majority in principal amount of the security holders, cooperation by the holders may serve to prevent hasty suits or will contribute to determination of the proper remedy to pursue and the appropriate time and method for instituting suit.

2. Waiver of default.   In addition to the right to direct the time, method, and place of conducting proceedings for enforcement, a majority in principal amount of the security holders have the right to waive any past default and its consequences under the indenture, other than a default in principal or interest. Such waiver will be binding on all holders.[23]

This provision can be extremely helpful in working out a readjustment plan wherein waiver of existing defaults is essential and consent of all holders could not be obtained. Such waiver could also apply to past sinking fund or purchase fund installments, even though extension of maturity, change in interest rate, or other prospective substantive change in the indenture could not be made.

Any such change requiring modification or amendment of the indenture can be accomplished only with the consent of the percentage of the holders required by the indenture. As previously indicated, this would not include extension of maturity of principal, reduction in interest, or change in future sinking fund requirements.

3. Removal of trustee.   Another remedy available to security holders, acting collectively, is removal of the trustee. The indenture will customarily provide that the trustee may be removed, and a new trustee substituted, by the action of a specified percentage—usually a majority in principal amount of the security holders. Where a new trustee is appointed pursuant to such action, the court will not disturb the discretion of the security holders and must recognize the new trustee so appointed.

Instances where exercise of this remedy would be beneficial are the trustee's neglect or refusal to take remedial action, or the existence of some conflicting interest that make appointment of a successor advisable.

The right may not always be an unmixed blessing, however. It may be possible for a group of holders to acquire a majority in principal amount of the bonds for the purpose of obtaining control of the obligor in default and then use such control for purposes not related to protection and enforcement of their rights as security holders. The trustee, with the

---

[23] TIA sec. 316(a)(1)(B). *See also* sec. 316(c) for provisions relating to record dates for solicitation of consents.

rights of the minority in mind, might refuse to accede to the demands of this group for particular action. It could then be removed pursuant to the indenture and a new trustee appointed that would join in the action of the majority. The right of removal by the requisite percentage of holders is absolute.

Problems arise if there is not an appropriate indenture provision, or if demand by the requisite percentage cannot be obtained. Where a trustee refused to comply with an order of a court in a foreclosure proceeding, it was held that it could be removed at the suit of an individual bond-holder. A trustee will not be removed, however, if minority holders merely disagree with its policy, or by reason of the fact that it is a general creditor of the obligor.

4. Protective committees.   As a practical matter, the organization of security holders in such a manner as to secure unanimity of a majority to direct or assist the trustee is not an easy task. The principal advantage lies in the ability to obtain consents and permit some form of voluntary readjustment in cases where default is not too serious and where liquidation and reorganization can be avoided.

The delay necessarily involved means, however, that the trustee must determine for itself the initial steps that must be taken and must proceed to the initiation of such action.

The historical way in which bondholders have been organized was through creation of protective committees. A small group, usually representing the more substantial holders, would form a committee, select a depositary, and request all holders to deposit their bonds pursuant to an agreement that gave the committee broad powers of representation. This arrangement was time-consuming and expensive and has fallen into disfavor. The customary practice today is for the committee to request proxies or powers of attorney authorizing it to represent assenting holders. The difficulty with this arrangement is that there is no way of establishing, at a given moment, just how much in principal amount of bonds the committee represents. The trustee represents all the security holders and must always be alert to the interests of the minority. While it can help to facilitate the creation of such a committee, and cooperate with it, it should maintain its independence at all times.

The trustee should not be a member of such committee, although it clearly should be aware of its proceedings and support its efforts, but only to the extent that it does not conflict with the trustee's fiduciary responsibility to represent the *entire* class of security holders.

THIRTEEN

Bankruptcy and Reorganization

A corporation may become a debtor under the Bankruptcy Code[1] either through insolvency, by reason of an inability to pay its debts as they mature, or as the result of an involuntary petition filed by its creditors. Insolvency is not, however, a precondition to a filing, and a solvent entity can in fact file a voluntary petition. When such a situation occurs, a major default under the indenture results. Before the enactment of the Code, such event usually triggered the remedial provisions of the indenture and could result in the actual liquidation of the business of the obligor and sale of the properties mortgaged or pledged for the benefit of the security holders.

From the perspective of a secured creditor (*e.g.*, a mortgage bond-holder), and a senior debenture holder, actual liquidation may represent the best opportunity to recover, but as a result of the diverse creditor and equity constituents and the Code's protective umbrella of the "automatic stay," this is seldom possible now. Although not stated, it is evident that the underlying policy of the Bankruptcy Code is to favor rehabilitation of the debtor even if such does not assure the maximum recovery by creditors holding senior debt. In addition, despite the loss in security values that may accompany the commencing of a case in bankruptcy, it is usually in the interest of security holders, as well as obligor companies, that the latter's capital structure be readjusted and its business continued on a solvent

---

[1] Pub. Law 95–598, 92 Stat. 2549 (1978), which codified and enacted Title 11 of the United States Code—Bankruptcy. Section numbers hereinafter referred to are to Title 11.

and viable basis. The object of most proceedings is some readjustment or reorganization of the obligor's affairs, brought about by extension, conversion, compromise, or in some cases, expungement of the rights and claims of indenture security holders and other creditors.

Reorganization may be accomplished either through a compromise between the obligor and its creditors without a court proceeding or through the process of a judicial reorganization. Where the affairs of the obligor are undergoing only a temporary strain and it is basically solvent, every effort should be made to achieve some adjustment without resort to court proceedings. However, even temporary relief may not be achievable in some cases without judicial intervention. Conversely, it may be possible to have major structural changes effected in the corporation's finances without the aid of a court (e.g., a tender and exchange offer to public debt holders). The indenture trustee usually does not, however, have the authority to allow the debtor the necessary accommodations for any out-of-court voluntary adjustment. As indicated in the preceding chapter, most indentures do contain provisions permitting certain percentages of security holders to waive a past default or even to extend the time for payment for interest for a limited period of time.

Permanent adjustments are usually difficult to accomplish, however, unless the security holders are few and easily accessible. Under ordinary circumstances the rights of an individual holder cannot be changed without such holder's express consent. Where a permanent adjustment in the terms of securities is required, it is usually necessary to have recourse to some form of judicial proceeding. It may be possible, however, for the bondholders, acting in accordance with the relevant provisions of the indenture, to agree to accept new securities in exchange for the old, without the intervention of a court proceeding.

Much has been written on the various bankruptcy and reorganization statutes, and neither time nor space will permit a detailed discussion of this subject matter here.[2] Most indenture administrative officers will at some time be faced with the very serious problems involved in these proceedings, and a brief review of the principal statutory provisions in a

[2] For those interested in a greater and more detailed understanding of the present bankruptcy law, see Klee, *The New Bankruptcy Act of 1978*, 64 A.B.A.J. 1865 (1978); King, *Chapter 11 of the 1978 Bankruptcy Code*, 53 Amer. Banker L.J. 107 (1979); Rome, *The New Bankruptcy Act and the Commercial Lender*, 96 *Banking* L.J. 389 (1979).

historical perspective and the position of the indenture trustee in such proceedings may be beneficial.

HISTORICAL BACKGROUND

The U.S. Constitution specifically grants to Congress the right to enact bankruptcy legislation.[3] Such power was exercised with the passage of the first National Bankruptcy Act in 1800, the Bankruptcy Act of 1898, and the Bankruptcy Act of 1934. Before the enactment of Sections 77 and 77B of the latter statute, there was no statutory authority for reorganization as opposed to liquidation of a debtor corporation.[4] Because liquidation was impossible in many cases for various reasons, the necessary result was accomplished through resort to an equity receivership proceeding.

Such proceedings, as developed by the federal courts, were generally instituted by the filing of a voluntary petition by the obligor, or a general creditors' petition, resulting in the appointment of a general receiver of all the property of the obligor company. Under its general equity power, the court would enjoin all individual suits by creditors and the filing of any additional suits.

The extensive development of the creditors' "protective committee" took place in connection with these proceedings and was essential to their successful culmination. Committees would be formed for each class of securities of the obligor company. A depositary would be selected and security holders would be requested to deposit their securities, receiving in return a certificate of deposit that could be negotiated in the same manner as the original security. Committees usually took title to the deposited securities and acted under deposit agreements that gave them very broad powers.

A reorganization plan would be worked out through a compromise of the various creditor representatives. Once agreement was reached, the plan was submitted to the court for approval.

The development of the equity receivership form occurred largely in connection with railroad organizations, although it later came to be used extensively by other types of business corporations.

Whereas, in general, the equity receivership was successful in ac-

---

[3] Art. I, sec. 8, clause 4.
[4] Such provisions are now contained in Chapter 11.

complishing the essential purposes intended, there were a number of disadvantages that needed correction:

1. Where the debtor's property was located in more than one federal judicial district, it was necessary for ancillary proceedings to be initiated in each separate district. This resulted in a great deal of time-consuming and expensive collateral litigation.
2. The necessity for a judicial sale of the properties frequently involved difficult problems.
3. There was no way in which dissenters could be compelled to participate. Those who failed to do so because of ignorance or inadvertence were often accorded harsh treatment. Professional dissenters sometimes had a field day, and the fact that their efforts were often successful made subsequent proceedings more difficult.
4. It was possible for the debtor and its senior creditors to conspire against the interests of public debt holders, which caused a great deal of concern to the judiciary and to institutional investors in particular.
5. Finally, consummation of the reorganization seldom provided a permanent solution. Each decade seemed to produce a new wave of equity receiverships, many of them involving the identical companies or their reorganized successors.

In an effort to cure some of the imperfections in the equity receivership arrangements, Congress in the mid-1930s added Sections 77 and 77B to the bankruptcy statutes to provide for statutory reorganizations. These were not bankruptcy statutes in the true sense, for they provided for reorganization rather than liquidation of the assets of the debtor. They were in effect an effort at codification of the essential features of the former equity practice.

The first of these statutes was Section 77, first enacted in 1933 and substantially amended in 1935. It was designed to provide for reorganization of railroad corporations, a number of which were then in equity receivership.

The necessity for ancillary proceedings was eliminated, the single court being given full jurisdiction over the debtor, all its property wherever located, and all its creditors. It was no longer necessary to go through the formality of a judicial sale of the property. If the plan was approved by two-thirds of the creditors and stockholders of each class affected, it was binding on dissenters and they could be forced to accept the same securities of the new company allocated to other holders of their class under the plan. It was further provided that even if the required two-thirds approval was not obtained, the plan might still be confirmed if the court found the rejection of the plan by a particular class was not reasonably justified.

In actual practice and operation, Section 77 fell far short of the expectation of its framers.

One of the most objectionable features was the time required to consummate a reorganization, the principal cause being the substantially concurrent jurisdictions of the reorganization court and the Interstate Commerce Commission ("ICC") that had jurisdiction over railroads, and the procedure that each established for carrying out its respective functions under the act. The result was a constant shuttling of the plan between the two bodies and an unnecessary and time-consuming procedure each time this was done.

Another major problem arose from the substitution of the dictates of the ICC for the results achieved by negotiation among representatives of security holders and creditors. Under the equity receivership process, the plan was usually the outcome of extensive negotiation among various creditor interests. Although this caused delay and litigation, the result achieved was in most cases more equitable to the various classes of claimants than that of the Section 77 proceedings. In many instances plans were approved by the ICC and confirmed by courts, over objections of dissenting creditors, that wiped out substantial values and left the affected security holders no recourse whatever.

Another concept that developed under Section 77 proceedings was the paramount importance accorded the "public interest," as opposed to the interests of creditors and stockholders. During the pendency of a Section 77 proceeding, creditors were enjoined from realizing on their security. The primary objective of the court, and the court-appointed trustee, should have been to provide protection of creditor rights until a fair and equitable reorganization was brought about. However, the reverse often happened. In one notable proceeding, over the repeated objections of the indenture trustees during a fifteen-year period and despite statements of the ICC that no plan of reorganization was feasible, the court refused to authorize a petition for abandonment and liquidation. When the proceeding was finally terminated and the remaining properties sold, the monies realized were insufficient to pay administrative expenses incurred by the court-appointed trustees during the proceedings, despite the fact that substantial amounts might have been realized by the security holders, even on a salvage basis, if they had been permitted to foreclose when it first became apparent that reorganization was impossible.

Section 77B was added to the Bankruptcy Act in 1934 to provide for a substantially similar procedure for the reorganization of non-railroad corporations, which could not file under Section 77. In 1938 this section was repealed and Chapter X substituted.

The proceedings under Chapter X were in many respects similar to those under Section 77. A trustee appointed by the court was required to file a list of the creditors of each class and of the stockholders and a statement of the property, liabilities, and financial condition of the debtor, the operation of the business, and the desirability of the continuance thereof. The court also fixed a time within which the trustee was to prepare and file a plan. Upon the filing of the plan, the court conducted hearings thereon, at which time any creditor or stockholder could appear and file objections or amendments thereto. If the court found the plan worthy of consideration, it had to be submitted to creditors and, unless the debtor was found to be insolvent, to stockholders. On its acceptance by creditors holding two-thirds of claims of each class, and by a majority of the stockholders (if they were entitled to participate), hearings were held on confirmation of the plan. If two-thirds of any class of creditors did not accept the plan, adequate provision had to be made for the realization by creditors of such a class of the value of their claims. If the court found that the provisions of the plan provided such protection, the plan could be confirmed despite the failure of two-thirds approval.

The role the ICC played in Section 77 proceedings was delegated to the SEC under Chapter X, with a few significant differences. The plan had to be submitted to the SEC and could not be approved by the court until the SEC submitted its report thereon or advised the court that it would not file a report or until the time fixed for filing of such a report expired. One significant difference from Section 77 was that under Chapter X, the SEC could intervene in the proceedings and thereafter was deemed a party for all purposes, except that it could not appeal from any orders entered.

Viewed in the most favorable light, the old statutory reorganizations fell far short of realizing the objectives intended. They delayed rather than accelerated consummation of plans, and the resulting loss to the real parties in interest was far greater than was necessary. Despite the acknowledged good faith of the administrative agencies involved, it is questionable whether substitution of their judgment for that of the real claimants was beneficial to debtors or creditors or to the public interest.

THE BANKRUPTCY REFORM ACT OF 1978

In view of the shortcomings discussed above, an effort to overhaul the bankruptcy laws was undertaken with the result that on November 6, 1978, Congress enacted the new Bankruptcy Code, and it became effective on October 1, 1979.[5]

The Code has seven chapters numbered: 1. General Provisions; 3. Case Administration; 5. Creditors, the Debtor, and the Estate; 7. Liquidation; 9. Adjustment of Debts of a Municipality; 11. Reorganization; and 13. Adjustment of Debts of an Individual With Regular Income.

The filing of a petition under Chapters 7, 9, and 11 operates as an automatic stay, applicable to all creditors, of any action against the debtor.[6] The purpose of such is to prevent the continuation or commencement of any action, judicial or administrative; the creation, perfection, or enforcement of a lien against the debtor; or any action to collect, assess, or recover a claim or set off a claim by a debt owed to the debtor. Such stay will continue until the case is closed, dismissed, or a discharge is granted or denied, unless a creditor or any other party affected by the stay petitions the court for termination or modification. After due notice and a hearing, the court may continue the stay, modify or lift it against the lien or claim enforcement, or require that adequate protection be given to the creditors.[7]

The result will be to protect the debtor and its property, from the time of filing, against any action that would enable a creditor to establish or improve its position. Thus the bankruptcy court becomes the pivotal

[5] Note 1, *supra.*

[6] 11 USC 362(a) and 922(a). Section 362(b) excepts certain actions from the stay, including: acts to perfect an interest in property of the debtor to the extent that the bankruptcy trustee's rights and powers are subject to such perfection; the commencement or continuation of an action by a governmental unit to enforce its police or regulatory powers; and the setoff by certain financial market participants of mutual debt or claim arising in connection with certain financial market contracts. Section 1168 expressly provides an exception for "rolling stock," which affects railroad reorganizations.

[7] *Id.* sec. 362(d). See, however, sec. 362(f), which permits the court, without a hearing, to grant relief from the stay, if "necessary to prevent irreparable damage to the interest of an entity in property. . . ."

point for the resolution of all issues and differences involved in determining whether any particular creditor may move to protect or improve its position.

Under Section 362, it would appear that the acceleration of the primary debt may be precluded upon the filing of a petition. It is nevertheless generally believed by members of the bankruptcy bar that such filing or the entry of an order for relief would be deemed an acceleration event, for all claims are treated as accelerated until deaccelerated under Section 1124. The question arises in connection with guaranteed debt whether the guarantor is obligated to pay the entire unpaid principal and interest as though the primary debt had been accelerated or whether the guaranty obligation relates solely to installments of principal and interest that may be due or that may become due following filing of a petition. To significantly address the effect of a stay on the acceleration of the primary debt it may be necessary to revise the language contained in most existing guaranty agreements. Any resolution of this issue involves a substantive adjustment of rights as between the guarantor and the security holders. A question is thus raised about the propriety of the indenture trustee suggesting a resolution of this issue if the parties have not done so. The indenture trustee may find itself involved in a dispute about enforcement of rights under the guaranty if the guarantor is called upon when the ability to accelerate the underlying debt is stayed. Conversely, if the indenture trustee suggests a clarification of this issue in drafting the guaranty, it will, of necessity, require that one side or the other surrender what may be deemed to be a substantial right. Nevertheless, it is desirable to include provisions in the indenture that would result in an automatic or deemed assumption of the debt without a release of the principal obligor, if the principal obligor becomes a debtor under Title 11.

Chapter 7 now contains the basic provisions governing the collection, liquidation, and distribution of the estate in a liquidation case. It takes the place of the straight or "ordinary" bankruptcy under the former act. In such a proceeding, a trustee will be elected by the creditors to collect and reduce to money the debtor's property and to close up the estate as quickly as possible as is compatible with the best interests of the creditors. If necessary, the trustee will examine proofs of claims and object to the allowance of any claim that is improper and will file a final accounting of the estate with the court.[8]

[8]*Id.* sec. 702, 704.

Chapter 9 provides a municipality[9] with the sole right to institute a proceeding. There are no provisions for the creditors of a municipality to institute an involuntary proceeding.[10] It must, however, demonstrate that it is either insolvent or unable to meet its debts as they mature, that it is specifically authorized by state law to be a debtor, and that it desires to enter into a plan to adjust such debts. Under the Code, it must be shown that the municipality: (1) has obtained agreement, or having negotiated in good faith has not been able to gain agreement, from the creditors who hold a majority of the amount of claims of each class that would be adversely affected; or (2) is unable to negotiate with its creditors, because such negotiations are impractical; or (3) reasonably believes that a creditor may attempt to obtain a preference.[11] Notice must be given of (1) the commencement of a case, (2) the granting of an order for relief, and (3) any dismissal of a case. Such notice must be ''published once a week for three successive weeks in at least one newspaper of general circulation published in the (judicial) district in which the case is commenced and in such newspapers having general circulation among bond dealers and bondholders as the court designates.''[12]

Chapter 9 was amended in 1988 to overcome certain structural problems in public ownership of municipalities. A category of ''special revenues'' was defined which included: receipts derived from the ownership or operation of projects or systems of the municipality primarily used for transportation, utility, or other services, special excise taxes, incremental excise taxes, other revenues derived from special functions of the debtor or specially levied taxes, but excluding receipts from general property, sales, or income taxes levied for the debtor's general purposes. These special revenues are subject to a postpetition lien notwithstanding Section 552, which ordinarily defeats such liens. In order to ensure continued operation of essential services, Section 928 provides that the lien on special revenues is subordinate to the operating expenses required, for example, for electric generating facilities. The amendments also insulate a bondholder's receipt of payments on its revenue bonds from the recapture provision of Section 547, if such funds are received within ninety days of the filing of the municipality's Chapter 9 petition.

Chapter 11 is the sole reorganization chapter in the new Code avail-

[9]*Id*. sec. 101(29). Defined as a ''political subdivision or public agency or instrumentality of the state.''

[10]*Id*. sec. 109(c), 901(a).

[11]*Id*. sec. 109(c)(5).

[12]*Id*. sec. 923; *see also* Rule 2002, Rules of Bankruptcy Procedure.

able to nonmunicipal corporations and represents a consolidation of Chapters VIII (which included Section 77 railroad reorganizations) through XII of the former Bankruptcy Act (except for Chapter IX which dealt with municipal reorganizations). It forms a single system for the rehabilitation of a debtor and the adjustment of all claims against the debtor and its assets, secured and unsecured, as well as equity interests. In attempting to balance more equitably the competing rights of debt holders, secured and unsecured creditors, and public holders of corporate securities, it strives to make the reorganization process itself more expeditious, less expensive, and more in line with the realities of the competing interests.

In essence, Chapter 11 affords the debtor an exclusive opportunity to file a reorganization plan during the first 120 days after the court has ordered Chapter 11 relief. However once a reorganization trustee is appointed in a Chapter 11 case, the debtor loses its exclusive right to file a plan. Any other party in interest, including an indenture trustee, may file a plan if (1) a reorganization trustee has been appointed; (2) the debtor has not filed a plan before 120 days after the date of the order for relief; or (3) the debtor has not filed a plan that has been accepted before 180 days after the order for relief. It usually happens that the court, after notice and a hearing for good cause, will extend both the 120-day and 180-day periods.

Section 1125 requires that a written disclosure statement, as approved by the court after notice and a hearing, be sent to all holders of claims or interests, together with the plan or a summary of the plan, in cases under Chapters 9 and 11. No solicitation of acceptances (or rejections) of the plan may be made until the disclosure statement is sent out to each member of each class. It is recognized, however, that different disclosure statements may be sent to different classes, the test being whether the particular class has received adequate information of a kind and in sufficient detail that a hypothetical reasonable investor typical of that class can make an informed judgment about the plan.[13]

Although the provisions relating to the confirmation of a plan are detailed and complex, in general a plan can be confirmed if each class has either accepted the plan[14] or (1) if impaired will be treated at least

[13] See Rule 3017, Rules of Bankruptcy Procedure, for court considerations of disclosure statements.

[14] The requisite majorities for acceptance by a class are at least two-thirds in amount and more than one-half in number of the allowed claims of such class that vote on the plan. (Section 1126(c).

as well under the plan as if the estate were liquidated under Chapter 7, and secured creditors receive value equal to interests in property securing their claims[15] or (2) is not impaired under the plan. The concept of "impairment" is a new statutory concept, although it does have antecedents in Chapter XII of the old Act. A class of claims or interests is deemed impaired under the Code unless the plan treats such claim or interest in a manner that provides full and complete recovery, in cash, of the creditors' claims or interest, leaves unaltered the legal, equitable, and contractual rights of the holders of the claim or interest, or restores full rights of interest in the debtor's property.[16] In effect, plan proponents may continue unaffected existing credit relationships and by doing so disenfranchise such creditors from voting on the plan. When a class does not accept the plan it may still be confirmed if it provides certain prescribed treatment for such nonaccepting classes. Generally, if the proponent requests and if all other confirmation requirements are met except that all impaired classes have not accepted the plan, the court must confirm the plan if, with respect to each nonaccepting impaired class, the plan does not discriminate unfairly and is fair and equitable to each such class. In any event, at least one nonimpaired class must accept the plan. This concept of confirmation over nonaccepting classes has been aptly dubbed "cramdown" and essentially involves satisfying the claims of dissenters in accordance with the absolute priority rule, which provides that any nonaccepting class be satisfied in full before any junior class shares under the plan. The prospect of cramdown and the desire of existing management to retain equity in the reorganized entity has an unmistakable bearing on the development of a consensus in producing a final plan of reorganization.

Some of the other significant provisions that directly relate to indenture trustees are (1) Section 364, which allows the debtor to incur unsecured debt[17] as an administrative expense without a hearing; (2) Section 364, which also permits the debtor under certain circumstances to obtain credit or debt secured by a senior or equal lien on property of the estate that is subject to a lien;[18] (3) Section 503, which provides

15 11 USC sec. 1126(c), 1129(a).

16 *Id.* sec. 1129(a). *See* sec. 1124 for specific criteria for determination of nonimpairment.

17 A court will allow such action only in extraordinary circumstances and only if the interests of the original secured creditors are protected.

18 Such postpetition debtor-in-possession (or DIP) financing is of vital importance to the debtor to enable it to stabilize its operations in the very early days following the filing of the petition for relief. A debtor may also obtain unsecured credit upon order of the court, even if not in the ordinary course of business. *Id.* section 364(b).

reasonable compensation to an indenture trustee for services rendered in making a substantial contribution in a Chapter 9 and 11 case, including actual, necessary expenses and reimbursement of its counsel's fees and expenses; (4) Section 547, which permits a debtor to avoid any transfer of property made to or for a creditor of an antecedent debt within ninety days before the filing of a petition (such preference period is extended to one year if the creditor was an ''insider'' and had reasonable cause to believe the debtor was insolvent at the time of the transfer, or the transfer was fraudulent);[19] (5) Section 548, which permits the trustee in bankruptcy to avoid fraudulent transfers by the debtor of an interest in its property, if, at the time of the transfer, there was an actual intent to hinder, delay, or defraud an entity to which the debtor was or became indebted, or if the debtor received less than reasonably equivalent value in exchange for the transfer and the debtor was or became insolvent at the time of, or as a result of, the transfer; (6) Section 552, which appears to render after-acquired property clauses in indentures automatically inoperative as of the date of commencement of the bankruptcy case;[20] and (7) Section 1102(a)(i), which directs the United States Trustee to appoint a committee of unsecured creditors as soon as practicable, it being intended that the committee oversee the debtor and the reorganization process, as distinguished from the court's involving itself in the everyday affairs of the debtor.[21]

The appointment of committee members rather than their election, in Chapter 9 and 11 proceedings differs from the former Bankruptcy Act, and is to ensure that the committees are fairly representative and not solely controlled by attorneys seeking counsel position. If a prepetition committee does not exist, the United States Trustee is required to select the seven largest unsecured creditors willing to serve. It is also recognized that because Chapter 11 can affect secured creditors and shareholders, as well as different classes of unsecured creditors, additional committees may be necessary. The appointment of such additional committees is not, however, automatic but requires a conclusion by the court, upon application, that the particular committee requested is necessary to assure adequate representation.[22] The importance of providing

[19] *Id.* sec. 547, 548.

[20] The applicability of Section 552, in the event of a municipality bankruptcy, has been curtailed by the addition of Section 928(a).

[21] Congress has established on an experimental basis a U.S. Trustee's system. The U.S. Trustees generally have responsibility for administering the cases and aiding the courts in other ways. U.S. Trustees have a fair amount of influence in bankruptcy proceedings.

[22] 11 USC, sec. 1102(a)(2).

for "official" or "statutory" committees is that the members, and the persons employed by such a committee, e.g., attorneys, accountants, financial advisors, are entitled to compensation from the estate based on time, nature, and value of their services in relation to the cost of comparable services in a nonbankruptcy case. In actual practice, it is unusual and difficult to get such a special committee appointed. Usually there will simply be a representative of debenture holders appointed to the prepetition committee along with secured and other senior creditors.

Chapter 11 does not require the appointment of a reorganization trustee but assumes the continuation of the debtor-in-possession. Any party in interest may, however, apply to the court for the appointment of such trustee to operate the business. The request will be granted if the court finds that there are reasonable grounds for the appointment, which might include allegations of fraud or mismanagement on the part of the debtor, or that it is in the best interests of the creditors or stockholders.[23] It should be noted that the appointment of a reorganization trustee automatically deprives the debtor of the exclusive right to file a plan. If such trustee is not appointed (*i.e.*, the debtor remains in possession and continues to operate the business), any party in interest may request the court to appoint an examiner, which request will be granted if it is in the interests of the creditors or if the debtor's nontrade, nontax unsecured indebtedness exceeds five million dollars.[24] The role of the examiner is to investigate the debtor with respect to any adverse allegations, such as fraud or dishonesty, the financial condition of the debtor, and any other matter relevant to the proceeding or formulation of a plan.

The Indenture Trustee and Security Holders in Reorganization Proceedings

The rights and functions of indenture trustees in connection with reorganization proceedings still have not been completely defined. Whereas they are recognized as representing the indenture security holders, such rights of representation are strictly limited. In general, any matter relating to the security lien or priority of the indenture securities requires the indenture trustee's vigilance. On the other hand, it has no power or

[23]*Id.* sec. 1104(a).
[24]*Id.* sec. 1104(b).

authority to compromise the claim of the security holders and, accordingly, the extent to which it may properly participate in the formulation or advocacy of a plan that effects such a compromise is questionable. Nevertheless, absent an actual bondholder on a creditor's committee, the public debt holder—apart from the trustee—often will have no voice in the development of the plan.

Notwithstanding the broad limitations imposed by the automatic stay on actions to enforce contractual rights and the prohibitions against contract rejection based solely on the filing of a bankruptcy petition, the filing of such petition, voluntary or involuntary, is invariably an Event of Default under most, if not all, corporate bond indentures. Upon such default, the trustee's standard of conduct with respect to its rights, duties, and obligations is thereby raised to that of a "prudent man" and, while not required to participate in statutory creditor committees, many corporate trustees of public debt, in furtherance of their duties, do serve on such committees.

The right of the indenture trustee to be heard on all matters arising during the proceedings has been specifically recognized in Chapters 9 and 11. The indenture trustee may file a petition against a debtor, may intervene in any such proceeding as a matter of right, and is entitled to receive notice of all important matters arising during the proceedings.[25] These rights are recognized by the Code and are independent of the trustee's decision to participate as a member of a creditors' committee.

The specific provisions of the Code and the TIA with respect to the rights of the indenture trustee have not enlarged its authority to represent individual security holders. They have recognized the importance of the indenture trustee as an agency for the representation of the interests of security holders as a class during the proceedings, but the importance of representation by the security holders themselves has also been recognized and emphasized.

This emphasis on the individual holder has not, however, minimized the importance of collective action by security holders through committees. The right of any creditor to be represented in a Chapter 11 proceeding by a committee is specifically recognized in Section 1102. Because of the complexity of the usual reorganization and the lack of information available to an individual holder, as well as the substantial expense involved, it is impractical for most individual holders to appear personally in the proceeding. In addition to facilitating conduct of the proceed-

25 Section 1109 and Rule 2202(f), Rules of Bankruptcy Procedure.

ings by having the various classes of creditors represented by committees rather than by a number of individuals, an objection that may be raised will be more persuasive if it is entered collectively by a large number of a particular class. A committee will also be able, as a rule, to intervene in the proceedings, a privilege that offers a much greater opportunity for participation than the general right of individual holders to be heard. If anything, the importance of collective action has now been increased by reason of the fact that acceptance of a plan by two-thirds of the creditors of any class will bind dissenters of that class. Therefore, a dissenting minority now has more at stake and should organize to protect itself. Since the activity of these committees is now subject to court supervision, security holders should be better protected in being represented by a committee. However, although the committee "represents" holders, it does not have any rights that belong to the individual creditors.

GUIDANCE AND GUIDELINES

The following are suggested as general guides to indenture trustee administration officers in connection with reorganization proceedings. The circumstances of each individual case will be controlling, but these suggestions should apply in most situations:

1. Despite imposition of the prudent man standard of conduct and an understandable inclination of the indenture trustee to protect itself by court proceedings, filing of a petition for reorganization by an indenture trustee should be the last step to be taken. Experience has demonstrated that with few exceptions such proceedings result in substantial delays and losses to indenture security holders. Every effort should be made to work out with the obligor and, to the extent possible, with a majority of the security holders, an interim arrangement whereby the business can be continued and the rights of security holders protected. Filing of a petition under the Code should be regarded as an act of desperation and resorted to only when no other means are available for protecting the inherent rights of the indenture security holders.
2. When a petition is filed by the debtor or by other creditors, the indenture trustee should file an appearance promptly so that it will receive notice of all matters presented to the court, including

the disclosure statement pursuant to which the plan solicitation occurs. The trustee should consider also, with the advice of counsel, whether and to what extent it should send periodic information updates to the bondholders. In any event, only such information as is both factual and "public" should be included in any such report.

3. The administration officer should make certain that every department of the bank is aware of the pending proceedings and is familiar with the general prohibitions against any dealing in securities represented in the proceeding by the indenture trustee.

4. One important duty the indenture trustee should perform is the filing of a proof of claim on behalf of all indenture security holders. Express authority to do so is usually included in most indentures, but the indenture trustee undoubtedly has implied authority even in the absence of such provision. Under rules in Chapter 9 and 11 reorganization cases "[e]very person . . . representing more than one creditor or equity security holder and, unless otherwise directed by the court, every indenture trustee shall file a verified statement with the clerk . . . ."[26] Such statement must include the security holders' names and addresses, a description of the claims, including the time of acquisition and facts surrounding the employment of the indenture trustee, including a description of any claims or interests owned by the indenture trustee. The statement must be amended to reflect any changes in relevant facts after the initial statement is filed. One of the sanctions for failure to comply is that the court may refuse to permit the indenture trustee being heard or from intervening in the case. The Code has replaced the Bankruptcy Act's concept of "provability of claim" with that of an "allowed claim." This basically means that, unless objected to by the debtor or a party-in-interest, the amount of the claim is allowed as filed. The trustee should keep in mind the problems created by an original issue discount, which is characterized as unmatured interest and is therefore disallowed under Section 502(b) of the Code.

5. Where the indenture is a lien on the principal fixed properties of

---

[26] *Id.* Rule 2019. The filing of the verified statement makes available to the Court and, consequently, to interested parties, the names of the debt holders. The requirement does not override the indenture requirements for obtaining bondholder lists prescribed by the TIA. Nevertheless, attempts to impound a list of creditors have been disallowed by the courts; *see* In re Itel Corp., 17 B.R. 942 (Bkrtcy. App., 9 Cir. 1982).

the obligor and grants the trustee right to income after a default, a petition should be filed promptly seeking the segregation of all income for the benefit of the indenture trustee and the security holders. This is important, for it may seriously affect the rights of the security holders under the plan when it is presented or the right of the indenture trustee to object to the disposition of accumulated income during the proceeding.

6. The reorganization trustee or debtor-in-possession may present an application for an order authorizing it to sell or dispose of specific items of property free and clear of the mortgage indenture and without seeking a release from the indenture trustee. The indenture trustee should insist that there be included in the order approving this petition a provision that the proceeds of any sale be held in escrow subject to the same liens and priorities as existed on the property disposed of and that such funds should be used only for the purpose of acquiring additional collateral. On petition for approval of individual sales under such general order, the indenture trustee should require presentation of appropriate evidence of the sufficiency of the consideration for any such sale.

7. Every petition filed in the proceedings should be examined carefully. A majority of these will deal with routine administrative matters and will require no action or statement of position by the indenture trustee. The objective should be to maintain the priority lien position of the indenture on the debtor's property until a reorganization is consummated. Any proposed action that seems to affect such a position should be examined carefully, and if it appears likely to prejudice such a position, it should be opposed vigorously.

8. The indenture trustee's primary responsibility is to the maintenance and preservation of the bondholders' security. The trustee should initiate any action that seems appropriate or necessary for the protection of the security. In particular, it should endeavor to prevent the diversion of the proceeds of sale or liquidation of any of its security to purposes not of direct benefit to security holders. Where the indenture is unsecured, it is especially important that the indenture trustee be certain that the estate is not dissipated or, if it is, that as much of it as can be recovered is recovered.

9. Any application by the reorganization trustee for authority to incur debt or to issue certificates of indebtedness should be examined carefully. These obligations will constitute a claim with

priority over any prebankruptcy obligations. If a substantial amount of postpetition indebtedness is created, the security holders' position in the reorganized company may be weakened.

10. Where a number of different lien positions are involved, as is frequently the case in railroad reorganizations, it may be necessary for the reorganization trustee to prepare segregation formulae for the allocation of earnings and expense among the various segments of the line subject to different lien priorities. Any new securities issued on reorganization must bear a direct relationship to prospective earnings, and indeed development of proper formulae for allocation of such earnings frequently being one of the most important activities during the entire proceeding. Accordingly, the indenture trustee should participate actively in all discussions and hearings relating thereto. This is a matter for experts, and in an appropriate case the indenture trustee is well-advised to employ expert assistance to support its case.

11. Whereas committees to represent security holders' interests directly are usually of great importance, the indenture trustee should not organize a committee or take an active role in such organizational efforts unless, with the advice of counsel, this is necessary or desirable under the particular circumstances.[27] If the indenture trustee is in possession of lists of security holders, these should be delivered to the reorganization trustee or filed in court, and access of individuals attempting to form committees should be to lists on file with the court. The trustee should not make such information available directly except with the approval of the court.

12. Once a committee has been organized and has intervened in the proceeding, the indenture trustee should try to work closely with it on all matters relating to protection of the security holders as a class. Where the class does not include different levels of debt the interest of the indenture trustee and the committee usually will be identical. Under the statutory provisions, the interests of the unrepresented security holders are usually the same as those represented by the committee, for all will now participate to the same extent and in the same manner under the plan finally approved. In the normal situation, therefore, no position adverse to the committee is normally necessary for protection of the minor-

[27] For case law on the problem of the indenture trustee being on a creditors' committee, see Wood v. City National Bank & Trust Co., 312 US 262 (1941). Courts have also recognized that an indenture trustee may serve on a committee in a voting capacity; see In re The Charter Company, 42 B.R. 251 (Bkrtcy, M.D. Fla. 1984).

ity. The indenture trustee should always bear in mind, however, that it represents *all* the security holders. While cooperating with a committee in every way possible (including serving as a member of the committee), the indenture trustee should never surrender its position of independence or prejudice its right to take a contrary stand. This is particularly true where the principal holders represented by a committee are interested in issues other than the indenture securities. It must be mindful also of the potential conflicting interests between the professional bargain hunters who acquire the securities at severely reduced prices, and those investors who were prebankruptcy debtholders.

13. The indenture trustee should take an active interest in all matters relating to preparation and adoption of a plan, including a careful review of the disclosure statement. Appropriate objections should be made if the indenture trustee believes the statement is inaccurate, incomplete, or inadequate for the class of creditors it represents. Many trustees, conscious of their lack of authority to compromise the claims of security holders, have taken the position that negotiations on a plan are a matter for the security holders and their committees and that the indenture trustee should play a passive role. Such an attitude is shortsighted and unrealistic. It is true that indenture trustees cannot make a commitment binding on their security holders, nor can anyone else. This is a matter for individual holders who must be given the right to express their approval or disapproval by vote once a plan is disseminated for acceptance. The indenture trustee has no right to vote on a plan, but it should feel free to participate to the same extent as other parties, including committees, in all discussions leading to agreement on a plan. Participation will not foreclose its right to object to confirmation of a plan that appears to it unfair or inequitable or that its security holders subsequently reject. Under normal circumstances, the indenture trustee should not itself endeavor to prepare and file a plan. The only authority for it to do so is contained in Section 1121 of Chapter 11, which refers to situations when a reorganization trustee is appointed or when the debtor does not file a plan and obtain acceptances within specified time limits.

14. The indenture trustee should insist that the final order of the court directing and providing for consummation of the plan contain a specific discharge of the indenture and it. If this is done, the canceled indenture securities may be properly disposed of by the distribution or exchange agent appointed by the court without

being returned to the indenture trustee for cancellation and discharge. Unless this is done, the indenture trustee may find itself called upon to perform a great deal of unnecessary, detailed work for which it will receive no compensation.

15. The Code specifically authorizes the court, in directing consummation of a plan under Chapters 9 and 11, to set a period of time during which all claimants must present their securities or claims for exchange. At the expiration of this period the estate is closed and all claims for unexchanged securities become void. Any property left in the hands of the exchange agent reverts to the debtor or to the entity acquiring the debtor's assets under the plan.[28] This is an important provision and is usually contained in all final orders of the reorganization proceedings. Failure to so provide may mean that an estate may never be closed.

16. Where a debtor has been through a previous reorganization without provision for a final termination of an estate, a current proceeding provides an opportunity to secure an appropriate order and dispose of remaining property that may be held for exchange for old securities still outstanding from the previous reorganization. At the time of entry of the final order in the current proceeding, an effort should be made to secure court authority for terminating remaining matters in all previous proceedings.

17. Where the proceeding is in Chapter 7 (Liquidation) rather than reorganization, an order setting a limited period within which claimants must present their securities to receive their distributive share of the proceeds should also be obtained. Because in this situation there is no reorganized company to receive the balance of proceeds, a procedure that has been used successfully is to provide for a second *pro rata* distribution among holders who, during the period provided, did present their claims and receive the initial distribution. This enables the indenture trustee to close the estate within a reasonable period of time and is the most equitable disposition that could be made of the remaining funds. It is essential, however, that such a method of distribution be incorporated in the initial order for distribution. In one case where this was attempted by a subsequent order, a state successfully intervened and claimed a vested interest in the remaining funds under an abandoned property law. Where provision is contained in the initial order for complete distribution of all proceeds, no such rights can vest in the state.

28 11 USC sec. 347(b).

COMPENSATION AND RECOVERY OF EXPENSES

Almost every indenture contains provisions giving the trustee a contractual right to seek payment of its fees and recovery of its expenses from the obligor. Even where the obligor is in a bankruptcy proceeding, there has been express recognition of this contractual entitlement.[29] Thus, the trustee should always file a proof of claim for its prepetition fees and expenses and also for any contractually based fees and expenses which are incurred postpetition. Such claim, when settled, would receive consideration at the same level as any other unsecured creditor. However, given the uncertainties of a recovery, the trustee should also pursue a claim under Section 503 of the Bankruptcy Code. This section allows a court to reimburse the indenture trustee for the actual and necessary *expenses* incurred in making a substantial contribution to a Chapter 9 or Chapter 11 case,[30] and to pay the trustee "reasonable *compensation* for services rendered by [it] in making a substantial contribution in a case under chapter 9 or chapter 11 of this title, based on the time, the nature, the extent and the value of such services, and the cost of comparable services other than in a case under this title. . . ."[31]

Unfortunately, indenture trustees have not fared well in recovering either their fees or their expenses (which are primarily counsel fees). The award of fees and reimbursement of expenses under Section 503(b) is deemed to be an administrative expense of the bankruptcy proceeding, and as such is given a priority status. Because payment of these expenses will reduce the amount available to creditors and claimants, the section has been construed very strictly and narrowly by the courts. Most troublesome of all the cases denying recovery to indenture trustees is an Eighth Circuit Court of Appeals decision which held that the indenture trustee by merely performing its duties to its bondholders, even in a satisfactory manner, pursuant to its obligation to act as a "prudent man" was not, as a matter of law, entitled to compensation or recovery of expenses.[32] The court also concluded that the "bankruptcy estate should not have to pay for services which primarily benefit the debenture holders and only incidentally benefit the bankruptcy estate".[33] This decision places the trustee in a most difficult (some argue

[29]*In re Flight Transportation Corporation Securities Litigation*, 874 F.2d 576, 583 (8th Cir. 1989); *In re Revere Copper & Brass Incorporated*, et al., 60 B.R. 892 (S.D.N.Y. 1986).
[30]11 USC sec. 503(b)(3)(D).
[31]*Id.*, sec. 503(b)(5), emphasis added.
[32]*In re Fight Transportation Corporation, supra*, note 29, at 581.
[33]*Id.* at 591.

"impossible") position. It must, as a matter of law under the TIA, actively discharge its obligation under the indenture as an advocate for its bondholders even if it means that other creditors might receive less in any reorganization, but if it does so perform, the bankruptcy court will likely deny its claim for fees and expenses. It is also quite evident that the indenture trustee must do a great deal more than simply file a claim on behalf of its bondholders and otherwise perform in a perfunctory manner. Presumably, if the trustee can show (i.e., prove) that its services provided a direct, significant, and demonstrable benefit to the entire estate, were not of a routine nature, and were not duplicative of services rendered by other parties in the proceeding, it would stand a much better chance of receiving payment of its fees and reimbursement of its expenses.

Existing cases do not provide a definitive answer to this problem, nor do they even articulate an understanding of precisely what the nature and extent of the trustee's performance must be in order to recover from the bankrupt estate. The SEC, however, has articulated a formulation of what it believes should be the appropriate legal standard, stating: ". . . the Commission urges that an indenture trustee be entitled to compensation as an administrative expense pursuant to the substantial contribution test of Section 503(b) if its satisfies the following test:

(1) the indenture trustee has, through its representation of the interests of bondholders, made demonstrable efforts towards furthering the reorganization process; and

(2) the indenture trustee's services or those of its counsel do not duplicate the services of official participants or other indenture trustees."[34]

As a last resort, the trustee can attempt to recover under its lien against any distributions under an approved plan prior to distribution to the bondholders. It must be understood, however, that the parties in interest may be authorized to review the proposed deduction for reasonableness. Since the amount of the proposed deduction may be material to the bondholders' decision to accept or reject the proposed reorganization plan, it behooves the trustee to include a description in the disclosure statement of its plans for obtaining compensation from the bondholders' distribution. This will avoid the very real possibility that after confirmation of the plan, the bondholders will be unpleasantly surprised by the indenture trustee's action. As long as any cash distributions exceed the trustee's claim for compensation, a dollar-for-dollar

[34] Brief of the SEC, *In re Baldwin-United Corporation,* Case No. C–1–88–0056 (S.D. Ohio 1988), appeal settled and dismissed, BR Case No. 1–89–02495 (S.D. Ohio 1989).

deduction will be easy to implement, if the court approves. However, where the available cash is insufficient and the distribution consists of new debt and/or equity securities, the trustee may be in the rather unpleasant position of having to initiate a procedure before the court to value the noncash consideration received and to determine the appropriate deduction to be made. Given the additional potential for dispute with bondholders over valuation, it is unlikely that most trustees would pursue this route.

FOURTEEN

Specialized Trusts and Agency Appointments

In the preceding chapters, we considered the more important duties and responsibilities of trustees under the customary indenture and private placement contract. Even these vary, however, because of differences in types of financing, the nature of the security, particular indenture provisions, and other factors. In general, these differences constitute matters of detail rather than a change in basic function or responsibility.

From time to time, a bank performing the corporate trust function is called upon to serve in a somewhat different or more limited capacity. Six of the more significant of these trusts and/or agency appointments are discussed below.

MUNICIPAL TRUSTS/REVENUE BONDS

During the past decade a major portion of all tax-exempt financing has been in the form of revenue bond issues. In such instances, it has become customary to appoint a bank as trustee pursuant to a bond resolution of a municipal development authority. Three of the more common types have been for the construction of hospitals, educational facilities (including dormitories), and housing units. In addition, issues of industrial revenue bonds have been used for a myriad of purposes under legislation permitting the use of the tax-exempt bonds to build or modernize plant facilities of private corporations.

As with any document related to the particular financing, the trustee should carefully examine, in conjunction with its counsel, the relevant bond resolution, feasibility study (if one has been prepared), the preliminary official statement, the opinion of bond counsel, and the bond purchase agreement.

In addition to the trustee appointment, the particular bank is appointed as paying agent. As the result of TEFRA,[1] the appointment as registrar, as well, to provide the traditional registration of transfer services becomes of paramount importance. This appointment also involves the accounting for and destruction of canceled certificates.

The traditional long-term, fixed rate, semiannual interest payment transaction consisting of serial maturities and term bonds, once referred to as a "plain vanilla deal," gradually changed shape during the 1980s. Soon after trustees and paying agents managed to enhance system capabilities to service the addition of capital accumulator or zero coupon bonds to financing structures, fixed rate transactions rapidly became a vehicle of the past and variable rate securities with demand features grew in popularity. With the enactment of the Tax Reform Act of 1986 (86 Act),[2] severe restrictions were placed on municipal debt, including (among other things): restrictions on the amount of tax-exempt debt that any tax-exempt organization[3] can have outstanding at any given time; the institution of state volume caps for private activity bonds; requirements for issuers to perform complex arbitrage rebate calculations; and restrictions on the percentage of gross proceeds allowed to be applied to the costs of issuance.

As the industry approached the decade of the 1990s, municipal revenue bonds began to closely resemble securities generally associated with the corporate sector. Multi-modal, variable rate, variable term, variable interest and principal payment instruments (similar to commercial paper), and medium term notes, and even taxable municipals emerged.

Municipal Pool Financing

The basic objective of any borrowing entity is to raise funds at the lowest possible cost. Three key factors in achieving this objective for issuers of debt securities are: to obtain the most favorable interest rate possible, to structure the financing to appeal to a wide market, and to

---

[1] See note 6, chapter 2, *supra*.

[2] Pub. Law 99–514 (1986).

[3] See Internal Revenue Code, sec. 501(c)(3) for specific types of organizations.

limit the costs associated with the actual issuance of the securities. One mechanism for lowering the cost of borrowing is for entities to apply for a loan from a state, county, or city tax-exempt bond issuing authority, such as a state bond bank—each authority determining its eligibility rules. The proceeds from the sale of bonds by the issuing authority are loaned to the entity at a more favorable tax-exempt rate than if it had borrowed in its own name. Loan repayments as provided for in the loan agreement between the issuer and the borrowing entity are deposited in a bond fund established in accordance with the trust indenture and used to pay the debt service on the bonds.

Smaller entities making application to the issuing authority could be at somewhat of a disadvantage. The interest rate may not be as favorable as a larger entity could obtain and the cost of issuance charges could at times actually be prohibitive. Additionally, market interest in purchasing the securities could be relatively limited. A financial structure designed to address the needs of both the smaller and larger eligible borrowing entities is the loan pool vehicle. Proceeds from the same pool of bonds are loaned to multiple similar entities having comparable financing needs, such as a group of hospitals or school districts desiring to finance capital improvements. Each entity, having first been approved for a loan by the authority, then draws (borrows) against the pool of funds. The costs of issuance are therefore distributed pro rata among the borrowing entities and a more favorable rate is generally obtained.

The 86 Act eliminated what were referred to as "blind pools." In many cases, a large percentage of the proceeds from the pool bond issuance was not loaned, resulting in early calls for redemption of the bonds and arbitrage on the bond proceeds. Under the new regulations the issuing authority must have a reasonable expectation that a major percentage of the proceeds will be expended (loaned) within a specific time frame. Consequently, the issuing authority must obtain firm commitments from the entities wishing to borrow funds from a specific pool before the bonds may be issued.

Pool financing transactions place additional accounting and record-keeping responsibilities on the trustee. In addition to the normal accounting functions involving the custody of collateral and the maintenance of funds established in accordance with the indenture, the trustee also must provide a loan administration and accounting function. Each borrowing entity's loan must be administered and accounted for separately. The loan repayments are collected from each entity and the aggregate funds are then transferred to the appropriate debt service accounts.

Anticipation Notes

In chapter 1, the problems corporations encounter in financing the short-term working capital needs of corporations were discussed. Municipalities face similar challenges. Although operating expenses must be paid throughout the year, major income items such as property taxes are often collected at stated intervals during the year. Through the issuance of tax anticipation notes (TANs) and other revenue anticipation notes, the municipality is able to finance working capital during periods of cash flow shortage. Generally, if the anticipation note is not outstanding for more than thirteen months and the principal amount of obligations issued is less than the anticipated maximum cumulative cash flow deficit,[4] the issuer is permitted all the proceeds at an unrestricted yield.

Anticipation notes are issued in accordance with a resolution generally requiring the services of a paying agent, since a trustee appointment is not normally utilized. As discussed later, the benefit of pool financing combined with unrestricted yield from the investment of the proceeds of anticipation notes, among other things, have resulted in programs that may require the services of an indenture trustee.

Master Trustee

Another mechanism for pooling like entities together for the purpose of borrowing to meet capital needs is through the formation of an obligated group. There is no requirement that the members of such a group be affiliated entities; however, for practical reasons this is virtually always the case. Health institutions with multiple facilities are the predominant users of this type of structure. Individual entities become members of the group (i.e., obligated issuers) by executing a note issued in accordance with a master trust indenture. By executing the note, each obligated issuer agrees that it will duly and punctually pay the principal and the interest in accordance with its terms. Additionally, each obligated issuer jointly and severally guarantees and promises to pay any and all amounts payable under any note issued in accordance with the master trust indenture.

---

[4] Maximum cumulative cash flow deficit is defined as the sum of: (1) the amount the issuer will expend, from the beginning of the period to the computation date, that would ordinarily be paid out of or financed by anticipated tax or other revenues, plus (2) the amount of the anticipated expenditures for a period of one month after the computation date, minus (3) the sum of the amounts (other than the proceeds of the issue in question) that will be available for the payment of such expenditures during such period.

The master trustee is responsible for performing the note registrar function, enforcing the covenants of the master indenture, and, in some instances, collecting the principal and interest payments on the notes. Master notes are frequently issued in conjunction with one or more revenue bond transactions. The master notes are then registered to the issuer of the revenue bonds in the same aggregate principal amount as the bonds issued under the indenture. All the right, title, and interest of the issuer in the master notes is then placed and assigned by the issuer to the bond trustee. If there is more than one related revenue bond financing, the same procedure applies to each of the issuers and bond trustees. The payments by the obligated issuers in accordance with the provisions of the master note are then made directly to the bond trustee or trustees to provide for debt service. Because the master trustee must take prompt action in the event of default, it is of utmost importance that it establish procedures with the related bond trustees to ensure that it receives prompt notification of a default on any note payment. Because a potential for conflict exists between the role of the bond trustee and the master indenture trustee, the same entity generally should not act in both capacities.

Advance Funding Program Notes

Tax-exempt issuing authorities also pool similar borrowing entities through the issuance of advance funding program notes. The proceeds from the sale of the program notes are advanced to participating entities to resolve cash flow deficiencies in the current fiscal year. Entities participating in the program issue TANs that are purchased by the issuer. Each participating entity pledges to the issuing authority a security interest in all revenues derived by it from taxes and other revenues, by executing an advance refunding agreement. The program notes issued through the authority must comply with the anticipation note regulations (referred to previously) in order for the proceeds to be treated as invested during a temporary period in accordance with the Internal Revenue Code.[5] The repayments by the participating entities of the tax and revenue anticipation notes plus the interest earnings on any funds held in accordance with the trust indenture are transferred to the debt service fund to provide for the payment of the principal and interest on the program notes as such becomes due.

As with other types of pooled arrangements, the trustee may be

[5] Sec. 1.103–14(c).

required to perform loan administration and loan accounting functions in addition to its normal duties as indenture trustee, registrar, and paying agent.

VARIABLE RATE SECURITIES

Since the early 1980s, various forms of this type of security have been popular investment vehicles in the tax-exempt market. The earliest issues paid an interest rate based on a percentage of an agreed upon index, often a particular bank's prime lending rate. These issues were typically private placements that rarely were sold or bought in the open market.

The next development involved bonds that allowed bondholders to tender their bonds back to the issuer at par through a "put" or "demand." The benefit to the issuer was that it only had to pay a short term interest rate (largely based on the time period between tenders) instead of the usual long term rate based on the maturity of the bonds. The spread between the short term variable rate and the long term fixed rate results in a saving to the issuer, which is somewhat offset by the fees of the various agents required to run the program. It is axiomatic that the greater the spread between short term and long term rates in the credit markets, the more likely is the issuance of variable rate issues.

Involved in the processing of this investment vehicle can be a "re-marketing agent," a "liquidity facility" provider, and a "tender agent." The remarketing agent, usually an investment bank, is responsible for setting new interest rates, for remarketing or reselling any bonds that are tendered, and for giving the new registration information and remarketing proceeds to the tender agent. Except in unusual circumstances, they are almost always successful in selling the tendered bonds to new buyers.

The liquidity facility can be provided in various forms, including letters of credit("L/C"), insurance, or standby purchase agreements. Letters of credit are by far the most popular method of providing liquidity. Letter of credit banks in effect "guarantee" that in the case of the failure to remarket these bonds by the remarketing agent, the L/C bank will step in and purchase the bonds. This "guarantee" of liquidity on a tendered bond helps to keep the interest rate low. It should be noted that the rating of the bonds is therefore usually the same as the rating of the liquidity facility provider and the "guarantee" is only as strong as the ability of the liquidity facility provider to make payments if called upon to do so.

The other important agent is the tender agent. The tender agent receives notices of tender from bondholders, notifies the remarketing agent, liquidity facility provider, issuer and trustee of receipt of the notice and the bonds being tendered, pays the tendering holders with the appropriate funds, and in a co-registrar capacity, reissues new securities to the new purchaser. On some issues, the tender agent functions are performed by the bond trustee. Tender bonds are generally viewed to be one of two types. The first is a "put" bond, where the bondholder can tender bonds only during certain preset times, usually between fifteen to thirty days prior to the payment date. Semiannual and annual tender bonds are the most common examples, but in some issues, only in designated multiple years is the "put" option permitted to operate.

The other type of tender bond is the "demand" bond, whereby the bondholder can demand payment at any time upon giving proper notice. These are often called Variable Rate Demand Bonds (VRDBs), of which weekly demand bonds are the most popular. Others include daily and monthly demand bonds. A weekly VRDB is structured with an interest rate that is reset each week by the remarketing agent at a rate that will allow the bonds to be remarketed at par. This ability to reset the rate helps the remarketing agent resell bonds that are tendered.

"Commercial paper mode" bonds are a hybrid of the two types of tender bonds. During their existence in a commercial paper mode, bonds can be issued with maturities ranging anywhere from 1 to 270 days, as in regular commercial paper programs. The major difference is that these bonds are registered instead of being in bearer form. An issuer benefits with commercial paper mode bonds by gaining the flexibility to use shorter or longer mandatory "tender" dates. These dates would be determined during remarketings based on buyer demand and current or anticipated changes in the interest rate. An interesting feature of most variable rate bonds is the ability to convert from one rate mode to another. For example, a weekly mode bond can be converted to a fixed rate mode or a daily rate mode. Some issues allow for only a single conversion, to a fixed rate, but most provide the flexibility to change into any one of a myriad of modes. This change in modes is accomplished through a mandatory tender. When a bond issue is set up so there may be portions of the issue in different modes at the same time, the issue is designated a "multi-modal" structure instrument.

A typical tender by a holder occurs as follows. Bondholders, having chosen to tender their bonds, give the tender agent or trustee a notice or demand stating their irrevocable intention to tender a specific principal amount of bonds for settlement on a specific date. This notice usually includes the numbers of the bonds being tendered. The tender agent or the trustee then notifies the remarketing agent, liquidity facility provider and the issuer of the receipt of the notice. At this point, the remarketing agent looks for a new buyer of the bonds. If successful in selling the bonds, the proceeds are forwarded to the tender agent or trustee to pay the tendering holder upon presentation of the bonds. In the case of an unsuccessful remarketing, the tender agent or trustee will draw upon the liquidity facility provider to pay for the tendered bonds. New bonds are then registered in the new buyer's or the liquidity facility provider's name, whichever is appropriate.

ASSET-BACKED SECURITIES TRUSTS

Asset-backed securities, a term generally used to describe debt issues secured by assets other than those securing the traditional mortgage bond issue, have become a major factor in the capital markets during the past several years. The relative newness and complexities of this type of financing and the additional duties and responsibilities required of the trustee should be completely understood prior to accepting the trusteeship of any type of asset-backed bond issue.

While such issues that are sold publicly are required to be registered under the 33 Act, and are subject to the disclosure and reporting requirements of the 33 and 34 Acts, the structure of the particular issue will determine whether the TIA is applicable. If the underlying assets which are being securitized (typically, pools of mortgages or receivables) are sold to a trust, the debt securities issued by the trust constitute an undivided interest in the trust and are exempt from the provisions of the TIA.[6] With this type of structure, where the trust is the issuer, a bank will be appointed as trustee under a Pooling and Servicing Agreement,[7] such agreement not being considered to be an "indenture," even though many of the standard provisions of corporate indentures are included.

[6]The SEC has taken the position that such trust certificates are deemed to be equity securities, thus being exempt under TIA sec. 304(a)(1).

[7]A Pooling and Servicing Agreement will be executed by the seller (i.e., the entity selling the mortgage or receivables pool to the trust), the servicer or master servicer, and the bank as trustee.

The pooling of mortgage loans by the Government National Mortgage Association (GNMA or "Ginnie Mae") in 1970 was the earliest use of the securitization of a pool of assets and the issuance of securities backed by that pool. Securitization is simply the process under which pools of individual loans or receivables are packaged, underwritten, and sold to investors in the form of negotiable securities. The theory behind this financing technique is simply that the cash flows (which are generally predictable) from the underlying assets are used to pay the interest and principal on the securities. Until 1985, almost all the asset-backed issues were basically mortgage-backed securities issued by GNMA, FNMA, and the FHLMC. Thereafter the market expanded rapidly as a myriad of diverse asset pools were securitized. While principally utilizing automobile loans and credit card receivables, other issues were backed by computer leases, loans against insurance policies (i.e., "death-backed bonds"), loans supporting employee stock option plans, home equity loans, hospital receivables, and even high- yield debt securities!

Description and Structure

The basic rationale behind this type of financing vehicle is that the issuer, sometimes referred to as the "seller" (primarily banks, finance companies, and insurance companies) can positively affect its balance sheet by reducing its assets, which are securitized, with the resultant reduction in the need for and cost of capital to support those assets. Second, asset-backed securities can usually be funded at a lower cost, as they are typically structured to receive at least a "AA" bond rating; thus the issuer is able to borrow at lower cost than if it borrowed on its own credit.

Generally, investment bankers will identify the specific assets to be pooled, with two primary criteria. First, they must be homogeneous in order to facilitate structuring so that the cash flows are smooth and generally follow projections. Second, collateral will be selected that spreads the risk by limiting geographic—or, in the case of high-yield debt, industry—concentrations, so that a particular area is not overly represented. Spreading the risk of default linked with an economic downturn in a particular industry or geographic region enables the asset pool to better absorb payment defaults, thereby reducing risk to the bondholders. The selection of assets alone is not enough to obtain a high rating, so other forms of credit enhancements may also be used. These credit enhancements may come in the form of the issue structure itself, e.g., a senior/subordinate structure, over-collateralization and reserve accounts; or a third-party enhancement in the form of a letter of credit or some form of bond insurance.

Investors find asset-backed securities attractive because of the high ratings and the "bankruptcy remote" nature of the securities, which results from the absolute separation of the claims of the bondholders against the assets from the credit of the originator of the assets backing the bonds. The creation of an "issuer" of the asset-backed security is the mechanism that accomplishes this result. The issuers are usually special purpose vehicles that are created especially for the purpose of issuing the securities. An essential part of initiating this type of transaction is the sale of the assets to the special purpose entity. Such special purpose entity can take the form of a corporation, a partnership, or a trust created to hold the assets on behalf of the beneficial owners of the asset-backed securities. If a grantor trust is utilized, the owners of the asset-backed securities are also the owners of undivided interests in the asset pool. Such trusts are usually issued in pass-through form. If an owner trust form is used, the trust itself owns the assets and issues the more traditional type of debt securities that are simply collateralized by the assets. By the use of a special purpose vehicle, the cash flows can continue to service the securities even if the originator of the transaction files for bankruptcy.

Asset-backed securities issues have been marketed in a variety of forms, the primary ones being: pass-throughs, in which the payments on the underlying assets go directly through to the bondholders; pay-throughs, where the payments on the underlying assets are the basis for the cash flows supporting the debt service on the outstanding bonds, such flows being capable of being structured to meet investor needs; and collateralized debt obligations, where the debt of the issuer is collateralized by the assets directly, but the payments received on those assets are not dedicated to the payments on the bonds.

Most asset-backed transactions require a servicer. The servicer is basically responsible for tracking and collecting the payments due on the assets, for making the tax and mortgage payments on the mortgaged property, and for taking necessary collection measures against the borrowers who fail to make payments on time. The servicer is also responsible for forwarding reports documenting the performance of the assets to the trustee. The servicer's responsibilities may or may not include calculating the payment to be made to the bondholders.

In those transactions where more than one servicer is appointed there will also be a master servicer, whose role is to aggregate the information received from the subservicers and forward it to the trustee.

The Trustee's Role

Because there is limited recourse to an issuer for asset-backed securities, the trustee's role becomes more crucial than that in a traditional form of debt financing. For the same reason that the issue is "bankruptcy remote," it could also be considered to be "issuer remote." Once the bonds are sold, there are few entities that remain connected to the transaction, which necessitates that the trustee assume responsibilities normally reserved to the issuer. While the trustee normally has little discretionary power and limited authority, trustees for asset-backed securities are frequently called upon to make decisions involving the collateral,[8] to assume expanded responsibilities, and to advise, hire, and fire other parties to the transaction. For these reasons the account officer and administrator must clearly understand all the details of the particular transaction, including the cash flows and the collateral involved. It is essential that the documents associated with the financing, including the trust indenture and the pooling and servicing agreement, be carefully studied so as to identify any nontraditional functions the trustee may be asked to perform.

When reviewing the documents, the account officer should prepare a "flow diagram" of the transaction to determine whether the required reports and cash flows will work operationally. For example, if the trustee is required to receive master servicer reports on the 18th of the month, but subservicers are not required to report to the master servicer until the 17th of the month, the parties will experience difficulties meeting debt service payment deadlines. All duties must be clearly identified, and there must be complete understanding as to which entity is responsible for each duty's specific performance. If this is not done before the financing is effected, it is likely that the task will devolve upon the trustee, without its having an opportunity to renegotiate either the mechanics or its fees.

The account officer must also carefully review the reporting requirements and sample formats in the agreements. Underwriters usually

---

[8] While the underlying documents usually indicate that the trustee is to work with the servicer and may rely on its recommendations, the trustee is nevertheless under a duty to independently exercise its discretion, especially when requested to release its lien on property that has not been paid in full.

require extensive reporting to the the trustee—it being essential that the trustee receive sufficient and accurate information to enable it to perform the necessary calculation of payments to the bondholders, or prepare other required reports.

One of the most critical responsibilities of the trustee in this type of financing is the tracking and monitoring of the servicer's activities, as asset-backed financing will work only to the extent that the servicer performs in a timely, accurate, and conscientious manner. For this reason, the servicers are often considered potentially the weakest link in the chain. In order to ensure that there is no interruption in servicing the underlying collateral if the designated servicer fails to perform or defaults, the trustee is normally appointed as the back-up servicer. Although investment banks and rating agencies perform due diligence reviews of the servicer, the trustee should also review the servicer against its own criteria prior to acceptance of the appointment.

While most corporate trust organizations will perform some sort of "credit review" prior to accepting a new trustee appointment, for asset-backed transactions the servicer should be reviewed as to the likelihood that it will be able to adequately and effectively perform its responsibilities over the term of the financing. Any such review should include a review of the servicer's management and information systems, as well as gathering statistical information, including delinquency ratios, which can then be compared to other servicers in the same industry. The rating agencies and investment bankers tend to focus on the ability of the servicer to service the assets. More critical to the trustee, and often overlooked by the other parties, however, is the servicer's ability to translate the servicing activity to meaningful data for investor reporting. An otherwise excellent servicer may prove to be a significant threat to the viability of an issue if it does not completely understand the issue structure or if its systems cannot generate required reports without significant enhancements.

Once the issue is closed the trustee must continue to monitor the servicer's performance by reviewing its reports and ensuring that the indenture covenants are met. As in the traditional indenture, all specified Events of Default and remedies must be carefully defined and described. In particular, the trustee should ensure that if the servicer's parent organization is placed in conservatorship, or its debt is downgraded, or if the servicer is put up for sale, the trustee must be in a position to know exactly what action it can take and what information it can and should disclose to the bondholders and the investor community.

Agency Functions

The usual appointments associated with asset-backed transactions include registrar and paying agent as well as collateral agent/custodian. They may also include responsibilities for bondholder payment calculations and for the preparation and filing of certain tax returns.

Asset-backed securities, such as federal agency–backed collateralized mortgage obligations (CMOs), mortgage pass-through obligations, and automobile and boat loan receivables, are backed by the same pool of assets over the life of the securities. Transactions backed by short-term assets, including credit card receivables, continuously pledge new assets to the pool as other assets are paid down. In both cases the trustee must periodically review the UCC financing statements or other appropriate documentation to ensure that the trust maintains its perfected security interest in the collateral.

In the case of home mortgages, government obligations (e.g., Sallie Mae's), high-yield debt securities, and boat loans, the trustee may be asked to physically hold the securities or loan documents, and to perform a due diligence review of the securities and the loan documents.

On or before the closing of a loan-backed transaction, the trustee or custodian may receive the loan documents which are pledged to the trust. The trustee must compare each loan file to the underwriter's listing and verify that all files have been received. Each individual file must be reviewed to verify that all required documentation is in the file; such documents usually include a mortgage note, mortgage, assignment of the mortgage to the trust, and title or other insurance policies.

After the due diligence is completed, the custodian must identify all discrepancies and work with all interested parties to "cure" the problems. There are typically specific time frames during which this activity must be performed, at the end of which loans having incomplete or incorrect documentation must be replaced or repurchased by the seller. The loan document files are then deposited in the trustee/custodian's vault, with the trustee continuing to work with the servicer to answer any questions that may arise, and to take any necessary actions.

Over the life of the bond issue, it can be expected that such actions will include responding to requests for mortgage assumptions, reamortizations, proofs of claim, satisfactions, easements, and other legal matters. The trustee must examine each request in the context of the relevant agreement, consult with counsel as required, and take appropriate action. In addition, where the trustee is physically holding securities as collateral, it will be responsible for collecting payments and for processing substitutions of collateral.

The assets in these transactions normally generate significant amounts of cash that must be deposited in a collection account held by the servicer or collection agent and properly invested. Payments received from assets such as automobile and boat loans, credit card receivables, and mortgages are paid directly to the servicer which will forward them, in accordance with the financing agreements, to the collection agent responsible for reconciling the cash actually received to the amount expected to be received. It is also the collection agent's responsibility to ensure that funds received between specific designated cut-off dates are properly earmarked for the correct payment date.

Very often the collection agent's credit rating will be considered in determining whether it is eligible to hold a collection account. The trustee must be diligent in monitoring the credit rating and take any required action (including replacing the collection agent) should its credit rating fall to an unacceptable level.

The trustee may also be asked to perform extensive calculations to determine the amount to be paid to the bondholders, based on the data furnished by the servicer. If this is the case, the trustee must ensure that the documents clearly delineate its responsibilities, that the data will be sent to it in a timely fashion and in a usable format, that the calculations are clearly defined, and that the appropriate level of expertise exists in its own organization to develop the necessary financial calculations.

One of the most significant problems in performing these calculations is accurately determining that portion of the periodic payment which represents repayment of a portion of the principal and payment of interest on the bond. Typically, these securities pay principal down during the life of the issue. Principal is paid based on a factor, which is a percentage applied to the original principal amount. The remaining principal amount is reported in terms of a factor, which when multiplied against the original face amount of the bond will reflect the current outstanding amount. There is usually little risk of a call on asset-backed securities; the only one that commonly happens is known as a "clean-up call." This will occur when 90 percent or more of the principal amount has been paid down, i.e., the factor on the issue has fallen to .1 or less. In addition to the usual Form 1099 tax reports, trustees may be required to perform REMIC[9] tax reporting, the latter involving the

[9]Real Estate Mortgage Investment Conduit, as provided for in the Tax Reform Act of 1986.

preparation and filing with the IRS of the trust's initial information return as well as its quarterly and yearly tax returns.

The trusteeship of an asset-backed security financing represents a complex appointment to administer, one that entails significantly greater risk and a higher level of liability than almost every other debt trusteeship. Over the past few years, the trustee's role has broadened considerably, requiring judgment calls and decisions that trustees, in general, have not had to make in the past for the more traditional corporate and municipal debt financing transactions. With the level and volume of new issuances expected to grow significantly over the next several years, compared to the level of unsecured debt financings, the competition (including pricing) among trustees for these appointments will undoubtedly increase. It is hoped that trustees will not permit any erosion in the level of controls or timely resolution of accounting differences to occur.

EQUIPMENT TRUSTS

A special form of contract has been developed for the financing of the purchase of equipment by railroads and, since 1970, for the financing of aircraft by the major airlines.

The basic concept of the equipment trust is ownership of the equipment by the trustee during the life of the loan. The obligations are in the form of equipment trust certificates, executed by the trustee, which represent a *pro rata* interest in the rentals and other proceeds received by the trustee through lease of the equipment to the user corporation. The proceeds received from sale of the certificates are used to purchase the equipment, and a lease thereof is executed by the trustee to the user corporation. This is a net lease calling for payments of rental over an eight- to fifteen-year period sufficient to pay all interest and principal on the certificates. In the case of railroads, the certificates mature serially and the obligations are retired more rapidly than normal depreciation on the equipment. Because the corporation (or as more recently seen, an institutional investor) provides equity in an amount equal to 20 to 30 percent of the purchase price of the equipment, and because most of such equipment is considered salable, these obligations command a ready market and usually a better price than the credit of many railroads or airlines alone would warrant.

In addition to its obligation to make the rental payments under the lease, the user corporation executes a guaranty on each certificate that runs directly to the certificate holder.

Normally, administration of these trusts is somewhat easier than the average trust indenture, although the initial documentation tends to be much more complex and very special problems are created if a default or equipment loss occurs under the lease.

CONSTRUCTION AND BOND FUND TRUSTS

Although occasionally an indenture requires administration of a construction fund in connection with a new bond issue as part of the other duties of the trustee, the type of trust considered here is somewhat unique. It may occur in connection with a revenue bond issue of a state or municipality or a public or quasi-public body created for a special purpose. Power districts, sewer districts, turnpike commissions, and similar entities are typical examples. Inasmuch as the security for the bonds issued consists of the revenue to be derived from the project to be constructed, the bond proceeds are required to be segregated and held in trust solely to pay the construction costs of the project.

The function of the construction fund trustee is to hold such proceeds, make investment thereof in such manner as to provide the greatest return consistent with the requirement for paying them out over a predetermined period, and disburse the funds and the income thereon for the construction cost of the project. Disbursement is made against certifications by the project engineers of actual expenditures made or obligations incurred for construction purposes. Although the trustee is entitled to rely on these certifications, it should check them in sufficient detail to satisfy itself that the expenditures listed are of the type properly chargeable against the construction monies. In addition, the trustee should ensure that the types of investments are those specifically authorized by the indenture or bond resolution. As a practical matter it is desirable to limit these to obligations of the United States or its agencies or to certificates of deposit in prime money center banks.

One very important consideration in establishing a construction fund is to provide for a revolving fund in a sufficient amount to take care of ordinary day-to-day disbursements for a reasonable period of time. This permits all miscellaneous disbursements to be included in one certificate at monthly or other periodic intervals, at which time the revolving fund is replenished.

Once the project has been completed and an appropriate certificate to this effect received, the duties of the construction fund trustee are finished. Any disbursed funds are usually turned over to the bond fund trustee and used to retire a portion of the debt.

In addition to a construction fund trustee for a revenue project, it is also necessary to designate a bond fund trustee. These may be separate institutions, or one trustee may be designated to perform both functions.

The duties of the bond fund trustee relate solely to receipt and disbursement of the revenues of the project once operation commences. Varied types of special funds are usually created to provide for operating expenses, maintenance, bond service, reserves, and major replacements, additions, or extensions to the project. The revenues are received directly by the trustee and allocated to each fund according to the formula set forth in the indenture. The funds are then disbursed for the proper purposes either according to a predetermined schedule or against certificates of the proper officials of the district, commission, or authority.

A bond fund trustee has no power of enforcement or other rights in the event of default or insufficiency of the revenues. If the revenues or other payments due should be withheld wrongfully, it could undoubtedly bring suit to recover them. Its duties relate solely, however, to the revenues or other funds provided to be paid to it. It is not a representative of the bondholders for purpose of enforcement.

ESCROW AGENT

The significant growth in the number and type of innovative financings has also increased the need for an escrow agent in many transactions. Essentially, such agent is a disinterested party that holds something of value for two or more other parties in interest, until a specified time has passed or until a specified event has occurred.

This type of "custody" arrangement has been used to hold the down payment toward a purchase of a plant facility, to secure a portion of the purchase price in a merger or acquisition transaction pending the execution of specified representations and warranties, to hold investor payments for subscription to securities, to hold life insurance policies covering the principals of closely held companies, and even to hold the source code documentation for computer software to assure users of continued software support by the developer.

It is essential that the escrow agreement clearly identify the parties in interest, accurately describe the property to be held, and specifically set out the circumstances of the release of the property from the escrow. If the property consists of cash and/or marketable securities, the escrow agent's duties and responsibilities regarding investment, reinvestment, collection, and disposition of income, registration of the securities, voting rights (in the case of stock), valuations, and reports should be carefully spelled out.

Appropriate provisions should also be included covering notifications and required methods of delivery, resolution of disputes, the governing law, and the resignation, removal, and succession of the escrow agent. It is equally important to provide for full indemnification of the agent against all loss, cost, damage, or expense that may arise or result from the performance of the agent's duties—its liability being only for gross negligence or willful misconduct.

UNIT INVESTMENT TRUSTS

During recent years, with the increased interest of private investors in the bond market and the desire to provide for portfolio diversification, offerings of a "pooled" portfolio of bonds much like mutual funds for stock issues have increased dramatically.[10]

An investment firm acting as a sponsor buys a selection of bonds for a particular UIT portfolio, and then offers shares or "units" of the fund for sale to investors. Each unit represents a fractional, undivided share of all the bonds in the portfolio. This selection is determined by the type of fund the sponsor seeks to sell to investors. It may consist entirely of tax-exempt bonds of a particular state, or of debt obligations of a particular industry, or may be funded with securities of "growth" companies or, conversely, with debt obligations that provide high-income yield. The nature and type of the underlying portfolio are limited only by the ingenuity of the sponsor and its perception of the needs of potential investors.

Because a UIT both issues securities and uses the proceeds to buy the underlying portfolio, it falls within the definition of an "investment company" in the Investment Company Act of 1940 (40 Act).[11]

[10] This investor interest has also resulted from the liberalization of tax legislation and regulation related to the establishment and funding of Investment Retirement Accounts and "Keoghs."

[11] 15 U.S.C.A. Sec. 80a–3(a)(1) and 3(a)(3). UITs are also subject to the 33 Act but are specifically exempted from the TIA by its Sec. 304(a)(2).

The structure of the trust is governed by a trust indenture that designates the trustee, the sponsor, and the evaluator and that delineates their responsibilities. The indenture will also set forth the duration of the trust and the conditions under which it may be terminated early.

Section 26 of the 40 Act prescribes the minimum requirements for the indenture, stating that: (1) the trustee must be a bank having aggregate capital, surplus, and undivided profits of not less than $500,000; (2) the trustee cannot resign until the trust has been liquidated or a successor trustee appointed; (3) the fees available to the trustee, sponsor, and evaluator must be set forth, and; (4) the sponsor must maintain appropriate unitholder records and notify the holders in the case of substitution of any portfolio security.

The bonds are deposited with a bank as trustee which will perform a variety of duties, including safekeeping of the securities until redeemed or called; the collection of interest on the securities and their principal if called or redeemed; the issuance to each investor of a registered certificate of ownership or the provision for a book-entry record of such holdings; the distribution of checks representing income on the shares on a monthly, quarterly, or semiannual basis, or the reinvestment of such; and the redemption of the trust's shares upon request by the investor.[12]

12 For a detailed discussion, *see* Gould and Lins, *Unit Investment Trusts: Structure and Regulation Under the Federal Securities Laws*, 43 *Bus. Law.* 1177 (August 1988).

FIFTEEN

Servicing Debt Securities—Agency Functions

Corporate trust officers must be concerned not only with protecting the security of the indenture and administering its provisions but also with providing facilities for performance of the many responsible and detailed duties involved in the handling of the securities themselves, from the time of their issuance until they are finally retired and disposed of. In the larger institutions that handle a substantial volume of corporate trust business, these "operating" functions are usually performed by a separate staff under the management of a senior officer experienced in operating procedures and systems. In the smaller banks, however, which constitute a majority, a single officer may be responsible for both indenture administration and securities servicing activities. Even in the large institutions, an administrative officer cannot discharge his/her functions properly unless there is an understanding of the basic problems involved in servicing debt securities.

These functions are separate and distinct from the specific duties of the trustee, although of necessity the responsibilities overlap at many points. However, they are performed by the bank in an agency capacity, and separate appointing documents and instructions should be received. Because the relationship involved is essentially that of an agency, it may be terminated by the issuer at any time without a change in the basic trustee relationship.

As between the issuer and its agents, the obligation is to exercise good faith and due diligence—an obligation that under the UCC cannot be varied by agreement, although standards of performance may properly be subject to negotiations among the parties. The agent is also properly entitled to full protection and indemnity for any action taken or omitted to be taken on the instructions of the issuer, as long as the agent acts in good faith with due diligence and without negligence or misconduct.

Each agent has, with regard to the particular function it performs, the same obligation to the holder or owner of the security and has the same rights and privileges as the issuer has in regard to those functions. The net effect is that the agent has the same liability as the issuer and is subject to suit by a holder regardless of whether or not the issuer is also sued.[1]

The bank designated as corporate trustee is usually appointed principal agent of the corporation to service the indenture securities, and in most instances such designation facilities handling the many problems involved. The issuer may, however, and sometimes does, designate other banks to act in one or more agency capacities.

New York City is the principal financial center in the country, and many purchasers of securities prefer to have facilities provided there for the servicing of their securities. Because many millions of bonds are held in custodial or depository arrangements in New York, a great deal of expense is avoided if shipment to other areas of the country is made unnecessary. Accordingly, many indentures require the obligor to designate an office or agency in New York City where demands or notices may be served and where the securities may be presented for payment, registration of transfer, exchange, and so on. When a bank outside New York City is named trustee, it is quite common to designate such a bank as the principal agent to service the securities with a New York bank named as either co-agent to perform all requisite agency functions or as drop agent to receive items on behalf of the principal agent. These include an appointment as authenticating agent for the trustee to authenticate securities to be issued on registration of transfer, exchange, or partial redemption. Occasionally, a co-agent is named in one or more cities in addition to New York. The activities of all the agents must be closely coordinated, and appropriate controls should be maintained by the trustee and principal agent, with the other agents reporting and accounting to it.

Procedures tend to vary widely, depending on volume handled, local practices, and in some cases, requirements of specific laws and regula-

[1] For an excellent review of the cases and decisions related to these services, see Gutman, *op. cit, supra* note 35, chapter 2.

tions. This chapter focuses therefore on the more important aspects of the particular agency appointment, and the relevant duties and responsibilities incident to such appointments. These securities processing services are bond registrar, interest paying agent, principal paying agent, exchange agent, conversion agent, and accounting and destruction agent.

APPOINTING DOCUMENTS

The only documents normally required to support an agency appointment are (1) a resolution of the company's board of directors; (2) a copy of the indenture or supplemental indenture creating the issue (or in the case of a municipal bond issue, a copy of the bond resolution or ordinance); (3) incumbency certificates; (4) a specimen of each authorized denomination of the bond or debenture; and (5) such supplemental instructions from the issuer as may be required to set forth the specific duties and responsibilities of the agent. Where the agent is also the trustee, most of these documents will have been received by the trustee and duplication is unnecessary.

When the agent is designated by name in the indenture itself, a general resolution approving the indenture is all that is required, although it is a desirable practice to have the resolution sufficiently broad to cover each agency appointment specifically. No special form is required, but it is suggested that the text of the resolution follow the indenture language as closely as possible to indicate that this is the specific appointment the company convenanted to make. It is also recommended that the resolution contain general language designating the company officials (by title) who are authorized to issue instructions to the agent. While it is not necessary to name the agents in the securities themselves, it will facilitate subsequent processing if the bond contains the name of the bank to which it should be presented for payment, registration of transfer, and so on.

The incumbency certificates should include specimen signatures of the officers of the issuer, particularly those who signed any of the bonds or debentures. If facsimile signature are used, the specimen bond suffices for this purpose, but the agent should still have the signatures of the officers authorized to instruct it. If the agent is a bank other than the trustee, it should also have specimens of the signatures of all officers of the trustee that authenticated the bonds.

Finally, the agent should obtain such detailed instructions from an authorized official of the obligor as are necessary to enable it to carry out its duties expeditiously. This would include such things as source of funds to pay principal and interest, disposition to be made of canceled securities, statements and reports to be rendered, and so on. As a practical matter, because the agent wishes to fit this agency into a customary pattern and usually knows more than the issuer about what should be done, it is customary for the agent to outline to the issuer the procedure it intends to allow and to request the confirmation and approval of the latter.

BOND REGISTRAR

Before the adoption of the UCC, there was no statutory requirement that corporate issuers maintain "books of record." However, for almost all publicly sold debt issues the issuers assumed a contractual obligation to do so in the indenture pursuant to which the securities were issued and which provided for an office or agency where registrations of transfer and payment could be effected.

The registrar appointment is of great importance in the modern fully registered issue, and there are many reasons why the trustee should be designated as principal registrar to maintain the record of registered holders and of registrations of transfer. The list of holders is essential for other purposes, such as selection of bonds for partial redemption and mailing of notices. Both time and expense are saved if the trustee is made responsible for maintaining this record. Interest and principal payments are usually made by check, and it is important that this be done by the bank that maintains the record of holders. In the event the trustee is not located in New York City, it will be necessary for actively traded public issues to have facilities provided for either transfer or receipt of registered bonds in New York. In particular cases it may be desirable to provide such facilities in one or more other financial centers. In any place where registration facilities are required that is not also the location of the trustee, the registrar or co-registrar should also be given the necessary authority to "authenticate" the obligations. This is an agency function and the granting of this authority constitutes an appointment in addition to the registrar function.

Whereas a number of unlisted stock issues have no New York City transfer facilities, the situation is different in the case of bonds because of the accrued interest factor and the fact that the average bond transaction involves a substantially greater dollar value. Where the trustee is not located in New York City, facilities should be provided to accommodate the New York securities market. One procedure, if allowed by the laws of the state of the principal agent, is to appoint a New York registrar as an agent of the trustee to authenticate the bonds to be issued on registration of transfer. Such agent enters into an agreement with the trustee indemnifying it with respect to exercise of such authority by the agent. This function has been in existence since the early 1970s and has proved to be a very efficient and effective method to avoid any delays in consummating registrations of transfer and interdenominational exchanges. Another arrangement is to designate a New York drop agent to receive items on behalf of the trustee/transfer agent. The drop agent forwards items to the principal agent generally on the same day the items are received. While transfer agent regulations do not deem the "drop" to be equivalent to the principal agent's premises where transfer functions are performed, such agent must have appropriate procedures to assure that items are promptly forwarded to it.[2]

Authentication on original issuance should be only by the trustee, as should the authentication of bonds in replacement of mutilated, lost, stolen, or destroyed bonds. These transactions involve creation of additional indebtedness with respect to which the trustee has special fiduciary responsibilities. However, authentication of securities on transfer, exchange, or partial redemption does not involve the same degree of responsibility and, where desirable to avoid unnecessary expense to holders, may properly be done by a responsible institution other than the trustee under appropriate safeguards.

Many existing mortgage indentures are intended as permanent financing media, and some questions may exist about whether an authenticating agent can be appointed for additional series of bonds to be issued under these indentures by reason of certain language in the original indentures. This is an example of the type of inflexibility that should be avoided in drafting indentures. In such indentures, every effort should be made to find a legal resolution, for it is obvious that the rights of holders of existing obligations will not be affected. If these legal questions cannot be resolved, simplified procedures for obtaining consent of the requisite percentage of holders should be considered.

A fully registered bond means that both the principal and interest are registered in the holder's name. From the standpoint of such holders,

---

[2]*See* SEC Rule 17Ad–1(g), 17 CFR 240.17Ad–1, and Question (28) in SEC Interpretative Release 34–17111 (Sept. 2, 1980).

there are a number of advantages to registration. Negotiability is restricted, and, in the case of theft or loss, the expense of replacement is reduced and the risk of total loss of investment almost eliminated. Interest is paid by check, and the chore of detaching and collecting interest coupons every six months is eliminated. In the event the bond is called, or the trustee or issuer wish to communicate with the holder, a notice or letter can be mailed directly to the registered holder. The principal disadvantage is that the bond cannot be disposed of by delivery to a purchaser but must be surrendered to the registrar to effect the registration of transfer.[3]

To effect a registration of transfer, the bond must be accompanied by a form of assignment that has been executed by the transferor, assigning the holder's interest in the bond in blank or to a specified transferee. The registrar will require that the holder's signature to the assignment be guaranteed. Most major bond registrar banks normally require that the guaranty be by a member firm of the New York or American stock exchange or other acceptable regional stock exchange, or by another commercial bank or one of its correspondent banks. Other registrars have similar requirements, modified to meet their particular needs and operating policies.

Registration of both principal and interest requires that a new bond or bonds be prepared and issued on every transaction, such being usually issuable in any denomination that is a multiple of $1,000 (or in the case of municipal bonds, in multiples of $5,000). If the registrar has been appointed as authenticating agent, it authenticates the new certificates, under advice to the trustee that it has canceled (obligor's signature only) an equal principal amount of bonds, including in the certification the serial numbers of the certificates issued and canceled, and ships the canceled bonds to the trustee.[4] If the registrar is not an authenticating agent, both the old and new certificates must be delivered to the trustee, which will cancel its authentication certificate on the old bonds and authenticate the new ones to be delivered. Information on the particular transaction—including name, address, and taxpayer identification number of both the transferor and the transferee; the bond numbers canceled and issued; and the principal amount—must be input to the registrar's bondholder record file. A transfer or journal sheet is normally prepared

---

[3] See note 2, chapter 2, *supra*.

[4] It may be more desirable for the registrar to enter into an agreement with the trustee whereby the registrar destroys the canceled certificates, furnishing the trustee with an appropriate destruction certificate.

reflecting each day's activity for the particular issue. Although most major bond registrar banks maintain the permanent record as part of their computerized recordkeeping procedures, it may be desirable to produce daily "hard copy" of such transactions, either for research purposes if such is not otherwise readily available or to forward it to the obligor. Where more than one registrar is involved, only the principal registrar maintains individual registration records of the holders. All co-registrars must therefore furnish the information (usually a copy of their transfer sheets) to the principal registrar.

Almost all state and municipal debt securities issued before July 1, 1983, were in bearer form and many provided for the registration thereof at the holder's option. Most corporate obligations sold before 1968 were similarly issued. Such registration privilege could be as to principal only or as to both principal and interest. In the case of corporate issues, the privilege had, however, to be set forth specifically in the indenture.

Registration as to principal only means the principal of the bond is registered in the holder's name. The bearer interest coupons remain attached and are used for collection of the semiannual interest in exactly the same manner as if no registration had occurred. Registration of such bonds is also accomplished by presenting the bond to the registrar accompanied by an executed assignment, with the signature guaranteed in the same manner as a fully registered bond. The registrar enters the date and name of the registered holder on the special registration panel on the back of the bond, and the registration is authenticated by the signature of an authorized officer of the registrar opposite the name of the holder. A special transfer sheet is usually prepared by the registrar showing the bond number and a transfer from "bearer" to the name of the holder. This transfer is posted to a subsidiary record file (or ledger sheet) under the name and address of the holder, which shows the date, number, and principal amount of the bond registered as to principal in the holder's name. Any subsequent registration as to the principal of bonds of the same issue in that holder's name will also be posted to the particular record file by showing a debit to the transferor and a credit to the transferee.

A release of a bond registered as to principal is accomplished in the same manner as a transfer, except that the word "bearer" instead of the name of a transferee is entered in the registration box. Full negotiability by delivery is then restored. An assignment in blank by the former registered holder is required to effect such "deregistration."

No posting to the trustee's principal record of bonds issued file is required in the case of registration as to principal only, or on transfers of such bonds, for no change occurs in the serial number or principal amount of bonds outstanding.

Payment of Interest

The first obligation of the agent is to make certain that requisite funds are obtained before each interest payment date. Many banks follow the practice of billing their principals for all interest payments due. This is an expensive but sometimes necessary step. (The obligation of the issuer to provide the necessary funds is an absolute one, and their officials should be capable—without reminder—of making funds available on time and in the proper amount.) When deposit with the paying agent is by check, it should be in sufficient time to enable the agent to complete collection of the check and have available funds on the payment date. When the paying agent is willing to accept deposit of immediately available funds on the payment date, extreme care should be exercised in following the usual and customary practice of mailing the interest checks on the business day preceding the payment date. Such decision, including the advance mailing of such checks on a staggered basis, should be made only after full consideration of the possible consequences of the obligor's failing to deposit the requisite funds on the payment date.

Although almost all indentures provide for the payment of interest by check (occasionally one does see the use of "drafts" permitted), it is probable that in the future there will be an increasing use of wire transfers and direct deposit credits thorough automated clearing house ("ACH") mechanisms.

Under qualified indentures all funds deposited for payment of interest must be held in trust, whether or not they are held by the trustee. If the agent is a bank other than the trustee, it must—at the time of accepting its appointment—execute a letter of undertaking to the trustee to hold in trust for the benefit of the security holders all sums deposited with it for the payment of principal or interest on the securities and to give prompt notice to the trustee of default by the obligor in the making of any such payment.

The responsibility of the paying agent is further complicated by the necessity of complying with the relevant provisions of the Internal Revenue Code and with the regulations of particular taxing jurisdictions.

All payments of interest on taxable bond issues in excess of ten dollars must be reported to the federal government, and under specific provisions of the Interest and Dividend Tax Compliance Act of 1983, the paying agent may be required to withhold a portion of the payment.[5] For bond issues sold before July 18, 1984, it is also necessary to withhold the requisite taxes on all payments to nonresident aliens and to process and file with the federal government the appropriate tax forms.

The requirements of particular state tax laws must also be taken into consideration. For example, any corporation incorporated in Pennsylvania or with a treasurer's office in that state is subject to the Pennsylvania Corporate Loans Tax. Unless the tax is assumed by the corporation, it must be withheld from all payments to Pennsylvania residents. The corporation is entitled to a credit with respect to payments to all non-Pennsylvania residents, but proof of such payments must be supplied. The agent must, therefore, obtain evidence on the residence of each holder to whom payment is made, so that the necessary proof to support the corporate return may be supplied. In the case of bearer bonds, this is accomplished through the use of a memorandum certificate of ownership. (*See Exhibit 16.*)

Payment of Registered Interest

Interest is usually payable semiannually, although in recent years a number of variable rate issues have provided for quarterly and monthly payments. Such interest will be due and payable on fixed dates, all accruals of such interest being for the prescribed periods. A transfer of the obligation normally transfers the right to any interest accrued, the purchaser paying this amount as part of the purchase price.

In order to provide the paying agent sufficient time to effect payments of interest on registered bond issues, without any disruption in the trading of such securities, a procedure was developed in the late 1960s whereby the contract between obligor and holder provides for a record date before the end of the accrual period for determination of holders entitled to the payment.[6] As a result, the transfer books need not be closed at all during this period.

5 See note 10, chapter 12, *supra.* Such withholding, referred to as "backup withholding," is imposed if a nonexempt payee fails to furnish the payor with an obviously correct taxpayer identification number and, for accounts opened after January 1, 1984, with a statement that such holder is not subject to backup withholding. Both statements must be certified under penalty of perjury.

6 The Municipal Securities Rulemaking Board (MSRB), with the concurrence of the SEC and the Government Finance Officers Association, strongly recommended the use of the

Inasmuch as the basic obligation calls for payment of interest on the interest payment date, and the full six months' interest does not become payable as a debt until such date, the obligation to pay on such date to holders of record as of a preceding date must be set forth clearly and unambiguously in the indenture and on the face of the bond.

The standard uniform record date for interest payable on the first day of a calendar month is the close of business on the fifteenth day of the calendar month preceding the date of payment. If interest is payable on the fifteenth, the record date is the close of business on the last day of the calendar month next preceding. In the event of a failure to pay on the due date, the established record date is of no effect and the transfer of the bond will transfer all rights of the holder for the defaulted interest to the transferee. This should be set forth clearly in the indenture and provision should also be made for determination of the persons entitled to payment of such defaulted interest. It is recommended that, upon receipt of notification of intention to pay the defaulted interest on a certain date (including arrangements satisfactory to the trustee for the deposit of the funds), the trustee establish a special record date, which should be not more than fifteen nor less than ten days before the proposed payment date and not less than ten days after receipt of the notice of proposed payment. Notification of the proposed payment and of the special record date should be mailed to the bondholders by the trustee not less than ten days before the special record date.

Interest so payable to the "record date" holders of fully registered bonds is made by check issued and mailed to them, as shown by the registration records. If the interest disbursing agent is other than the registrar, the latter will prepare a certified list of registered holders, as of the record date, with the total holdings of each, and deliver it to the disbursing agent. These checks are usually mailed on the business day preceding the interest due date to ensure that in most cases the check will be received by the holder on the date the interest is due.

The total amount to be disbursed should be proved to the trustee's registered bond control record to ensure that the registrar's bondholder records are in proof with the trustee's control. Each transaction involving a change in the outstanding principal amount of bonds should be posted to the trustee's record of bonds issued file, and the requisite control may be provided by use of such record. Where, however, an issue is outstanding in both bearer and registered form, it is necessary to

---

standard record dates for registered tax-exempt issues, in *Notice Concerning Recommended Standards on Registered Municipal Securities* (May 6, 1983).

maintain a subsidiary control of the outstanding fully registered bonds. This practice facilitates a quick proof of registered interest disbursements, certifications of registered bonds outstanding, and other transactions relating to such bonds. This record may be maintained as part of a computerized securities transfer system or off-line in a manual ledger record. In the latter case it is maintained by posting from a daily journal covering all registration activity for each day. This journal records the total principal amount of fully registered obligations canceled or discharged or issued during the day for each separate issue on which there was activity. The totals are the posted to the registered bonds outstanding control record for each such issue.

Payment of Bearer Interest

Because most corporate debt obligations issued before 1968, and almost all state and municipal obligations issued before July 1, 1983, are outstanding in bearer form, it is necessary to examine in some detail the means whereby interest is collected by the holders thereof. This is accomplished by attachment to each such obligation of a sheet of bearer coupons, one for each interest payment date to, and including, the date of maturity of the principal obligation. Until they become payable, these coupons are an essential part of the bond itself and together with it constitute a single obligation.[7] Once they have matured and become payable, however, they constitute separate and distinct obligations and may be transferred by delivery separate from the bond itself. Payment to bearer, even though other than the holder of the bond, will discharge the debt represented thereby.

As noted before, interest is usually payable semiannually, although infrequently provision is made for payment at different intervals. On a twenty-million-dollar, twenty-five year bond issue consisting of all bearer bonds of $5,000 denomination that remain outstanding to maturity without interim sinking fund or redemption payments, 200,000 separate interest obligations will have to be processed. It follows that the function of the coupon paying agent is one of the more important to be performed in servicing the pre-July 1, 1983, obligations of state and municipalities, old corporate bond issues, and the so-called Eurodollar issues.

[7] It is, however, possible and perfectly proper to have the bond "stripped" of its coupons with the principal sold at a discount (much like a zero coupon bond) with the coupons sold as a separate instrument. In the latter case, the investor receives semiannual payments representing in effect the amortization of investment plus interest on such investment.

Because the coupon, when due, will become a separate obligation, it must incorporate a separate and distinct promise to pay. Where the bond is subject to prior redemption, all coupons maturing after the first possible redemption date should have this promise qualified by language such as: "Unless the bond hereinafter mentioned shall have been called for previous redemption and payment of the redemption price thereof duly provided. . . ." Each coupon will contain the name of the issuer, the date on which it will become due, the specific amount due thereon, the place of payment, and a statement that it represents interest for a specified period on the bond designated by serial number. The coupon will be validated by the signature (usually facsimile) of the treasurer or other authorized official of the issuer. To facilitate identification and processing, the coupons attached to each bond should be numbered in consecutive order, the first maturing coupon being Number 1, the second Number 2, and so on. All coupons maturing on the same date from bonds of the same issue will bear the same coupon number.

The holder of a bond may detach the coupons and forward them directly to the paying agent and receive a check in payment. Because this check must also be processed, this method of collection will delay receipt of usable funds by the holder, and it is not the method most frequently used. From the viewpoint of the agent, it is the most expensive way in which payment has to be made. The normal collection procedure follows the same pattern as is used in processing checks, except that credit is usually not passed to the depositor's account until collection is actually made. Each bank provides special envelopes (generally referred to as "shells") for its depositors in which coupons may be enclosed and deposited for collection. The holder writes his or her name, address, and taxpayer identification number on the shell, together with a description of the bond, the denomination of the coupon, and the total face amount of coupons deposited. The bank of deposit then forwards the shell, together with all shells received from other depositors, to its correspondent bank in the city of collection. The latter accepts it as a deposit from the forwarding bank and assigns a collection number to the total deposit, which may represent many coupon shells for many different issues. After proving each collection, this bank then sorts the shells by issues and paying agents and presents the coupons to the respective paying agents. Most of this processing takes place before the maturity date, and the paying agent accepts coupons for processing about a week before the actual due date. On the due date the paying agent makes payment to the presenting bank for all coupons presented, up to and including such date. On the same date each bank through which the coupon has been processed passes the preestablished credit to its depositor.

Where default has been made in payment, or where a particular coupon is mutilated or is otherwise irregular or has been detached from a previously called bond, it must be returned through the same channels used in its collection and each depositor's account must be charged back for the amount of the item.

In New York City the major banks, and banks in certain other cities, provide for collection of all coupons through a central clearing house. Each morning all collecting banks transport all their collection items to the clearing house, where they are delivered to the paying banks. For the total deposits and receipts, a net credit or debit is made to the bank's account at the Federal Reserve Bank. The aggregate of return items that have to be charged back is handled in the same manner. This arrangement facilitates the collection process and reduces to a minimum the number of checks that have to be prepared and issued by the agents. Together with the preliminary work performed by the banks in their capacity as collecting agent, it has also minimized the costs to issuers for servicing of their coupons.

The paying agent must examine each separate coupon presented to see that it is a valid obligation, that it is a matured obligation and one the agent is authorized to pay, that the bond from which it was detached has not been previously called for redemption, that the coupon has not been canceled, that it is not otherwise mutilated, and that no stop order is on file with respect to the particular coupon. Each separate shell and collection item must also be proved for amount. If everything is found to be in order, the coupons are canceled by perforation. The total of all coupons for each issue received each day is proved to the total collections received and the appropriate account charged for the total payments. If payment is refused for any reason, the coupon is returned uncanceled to the presenting bank (or to the presenter if not a collecting bank) and, if an aggregate credit has been made, against an appropriate charge back. When a clearing house arrangement is utilized, all coupons are usually processed and paid on the same day they are presented to the agent. Any coupons or shells being returned for the reasons indicated above should be returned immediately or, if presented through a clearing house, in the next day's clearing.

Most coupons are payable on the first or fifteenth day of the month, and the few days immediately preceding and following these dates are periods of heavy volume. During the remaining days of the month, the work processed during these periods is audited and verified by personnel other than those who handled the payment. In this operation the coupons are broken down by the maturity date, and the total coupons paid for a designated period (usually monthly) are proved to the total charge made during the period to the coupon account.

Some banks still follow an expensive practice of maintaining a separate cash account for each interest maturity. Because it is necessary in any event for the coupons to be segregated by coupon number (or maturity date), it is much easier to maintain the appropriate breakdown by subsidiary data record. Where a single obligor has a number of separate issues of securities outstanding, it is entirely appropriate to maintain a single cash account for all issues and to provide the necessary breakdown by issue and maturity by subsidiary records.

Where a great volume of coupon payments is handled, the responsibility of the administrative officer is to furnish operations personnel with essential instructions and information in as concise and clearly understandable manner as possible. Any information that facilitates ready verification of the validity of the obligation is helpful.

A corporate issuer is required under qualified indentures to maintain a list of all information coming into its possession of names and addresses of its security holders annually. If this information is derived from the collection of interest coupons, the agents must maintain it in current form for filing with the trustee. The information is derived from the shells in which the coupons are received.

Where two or more banks act as paying agents for a particular issue, arrangements must be made for appropriate coordination of the work of all the agents. The normal procedure is for one bank (usually the trustee) to be designated the principal agent and for all funds to be deposited with the bank. If the other agents are correspondents of the principal agent, authority is given for charging the account of the principal agent for payments by the co-agents, and the principal agent is responsible to the issuer with respect to all payments made. Once the coupons have been paid, verified, and canceled, and appropriate charge has been made to the coupon paying account, the work of the paying agent is concluded. The problem of making appropriate disposition of the canceled coupons still remains and will be discussed later in this chapter in connection with accounting and destruction procedures.

PAYMENT OF PRINCIPAL

Theoretically, the same principles that govern payment of coupons should apply to payment of the bonds themselves. The procedures followed are usually, however, quite different. In the case of bonds, the amount involved in the handling of each item is many times greater, and consequently the risk is substantial. Coupons are handled on a volume basis; bonds, on an individual basis.[8] Whereas the trustee is responsible for proper accounting for both bonds and coupons, the latter are usually accounted for by total amount by maturity date, while accounting for principal obligations is done individually, by serial number.

The bond payment personnel work from instructions prepared by the account administrator. Although in the case of coupons one set of instructions is normally sufficient for all maturities, it is usually desirable to prepare a separate set of instructions for each separate principal payment. These instructions should contain all essential information so that operations personnel do not have to refer to the indenture or other source material. In the case of a redemption payment, the amount of the premium payable must be shown, as well as the specific serial numbers of the particular bonds called.

Because payment for principal obligations is made by check, the identity of the individual presentor can be preserved.[9] During a heavy maturity period, each day's work represents a large dollar volume, and one of the essential factors in any procedure is maintenance of proper controls. In a large-volume operation, it is desirable to have control maintained separate and apart from the personnel making the actual payment. For each item presented, there is indicated on a control ticket the name of the presentor, a description of the issue and its CUSIP number,[10] the aggregate face amount of the bonds, and the serial num-

[8] Since the mid-1970s, a matured municipal and corporate bond clearing system has been used by members of the New York Clearing House, following procedures similar to the daily clearing of coupons.

[9] See note 10, chapter 12, and note 5, chapter 15, *supra*. In addition, payors are required under income tax regulations to report the "gross proceeds" paid to any non-exempt holder from the redemption of both corporate and municipal obligations.

[10] The term *CUSIP* is an acronym for the Committee on Uniform Security Identification Procedures, of the American Bankers Association. Since 1967, a standard alphanumeric numbering system has been used by all segments of the securities industry. The standard consists of nine characters, the first six being the issuer number, the next two being the issue number, and the last being a check digit. The numbers that appear on the face of each stock

bers thereof. One copy is given to the presentor (in the case of a window item), another is sent to a security control (audit) unit, the other two copies accompany the bonds to the payment desk. Here the bonds are examined to determine that they are valid, that they are in good order with no mutilations, and that no stop payment order is on file with respect to the particular bonds, and such other checks are made as may be indicated for a particular issue. The amount of the payment is computed and entered on the control ticket. The item is then reviewed by a second person, and a check is prepared on which the number of the control ticket is entered. The bonds are subsequently canceled and the check is returned through the control clerk for delivery against surrender of the receipt or for mailing to the presentor. The control clerk is responsible for seeing that a check is delivered for each control ticket processed. As a separate audit, another person proves the total bonds canceled for the day to the total funds disbursed. A copy of the control ticket accompanies each block of canceled bonds, and the original, with the number of the check issued entered thereon, is filed for record purposes.

Where part of the bond issue is called before its stated maturity, the particular serial numbers of the bonds presented must also be examined to ensure that they appear on the list of called bonds.

Care must be exercised that payment is made only to the registered holder or that an appropriate assignment is received. Where payment is made to the registered holder, no assignment is necessary. Registered bonds must also be delivered to the bond registrar for proper discharge from the registration records.

In the case of a partial call, most registered bonds of large denomination are called in part only. The holder of such an obligation is given a new bond for the unredeemed portion. Where there is a separate registrar, a special transfer sheet is prepared showing reduction in the amount of such registered bonds. It is important that the principal transfer agent communicate with all co-transfer agents prior to processing a partial call for redemption. All co-transfer agents should be required to submit journals to the principal agent no later than one business day after any transfer. The principal agent should post all activity before processing the call and notify the co-transfer agents that the books will be closed for a specified period.

---

and bond certificate are assigned by the CUSIP Service Bureau of Standard & Poor's Corporation under contract to the American Bankers Association.

Because all bonds are controlled on the trustee's principal record of bonds issued, one copy of the control ticket may be used to reflect the cancellation, reducing the trustee's control of outstanding bonds. Since for purposes of the indenture, bonds cease to be outstanding on the redemption date when the required funds are deposited in trust, the recommended procedure is for the entire principal amount called to be debited from the trustee's principal control record on the redemption date. A separate subsidiary control record should be established to reflect the actual surrender and payment of the bonds, and the cash balance reflected in this record should always prove to the funds in the redemption account.

Exchange Agent

The function of the exchange agent is similar to that of a registrar in that it involves the exchange of bonds of an issue for other bonds of the same issue provided such is permitted by the terms of the indenture. In actual practice, a separate exchange agent is usually not appointed, the registrar assuming this function.

One form of exchange is that of fully registered bonds for the coupon bearer type, or the reverse, for pre-1983 issues when such bearer bonds were authorized. Upon receipt of bearer bonds with a request for issuance of an equivalent amount in fully registered form, the former will be canceled and a registered bond or bonds prepared, with the transaction information input to the bondholder records file. The canceled bearer bonds and the registered piece are delivered to the trustee with a request for authentication of the latter. (If the registrar-exchange agent has been appointed as authenticating agent, it authenticates the registered bond, under advice to the trustee that it has canceled an equal principal amount of bearer bonds, including in the certification the specific serial numbers of the bonds issued and canceled.) On a reverse transaction, involving the issuance of bearer for fully registered bonds, the canceled registered piece is delivered to the trustee after discharge, and the appropriate number of bearer bonds are requisitioned. After detaching all coupons for which interest has been paid, the trustee (or the authenticating agent) authenticates and delivers the requisite amount of previously unissued bearer obligations. A number of issuers follow the practice of having the trustee "hold alive" any bearer bonds that have been surrendered for exchange, on the theory that on an exchange back to bearer form, a supply of certificates will be available. Although this does reduce the cost to the issuer in the event additional bonds must be printed, it adds substantial liability to the trustee, which must safely control the authenticated bearer bonds pending their possible reuse.

Most banks, however, follow the practice of canceling all bonds received for exchange so that no bonds bearing the same serial number can be reissued for any purpose. Where there is likelihood of frequent requests for exchange, a supply of unissued bearer bonds can also be lodged with the trustee for this purpose.

Where both coupon and registered bonds are authorized, special provisions must be made for the interchange of the two forms between the record and payment dates. The coupon for the interest payable on the payment date should be detached from the bearer bonds before their presentation for exchange, or delivery in exchange, of an equal amount of registered obligations.

The function of the interdenominational exchange agent is very important in fully registered issues to permit bondholders to "split" or "consolidate" the number of pieces they hold. In the case of securities issued in connection with a subscription offer to stockholders, denominations of $500, $100, and even $50 may be authorized. Frequently these denominations are freely interchangeable, although the more common provision is to permit consolidation into bonds of $1,000 denomination or multiple thereof, but no split of $1,000 bonds into smaller denominations. The reason for this limitation is the substantial cost of servicing small denomination bonds.

In recent years, many of the larger banks have acted as an exchange agent for securities of highly leveraged companies being financially restructured. These transactions typically involve the exchange of high-yield (i.e., "junk") bonds for cash, extended maturity and/or reduced–interest rate debt securities, and even common stock.

CONVERSION AGENT

The use of the convertible type of debt security has varied in popularity during the past twenty years, as changes in economic conditions and the market's receptivity to such "equity kickers" have waxed and waned. In the case of a corporation that is rapidly expanding or whose credit is not considered top tier by investors, such vehicle provides a means of raising equity capital, usually at considerably less cost than direct equity financing. During as period of rising stock prices, the conversion privilege is a valuable one, and many convertible debentures sell at substantial premiums in excess of the price they would command as straight debt securities. The usual security into which such an obligation is made convertible is the common stock of the issuing company.

The indenture controls the terms and conditions on which the privilege may be exercised, and these terms and conditions should also be set forth in the debenture itself in reasonable detail. The debenture may be made convertible into a fixed number of shares of stock, but the more usual provision is to fix a dollar price at which shares of stock may be purchased by use of the principal of the debenture. This price is subject to adjustment to reflect any change in the ratio of number of shares outstanding (other than through conversion of other debentures of the same issue).[11] Provision may also be made for an arbitrary increase in the conversion price at stated intervals during the life of the debenture, to encourage conversions during the earliest period. A common practice is to set the initial conversion price at a figure somewhat higher than the current market price of the common stock. This provides the advantage of the company's having a less expensive debt security for a period of time but one it will likely never be called on to pay, except through the issuance of common stock at a price higher than could be obtained by an immediate issue of such stock. To achieve the same purpose it is sometimes provided that the conversion privilege cannot be exercised until a stated time has elapsed after issuance of the debentures.

Upon the issuance of convertible debentures, the company must authorize and reserve for issuance of the maximum number of common shares that could be issued on conversion of the entire debenture issue. This authorization involves all the steps that would have to be taken if a number of shares were being concurrently issued publicly, including the necessary registration under the 33 Act and the listing of such additional shares on any securities exchange on which the stock is listed. The trustee should make certain that all proper steps have been taken.

The function of the conversion agent is to receive any debentures surrendered for conversion, compute the number of shares issuable, requisition such shares from the company's transfer agent, and, upon their receipt, cancel the debentures and deliver the shares to the presentor.

Often a fractional interest is involved, which may be handled in a

---

[11] For an excellent review of the problems inherent in drafting antidilution provisions, *see* Tomczak, *Corporate Trust and Commercial Finance Agreements* (1984), sec. 1.45 et seq.

number of ways. The almost universal practice, however, is to pay the value of the fractional interest in cash using the current market price of the stock to give the holder the equivalent value of the fractional interest. The indenture should set forth clearly the particular method to be followed.

Exercise of the conversion right is a privilege of the holder of the debenture, who has the option of deciding when to exercise the privilege. Conversion can frequently be forced by the company, however, by its calling the outstanding debenture issue for redemption. This places a termination date on the conversion privilege and, if conversion is favorable, results in conversion of the entire issue. If the conversion privilege is not favorable, there is seldom reason for a redemption call.

It is desirable to have the conversion privilege continue to the maturity or redemption date of the debentures. Some issues provide for an earlier termination date of convertibility, and invariably substantial losses are sustained by security holders who receive no actual notice or misunderstand the provisions of their security. There is usually no good reason for such earlier termination, for it is to the advantage of neither the company nor its security holders and should be avoided. The trustee should be diligent in endeavoring to change any such arbitrary provision. Where it does exist, the trustee should insist that every effort be made to inform security holders of their rights to minimize their losses.

A further problem to which attention should be paid is the matter of accrued interest to the conversion date. The problem may be handled in a number of ways. Occasionally an adjustment is made as between accrual of interest and accrual of dividends. This is an exceptional provision and is feasible only where the company has a fixed dividend policy with fixed dividend payment dates. The more usual provision is to state that no adjustment for accrued interest or dividends will be made. It is up to the holder to time the conversion in such a way as to be of the greatest advantage.

A convertible issue presents special problems where a record date is involved if a debenture is presented for conversion after a record date and before the interest payment date. Rather than suspend the conversion privilege during this period, the person converting should be required, as a condition to conversion, to deposit funds equal to the amount of interest that would otherwise be payable on the interest payment date on the debenture or portion thereof to be converted. These funds are then used to offset the payment that is made to the person in whose name the debenture was registered on the record date. This practice is especially desirable in a situation where the record holder has sold a debenture after the record date to an individual who converts before the interest payment date. As part of the sale, the seller normally delivers a check for the full interest due to the purchaser, conditional on the payment of interest by the obligor, with the expectation that the seller will receive this amount back on the interest payment date. The purchaser having received this check, deposits equivalent funds at the time of conversion.

The necessity for requiring such deposit can be illustrated by a hypothetical situation in which, after a record date, dealer A buys twenty-five $1,000 debentures from twenty-five individuals and exchanges them for five $5,000 debentures. Dealer A then sells the $25,000 principal amount to various other dealers, of whom dealer B, receiving $5,000 principal amount, decides to convert before the interest payment date. As the result, the obligor is not required to deposit funds for payment of interest on that $5,000 principal amount. Because the twenty-five individual holders of record are entitled to receive their interest on the payment date, the amount equivalent to interest payable of $5,000 debentures must be obtained from dealer B at the time the debenture is presented for conversion.

In the event that the obligor defaults in the payment of interest on the payment date, the funds so deposited would be repaid to the person effecting the conversion. The provisions in the indenture establishing this condition to conversion must, however, be qualified to the extent that such deposit need not be made if the obligation converted has been called for redemption on a date before the payment date. Since no obligation exists for payment of interest on an interest payment date on bonds called for prior redemption, there would be no record date for such payment. One question that may arise is the possibility of receipt from a debenture holder of a check that cannot be collected before mailing of the interest checks has to be made. If this check should prove uncollectible, a loss may result. This can be resolved by withholding delivery of the new securities for a sufficient period to allow for collection. Probably no special indenture language is required, but this problem should be borne in mind.

It should be noted that most convertible debenture issues provide for a sinking fund. It is both customary and proper to provide that the obligor will receive credit against its sinking fund requirement for all debentures converted into stock of the company.

SUBSCRIPTION AGENT

One of the collateral and important functions frequently performed is that of subscription agent in connection with the issuance of convertible debentures. In states where stockholders have preemptive rights, any issuance of stock or securities convertible into stock must first be offered to existing stockholders. Even where no preemptive right exists, such offering to existing stockholders is frequently the most feasible way of completing a successful offering.

The offering is made through the issuance of subscription warrants to existing stockholders. After the amount of the total offering has been determined, an appropriate ratio to existing shares is determined, and each shareholder is given the right to subscribe to a pro rata portion of the new offering. These rights are often valuable, the measure of value being the difference between the offering price and the market value of the debentures. Warrants are usually issued by the company's stock transfer agent and evidence the right to subscribe to a specified principal amount of debentures. The offer is normally underwritten, the underwriters agreeing to purchase all debentures not subscribed for through the exercise of warrants. Under the underwriting agreement, the life of the warrants is customarily limited to a period of two or three weeks from their date of issue.

The function of the subscription agent is twofold. First, it accepts and processes subscriptions to the debentures. This involves receipt of warrants with checks in payment of the subscribed debentures. When issuable, the debentures are requisitioned from the trustee and delivered to the subscribers.

The second function concerns the purchase and sale of rights. A stockholder who is unwilling to subscribe to the debentures is still entitled to the value of the rights represented by the warrant. Others may wish to exercise only a portion of their warrant and sell the balance of the rights, while some may wish to acquire a larger interest than their warrant entitled them to and therefore need to acquire additional rights. By reason of the large number of small holders, trading of such rights through normal brokerage channels might be very expensive. For the convenience of such holders the subscription agent is permitted to purchase and sell rights. It offsets purchase and sale orders for each day's activity and either purchases or sells the net position in the open market. The average price received on all transactions for the day is used to determine the price at which all purchases are computed. A small commission charge is imposed on the holders for this service.

PUT/DEMAND OPTION AGENT

For those issues which have a "put" or "demand" option, the paying agent must be prepared to accept the securities against payment, usually at par, to the registered holder. In some issues, the securities are purchased by a "remarketing agent" rather than the issuer itself.

ACCOUNTING AND DESTRUCTION

The purpose of every bond or debenture indenture is to secure payment of the obligations issued thereunder. Proper accounting for all such obligations is one of the important functions of the trustee. Provision must also be made for proper disposition of all obligations canceled because of transfer, payment, exchange, or conversion or for other reasons. These functions are usually performed by the trustee, but because a separate fee is charged for their performance, and because they may be performed by the operations staff, they are included among the agency functions.

Accounting for Interest Obligations

A fully registered bond represents the obligation for both principal and interest. When such a bond is surrendered and canceled, the trustee is entitled to assume that all amounts due with respect thereto have been paid or otherwise discharged. It is desirable, however, for the trustee to maintain a more current account of interest payments. Where it acts as registrar and interest disbursing agent, its own records will provide requisite evidence of payment of all amounts of registered interest due. Where the issuer or another agent disburses registered interest, the trustee should establish an appropriate procedure for ascertaining that all registered interest payments have been made. The most common and practical way to accomplish this is for the trustee to receive and rely on a certification by the disbursing agent of payments made. Whatever the form of the evidence received, it should be sufficient to establish the fact of payment.

Accounting for coupon interest is a different matter. The coupons represent separate and distinct obligations, and satisfactory evidence of their payment or cancellation should be received. A great deal of progress has been made over the years in simplifying the procedure of accounting for interest coupons. In the early days of corporate bond issues, a very elaborate procedure was followed. Large coupon ledgers were prepared that included a separate page for each bond issued. As the coupons were paid they were carefully pasted in the appropriate page on this ledger sheet, with the date of payment entered. This provided a complete record, but the expense involved was substantial. In most corporate issues this practice has been obsolete for many years, although it is still followed by a number of municipalities.

A major step forward was achieved when issuers permitted trustees to dispose of canceled coupons by completely destroying them (usually by cremation). An appropriate certification was prepared as evidence of such destruction. At first, cremation was witnessed by both company officials and the trustee; later, the trustee was permitted to perform this task alone. An elaborate exhibit was attached to the destruction certificate that described the coupons in detail. This included a description of the issue, the maturity date and amount of the coupons, and the bond serial numbers. This costly procedure necessitated that all coupons paid be sorted in numerical order so that they could be listed on the appropriate schedules.

In the late 1940s, a number of trustees began to question the necessity for such an elaborate procedure. Investigation revealed that these detailed schedules were seldom if ever referred to. Such detail was, therefore, unnecessary for proper accounting. As a result of these studies a major change in the accounting and destruction procedure was initiated. This accounting needs only to be done by total number of coupons and total dollar amount for each coupon maturity date. The necessity for sorting and listing of coupons by bond serial number is thus eliminated, although some banks using computer-generated payment records still follow this archaic practice.

To ensure proper accounting control, a subsidiary destruction ledger or computer file is maintained by the trustee. For each interest maturity date, the total interest due is entered. Credits against this amount are made for total registered interest disbursed and for total value of coupons of that maturity shown by each destruction certificate. The resulting balance, if any, shows the amount of coupons outstanding and unpaid.

Where paying agents other than the trustee pay a substantial percentage of the coupons, their subsequent shipment to and audit by the trustee involves an expensive and time-consuming arrangement. The trustee and the issuer should authorize the paying agents to complete disposition of the canceled coupons by satisfactorily destroying them. The certificate of such agent may be relied on by the trustee as evidence of such destruction.

Accounting for Principal Obligations

Each bond canceled for any reason must be included in an appropriate accounting. The destruction certificates covering principal obligations are similar to those covering coupons, except that the serial numbers of the bonds are shown on the certificate or the supporting schedule. There is no real need or purpose served in identifying and reporting the reason for the cancellation (*i.e.*, transfer, exchange, payment, etc.) except with regard to any remaining inventory of unissued bonds.

Registered bonds are handled in a different manner than coupon bearer bonds are. Where these are canceled because of transfer or for any reason requiring assignment of the bond, destruction is usually deferred for a reasonable period of time, usually one year, and a microfilm record is made of the bond and the assignment before destruction. Where assignment is received separate from the bond, it is usually microfilmed with the bond and destroyed with it, together with any documentation supporting a "legal" transfer (*e.g.*, one involving a corporation or a decedent). It is important that the laws of each particular jurisdiction be examined carefully in establishing canceled security retention and destruction periods. Exhibit 16 provides a matrix outline of recommended minimum guidelines.

LOST, STOLEN, AND DESTROYED SECURITIES

Securities are sometimes stolen or, more frequently, lost or misplaced by the holders. The holder then notifies the trustee (or, in the case of a tax-exempt bond, the fiscal agent or registrar) and requests that a stop order be placed against the particular bond or coupon. Care should be used in acknowledging any such request, for the trustee may be placed in a position where it cannot comply. Registered bonds that have been endorsed and bearer bonds and coupons are fully negotiable and as such are valid obligations in the hands of a bona fide purchaser.[12] The trustee or registrar (or fiscal agent) receiving a stop order should promptly note its records and communicate the information to all agents. In addition, the trustee or agent must promptly furnish such information to the entity designated by the SEC to receive reports of loss or theft.[13] That entity maintains a data base of such information in order to respond to inquiries by institutions involved in receiving, holding, or processing securities. Holders sometimes fail to notify the trustee that a lost security has been found, particularly in the case of coupons. Neither the trustee nor any agent should take it upon itself to remove such stop, even if a long period of time has elapsed, unless (1) the missing security has been surrendered to the trustee and is canceled by it, or (2) before the issuance of a replacement (or payment, as later discussed) the holder who requested the stop order notifies the trustee and requests that it be removed.

Where a stop order has been filed with the issuer (or trustee or agent) and the security is thereafter presented, the issuer or agent is permitted to discharge its responsibility for such adverse claim[14] in any reasonable manner. It is recommended that the procedure outlined in the UCC always be followed.[15] Notice to the adverse claimant must always be by registered or certified mail, and the person presenting the security must be named. This notice must also grant the option of a court order or the filing of a sufficient indemnity bond.

Most indentures provide for replacement of securities that have been lost, stolen, or destroyed upon the furnishing of satisfactory indemnity. Such indemnity is usually a bond executed by the holder and a surety company, satisfactory to the obligor issuer and the trustee. Some outstanding security issues have no provision for issuance of replacement certificates, including a number of municipal and other public and quasi-public issues.

Under the UCC, the issuer (and the trustee) must issue a new security in place of the original if the owner (1) so requests before the issuer has notice that the security has been acquired by a bona fide purchaser, (2) files with the issuer a sufficient indemnity bond, and (3) satisfies any

[12] Defined in UCC Article 8 as "a purchaser for value in good faith and without notice of any adverse claim. . . ."

[13] Rule 17f–1 (17 CRF 240.17f–1, July 1, 1979).

[14] A claim by someone not in possession of the security. It includes a claim that a transfer was or would be wrongful or that a particular person is the owner or has an interest in the security.

[15] UCC sec. 8–403.

other reasonable requirements imposed by the issuer.[16] There are two conditions that preclude the owner from receiving a replacement security. These are a failure by the owner to notify the issuer within a reasonable time after the owner has notice, and registration of a transfer of the original security before the issuer receives notice. If the original security when presented was properly endorsed, the issuer is protected under this rule and may refuse the demand for a replacement.

If, after the issuance of a replacement security, a bona fide purchaser presents the original for registration of transfer or payment, the issuer must register the transfer unless registration would result in overissuance, in which case the issuer must either purchase and deliver a like security if reasonably available or, if not, pay the amount such purchaser paid for the security with interest from the date of demand. The issuer may recover the replacement security from the purchaser to whom it was issued (or anyone taking from such person except another bona fide purchaser) in addition to exercising any rights it may have under the surety bond.

Many indentures permit the obligor company to avoid the complications of issuing a replacement security by paying the lost bond or coupon if it has, or is about to, become due and if the other conditions related to replacement are complied with. In the case of a convertible debenture, the indenture should specify that the right to convert is not destroyed by paying instead of issuing a new debenture.

MISCELLANEOUS FUNCTIONS

Certain other functions may be required to be performed by the trustee or the company's agents, depending upon the terms of a particular issue. The more significant of such subsidiary functions are outlined below.

Validation of Bonds and Coupons

Where a bond is mutilated for any reason, the easiest solution is to cancel it and issue a new bond in replacement. Where mutilation relates only to a single coupon, however, it is much simpler to validate such coupon. This may be accomplished by having an official of the company sign a statement on the back of the coupon to the effect that it is a valid obligation. If this procedure is not feasible, the trustee itself may validate the coupon. The language used should be substantially as follows:

---

[16]*Id.* sec. 8–405.

"This coupon belongs to Bond No. ――― and is a valid obligation of the obligor." The bond itself should always be examined to ascertain that it is in fact a valid obligation.

Exchanges Under Judicial Reorganization or Recapitalization Plans

An important function is involved in consummating a reorganization or recapitalization plan. The agent is in effect acting for the reorganization managers or the court and is usually appointed by court order. The work involves receipt and cancellation of all claims recognized in the reorganization proceedings and delivery of the cash and securities authorized in respect thereof.

Because of the complexity and diversity of such plans and arrangements, no effort will be made to describe the procedure in detail. In considering acceptance of any such appointment, the agent should ensure that the plan has been validly confirmed by appropriate court order, that the claims and distributions schedule is clear, that proper direction and instructions about its functions have been received and approved by the court, that a definite termination date for the exchange is set, and, most importantly, that the compensation to be paid for its services is sufficient to cover the expense and detail of the work involved.

Agent for Securities Not Issued Under an Indenture

The most important securities of this type are those issued by states, municipalities and authorities. Generally the same services are required as in the case of corporate obligations, with, however, a much greater emphasis at present on the paying agent and registrar functions. The procedures followed are similar except that the canceled securities are either shipped to the finance officer of the state or municipality, or the agent itself performs the accounting and destruction service customarily performed by the trustee in the case of corporate obligations.

In connection with direct placement financing of corporations, long-term notes are sometimes issued under purchase agreements not requiring the service of a trustee under an indenture. A bank is frequently, however, appointed agent of the obligor company to service such a note issue. It maintains a record of the note holders, makes interest payments, determines allocation of periodic sinking fund installments, acts as exchange agent, and in general performs all the ministerial details that the company itself would otherwise be required to perform.

LEGISLATION AND REGULATION

Partially as a result of the intense criticism of the securities processing industry arising out of the heavy volume in securities trading during 1968–1970, a number of studies by Congressional committees were made to determine the nature and extent of any additional legislation that would improve the clearance and settlement of securities transactions.[17] The most significant result was the enactment of the Securities Acts Amendments of 1975.[18] The main thrust of this legislation was to authorize the establishment of "a national system for the clearance and settlement of securities transactions and the safeguarding of securities and funds related thereto."[19] To implement this objective, the 34 Act was amended by adding section 17A[20] to provide for the federal regulation of clearing agencies and transfer agents. The SEC and the federal bank regulatory authorities were given the authority to adopt rules and regulations governing the conduct of transfer agents and to enforce compliance.[21]

Pursuant to its authority, the SEC has promulgated rules implementing the registration of transfer agents;[22] requirements for the almost universal fingerprinting of all persons engaged in the sale of securities, those who have access to the handling or processing of securities, monies, or books and records relating thereto, and those who have direct supervisory responsibility over persons engaged in such activities;[23] the promulgation of minimum performance standards and recordkeeping requirements for all registered transfer agents, including transfer turnaround requirements;[24] the establishment of a reporting and inquiry system for all lost, stolen, missing, or counterfeit securities, the prime objective of which is to prevent the misuse or fraudulent use of such securities particularly as it relates to collateralizing of loans;[25] regula-

[17] In particular, Rpt. of the Subcomm. on Securities of the Senate Comm. on Banking, Housing and Urban Affairs, 92d Cong., 2d Sess. (1972); Rpt. of the Subcomm. on Commerce and Finance of the House Comm. on Interstate and Foreign Commerce, 92d Cong., 2d Sess. (1972).

[18] Pub. L. No. 94–29 (June 5, 1975).

[19] *Id.* sec. 2.

[20] *Id.* sec. 15.

[21] Securities Exchange Act of 1934, sec. 17A(d).

[22] Rule 17 2–1 (17 CFR 240.17 2–1, October 22, 1975).

[23] Rule 17f–2 (17 CFR 240.17f–2, March 16, 1976).

[24] Rules 17Ad–1/7 (17 CFR 240.17Ad–1 to 7, June 16, 1977).

[25] Rule 17f–1 (17 CFR 240.17f–1, July 1, 1979).

tions governing the maintenance of accurate security holder files and safeguarding of funds and securities;[26] a requirement that any registered transfer agent acting as a depositary in the case of a tender offer (or as an exchange agent in the case of an exchange offer) must establish special designated accounts with the national securities depositories to permit securities to move to and from the tender/exchange agent through a book entry mechanism;[27] the timely mailing of transfer agent journals by a co-transfer agent to the recordkeeping transfer agent and a maximum time period in which to respond to dividend and interest inquiries;[28] and a requirement for the filing of an annual report on form TA-2.[29]

It can be expected that as new concerns and problems present themselves, additional regulations will be promulgated—unless the securities industry itself is able to resolve these to the satisfaction of the federal regulatory agencies. Quite possibly these agencies will seek to have a "transfer agent self-regulatory organization" created. This entity would then have the power to regulate registered transfer agents, with appropriate disciplinary authority similar to the municipal Securities Rule-making Board (for municipal bond underwriters and dealers) and the National Association of Security Dealers.

Municipal Securities and the Depository

Certificate Immobilization

The potential benefits of certificate immobilization and centralization have been understood in the corporate security sector for many years. However, until the enactment of TEFRA[30] legislation, municipal securities issuers possessed little knowledge of fully registered instruments, as bearer bonds were the norm—municipal trades traditionally being settled by physical delivery versus payment (known as "DVP") at the premises of the purchaser. Anticipating the potential impact of DVP for registered municipal securities trades, the Municipal Securities Rule-making Board established regulations to automate settlement practices.

One of the rules that impacted bond registrars required the usage of

26 Rules 17Ad–9/13 (17 CFR 240.17 Ad–9 to 13, June 21, 1983).
27 Rule 17Ad–14 (17 CFR 240.17Ad–14, January 19, 1984).
28 Rule 17Ad–10 (17 CFR 240.17Ad–10, April 1, 1986).
29 Rule 17Ac2–2 (17 CFR 240.17Ac2–2, May 5, 1986).
30 See note 7, chapter 2, supra.

book-entry delivery systems in order to expedite the settlement process.[31] This required, in part and allowing for specific exceptions, that interdealer transactions be settled by book-entry delivery in a registered clearing agency (i.e., depository). Since then most publicly traded municipal security issues have settled through a depository, the most significant being the Depository Trust Company in New York City. When a security obtains eligibility, the underwriter directs the trustee/bond registrar to register the securities in the depository's nominee name. Securities are then delivered to the depository against a trust receipt, generally one business day prior to the closing date. The depository assumes custodial responsibility for the securities by placing the physical securities in its vault. Upon joint notification by the trustee and the underwriter that all conditions precedent to the issuance of the securities have been met (i.e., that the bond issue has closed), the depository will credit the appropriate value of the bonds to the lead managing underwriter's account and process book-entry deliveries to the accounts of the syndicate members and other purchasers of the issue. Subsequent transfers of ownership may be affected either through book-entry notation on the participant's records or through withdrawal of physical securities from the depository's vault to be reregistered in the name of the purchaser or purchaser's representative, a process referred to as "withdrawal by transfer." At the end of each business day, the depository nets all trades for each participant and either collects funds from or pays funds to them, depending on their net position.

Book-Entry-Only Securities

Municipal certificate immobilization through depository settlement gained momentum and quickly expanded to a procedure that had been employed by the U.S. government securities market for many years: book-entry-only issuance ("BEO"). This program requires that issuers create a single "global" certificate for each maturity within a specific bond issue. The underwriter instructs the bond registrar to register the global certificates in the nominee name of the depository, the certificates to be held in the depository's vault until final maturity or redemption. Any reduction to the authorized principal amount of bonds outstanding, usually the result of a partial call for redemption, will be posted on the depository's records and on the records of the trustee and bond registrar. No physical securities change hands until the issue is paid in full at

31 MSRB Rule G–12(f)(11), effective Feb. 1, 1985.

which time the trustee or bond registrar will cancel and dispose of the global certificates.

The purchaser of BEO securities receives a confirmation of any trade from its broker-dealer or bank. Subsequent activity, such as payments of interest and principal, is reflected on the customer's account record evidence by periodic statements furnished by the broker-dealer or bank. Until the securities are sold or otherwise disposed of, the security position will remain on the broker-dealer or bank's participant account record at the depository. Transfers of ownership will occur only thorough book-entry debits and credits to the purchaser and seller participant account records.

In this environment the trustee must recognize and prepare for the challenges presented by the issuance of BEO securities. Obviously, a lost revenue opportunity will impact the profitability of the organization, but of additional importance is the loss of the capability of direct contact with those whom the trustee represents—the bondholders.

The depository generally will not release participant records information without the written consent of the issuer. Consequently, it is essential that the trustee obtain blanket authorization from the issuer consenting to the release of information by the depository upon the request of the trustee. In a default situation, the trustee must have the ability to reach bondholders in order to obtain direction or consents and to provide critical information in a timely manner.

The need to standardize the processing practices of the trustee and bond registrar has increased significantly with the growth of depository-eligible municipal securities. In order for a new security issue to be accepted as eligible by the depository, the trustee or agent may be required to execute an operational agreement which sets forth, inter alia, required procedures governing delivery of original issuance securities, timeliness of certificate transfers, reporting and notice formats and time frames, methods of transmitting interest and principal payments, and municipal call processing procedures.

It is important that the appointed trustee and bond registrar use their best efforts to comply with the terms of the arrangement to ensure the continued eligibility of the issue for which they act. The depository will generally provide trustees and bond registrars with periodic performance reports so that any processing concerns can be identified and resolved in a timely manner.

II

Management

A social organism of any sort whatsoever, large or small, is what it is because each member proceeds to do his own duty with a trust that other members will simultaneously do theirs.

—William James, 1842–1910

Management is tasks. Management is a discipline. But management is also people. Every achievement of management is the achievement of a manager. Every failure is a failure of a manager. People manage rather than "forces" or "facts." The vision, dedication, and integrity of managers determines whether there is management or mismanagement.

—Peter F. Drucker, *Management*

Introduction

During many years of involvement in the corporate trust industry, I have observed that few people hired as "corporate trust administrators" or "management trainees" are provided with orientation, structured training, or a real understanding of the managerial or human side of the enterprise. Their training and development is almost always limited to the technical aspects of the job, often on a transactional basis, designed to get them working as quickly as possible. Whereas this may achieve the desired work results within a relatively short time, it becomes exceedingly difficult for them to develop an understanding of the relationship of their job and its responsibilities to the overall corporate trust function and the business plan that drives it. The development and utilization of a planned training program that links the organization's strategy and business plans to individual job requirements and accountabilities can become the vehicle to help them grow and to be an even greater asset to the organization, as well as fulfill their own potential.

The human side of the enterprise includes managerial issues and concerns incident to the several components of the business, *i.e.*, what are the organization's strategy and planning philosophy, process, and techniques; what is the organization of the work and the resultant structure; what is the overall action plan for personnel training and development; and, finally, what means are used to evaluate performance and identify needs for improvement, including advancement opportunities.

Unfortunately, as I have discovered in leading numerous seminars and workshops, relatively few people who have worked in the business even for several years have a sufficient understanding of these issues and, more importantly, lack the training necessary to deal with them. In fact, many supervisors and managers still "wing it," relying on their own transactional experiences and a few general management courses to help them deal with people issues. Because these issues are usually believed to be within the prerogative of senior management and are subject almost exclusively to the policies and procedures (if they even exist) of the individual bank, little attention has been paid to them in the context of the development of the corporate trust professional. Management is a skill and a responsibility that must be learned and experienced at all levels, starting with the taking of responsibility for managing oneself and one's own activities. As the individual assumes greater responsibility for the work of others, these skills become the basis for helping others achieve a better perspective of their role in the overall function.

The ensuing chapters, which are relatively brief, are not designed to teach the profession of management or to be an exhaustive "how to" treatment of the subject matter. They are simply a framework within which corporate trust administrators and account officers, operations supervisors, and managers can begin to appreciate and understand the dynamics and complexities of operating in a truly professional environment. They can, as a result, develop the necessary action plans and programs to fit their particular needs and the needs of the organization.

It must be understood that management is an interactive process, requiring trust, cooperation, and understanding between managers and subordinates. To be a truly effective process it will operate on three levels: manager to subordinate ("managing downward"), subordinate to manager ("managing upward"), and manager to manager and subordinate to subordinate ("managing laterally"). Thus, this material should be of as much value to the new administrator as to the experienced manager. In fact, as a result, some managers may even be encouraged (or forced) to respond to their subordinates' questions on these matters.

The structure and size of the particular organization will clearly affect the implementation and use of any of the ideas, guidelines, and suggestions set forth. The basic assumptions and premises should not, however, be affected by numbers of people or levels of management hierarchy. The usefulness of this material will be determined by the degree of interest of those who seek to learn more about the management aspect of the function and by a desire to enhance their value to their organization. It is obvious, however, that the level of interest and inclination of the managers who are in a very real position to influence or determine the desired outcome will be a key factor in the training and development of the people in the function.

For those who wish to explore this subject in a much broader context, there has been included in the bibliography a small selection from the myriad of books and articles on management issues that I have found to be germane and helpful. In particular, I would recommend that every manager (and all who would like to be one) read, study, and use the concepts, principles, and approaches in the following books: *The Concept of Corporate Strategy* by Ken Andrews is a relatively short book (132 pages), that provides an excellent, thoughtful, and very useful discussion of both the formulation of corporate strategy and its implementation; *Coaching For Improved Work Performance*, by Ferdinand F. Fournies, is an eminently readable and practical approach to dealing with the obstacles to work performance and the ways and means to counsel and coach employees in overcoming problems that hinder or block their development and future opportunities; *A Passion for Excellence* by Tom Peters and Nancy Austin complements the other two works; it is an extremely well written commonsense analysis that highlights the methods and accomplishments of those companies that have demonstrated superior service to their clients and customers, a constant level of innovation, and a consistent approach to internal corporate entrepreneurship.

Strategic and Tactical Planning

As we begin to examine the management aspects of the corporate trust function, it is necessary to take a view of the function as being a separate business or product line within a larger financial services institution. Thus it follows that it *should,* in fact, be so managed. For any business to survive and succeed, it must be driven by a strategy that clearly defines its purposes or goals so that it keeps moving in a deliberately chosen direction. The resultant structure of the organization must in turn support that strategy. No student of management or of organization development would, however, suggest that strategy is a static, immovable force. It and the structure must be adaptable to change; it must be flexible enough to permit the organization to modify its approach, and even to dramatically change direction as the needs of *its* market, and of the environment in which it operates, change.

Corporate strategy has been defined as "the pattern of decisions in a company that determines and reveals its objectives, purposes, goals, produces the principal policies and plans for achieving those goals, and defines the range of business the company is to pursue, the kind of economic and human organization it is or intends to be, and the nature of the economic and noneconomic contribution it intends to make to its shareholders, employees, customers, and communities." [1]

Another excellent definition was written by Alfred D. Chandler in *Strategy and Structure* in which he postulated that is ". . . the determination of the basic long-term goals and objectives of an enterprise and

---

[1] Andrews, *The Concept of Corporate Strategy,* p. 13.

the adoption of courses of action and allocation of resources necessary for carrying out these goals." [2]

The strategic business plan of an organization is based on its articulated strategy—expressed in terms of long-range direction, purpose, and corporate culture. One of the best known and most widely read authors on management is Peter Drucker. In his landmark study of the subject he observes

> 1. It is not a bag of tricks, a bundle of techniques. It is analytical thinking and commitment of resources to action. . . . 2. Strategy planning is not forecasting. It is not masterminding the future. . . . 3. Strategic planning does not deal with future decisions. It deals with the futurity of present decisions. . . . 4. Strategic planning is not an attempt to eliminate risk. It is not even an attempt to minimize risk. [3]

"Strategy . . . answers the questions. What is our business, what should it be, what will it be. . . . It thereby determines what the key activities are in a given business or service institution. Effective structure is the design that makes these key activities capable of functioning and of performance. . . ." [4]

Strategy is thus the driving force from which all else in the organization flows and is the means to direct the organization in the pursuit of its mission, the components of which are discussed below.

The strategic plan for the corporate trust business must flow from both the strategy and the strategic plan of its parent institution. Because the corporate trust function is not a fully independent entity, its strategy and planning process will be guided by the institution's direction and demands, its guidelines, and its policies. Within any such parameters, however, corporate trust managers will be responsible for developing its culture, plans, objectives, and supporting structure. It is they, together with the members of the corporate trust organization, who must drive the business within the context of its business plan. Axiomatic is the policy that "those who *implement* the plans must *make* the plans." [5]

[2] Chandler, *Strategy and Structure*, p. 13.
[3] Drucker, *Management*, p. 123.
[4] *Id.*, p. 523.
[5] Texas Instrument's Patrick Haggerty quoted in Peters and Waterman, *In Search of Excellence*, p. 31.

THE NEEDS ANALYSIS

Before developing a strategic business plan it is necessary to establish a process whereby each of the essential elements will lead into and influence the others. Included at the end of the chapter is a diagrammatic model (Figure 1) depicting this process flow and the interrelationships of the strategic and tactical business plans.

This process will include an issues and needs analysis covering an "environmental scan" of the corporate trust and securities processing business, the present and projected economic capital financing environment, the nature and extent of the competition for corporate trust appointments, the strategic posture of the institution, and the present state of the corporate trust function.

The "critical issues analysis" is simply an understanding and evaluation of those conditions under which the corporate trust function is operating and can expect to operate during the next three to five years.

The framework for such an analysis should focus on three levels:

1. *The Industry* (a) What are the significant technological changes taking place in providing trustee and securities servicing activities? (b) What legislation and regulation is significantly impacting the development, production, and delivery of the services? (c) What is the effect of judicial decisions on the evolving role of an indenture trustee? (d) What changing economic conditions and changes in the capital markets, including types of financing vehicles, must be met? (e) What is the competitive environment for obtaining profitable appointments? (f) What is the impact of changing demands and expectations of the clients and the security holders?

2. *The Bank* (a) Does the bank's strategy enhance or detract from the corporate trust business? (b) Will the bank's response to changes in limitations on or expansion of the permitted scope of its activities help or hinder the function? (c) Does the management of the bank actively support or simply tolerate corporate trust activities? (d) What demands does the bank's senior management place on the corporation trust function as a *profitable* business line? (e) To what extent do other areas of the bank provide product and market development support? (f) To what extent does the bank provide resources to support and grow the function?

3. *The Corporate Trust Function* (a) What is the *financial* impact resulting from technological changes in the industry, from a changing

and volatile economic environment, from increased levels of regulation and government intervention, from increasing competition, and from greater demands by clients and security holders? (*b*) At what stage is the function in terms of its *organizational development,* including necessary managerial and technical/professional staffing; personnel training, development, and evaluation; and meeting the needs and demands of a changing work force?·(*c*) What is the underlying basis for the development of new business, *i.e.*, its *marketing* responsibilities, and to what extent is it dependent upon the sales solicitation efforts of noncorporate trust people? How is the internal sales effort managed? How do new services or modifications of existing services get developed? What is the impact on the marketing and sales efforts resulting from the bank's relationships with its corporate and municipal clients? (*d*) What is the state and extent of the existing *technology* supporting the function? What are the major shortcomings or deficiencies of the processing and information systems? What level of support can be reasonably expected from the institution's systems development staff? What major changes or enhancements to the existing systems are needed to remain price and market competitive? What impact will the greater use of microcomputers and remote processing have on the delivery and cost of agency services?

Once the answers to these questions have been set forth, the next step in the process is to develop a "critical needs analysis." In this instance, the issues that were identified earlier and the related responses can be divided into two categories, those having a longer range impact, which should be addressed over a three- to five-year time frame, and those that must be addressed within a one- to two-year period. Within each time category, the critical needs can be grouped as follows:

> Financial Management
> Marketing Development
> Technological Development
> Organizational Development
> Organizational Structure

The result of this part of the planning process will be to establish identified issues and needs that become the key ingredients in developing both the strategic and annual business plans.

THE STRATEGIC PLAN

As discussed earlier, the components of the plan will be an evaluation of the present state of the business ("what are we doing?"), an understanding of what the business will be like ("what will we be doing?"), and a definitive posture reflecting what direction the business should go ("what do we want to be doing?").

In addition to the development of the critical issues and needs, it is necessary to examine the various services offered and the particular markets for such services. This analysis can be done by matrixing the various trustee and agency services against the several target markets, indicating for each: (1) whether the service/market exists [E], is planned [P] or is possible[?]; (2) the attractiveness of the service/market on a scale of 5 down to zero, in terms of profitable business and opportunity to increase volume and/or market share; and (3) the perceived competition for the service/market on a scale of five down to zero.

Such a matrix for the Paying Agent service might look like this:

Service	Corporations	Governments	Banks
Paying Agent	E-5-4	E-4-5	P-3-5

A further refinement of this matrix would include an analysis of the financial components affecting each service/market in terms of: (1) the relative significance of the cost components, high-medium-low, of both fixed and variable cost; and (2) the relative significance of the profit margins, high-medium-low, on an incremental and fully absorbed cost basis.[6] Thus, our Paying Agent example might look like this:

	Cost Fixed/Variable	Profit Incr./Fully Abs.
Corporations	M/M	H/M
Governments	M/H	H/M

In reviewing the existing and potential corporate trust business an analysis should be done for each of the major service/market categories: trustee for debt issues of corporations, governments, and other banks; bond registrar for corporate and government debt issues; transfer agent

---

[6]Incremental profit is the gross income minus fixed expense and corporate overhead that is allocated to the function. Fully absorbed profit (sometimes referred to as "NIBT," net income before tax) is gross income minus the total of all expense (variable, fixed, direct, indirect, or allocated) attributable to being in the particular business.

(and registrar) for corporate equity issues; and paying agent for corporations and governments. For each of these components, an analysis can be made of: (1) the historical size and direction of the market and the environmental factors influencing the numbers and the direction (e.g., unsecured versus secured debt, straight versus convertible, fixed rate versus floating rate); (2) the nature and extent of the existing and projected competition for such appointments and of the perceived strengths and weaknesses of the most significant competitors; and (3) the major existing and projected strengths and weaknesses of the corporate trust function in providing such services against the competition.

The result of all these analyses will be to establish the realistic parameters and opportunities for the business. The analyses may also result in a decision by the senior management, not to "grow the business," but either to let it run down or simply sell it off. (This obviously is the risk inherent in fully understanding the dynamics, components, and profit potential in any business line!)

On the assumption that the signs are favorable, and the risk/reward analysis is positive, the next step would be the articulation of a "strategic overview and posture," which would include a statement of the function's key objective or mission; a delineation of the services that are to be offered to the particular identified markets; the strategic theme reflecting what level of *emphasis* will be placed on particular services and markets; the business objectives in terms of market share, profit margins, year over year profit dollar growth, return on expense investment, or any other determinant or standard the institution establishes for its business lines.

While not intended to be a definitive statement of the overall mission or goal of the corporate trust function, it is evident that this overview should include making a contribution to the growth and profitability of the bank by providing professional corporate trust services to its clients on a cost effective and profitable basis.

The strategic overview of the function having been established, this should then be translated into the strategy to be applied to the continuation of existing services and markets, the enhancement of such services and the broadening (or narrowing) of the target markets of each, and the planned development and delivery of new services to the same or different prospective markets. Inherent in this part of the strategic business plan would be consideration and projection of resources needed to accomplish the plan. The resource needs can be categorized into staff (number, type, mix), space (how much and where), and furniture and equipment, including appropriate technological support.

Also to be considered are the projected organization structure necessary to support the plan and the relationships and interdependencies of the various units involved in developing, producing, implementing, and delivering the various services.

The final part of the strategic business plan should address alternative and contingency planning. The previous parts of the plan were based on certain assumptions, which might not prove to be either accurate or viable. It is therefore essential that consideration be given to alternative strategies that could be adapted and/or adopted as the need arises. Those areas that would seem most susceptible to this possibility and for which it would seem, therefore, most necessary to have contingency plans include economic environment, legal and regulatory restrictions, competition, automation technology, and availability of trained staff.

The Annual Business Plan

Each institution will, of course, establish the framework and process for its annual planning cycle, as well as the parameters covering the type and detail level of the plan itself. Within that context, however, it is evident that *the plan* will include several separate but interrelated subplan components. These would be a marketing plan, an activity/volume plan, an automation technology plan, a human resources plan, and, certainly, a financial plan.

The marketing plan includes not only the "how, when and where" of the planned effort but also the results sought to be accomplished. In effect it constitutes the sales objectives that are believed to be viable and realistic.

The activity/volume plan is simply a projection of the extent to which the existing and planned book of business will result in certain types of activity and the volume of each such activity. This would run the gamut from the number of projected new trusteeships to the projected volume of certificates to be issued and canceled as transfer agent. These data are essential in evaluating and assessing the needs for resource support, as well as the development of the income and expense plan.

The automation technology plan addresses the needs of the business in being able to efficiently and effectively deliver its services. It would delineate what systems maintenance or development efforts are necessary, what additional hardware and equipment are required and what the projected cost benefits of the investment are.

The human resource plan will focus on the identified personnel needs of the function and its staff in accomplishing its business goals. This will include an assessment of the present staff, its adequacy in terms of numbers and level of expertise, the training and development needs, and an appropriate compensation program. It will also provide for a process wherein the identified needs are translated into organizational objectives, as well as personal improvement objectives for the staff members. In the following chapters, the essential elements of organization and structure and the establishment of training and development programs and an evaluation process are discussed.

The final part of any annual business plan will address the financial objectives of the function. It will cover the expected income from each of the major services provided and is usually quantified on a quarterly basis. The expense side will reflect the allocation and use of all resources required to meet the income objectives. In almost every institution this will require a detailed analysis of the fixed (*e.g.*, space) and variable (*e.g.*, overtime) costs incident to the business. Certain of these expenses will be charged directly to the function as a profit center, while others (*e.g.*, corporate overhead) may be allocated on an indirect basis through the institution's cost allocation systems.

The most significant expense, usually running between 70 and 80 percent of total expense, relates to people. It therefore receives the most attention from managers as they seek to achieve increased productivity. Because of the major impact that training, development, and performance planning can play in achieving higher levels of productivity, chapters 18 and 19 address these topics in some detail.

Before discussing in the next chapter what are some of the typical arrangements and functional relationships in corporate trust, it is necessary to fully understand that the structure of the particular organization must flow out of both the nature of the business itself and the strategy that drives the business. Peter Drucker puts it this way: 'Organization is not mechanical. It is not "assembly.' It cannot be prefabricated! Organization is organic and unique to each individual business or institution. For we now know that structure, to be effective and sound, must follow strategy. . . .''[7]

[7]Drucker, *Management*, p. 523.

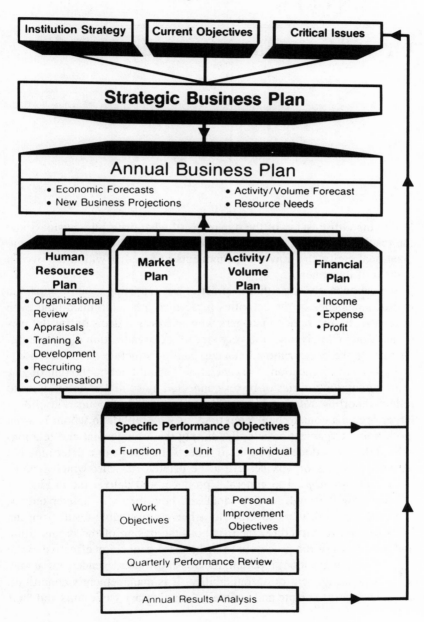

FIGURE 1
Planning Process Flow

SEVENTEEN

Organization and Structure

Following a discussion of the dynamics of what drives the business and the resultant planning process, it seems appropriate to look at the organizational entity and how the components fit together within the overall context of its strategy.

It is abundantly clear that in practice the reporting relationships and interdependencies of the activities performed are determined (and even governed) by the senior managers who make such decisions at the particular time. Clearly also, the very size of the organization directly influences both the organizational makeup and the structure of the function.

In its basic application, "organization" should not be thought of as a chart containing a series of boxes connected by solid and dotted lines to reflect reporting relationships. (Such a chart is, of course, useful in larger organizations to help keep track of who reports to whom in what work unit.) Organization is rather simply the arrangement and relationship of the work done by people. It reflects the results of a determination of what products or services are to be offered for sale; which type of work units are needed to generate, produce, and deliver the product or service; how they will receive input and how they will deliver output; and how they will work together to achieve a profitable result from the labor expended. Structure, then, is both the design of the organization and the design of the processes to make the organization effective in the areas of communication, reporting relationships, interdependencies among units, and assignment of accountability. It is management's conclusion about how best to create and maintain the necessary work units and their relationship to each other, at that particular time in the entity's existence.

For the purpose of discussing organization and structure, it is assumed that the function includes the following key business activities: administration of trust indentures and other debt financing instruments and agreements, as well as agency servicing agreements; operational servicing and processing of debt and equity securities and maintenance of related records and data files; and marketing of both trustee and agency services to existing and prospective clients. In essence this arrangement is often referred to as "product divisionalization", *i.e.*, the corporate trust function as an integrated business line or product center is a relatively self-contained business unit. Each of the key business activities interfaces with the others—the natural order of the work required to be accomplished flows between and among them. The output of one becomes the input of another. The final product, or output of the function, is thus the result of the efforts, and value added, of each and all of the work units in the process.

As an integrated function, it is responsible and accountable for the expenses it incurs (including the overhead of simply being part of a larger organization) and the income it produces, resulting in a profit contribution to the bank. In many banks where all the work units are not under "corporate trust management," an effort is made through the practice of transfer pricing to charge the income-producing center with the expense of the work performed by any noncorporate trust work units. This approach is valid only if: the rates to be charged are negotiated in advance; the activity volume is accurately captured; the resultant expense is monitored and evaluated on a regular basis; and it is, in fact, a cost-effective means of producing and delivering the services. It does not, of course, address the real people issues of full product ownership or the developmental options of the employees or the managers—a discussion of which is set forth in chapter 18.

Within the corporate trust organization itself, it is generally agreed that a "functional" structure best achieves the overall business goal indicated earlier. The integrated functional structure provides the greatest number of options for the most effective management of the people and the work involved. The classic problem of "we versus them" is greatly mitigated when all parts of the business line operate in a common environment under a management team that is responsible for the entire corporate trust function. On such a basis the structure of the line units would then be:

Function Head

Marketing	Administration	Operations
Product Development	Trustee	Securities
Research	Agency	Processing
Sales		Funds and
		Payments
		Records

with such staff support units as are necessary.

(In a few very large corporate trust banks the product divisionalization is carried even further, so that separate product centers are established—each having marketing, administration and operations responsibilities—all within the overall corporate trust function.)

This arrangement, reflecting the major responsibilities of the business and the resultant interdependencies and accountabilities, is not, however, universal among the corporate trust banks. In fact, in some banks, each of the three main components is in a separate department—the only common manager being the bank's president! In those banks corporate trust is usually defined as, and limited to, the administration activity. However, even in this instance, attention to the organization and structure of the unit is critical.

Even under an integrated functional structure, corporate trust is not a completely stand-alone business, *i.e.*, fully integrated both horizontally and vertically. It still requires the support of other line and staff organizations within the bank, including money transfer, check reconcilement, personnel, and commercial banking units for marketing support.

Having looked at the corporate trust function as a whole, an examination of each of the three main components follows.

MARKETING

New business is the lifeblood of the function; there must be continuous infusions of new appointments. Without the continued inflow, the organization will simply not survive—fixed expenses will continue to be incurred to a point where the function cannot produce income that covers both the variable expenses and the overhead. It is evident also that no successful institution is going to indefinitely offer a service for which the profit levels do not justify the investment in space, equipment, and people. Today, most successful banking organizations also demand that the business line evidence a year-over-year growth in its profit contribution. It must be recognized, however, that some banks still view the function as an accommodation service—something it must offer to be perceived as a full-service financial provider—even though it does not contribute to the bank's net earnings.

The marketing of corporate trust services, like most other nonasset-based banking functions, must be done on two different levels. First, efforts must be made by corporate trust in marketing to the commercial banking officers who form the first line of salespeople in generating corporate trust appointments. Second must be the direct marketing by corporate trust personnel to corporate and municipal issuers and to financial intermediaries. In the former instance, the banking officers become the eyes and ears of the corporate trust selling effort. Such officers are usually in a position to most effectively determine whether their clients will need corporate trust services because of their more frequent calls on such clients. Unfortunately, they are also called upon to do the same for all (or most) of the other services being offered by the bank—and it must be recognized that corporate trust appointments may not be uppermost in their minds in seeking additional relationships with the client.

It is for this very reason that such officers must be made aware of the corporate trust services offered, be comfortable in seeking such business, and know whom to call for technical sales help or to whom to refer a potential appointment. Thus it becomes essential that a great deal of the corporate trust marketing effort be organized to ensure that these matters are addressed to as many commerical banking officers as possible. One easy way to accomplish this is to "take a banker to lunch" and review the potentially profitable opportunities for the bank (thus enhancing that particular banking officer's value to the bank as well).

It is not always possible to accomplish the desired marketing objectives by relying solely on others to do the sales work. In those instances where the corporate trust function has the only relationship, or where a technical sales call for a particular transaction would be more directly productive, this should be done by a knowledgeable corporate trust officer.

In either case, however, the responsibility for product development (*i.e.*, what new or modified service to what market segment) and basic research must be assumed by those people who have the greatest knowledge of the nuances of the service and the capabilities of the function. Whether or not the marketing activity is specifically within the corporate trust structure, the expertise and knowledge required does not change.

The requirement to fully understand the nature and workings of corporate trust activities and the function's ability to deliver the services with a resultant profit is essential to successfully accomplish any marketing objectives.

ADMINISTRATION

Once the appointment has been obtained, it must be administered in a professional manner, consistent with the particular duties and responsibilities of the appointment and with knowledge of the potential liabilities involved. In essence, the organization and structure of the administration function is to provide for one or more account officers and/or administrators (or teams of such) who are accountable for discharging the bank's duties and responsibilities under the particular appointment documents. This can run the gamut from a one-person unit to a structure that uses many people organized into discrete work units or teams. In the latter case, this can be accomplished by organizing in one of two basic ways: (1) allocating the work on a functional or product basis, with a separate team handling each different type or appointment (e.g., being responsible only for municipal housing issues) or just one aspect of the work involved in all accounts (e.g., giving comments on indentures or handling the various sinking funds) or (2) on a divisional basis where each team is fully responsible for all aspects of a diverse set of trustee and agency appointments. In actual practice few corporate trust functions are organized purely on a functional or divisional basis but somewhere on the spectrum between them. In the smaller banks, the tendency is toward the divisional structure, wherein a few account officers and administrators do everything. In the larger banks, which probably have a very heavy volume of diverse appointments, more specialization tends to be the case, the result being a structure more reflective of a functional or product approach.

OPERATIONS

In almost every organization, the operations function was not created *de novo* but grew piecemeal with a structure that responded to the type and volume of appointments over a period of years. The advent of the all fully registered corporate bond issues in the late 1960s, the proliferation of tax-exempt issues and creative financing vehicles, the increased numbers of smaller companies selling debt and equity securities, and the widespread use of computerized systems have all had a significant impact on the organization of the function and its resultant structure.

It is not really possible to articulate a precise model—given the great diversity of activities that may be performed within the operations function. Despite that drawback, it is possible to describe generally the basic areas of activity that are usually found in a corporate trust operations organization. These would include (1) the processing of securities, (2) the receipt and disbursement of funds, and (3) the maintenance of records and data files.

With respect to securities processing, the organization of work performed will follow from the logical flow of the work required to be done. This normally follows a pattern that includes:

1. receipt of the securities
2. examination of the securities
3. input of data to debit and credit security holder accounts
4. cancellation of the incoming securities
5. issuance of new securities and/or payment vehicles
6. delivery of new securities and/or payments

Each of these key activities is involved in both the receipt of work and the output of work—in effect each of the parts must be organizationally structured so that maximum efficiencies can be achieved.

The receipt of securities may be either through a collection or clearing system, which generally involves a bulk shipment of securities for the agent to process, or directly from an individual security holder (or broker) by mail or in person. The next step in the process is the examination of the particular securities to ensure, among other requirements, that it is in appropriate form for the action requested to be effected, i.e., registration of transfer, exchange, payment, and so forth. On the assumption that the item is not defective and the action requested can be effected, it then goes to operations personnel who make the necessary changes in the security holder file. In the case of the registration of a transfer, an appropriate debit is posted to the transferor's account with an offsetting credit to the transferee's account, or in the case of a new account, the posting of new account information. At the same time, systems are activated to produce new certificates in the name of the transferee. If the transaction is a redemption or maturity, the offsetting credit to the account debited is the production of a check or other payment vehicle. For a convertible issue, the offset to the cancellation of the surrendered certificates is the production (or requisition from the stock transfer agent) of the appropriate number of full shares of stock. The incoming securities are then canceled and ultimately disposed of, the new certificates (or payment checks) being sent back to the person surrendering the securities in the first instance. This may include their direct mailing, their return over the window, or back through the particular collection or clearing system, thus completing the full cycle of the processing function.

The second major operational activity involves the receipt and disbursement of funds. In almost every corporate trust organization, specific people are designated to follow for, and book in, the required debt service funds or dividends as the case may be. Because the role of paying or disbursement agent is really that of a conduit, the other side of this activity involves the calculation of the funds required to be disbursed and the actual disbursement thereof. These typically include payments of interest on registered bonds and dividends on stock, payments of interest against surrender of bearer coupons, payments of principal on account of a partial redemption or upon the maturity of an issue. The activity is not performed in isolation but requires coordination between and among the account administrator and the operational units involved in the processing of the underlying securities.

The third major area of activity involves the maintenance of records. Whereas much of the information required to be maintained is an integral part of the securities processing and payment functions, other records must be kept, whether they are to establish appropriate audit trails, meet SEC reporting requirements, provide for accurate cash controls, perform the billing function, or simply to provide management information on levels of activity and volume. In addition, it is of paramount importance that every operations officer maintain a constant high level of attention to the entire range of proof and control activities within the function, including the daily reconcilement of all individual cash and securities transactions to the unit's control records. It is the functional need that must be appropriately integrated into the organization, rather than the identification of which people or units do what work.

In most institutions, the organization of this operational work is structured along functional lines under the management of an experienced officer. Ideally, this person should be a real people manager, capable of dealing with complex automation needs, processing procedures, and techniques, all in a fast-paced and action-oriented environment.

Within the context of the organization of the function and its resultant structure, we now turn to consideration of the requisite training and development needs of the staff involved in implementing the business plan.

EIGHTEEN

Training and Development

One of the key components of a manager's job, perhaps even the most important, is to establish and maintain an environment in which people are encouraged and helped to develop and improve their knowledge and skill competencies. It is generally agreed that to accomplish the desired results any developmental effort should be on a building block basis. The cumulative effect of such an approach will be that the individual becomes increasingly more knowledgeable and skillful (i.e., productive) in the existing position and is able to demonstrate potential for increased levels and/or scope of responsibility. The end result will be much more motivated persons who will have increased their individual value, and their value to the organization. This in turn will provide both the individual and the organization with more options for the type and nature of their future responsibilities and the position in the organization at which they work.[1]

The starting point for any manager is to do a manpower audit. Simply put, it evaluates the degree and breadth of knowledge and skill of the existing staff against the needs of the organization as determined by its strategic and tactical business plans (as discussed in chapter 17). Included in the analysis must be what numbers of people and what mix (specialists, generalists) are necessary, what the projected personnel turnover is, and what the personnel vulnerabilities are. This is in effect

[1] The Certified Corporate Trust Specialist designation offered by the Institute of Certified Bankers is intended to "hallmark" the industry's most experienced professionals. This program should also encourage other corporate trust practioners to increase their level of competence and technical knowledge through a program of continuing education and development.

a personnel needs analysis that highlights the particular recruiting, staffing, training, and development needs of the organization.

As discussed earlier, the increasingly complex nature of the corporate trust business has led to more and more specialization of work by administrators and account officers, particularly in the larger organizations. It is evident that, carried too far, it may over a longer period of time be counterproductive to the development of a well-rounded professional administrative staff. A great deal of learning experience may be sacrificed under the guise of efficiency. In such situations, individual training and development needs must be factored into a comprehensive training program to ensure that diverse learning opportunities are made available.

The major drawback resulting from training only specialists can, of course, be overcome through appropriate job rotation, provided it is in fact accomplished through a defined plan. The timing of rotational moves and attention to structured training experiences require careful follow-up by the manager for it to be effective. It seems evident, however, that any particular corporate trust organization is significantly better served and the individual is better equipped for greater responsibilities if he/she is not limited to a functionally driven set of accounts or work responsibilities but rather is thoroughly trained and experienced in all facets of administering debt and equity accounts, covering as wide a range of diverse types of appointments as is possible.

Before developing any type of comprehensive training program, it is essential to define the job, including its objectives, accountabilities, and the requisite knowledge and skill competencies. The competencies would be those related to technical, managerial (including self-management), and interpersonal factors. Incorporated in such a job description or position profile would be the essential elements of an account administrator's or officer's job as follows:

KEY OBJECTIVE: To contribute to the growth and profitability of the bank by providing expert innovative trust and agency services for issuers and holders of corporate, state, and municipal securities and by meeting the changing demands of the economy and of the banking and securities industry.

PRIMARY ACCOUNTABILITY: To represent the bank in all facets of corporate trust administration, including the review, negotiation, execution, and delivery of indentures and other financing agreements; the establishment and implementation of procedures relative to the administration of such agreements; the enforcement of the provisions of such agreements in accordance with the Trust Indenture Act and other securities laws and regulations, with emphasis on the rights of security holders and the risks and liabilities of the bank related thereto.

REPORTING RELATIONSHIPS: Reports to an administration manager. (For officers: has responsibility for supervising and training account adminstrators.)

INTERFACE RELATIONSHIPS: Interfaces with operations units, commercial banking officers, existing customers, correspondent banks, investment bankers, law firms, and underwriters.

ACCOUNTABILITIES: *(level of such as determined by training and experience)*

Account Acceptance Performance:

(1) Reviews, negotiates, and renders comments on new indenture and other financing instruments so that they meet the requirements for acceptance by the bank; (2) evaluates bank's duties, responsibilities, and potential liabilities; (3) handles all matters related to the closing, including the review of required documents, preparation of internal records, and instructions to operations units; and (4) develops and/or negotiates fees and pricing matters with client.

Account Administration Performance:

Completes the following administrative transactions, as applicable, in a timely and effective manner: (1) establishment, maintenance, and use of internal records, files, and instructions; (2) review of certificates and opinions; (3) analysis of financial statements; (4) receipt and movement of funds and collateral; (5) preparation of annual trustee's reports; (6) processing of sinking funds and redemptions; (7) investment of trust funds and valuations; (8) processing of releases and withdrawals; (9) processing satisfactions, resignations, change of corporate name and consents, and waivers; (10) security holder meetings; (11) successor trusteeships; and (12) mergers and acquisitions.

Planning Performance:

Develops specific objectives for annual performance, including: (1) recommendations in modification of policies, procedures, and methods to improve administration services; (2) planning and establishing priorities in workflow and organization; and (3) participates in revenue generating and expense reduction planning.

Human Resource Performance: (*for account officers*)

(1) Supervises the daily work flow of administrators and reviews all required documents; (2) provides training and development consistent with work standards and the training guidelines for administrators; and (3) conducts appraisals of nonofficial staff and provides appropriate assistance to administration management.

Marketing Performance:

(1) Promotes relationships with current customer base and other contacts; (2) contributes to the planning process by assisting in the identification of new prospects; (3) evaluates prospective new business in conjunction with administration management; and (4) participates in new product development.

KNOWLEDGE COMPETENCIES: (1) Principles of and developments in corporate and municipal finance; (2) federal and state securities statutes, particularly TIA and applicable provisions of the UCC; (3) federal and state securities regulations, particularly those of the Federal Reserve Board, SEC, and OCC; (4) structure and content of basic documents, including bond mortgage, debenture indenture, private placement agreement, agency agreements for debt and equity, leveraged lease documentation, commercial paper documentation, depository and escrow agreements; (5) applicable bank and administration policies and procedures; (6) trends and developments in corporate trust industry, including applicable court decisions, securities processing procedures and tax requirements; (7) administration's technical, managerial, and human resource planning process; (8) investment banking and underwriting functions; and (9) industry rules and practices, particularly those from NYSE and MSRB.

SKILL COMPETENCIES: (1) Effectively negotiates trust and agency agreement provisions and related fees to meet organization's standards; (2) administers trust and agency accounts in accordance with legal and bank policies and standards; (3) makes investments as directed by obligor/principal by completing appropriate instructions and accurately calculating discounts, interest, etc; (4) effectively and within specified guidelines manages default situations and bankruptcies; (5) provides operations units with timely and accurate instructions for processing for all account transactions; (6) effectively prepares, maintains, and utilizes internal administration records and files; (7) does appropriate research and develops timely response to customer inquiry on transactional project; and (8) carefully analyzes current and potential problems and makes sound recommendations/decisions based upon such analysis.

MANAGERIAL COMPETENCIES:

Planning

(1) Understands objective-setting process and establishes meaningful and realistic performance objectives with supporting action steps; (2) effectively ranks current and projected work responsibilities and assignments by priorities; and (3) assesses consequences of current and planned programs and work assignments.

Leading

(1) Effectively and efficiently trains and develops subordinates; (2) motivates subordinates to reach high standards of quality and to stretch own performance expectations; (3) develops and leads a transactional team or task force project; and (4) willingly delegates work and responsibility, including scheduling of work for maximum efficiency.

Organizing

(1) Manages own time, including scheduling and prioritizing of work to be done; (2) handles multiple assignments regularly and completes them in a thorough, timely manner; and (3) recognizes and uses staff support resources as needed.

Controlling

(1) Effectively monitors and controls work in progress; (2) implements administration performance standards and takes corrective action when necessary; and (3) effectively monitors and conserves allocated expense dollars and other resources.

INTERPERSONAL COMPETENCIES: (1) Performance results—desires to excel and perform above standards; (2) customer contact—establishes and maintains working relationships to assure responsiveness to customer concerns and inquiries; (3) problem solving—works with others in developing relevant information, reaching best solution scenario and implementing decision reached; (4) influence management—accomplishes desired results through others over whom there is no direct control, including desirable changes in methods and procedures; (5) communicating—achieves clear understanding through effective oral and written communication, on a timely basis, with subordinates, peers, superiors, customers, and security holders; (6) sensitivity—recognizes the needs, feelings, and expectations of others and manages the relationships to assure productive results; (7) professional image—presents a positive professional image, including oral and written communication and personal appearance, to customers and contacts.

In conjunction with the use of the position profile, it makes a great deal of sense to have in place also a fairly detailed articulation of the expected standards of performance for the position. Such a document can be extraordinarily detailed or simply focus on the significant duties and activities of the administrator.

The development of such a guideline is really the basic ingredient enabling a manager to determine, monitor, and evaluate what the expected results or outcomes of the training program are. It also provides the individual administrator and officer with full understanding of the expected standards of performance upon which he/she will be reviewed and appraised (as discussed in chapter 19).

These standards are derived from the organization of the work to be done, the relationship among the people involved in the process, the particular policies and procedures established by the organization, and the level of service quality that the organization desires to provide its clients. Table 1 shows a few examples of some activities and recommended standards that would be basic in almost every corporate trust organization.

The accountabilities and requirements of the position having been clearly defined, as established through a position profile and performance standards, the development of a training program simply flows from a logical analysis of how and when the particular components need to be addressed. The program itself should be comprehensive in its approach and detailed in its implementation. The application of each component will, of course, depend upon the results of the needs analysis from the perspective of the particular corporate trust organization and the needs of the individual involved. In first embarking on this endeavor, it might be useful to call upon an expert, experienced in designing and developing performance-based training programs. These professionals can usually be made available through the personnel department of the bank. The nature and extent of the administrator's educational background, his/her previous jobs, and familiarity with the subject matter, will permit the manager to tailor the comprehensive program to the identified needs of the particular person (being in effect an "individual educational prescription").

In addition to training in the technical aspects of the position, the

TABLE 1
Activities and Standards Compared

Activity	Standard and/or Time Limit
1. Preparation of Form T-1.	1. Completed and sent to Company at least 1 day before Company's need.
2. New Issue Closing *a.* Indenture comments.	*a.* Review for clarity, simplification, and workability and comment on timely basis as requested by Company.
b. Initial issuance list and security certificates.	*b.* To Operations 4 business days before closing
c. Execution copy of Indenture.	*c.* Line check as soon as possible but always before signing by Bank.
d. Completion of all items on Procedure Guide For New Issues.	*d.* 10 business days after closing with pending cards prepared for all open items.
3. Preparation of Internal Operating Instructions.	3. 2 days before issuance date.

4. Ticklers
   a. Preparation
   b. Funds
	a. 10 business days after closing.
	   b. Refer to account officer if money not received by day before disbursement date.

c. All others	*c.* Refer to account officer if not received or complied with on or before due date.
5. Review of Financials, Certificates, and Opinions.	5. Review for indenture compliance, including signature authority—3 business days from date of receipt.

6. Processing Investments
   a. Purchases/Sales
	a. Review for accuracy and authority. To Order Desk by
	   _____A.M. (telephone)
	   _____P.M. (confirmation)

b. Settlement Confirmation	*b.* Determination of correctness of transaction.
7. Processing Routine Releases	7. 3 business days from date of receipt.
8. Trustee Annual Report	8. Draft to obligor 4 weeks before mailing date. Followup 2 weeks before mailing date. Mailing instructions to Operations 1 week before mailing date.
9. Funds Receipt	9. If received before _____P.M., prepare tickets and deliver to Funds Desk by _____P.M. If received after _____P.M., prepare tickets and deliver to Funds Desk at opening of business next day.

10. Funds Transfers Between Accounts	10. If received before ____P.M., prepare tickets and deliver to Funds Desk by ____P.M. If received after ____P.M., prepare tickets and deliver to Funds Desk at opening of business next day.
11. Correspondence	11. Acknowledgement or response 3 business days from date of receipt.

12. Satisfactions
  a. Redemption/Maturity Instructions
  b. Document disposition
	a. Deliver to Operations 3 weeks before payment date.
	b. In accordance with Document Disposition Guide—2 weeks after date of satisfaction.

administrator may very well need additional instruction and/or coaching on such seemingly basic requirements as writing business letters and memoranda, effective verbal communication skills, and an understanding of basic economics, finance, and accounting.

Any training and development program should include as wide a variety as possible of the ways and means to achieve the desired results. It should also take place over a span of time during which it is reasonable to expect the desired knowledge and skill competencies to be acquired and effectively implemented. The components of the program could include, among others: use of a designated teacher-trainer; regularly scheduled individual training sessions or participation in transactional in-bank seminars and workshops; attendance at industry-sponsored schools, seminars, and conferences; use of an administrator's "handbook" containing relevant policies, procedures, and guidelines; availability of a library of appropriate books, articles, judicial decisions, statutes, and regulations; and orientation tours to other areas of the bank with which the corporate trust function interfaces.

Any and all of these teaching vehicles or resources should be combined with the essential element of on-the-job training (OJT). In point of fact, it is usually much better to use an actual transactional experience with appropriate reading and coaching, on the assumption that during the OJT the manager has clear standards and objectives against which to train. It is essential that the overall training program provide (and hold the manager accountable) for extensive coaching and counseling on the application and use of knowledge and skills required of the position. "Coaching goes far beyond the short-term need to help someone learn the mechanics of preparing a budget and setting a proposal up. It is the principal means through which people learn what makes the organization tick, what it stands for, and how they can contribute to it over time."[2]

As noted earlier, the establishment of an appropriate comprehensive training and development program must focus on both the content and timing of the subject matter to be covered. *Exhibit 18* sets forth a model for such an approach—covering a two-year period. The caveat is, of course, that its implementation must be clearly tailored to the individual, as determined by his/her previous experiences, identified needs, and demonstrated abilities.

Any training and development effort, however, will be only as effective as the system will permit and require, usually by holding people accountable for it, with appropriate positive and negative consequences as established through a performance planning and evaluation process.

[2] Peters and Austin, *A Passion for Excellence*, p. 329.

NINETEEN

Performance Planning and Evaluation

The effectiveness of any function rests not only on the design of the structure and the skills of the people but also on how the system combines these elements and develops a process that motivates and rewards people to reach the desired goals.

The discussion in the preceding chapters sets the stage for consideration of the dynamic interplay among structure, process, and people. In particular, the comments on training and development lay the foundation for the key ingredients upon which an individual's performance, skills, and productivity are effectively managed.[1]

Such a system, whether highly formalized or not, is derived from the business plan and concomitant objective-setting process—a plan for what people are required to do. Combined with a regular feedback mechanism, the organization can then determine how effectively the structure, processes, and people interact to meet the organization's business strategy.

This system is universally referred to as the employee evaluation or appraisal procedure. Performance appraisal is simply the process designated to identify, measure, and develop people. A well-defined process not only evaluates current performance but also should include mechanisms to reinforce strengths and correct problems for the benefit of future performance.

Whereas the preceding chapter strongly suggests the critical need to

[1] Although chapter 18 was addressed specifically to account administrators and officers, most of the discussion in this chapter is equally applicable to operations supervisors and officers.

identify knowledge and skills upon which to train people to perform their jobs as corporate trust administrators or account officers, the position profile alone does not suffice in giving the dynamic perspective of the job. It requires a concerted joint effort between manager and subordinate to reach understanding of the job required, the priorities necessary to meet tactical objectives, and the concerns of the individual for defining his/her career aspirations.

The interaction between managers and their subordinates can occur only in an environment where the managerial philosophy and the recognition of these facets of an individual's development process are fully supportive. It is not an easy task, and yet without it, there exists no applied management of people, either in their personal development or in the providing of assistance required to enable them to effectively contribute to the desired objectives of the organization.

The ensuing dialogue stemming from an environment where real people management exists will result in a climate of trust and confidence and, consequently, greater receptivity to the feedback required for continued growth.

The process of identifying job skills and training and development programs not only provides the initial understanding of the job but also provides for the definition and communication of job-relevant behavior, competencies, and skills as reflected in the business plan.

Once the organization's strategic business plan has been developed and communicated, specific annual objectives can be established. Flowing from the specific objectives statement is an identification of the tasks individuals need to accomplish. This level of planning is instrumental in allowing for congruency between organization needs and individual expectations.

> Planning enables us to make the most effective and economical use of manpower, equipment, facilities and money. If we identify in advance our needs for people, we can develop individuals inside an organization so that they will be ready when the opportunity for promotion appears. Planning makes it possible to let subordinates know what is required of them and to give them an opportunity to participate in the decisions that are made.[2]

Planning in this respect involves analyzing the needs of the organization and matching them to the strengths, talents, and expertise of the

[2] Allen, *The Management Profession,* p. 100.

people involved. Using a needs analysis approach, a manager will identify the specific areas in which each subordinate lacks the required knowledge and skill competencies for the job and/or does not meet the expected standards of performance. In addition such analysis should focus on the developmental opportunities that the particular administrator, supervisor, or officer needs to provide for his/her growth in the organization.

Such an analysis is best accomplished when there exists, in writing, the competencies, performance standards, and performance results *expected* of an incumbent in the particular position. The competencies should reflect the differing expectations as dictated by level within a job family. For example, distinctions need to be made between an administrator and a senior administrator, a senior administrator and account officer, and an account officer and a senior account officer. This also serves the purpose of communicating what performance expectations exist for the next higher level position. *Exhibits 19 and 20* set forth a model of minimum competency guidelines for those positions. The manager will assess and match the expectations against the strengths and weaknesses of his/her subordinate to establish the areas for development. This cannot be a unilateral effort but rather the result of understanding and agreement between the manager and subordinate.

In developing this analysis, both would review: (1) the position profile reflecting expected performance accountabilities, technical knowledge, and skill competencies, relevant managerial competencies, and interpersonal factors; (2) the specific objectives previously established; (3) the performance standards established for the various activities and duties incident to the position; (4) the reasons why expected work results or objectives were not accomplished or not accomplished on a timely basis; and (5) what obstacles are present preventing the expected growth and development of the individual. In essence this would also constitute the major points of review during an appraisal meeting, a subject discussed later in this chapter.

Because this process of performance review, identification of deficiencies and opportunities, establishment of personal improvement and work objectives, and implementation of training and development efforts constitutes a complete system circle, it is in effect a continuous cycle of planning, implementation, and review. In this regard, it is quite similar to the planning process described in chapter 16.

Now that the needs analysis has been completed and the specific areas in which the individual is deficient—or in which learning and

experience opportunities would enhance the individual's development—
have been identified, the next logical step would be the negotiation,
understanding, and the agreement between manager and subordinate
about the desired results of the training effort. This objective-setting
process is also effectively used in establishing the expected results of
designated performance reponsibilities and activities. In approaching
this effort, the individual and his/her manager must know where they
are going before they can expect to get there. The more clearly the end
result or outcome sought is visualized, the easier it is to determine the
best route, the best timing, and the best method of achievement.

Often this process becomes so overly detailed and extraordinarily
time-consuming that the participants rebel against it. They continue,
however, to go through the motions (because it is expected) and produce
nothing more than the same objectives year after year, or others that
neither stretch the individual's talents and abilities nor provide for
innovative or creative actions designed to resolve existing deficiencies
or meet changing performance expectations.

In this connection, the following guidelines should be helpful in
highlighting some commonly encountered difficulties:

1. Objectives should focus only on the position's most significant
   aspects and the individual's major developmental needs within the
   context of a year's period.
2. The very number of objectives should be manageable, even as few
   as one or two, but certainly not more than five or six.
3. Each objective should be articulated so that the result or outcome
   is verifiable at the end of a given period. The manager and the
   subordinate must be able to evaluate whether the objective was
   achieved or to what degree it was accomplished. This does not
   mean that all objectives, and especially those related to personal
   development and improvement, must or can necessarily be quantified.
4. To the extent that the result sought to be accomplished can be
   quantified, it should be; to the extent possible, in terms of quantity, quality, time, or cost.
5. The objectives should be challenging, yet reasonable, and should
   require stretch effort for their accomplishment. The writing of a
   "maintenance" objective reflecting no change from existing performance is simply a waste of time and effort.
6. The manager and subordinate should agree on the priorities of
   each objective on the basis of their relative importance.

7. The objectives should be reduced to writing and should include the results to be accomplished, the standards or means of validating the results, the action plan or program steps necessary to meet the objective, the expected timing or schedule for each action step, and, if applicable, the cost incident to the performance of each action step.

8. The manager should ensure that the objectives are consistent with the organization's business plan and that they, at the same time, will meet the deficiencies and opportunities identified in the needs analysis.

In essence, an objective is simply an important end result whose accomplishment adds value to the individual and to the organization. Without a process for the orderly and integrated development and implementation of the objective, it is evidence that the necessary congruence between the organization's business plan and its goals and the developmental needs of the individual may not be realized.[3] The establishment of objectives, whether directly work results-related or in the nature of a personal development need, must also include a regular feedback mechanism. Individuals must have a recognized and established opportunity for two-way communication to discuss and review the progress they are making (or not making) in achieving the desired results. "Each individual needs to get accurate information about the difference between what he is trying to do and how well he is doing it. He needs to be able to use this information to correct or change his actions. Then, basically, he is steering himself."[4]

Although almost every manager would insist that he or she provides feedback to subordinates, it is usually done on a transactional basis—the "one-minute praise" or, more likely the "one-minute chewing out." Instant evaluation of and comment on a subordinate's performance is, of course, important, desirable, and necessary, but it should not take the place of an organized, scheduled, and reasonably detailed review of an individual's overall performance results during a given period. Basic questions that need to be answered during such a review might include the following: (1) Does the subordinate know what is supposed to be accomplished? (2) Are there obstacles beyond his or her control? (3) Does the subordinate know how to do it? (4) Could the subordinate do it if he or she possessed additional knowledge and skill competencies?

[3] For additional discussion on this topic, see Drucker, *Management*, chapter 34 ("Management by Objectives and Self-Control").

[4] Lippitt, *Organization Renewal*, p. 78.

(5) What support should the manager provide? and (6) Is the originally conceived expected performance result or objective still viable and necessary?[5]

Such a review should not occur only once a year, during an annual performance appraisal meeting. The need to coach, counsel, and guide the subordinate's performance and developmental efforts requires a more frequent mechanism. In many organizations the manager, in the pursuit of excellence, will establish a quarterly performance review ("QPR") that provides an opportunity for the necessary two-way communications regarding subordinate's overall work performance, developmental results, identification of further needs, and review of the next quarter's action steps and expected results. Because external factors, including volume of work, situational conditions, and even a change in business plans may impact the individual's performance and objectives accomplishment, the QPR provides a timely basis for making adjustments and changes in direction, priority, and timing of the previously agreed to expected performance results and objectives.

QPR can be a very effective means of providing the manager with an opportunity to discuss the subordinate's performance and to further reinforce his/her commitment to support that subordinate's training and development process. If, in fact, performance is not up to standards or expectations, this also provides a vehicle for getting agreement that specific problems do exist, for discussing alternative solutions, for mutually agreeing on actions to be taken to resolve the problem, and for reaching an understanding that there will be further follow-up to ensure that the agreed-upon action has been taken.

To be really effective, the QPR should be just that, and not a spur-of-the-moment meeting. It should be held in a private, quiet area with sufficient time scheduled for an unrushed discussion. The manager should focus on specific performance results, with necessary supporting "data" or observations of behavior, and not on inference or evaluation of behavior. When reviewing the accomplishment of objectives, the manager should review the progress that the individual is making in completing (or not completing) the appropriate action steps. Discussion should also be held on the results of any specific training and development programs that occurred during the preceding quarter. Such a meeting also permits both manager and subordinate to reevaluate the next quarter's expected performance results and to make any necessary mod-

[5] See Fournies, *Coaching for Improved Work Performance*, p. 107, *et seq.*

ifications. In all of this, it should be evident that the QPR itself is an integral part of an overall developmental process.

At the completion of a business cycle, normally a year, a complete review of the subordinate's performance will take place. This annual appraisal should involve a review of all objectives, and of factors that contributed to the subordinate's meeting or not meeting the agreed upon expectations. The appraisal should include the evaluation of the subordinate's technical work performance, general performance factors, knowledge and skill competencies, completion of objectives, and a developmental plan for the ensuing year.

The annual appraisal process consists of three interrelated parts: (1) the completion of an appraisal document by the manager and the completion of the same form by the subordinate; (2) an appraisal meeting, similar to a QPR, in which the manager reviews both documents with the subordinate, focusing on the major differences between the evaluation and the self-assessment, as well as the demonstrated strengths and weaknesses of the subordinate; and (3) establishment of a developmental plan for the ensuing year, based on an understanding of and agreement regarding the needs of the subordinate and the organization.

Although the form of any appraisal document will vary widely from institution to institution, and even within an institution, the essential elements (or competencies) of the position, the necessary knowledge and skill competencies, the expected standards of performance, and the accomplishment of agreed-upon objectives will be included. *Exhibit 21* sets forth a model that would be applicable to account administrators.

III

Reference Material

Exhibits

Exhibit 1
Acceptance Form for New Appointments

SECTION I: *To be completed within 24 hours of being advised of new appointment.*

[New Relationship _____ Exist. Relationship—New Appointment _____]

OBLIGOR _____

PARENT, GUARANTOR, LESSEE _____

ISSUE DESCRIPTION (Include P.A., Interest Rate & Due Date)

_____

_____ CUSIP NO. _____

ACCOUNT MANAGER   ADMINISTRATOR   MARKETING OFFICER

_____   _____   _____

ISSUANCE INFORMATION:

OUR APPOINTMENTS: _____

PRIN. AGT. (IF OTHER BANK) _____

UNDERWRITER _____

COMPANY COUNSEL _____

BOND/UNDERWRITER COUNSEL _____

INITIAL CONTACT AND TEL. # _____

ANTIC. CLOSING DATE _____ T-1 NEEDED BY _____

SECTION II   *Credit Review—to be completed within one week of preliminary acceptance.*

Check one:

_____ Credit Review (Trusteeship). A review has been made of the latest financial statements and a check made of the management, underwriters/investment bankers (if applicable), law firms, and public accountants of the Obligor/Guarantor or Lessee. We find them satisfactory.

_____ Acceptance Review (Agency). In accordance with the current criteria for acceptance of new agency appointments, the appropriate review has been conducted and the criteria met.

Conflict Check Information *(indicate review completed by a ''√''):*

1. Interlocking Directors _____   2. Bank Underwriter _____
3. Other Relationships _____   4. Fiduciary Holdings _____
5. Lending Relationship _____   6. Can we act in applicable states if secured financing?   Yes _____   No _____

Marketing Officer s/ _____ Date _____

Acceptance by Senior Officer s/ _____ Date _____

SECTION III   *To be completed by administrator within 5 business days after closing.*

Billing Address:

_____

_____

Actual Closing Date _____ Int. Pay. Dates _____

Indenture/Agreement Dated as of _____

Fee Schedule: Attached _____ or in File _____

Acceptance Fee: _____ Administration Fee: _____

Other Fees for Initial Bill: _____

_____

Counsel Involved: Yes _____ No _____ If Yes, Bill attached? _____

Prepare the Initial Bill within 10 business days after receipt of fee information, including all out-of-pocket disbursements incident to closing and original issuance.

DATE _____ ADMINISTRATOR _____ ACCOUNT MGR. _____

EXHIBIT 2
Discharge of Fiduciary Obligations

I. *Acceptance of New Appointments*
    If the prospective obligor is not well known to the Bank, informal inquiries and

background information is to be obtained on the credit standing and reputation of the company and its management, as well as the general reputation of the underwriters and the attorneys involved.

Á "new name" trusteeship will be accepted if (a) the preliminary check reveals no adverse information and (b) either (i) no creditor relationship exists and there is no expectation of establishing such a relationship or (ii) acceptance of the appointment is also approved by the Banking Department because of the credit standing of the obligor even though a relationship exists. The pertinent credit files are to be noted as to the existence of the corporate trust relationship.

Any administrative officer may tentatively accept new accounts subject to final approval by a senior corporate trust officer and the Corporate Trust Committee. A written report indicating the review and acceptance of the appointment is prepared and filed in the account contact file.

As part of the determination of the Bank's eligibility and qualification to serve as trustee, a determination is to be made that the Bank is neither the obligor, nor a person directly or indirectly controlling, controlled by, or under common control with the obligor. In addition, a "potential conflict" check is to be performed covering, inter alia, trust appointments under other indentures with the same obligor, ownership of stock of the obligor and underwriter by the Bank and vice versa, common directors, and past underwritings by the Bank's underwriting affiliate.

The rights, duties, obligations, and responsibilities of the trustee under the proposed indenture and applicable statutes are to be reviewed by an administrative officer and by outside counsel and referred to a senior corporate trust officer for review if a problem is encountered.

II. *Annual Conflict Check*

A conflict check is to be made in conjunction with the annual report to the security holders:

1. to ensure the Bank's continued eligibility and qualification to serve as trustee under the indenture;

2. to determine the existence of any potential conflicts of interest as enumerated in section 310(b) of the Trust Indenture Act;

3. to ensure compliance with the reporting requirements of section 313 of the Trust Indenture Act.

III. *Corporate Trust Committee*

Established by the Bank's Board of Directors for the purpose of group consideration of matters arising in the course of the administration of corporate trusteeships, and the reporting thereof to the Board for its review of the administration of such accounts and the application of management policies to corporate trust matters. This Committee, which is composed of senior corporate trust officers, the group head as chairman, [and the head of the Fiduciary Department as an ex officio member,] is meet on the first [Wednesday] of each month.

The agenda for these meetings is to cover:

1. approval of minutes of preceding meeting

2. review of appointments and terminations since preceding meeting

3. report and review of active defaulted accounts (i.e., those in which an Event of Default has occurred, or those that are the subject of bankruptcy or reorganization proceedings)

4. review of other trustee accounts

    a. any account, although not in default, that in the judgment of the Committee warrants a monthly review because of existing financial or other special circumstances.

    b. each trust account on an annual basis (i.e. approximately 1/12 of such accounts are to be reviewed each month).

These reports are to be rendered by the accountable administrative officer, and in addition to any specific information for the accounts in category a. above, to cover the following matters:

    i) tickler items (i.e., whether action or submission of documents by and to the trustee has been timely in accordance with the applicable indenture or other agreement)

    ii) operational problems, if any

    iii) administrative problems, if any

    iv) potential TIA 310(b) conflicts

    v) prospects for new or additional business

5. report on agency account matters (i.e., those not involving a trustee appointment)

IV. *Performance Under Indenture Agreements*

A. All items requiring periodic attention and/or documentation under an indenture or other agreement are to be monitored through a tickler system advice to the account officer for followup and completion signoff each month. Items still open one month after action are required to be referred to a senior corporate trust officer.

B. All reports, opinions, and certificates received pursuant to an indenture requirement are to be reviewed for compliance, noted upon acceptance, and filed in the account document file. Any variances or problems are to be referred to a senior corporate trust officer for further action.

C. All initial releases and/or substitutions of property or collateral for a given account are to be referred to counsel for review. If subsequent such transactions conform to the requirements of the indenture and follow substantially the same format as the original one, they need not be submitted to counsel. Any transaction that in the opinion of the account officer is nonroutine is to be submitted to a senior corporate trust officer for review and, if a legal question is involved, referred to counsel.

D. Any variance in compliance with the provisions of the indenture or in the proper interpretation and application of pertinent indenture provisions to specific situations is to be considered by a senior corporate trust officer; by counsel, if a legal question is raised; and if necessary by the Bank's senior management. All important transactions or activities after a default occurs are to be reviewed by senior corporate trust officers with counsel. Appropriate review is to be made monthly by the Corporate Trust Committee.

E. The final satisfaction of an obligor's responsibilities under an indenture is not to be rendered until there has been strict compliance with the terms and conditions of the particular indenture or agreement. In the case of bankruptcy or reorganization proceedings, an appropriate discharge of the Bank's responsibilities is to be secured from the Court.

EXHIBIT 3
Checklist for New and Additional Issues Under Indentures

Obligor _____

Guarantors and/or Joint Issuers (if any) _____

Title of Indenture _____

415 Shelf-registration _____ Yes _____ No

Issue of $ _____ Under Article _____ Section _____

Description of Issue _____ CUSIP No. _____

Authorized Issue under Indenture $ _____ under this Section $ _____

Total issued to date, under Indenture
(including this issue $ _____ under this Section $ _____

Balance unissued under Indenture $ _____ under this Section $ _____

Indenture qualified under TIA? _____ Indenture subject to Streit Act? _____

OUR CAPACITIES

Indenture Trustee _____ Registrar _____ P.A.-Prin. _____ P.A.-Int. _____

Conversion Agt. _____ Fiscal Agt. _____ Owner Trustee _____

Destr. Agt. _____ Tender Agt. _____ Put Agt. _____

Ledger maintained by _____ Co-Agents _____

TIME SCHEDULE:

T-1 & T-2 to be prepared as of _____ furnished by _____ to _____

Registration Statement to be filed on _____ Registration Number _____

Information Meeting: Date _____ Time _____ Location _____

Bid Meeting: Date _____ Time _____ Location _____

Delivery of Bonds: Date _____ Time _____ Location _____

Delivery of Underwriters List: Date _____ Time _____

Indenture executed: Date _____ Time _____ Location _____

Preliminary closing: Date _____ Time _____ Location _____

Closing: Date _____ Time _____ Location _____

CONTACTS:

Banking Officer: _____ Tel. No. _____

Obligor: Name _____ Tel. No. _____
            Address _____

Obligor's Counsel: _____

            Name _____ Tel. No. _____
            Address _____

Underwriter: _____

            Name _____ Tel. No. _____
            Address _____

Underwriter's
(or Purchaser's) _____
Counsel:

            Name _____ Tel. No. _____
            Address _____

Our Counsel: _____

            Name _____ Tel. No. _____
            Address _____

Banknote Co.: _____

            Name _____ Tel. No. _____

Other: _____

            Name _____ Tel. No. _____

Enter the following symbols in the column at the left to indicate action taken with respect to each requirement:

√ = Completed   P = Pending   Ø = Not applicable
                        (Pending card prepared)

I. Prior to Filing:

_____ A. Obtain proofs of Indenture and other documents for review. Send copies to our counsel.

_____ B. Reserve rooms for meetings to be held at bank.

_____ C. Prepare New Appointment/New Issue Form and distribute to appropriate parties.

_____ D. Complete conflict check.

_____ E. Furnish _____ executed and _____ conformed copies of T-1 & T-2.

_____ F. Write memo for Streit Act file.

_____ G. Determine whether bank is qualified to act in all states in which mortgaged property is located and whether provision for individual or Co-trustee is required or desirable.

_____ H. Send list of documents we require (see Exhibit 7).

_____ I. If new Indenture is involved, ensure that fee schedule is sent to Obligor.

_____ J. Determine if we are to be appointed destruction agent.

_____ K. Prepare:

       _____ (a) Informal Credit Review—Memorandum
       _____ (b) Fees to be applied, and
       _____ (c) Memorandum accepting appointment, notifying Banking Department and Credit Files.

_____ L. Determine quantities of each denomination of securities and prefixes.

_____ M. Advise Banking Officer which officials from Obligor will attend information meeting.

II. Between Pricing and Closing:

_____ A. Inform Banking Department promptly if closing to involve funds paid by investment and brokerage firms.

_____ B. Verify schedule for receipt of securities and lists.

_____ C. Review proofs of each securities denomination.

_____ D. Have Trustee's Counsel review proof of the security to be issued.

_____ E. Have Operations Division review proofs of each securities denomination.

_____ F. Obtain Obligor's TPI number, advise Operations Division.

_____ G. Receive and review drafts of closing memo and closing papers.

_____ H. Obtain CUSIP number.

_____ I. Send instructions for original issuance to Operations Division (before receipt of securities and lists).

_____ J. Prepare and distribute Operations Instruction sheets.

_____ K. Determine when Indenture is to be executed and by which officials.

_____ L. Consider necessity of obtaining County Clerk's certificates on notarial acknowledgments.

_____ M. Determine whether issue is subject to Pennsylvania Corporate Loans Tax.

       _____ Make arrangements for withholding and filing of tax.

_____ N. Determine disposition of funds (Clearing House or Federal) to be received at closing.

_____ O. Advise Money Desk if funds are to be deposited with us. Prepare deposit slip.

_____ P. Determine whether certified copies of Bank By-Laws, Signing Resolutions, or other documents are required.

_____ Q. Prepare Authentication Certificate and any other papers or receipts required to be furnished by Bank.

_____ R. Open appropriate cash accounts.

_____ S. Open account for collateral.

_____ T. Advise Banking Officer which Company officials will attend closing.

_____ U. Check with Operations Division whether securities are ready to be released at closing.

_____ V. Instruct Operations Division to open appropriate accounts (interest, principal, cash in lieu of fractional shares, etc.)

III. At Closing:

_____ A. Obtain supporting documents.

_____ B. Deposit proceeds of closing and invest, if instructed by the Obligor.

_____ C. Obtain receipt for securities from Obligor.

_____ D. Receive, control, and deposit collateral.

_____ E. Release securities.

IV. After Closing:

_____ A. Obtain opinion of our counsel.

_____ B. Prepare closing memo and distribute.

_____ C. Prepare letter for Stock Exchange listing.

_____ D. Write Company for appointment as Fiscal Agent and Witholding Agent.

_____ E. Receive undertaking pursuant to provisions of Section 317(b) of TIA if Obligor appoints a paying agent other than the Trustee.

_____ F. Determine if issue is subject to Original Issue Discount.

_____ Instruct Operations to file 1099-OID.

_____ G. Write Company regarding lost security replacement procedure.

_____ H. If there is an individual trustee:

_____ 1. Obtain undated resignation.

_____ 2. Obtain power of attorney.

_____ 3. Prepare cards for Individual Trustee file.

_____ I. Enter record date for Trustee's annual report in Conflict check file.

_____ J. Prepare approved tickler register control list. Consider sending copy to Obligor.

_____ K. Prepare (or update) following office records:

_____ 1. Prepare authorities file.

_____ 2. Prepare Obligor Address file.

_____ 3. Update State of Incorporation file and Mortgage file.

_____ 4. Update Affiliates file from Company questionnaire.

_____ 5. Prepare Owner Trustee files if lease financing.

_____ L. If Supplemental Indenture, annotate reference copy of Indenture.

_____ M. Write prior lien trustees.

_____ N. Prepare pending card for first interest payment.

    _____ 1. If first interest period is short or long, advise Operations Division to place legend on check. Consider enclosure.

    _____ 2. Two months prior to first interest payment date, check that issue is on registered interest list.

    _____ 3. Write to Obligor regarding filing reports of interest paid to holders in particular states.

    _____ 4. If tax-exempt issue, advise Operations Division not to prepare 1099s.

_____ O. Prepare letter to Obligor to accompany initial bill and fee schedule.

    _____ 1. Receive counsel bill.

    _____ 2. Advise Billing Unit to prepare our initial bill.

_____ P. If a convertible issue and bank is Conversion Agent, send letter to Obligor requesting that Operations Division be advised in writing of record dates for stock; and minimum deposit of funds sufficient for cash payments in lieu of fractional shares.

_____ Q. Document closing papers. Send appropriate documents to archives.

_____ R. Obtain conformed copies of Indenture for reference file and to fill requests.

_____ S. Prepare pending card(s) to make arrangements for delayed deliveries.

_____ T. Receive recorded counterparts and legal opinion and file.

Date: _____ Prepared: _____ Approved: _____

Exhibit 4
Checklist for Agency Appointments

Obligor _____

Address _____

Agreement _____

Description of Issue _____

CUSIP NO. _____ Prin. Amt. _____ Int. Dates _____

OUR APPOINTMENTS (If Co-Agent so indicate):

Trustee, Fiscal Agent, or Principal Agent _____

   Ledger maintained by (Registrar) _____

(Co-)Registrar _____ Authenticating Agent _____ Conversion Agent _____

(Co-)Paying Agent: Interest _____ Principal _____ Tender agent _____

Accounting/Destruction Agent _____Other _____

OTHER AGENTS:

(Co-)Registrar _____

Authenticating Agent _____

Conversion Agent _____

(Co-)Paying Agent (Interest) (Principal) _____

Tender Agent _____

Accounting/Destruction Agent _____

Other _____

TIME SCHEDULE:	DATE	TIME	PLACE
Information Meeting	_____	_____	_____
Bid/Pricing	_____	_____	_____
Del. of Underwriters List	_____	_____	_____
Preliminary Closing	_____	_____	_____
Closing	_____	_____	_____

CONTACTS:

Obligor:	Firm _____
	Address _____
	Name _____ Tel. No. _____
Obligor's Counsel	Firm _____
	Address _____
	Name _____ Tel. No. _____
Bond Counsel	Firm _____
	Address _____
	Name _____ Tel. No. _____
Underwriter	Firm
	Address _____
	Name _____ Tel. No. _____

Trustee	Firm _____
	Address _____
	Name _____ Tel. No. _____
Trustee's Counsel	Firm _____
	Address _____
	Name _____ Tel. No. _____
Principal Agent(s)	Firm _____
	Address _____
	Name _____ Tel. No. _____
Banknote Company	Firm _____
	Address _____
	Name _____ Tel. No. _____

ENTER THE FOLLOWING SYMBOLS IN THE LEFT COLUMN TO INDI-
CATE ACTION TAKEN WITH RESPECT TO EACH REQUIREMENT:

√ = Completed   P = Pending   Ø = Not Applicable
                              (Pending card prepared)

BEFORE CLOSING

_____ A. Prepare "Acceptance Form for New Issues" and distribute to appropriate
parties.

_____ B. Consider fees and send schedule to Issuer.

_____ C. Obtain and review proofs of security certificates.

_____ D. Obtain CUSIP Number.

_____ E. Obtain Issuer's Taxpayer Identification Number.

_____ F. Determine quantities of each denomination of securities to be delivered to us
by Banknote Company.

_____ G. If we are to do the Original Issuance, verify with underwriter:

_____ 1. list of registered holders.

_____ 2. time and place for delivery of securities.

_____ 3. time and place of packaging and preclosing.

_____ 4. time and place of closing.

_____ H. Prepare and distribute Original Issuance Instructions to Opns. Div. if we are
Registrar or Co-Registrar.

_____ I. Prepare any documents we are to furnish at closing (e.g., signing resolutions,
incumbency certificate).

_____ J. Advise appropriate officers of the bank as to closing and who will attend
from the Issuer.

_____ K. Open appropriate cash and/or investment accounts.

_____ L. Prepare and distribute standing Account Operating Instructions.

_____ M. Check with Opns. Div. that securities are prepped and ready for release.

AT CLOSING
_____ A. Obtain required documents, including:

  _____ 1. documents appointing bank as Agent.

  _____ 2. executed (or conformed) counterpart of the Indenture or Agreement.

  _____ 3. incumbency certificate of Issuer's officers.

  _____ 4. specimen certificates of each denomination.

_____ B. Deposit proceeds of closing into appropriate account(s), or wire funds at written direction of Issuer.

_____ C. Obtain receipt for securities from Issuer.

_____ D. Release securities to underwriter/syndicate manager.

AFTER CLOSING
_____ A. Request appropriate documents from Trustee to complete our records.

_____ B. If original issuance was done as a courtesy for another Registrar, provide such with necessary information.

_____ C. Prepare Closing Memo and distribute. Ensure one copy is sent to appropriate banking officer and another put in the appropriate Contact File(s).

_____ D. Prepare letter to New York Stock Exchange, if securities are listed, covering supply of certificates held to facilitate transfers and exchanges by us as Registrar or Co-Registrar.

_____ E. Ensure we have instructions from Issuer or Principal Paying Agent as to:

  _____ 1. source of funds.

  _____ 2. disposition of canceled securities.

  _____ 3. where to send our bills.

_____ F. If we act as Paying Agent, write Issuer for appointment as Fiscal Agent and Withholding Agent and send appointment letter to the IRS.

_____ G. Prepare all internal office records, including ticklers (consider sending copy to Issuer).

_____ H. If issue includes a Put or Demand option, complete "Put/Demand Checklist."

_____ I. If we pay registered interest, prepare pending card for first interest payment.

  _____ 1. If first interest payment is short or long, advise Opns. Div. Also note on Instruction Sheet.

  _____ 2. Set up pending card to check that issue is on registered interest control list for first interest payment.

_____ 3. If tax-exempt issue, send memo to Opns. Div. not to prepare 1099 Forms; otherwise send memo to prepare the forms.

_____ 4. If subject to OID, instruct Opns. Div. to file 1099–OID and obtain appropriate information from Issuer.

_____ 5. Write Issuer regarding state reporting and pend to instruct Opns. Div. upon receipt of information.

_____ J. If we are Co-Registrar, obtain written instructions where to send transfer sheets and, if required, a supply of certificates from the Trustee. Confirm in writing who will be responsible for maintaining records as Registrar.

_____ K. Send letter to Co-Paying Agent(s) regarding procedure to follow if we are the Principal Paying Agent.

_____ M. If convertible issue and we are Conversion Agent:

_____ 1. Send letter to Issuer requesting notification of record date for their common stock.

_____ 2. Request notification from the Issuer of changes in conversion price, if any.

_____ 3. request from Issuer minimum deposit of funds sufficient to pay cash in lieu of fractional shares.

_____ N. Follow to ensure that initial bill is sent by Opns. Div.

_____ O. Document closing papers.

_____ P. Consider sending letter of appreciation.

Date: _____ Prepared: _____ Approved: _____

EXHIBIT 5
Requirements for Appointment as Trustee Under Corporate Indentures

["Company" includes any Obligor or Guarantor.]

PRIOR TO CLOSING

1. Drafts of the Indenture, any other governing agreements, and other closing documents, including proofs of the securities, in *triplicate,* as early as possible to facilitate their consideration.

2. A list of the working group with names, addresses, and telephone numbers, in triplicate.

3. A timetable for the offering, in triplicate.

4. For public offerings only: No later than three business days prior to closing, instructions from the Underwriters for preparation of the securities as specified in item 5 below.

5. A supply of the securities along with instructions for their preparation, including the following information with respect to each registration:

(a) the name in which the securities are to be registered;

(b) the address;

(c) the taxpayer identification number;

(d) the denominations in which the securities are to be prepared, the number of securities of each denomination, and the total principal amount of each denomination;

(e) the total principal amount of securities to be prepared for each registration;

(f) the aggregate principal amount of securities to be prepared for the entire offering.

6. Completed Company questionnaire.

AT CLOSING

1. Certificate of the Secretary of State of the jurisdiction of incorporation of the Company, under recent date, listing all charter documents of the Company on file and certifying that the Company is in good standing.

2. Copies, certified by the Secretary of State, of all charter documents of the Company.

3. Certificate of the Secretary of the Company, as of the closing date, certifying that:

(a) The charter has not been amended since the date of item 1 above;

(b) The by-laws of the Company attached as an exhibit to the Secretary's certificate have been duly adopted and are in full force and effect;

(c) The officers mentioned in the Secretary's certificate were duly elected and are qualified to sign the securities and any instructions and documents furnished to the trustee, until written notice to the contrary, and the specimen signatures shown in the Secretary's certificate are the signatures of the respective officers;

(d) The resolutions of the Board of Directors of the Company or issuer, as indicated below, attached as an exhibit to the Secretary's certificate, have been duly adopted and are still in effect:

From the Company, if it is not the issuer of the securities:

(1) authorizing the issuance of the securities and approving the terms thereof;

(2) authorizing the execution and delivery of the Indenture and/or any other governing agreements to which it is a party;

From the Company, if it is the issuer of the securities:

(1) authorizing the issuance of the securities and approving the terms thereof;

(2) authorizing the execution and delivery of the Indenture and/or any other governing agreements to which it is a party;

(3) designating an office or agency for presentation of notices or demands;

(4) appointing the paying agent, registrar, conversion agent, or any other capacity mentioned in the Indenture or any other governing agreements but not specifically designated therein;

(5) appointing the Trustee;

(6) requesting authentication and delivery of the securities in accordance

with the terms of the Indenture and any other governing agreements;

From the Issuer of the stock, if the securities are convertible:

(1) reserving the maximum number of shares of the stock issuable upon conversion and authorizing the issuance of those shares upon requisition by the Conversion Agent to the Transfer Agent;

(e) The resolutions or consents of the stockholders of the Company, attached as an exhibit to the Secretary's certificate, have been duly adopted and are still in effect (unless an opinion of counsel is furnished to the effect that none is required by law or by the Company's by-laws or charter);

(f) Attached as an exhibit are true and correct specimen securities of each denomination and each form of authorized securities;

(g) Attached as an exhibit are true and correct copies of the prospectus and registration statement in the form filed with the SEC (for a public offering only);

(h) No stop order has been issued by any governmental authority.

4. Copies of the Indenture and/or other governing agreements approved in the foregoing resolutions, certified by the Secretary of the Company to be in the form submitted to and approved by the Board of Directors or the stockholders, as appropriate, and still in effect.

5. Copies of orders required of any governmental authority, certified by the appropriate public official.

6. Opinion of counsel, addressed to the Trustee, to the effect that:

(a) The Company is a duly organized and existing corporation;

(b) The Indenture and/or any other governing agreements to which it is a party have been duly authorized, executed, and delivered and are valid and binding agreements of the Company enforceable in accordance with their terms;

(c) The securities have been duly authorized and executed by the Issuer and, when authenticated by the Trustee and delivered for value, will be valid and binding obligations of the Issuer enforceable in accordance with their terms;

(d) Any required approval of governmental authorities has been obtained or that no such approval is required;

(e) The execution and delivery of the Indenture and any other governing agreements, the execution, issuance, and delivery of the securities and (if applicable) issuance of stock upon conversion of the securities do not and will not conflict with or result in a breach of the terms, conditions, or provisions of, or constitute a default under, the charter or by-laws of the Company or any order, decree, judgment, statute, law, rule, regulation, agreement, or instrument to which the Company is subject;

(f) The registration statement under the Securities Act of 1933, as amended, is effective or that no registration is required under the act and stating the reason for the exemption;

(g) The indenture is qualified under the Trust Indenture Act of 1939, as amended or that no qualification is reuired under the act;

(h) Registration. qualification, or filing has been effected under all applicable federal or state statutes or that the issue is exempt under the terms of the applicable statutes, including the following:

(1) Securities Exchange Act of 1934, as amended;
(2) Public Utility Holding Company Act, as amended;
(3) Investment Company Act of 1940, as amended;
(4) Transportation Act;
(5) State securities laws;
(6) Laws requiring competitive bidding for securities;

IF A MORTGAGE, PLEDGE, OR SECURITY INTEREST IS CREATED IN RESPECT OF ANY PROPERTY, ALSO:

(i) The Company lawfully owns or has the interest specified in the property described in the Indenture as mortgaged or pledged, or as subject to a security interest, subject only to exceptions and encumbrances stated in the Indenture, and that the Indenture gives the lien which it and the securities issued under it purport to create;

(j) The amount of mortgage recording tax or other taxes, if any, payable upon the transaction, the recording of the Indenture or the filing of financing statements, and that such amounts have been paid, or stating that no such taxes are payable;

(k) Article 4-A of the New York Real Property Law (Streit Act) is or is not applicable;

(l) All recording or filing required to perfect, preserve, and protect the lien of the Indenture has been accomplished, stating the details thereof and what necessity exists for any periodic re-recording or refiling to preserve and protect the lien thereof, or that no such recording or filing is required;

IF THE SECURITIES ARE BY THEIR TERMS CONVERTIBLE, ALSO:

(m) The maximum number of shares of stock issuable upon conversion have been reserved for that purpose;

(n) The shares issuable upon conversion have been duly authorized, and when issued in accordance with the terms of the securities, the Indenture and any other governing agreements will be validly issued, fully paid, and nonassessable;

(o) The shares issuable upon conversion have been registered under the Securities Act of 1933, as amended, or that no such registration is required and stating the reason for the exemption;

(p) Any required approval of governmental authorities for the issuance of the shares issuable upon conversion has been obtained or that no such approval is required.

7. Order of the Issuer to the Trustee for authentication of the securities and delivery thereof to the Issuer, with reference to specific issuance instructions from the Underwriter to the Trustee, as appropriate.

8. Receipt to the Trustee from the Issuer for the authenticated securities.

9. Cross receipts signed by the Issuer and the Underwriter for the securities and the purchase price therefor.

10. Counterparts of the Indenture and any other recorded documents, bearing recorders' notations, and the secured party's counterpart of each financing statement stamped with filing data (if recording or filing is required).

11. An undertaking pursuant to section 317(b) of the Trust Indenture Act of 1939, as amended, if the Company appoints a paying agent other than the Trustee.

12. Executed counterparts of the Indenture and any other governing agreements.

13. Additional sets of specimen securities that may be required for any agents or coagents.

14. If required under the terms of the Indenture or any other governing agreements, the following additional documentation:

    (a) Any documents required as a condition precedent to authentication of the securities;

    (b) Any sums required to be deposited with the Trustee, together with written instructions for investment in accordance with terms of the Indenture and any other governing agreements;

    (c) Title policies;

    (d) Insurance policies or certification of such;

    (e) Collateral securities with assignments from the registered owner and its assigns, if any, with signatures guaranteed, accompanied by a corporate resolution and incumbency certificate;

    (f) Letter of credit accompanied by a corporate resolution, incumbency and signature certificate from the issuer of the letter of credit and any other appropriate documentation (e.g., evidence of authority of the issuer of the letter of credit and an opinion of counsel with regard to that authority).

15. Any additional documents required by the transaction.

AFTER CLOSING

1. Six conformed counterparts of the Indenture and any other governing agreements and any additional counterparts thereof that may be required for distrib·· .ion to any agents or co-agents.

2. Additional supply of securities necessary for effecting transfers.

EXHIBIT 6
Account Review Checklist

Account Name _____ Account Number _____

Public Issue/Pvt. Placement _____ Corp/Muni _____

Our Capacity _____

Descript. of Outstanding Sec. _____

· ·

REVIEW QUESTIONS	YES	NO
1. Is there any client service quality problem? If so, describe problem and action taken.	_____	_____
2. Have all account files been reviewed for completeness and accuracy?	_____	_____

With respect to the account/document files:

    a. In good order and in compliance with current policies?   _____   _____

    b. All investment authorizations have been approved and filed?   _____   _____

    c. All instruction sheets have been updated?   _____   _____

    d. Authorities file has been updated?   _____   _____

    e. Certificates, financials, etc. are being reviewed in accordance with current policies and performance standards?   _____   _____

    f. Documents have been sent to archives in accordance with current procedure guidelines?   _____   _____

3. Have ticklers been prepared and approved?   _____   _____

   Are ticklers up-to-date? If not, describe item, tickler date, and action taken.   _____   _____

4. Is underlying collateral securing the issue properly maintained?   _____   _____

   Is refiling of financing statements required?   _____   _____

   New refiling date is _____.

5. Are all investments authorized by operative documents?   _____   _____

6. Has Obligor/Issuer met all debt service deposits/payments in a timely manner?   _____   _____

   If not, describe problem and action taken.

7. Are there any significant administrative problems?   _____   _____

   If yes, describe problem and action taken.

8. Are there any significant operational problems, including out-of-proof conditions?   _____   _____

   If yes, describe problem and action taken.

9. Are there chronic overdrafts, either true or technical?   _____   _____

   If so, describe problem and action taken.

10. Indicate whether prospect for new or additional business (corp. trust or other).

Date of Review _____ Admr./Account Mgr. _____

EXHIBIT 7

Illustration of Allocation Formula for Pro-Rata *Redemption*

Objective: To select bonds for redemption in even multiples of $1,000 from all holders in such manner that all holders retain same proportion of outstanding bonds as nearly as possible.

Procedure: Prepare chart on which is listed for each outstanding registered holder (if more than one bond is registered in same name, determine if allocation is to be made separately for each bond or if holdings are to be considered in aggregate):

COLUMN A—The *original* principal amount.

COLUMN B—The *present* principal amount outstanding.

COLUMN C—The principal amount that *should* be outstanding after exact percentage allocation of all redemption payments including the present. This is determined by multiplying amounts in Column A by a percentage determined as follows:

$$\frac{\text{Sum of Column B—Current redemption payment}}{\text{Sum of Column A}}$$

COLUMN D—Exact *pro rata* allocation for each holding, determined by subtracting Column C from Column B.

COLUMN E—Adjusted to provide current *pro rata* redemption in terms of $1,000 and integral multiples for each holding.

Application of this formula may be illustrated by considering a $10,000,000 issue originally sold to ten holders. The indenture provides for an annual sinking fund computed on the basis of 3 percent of the original amount for the first two years and 4 percent for the third year. Allocation of the sinking fund payments for the first three years would be as follows:

First Year

BOND NUMBER	Column A original P/A outstanding	Column B present P/A outstanding	Column C 97% of Col. A	Column D Col. B minus Col. C	Column E pro rata redemption
1	$3,500,000	$3,500,000	$3,395,000	$105,000	$105,000
2	1,800,000	1,800,000	1,746,000	54,000	54,000
3	1,250,000	1,250,00	1,212,500	37,500	38,000
4	950,000	950,00	921,500	28,500	29,000
5	878,000	878,000	851,660	26,340	26,000
6	720,000	720,000	698,400	21,600	22,000
7	540,000	540,000	523,800	16,200	16,000
8	175,000	175,000	169,750	5,250	5,000
9	140,000	140,000	135,800	4,200	4,000
10	47,000	47,000	45,590	1,410	1,000
	$10,000,000	$10,000,000	$9,700,000	$300,000	$300,000

Second Year

BOND NUMBER	Column A	Column B	Column C 94% of Col. A	Column D	Column E
1	$3,500,00	$3,395,000	$3,290,000	$105,000	$105,000
2	1,800,000	1,746,000	1,692,000	54,000	54,000
3	1,250,000	1,212,000	1,175,000	37,000	37,000
4	950,000	921,000	893,000	28,000	28,000
5	878,000	852,000	825,320	26,680	27,000
6	720,000	698,000	676,800	21,200	21,000
7	540,000	524,000	507,600	16,400	16,000
8	175,000	170,000	164,500	5,500	6,000
9	140,000	136,000	131,600	4,400	4,000
10	47,000	46,000	44,180	1,820	2,000
	$10,000,000	$9,700,000	$9,400,000	$300,000	$300,000

Third Year

BOND NUMBER	Column A	Column B	Column C 90% of Col. A	Column D	Column E
1	$3,500,000	$3,290,000	$3,150,000	$140,000	$140,000
2	1,800,000	1,692,000	1,620,000	72,000	72,000
3	1,250,00	1,175,000	1,125,000	50,000	50,000
4	950,000	893,000	855,000	38,000	38,000
5	878,000	825,000	790,200	34,800	35,000
6	720,000	677,000	648,000	29,000	29,000
7	540,000	508,000	486,000	22,000	22,000
8	175,000	164,000	157,500	6,500	6,000
9	—[1]	—	—	—	—
10	47,000	44,000	42,300	1,700	2,000
11	105,000[2]	99,000[1]	94,500	4,500	[3]5,000
12	35,000[2]	33,000[1]	31,500	1,500	1,000
	$10,000,000	$9,400,000	$9,000,000	$400,000	$400,000

[1] Bond Number 9 for $132,000 (original $140,000) canceled and new bonds 11 and 12 issued for $99,000 and $33,000, respectively.

[2] 75 percent and 25 percent of $140,000.

[3] Determined by lot.

Exhibit 8
Release Check Sheet

Indenture: _____
Date and document number containing last approval of counsel of similar transaction

---

Check all items when completed. If inapplicable, so indicate.

I. IF RELEASE OF PROPERTY OTHER THAN CASH:

☐ A. Obtain and review executed originals of following documents:

   1. Resolution of company board of directors containing request for release and description of property to be released.

   2. Officers' certificate of compliance with all conditions precedent.

   3. Engineer's or appraiser's certificate of fair value of property to be released.

   4. Opinion of counsel on compliance with all conditions precedent.

   5. Other required documents, if any. List such documents herein.

   _____

   _____

   _____

☐ B. Require independent engineer's or appraiser's certificate if fair value of all property released during calendar year (including current application) is 10 percent or more of indenture securities outstanding, unless fair value of property in current application is less than $25,000 or less than 1 percent of indenture securities outstanding.

☐ C. Check statements in certificates and opinion on compliance with Section 314 (e) of Trust Indenture Act.

☐ D. Obtain deposit of cash equal to proceeds of sale or to fair value of property released, whichever is greater.

☐ E. Obtain approval of trustee's counsel. Required if no approval of substantially similar transaction on file; or if fair value of property released is 1 percent of indenture securities outstanding, or $100,000; or if transaction involves unusual or special circumstances.

☐ F. Compare description of property in release instrument to that set forth in resolution and engineer's certificate.

☐ G. Execute and deliver instrument of release. If proceeds not deposited with application, deliver in trust.

☐ H. Prepare special reports to bondholders if fair value of property released is 10 percent or more of indenture securities outstanding.

II. IF WITHDRAWAL OF CASH OR RELEASE OF PROPERTY ON BASIS OF CERTIFICATION OF PROPERTY ADDITIONS OR DEPOSIT OF COLLATERAL:

☐ A. Obtain and check

   1. Resolution,

   2. Engineer's or appraiser's certificate,

   3. Officers' certificate,

   4. Opinion of counsel,

   5. Other required documents, if any. List such documents herein.

_____

- ☐ B. Require independent engineer's or appraiser's certificate if: (1) within six months prior to acquisition by obligor such property was used by a person other than the obligor in a business similar to that in which it has been or is to be used by the obligor, or (2) if securities are being deposited, the fair value of such securities is 10 percent or more of the indenture securities outstanding, unless the value of such property or securities is less than $25,000 or less than 1 percent of the indenture securities outstanding.
- ☐ C. Obtain executed counterparts of supplemental indenture subjecting property to lien of indenture, unless opinion of counsel states property is subject to such lien without the necessity for any specific conveyance.
- ☐ D. If supplemental indenture is required, follow for receipt of properly recorded counterparts and further opinion of counsel on sufficiency of such recording.

III. IF COLLATERAL IS DEPOSITED:
- ☐ A. Check negotiability.
- ☐ B. Ascertain whether income is to be collected and determine its disposition.
- ☐ C. Consider nominee registration.
- ☐ D. Prepare requisite instructions re receipt and deposit.
- ☐ E. If collateral consists of purchase money obligations, check that such obligations and purchase money mortgage run to trustee or that appropriate assignment is received.

Dated: _____ Prepared: _____ Approved: _____

Exhibit 9
Full Redemption Procedure Guide

OBLIGOR_____

INDENTURE_____

ISSUE_____

_____ CUSIP NO._____

REDEMPTION DATE _____ MAIL and/or PUBLICATION DATE ____

REDEMPTION AMT. _____ PREMIUM (if any)_____

REDEMPTION PRICE AMT. _____ TOTAL FUNDS REQUIRED____

ACCRUED INTEREST (If any, indicate if paid in usual manner to holders on regular record date) _____

TRUSTEE'S COUNSEL _____ OBLIGOR'S COUNSEL _____

Enter the following symbols in the column at the left to indicate action taken with respect to each requirement:

$\sqrt{}$ = Completed   P = Pending   Ø = Not applicable
                                        (Pending card prepared)

I. PRIOR TO REDEMPTION

_____ A. Immediately upon notification of redemption from Company review time requirements of the Indenture for mailing and/or publishing of Notice.

_____ B. If OID issue, receive from Company revised OID figures. Notify Opns. Div. and send copy to IRS.

_____ C. Send preliminary memo to Opns. Div. that issue will be called.

_____ D. If any Co-Agents, notify them of redemption; review securities with stops.

_____ E. Draft Notice of Redemption and Letter of Transmittal and submit to counsel (if necessary) and Company for approval. (Be sure Notice contains CUSIP Number and language on tax information regarding backup withholding).

_____ F. If Notice of Redemption required to be published, prepare instructions to advertising agents about dates of publication and specific newspapers.

_____ G. By memo have Opns. Div. open cash account for specific redemption payment.

(Note: Until the notice is mailed or published, treat information as highly confidential.)

_____ H. Prepare and distribute Redemption Instruction sheets to Opns. Div.

(Note: If OID issue, OID amount m st appear on Redemption Instruction for backup withholding.)

_____ I. Send copies of Redemption Notices via Fax transmission to Depository Trust Company, Philadelphia Depository Trust Company, and Midwest Securities Trust Company.

_____ J. Prepare mailing instructions to Opns. Div. to mail Redemption Notice to the following:

   _____ 1. Company
   _____ 2. Registered Holders
   _____ 3. Names received from Company
   _____ 4. Names received from Paying Agent
   _____ 5. Names on two-year list
   _____ 6. Co-Agents
   _____ 7. Stock Exchanges, NASD, Moody's, Standard & Poor's, Financial Information, Inc., and Kenny Information System. For municipal issues: *The Daily Bond Buyer* and *Redemption Digest*.

_____ K. Obtain Affidavit of mailing, and, if requested, send to Company.

_____ L. Obtain Affidavit of publication and send, if requested, to Company.

_____M. Verify with Company amount of funds to be deposited and date of deposit required by the Indenture. Arrange for proper receipt and distribution.

_____ N. Send memo to Opns. Div. requesting them to keep records of time spent and to advise fee unit of any charges to be billed to Company upon completion.

_____ O. Make arrangements for funds with any Co-Agents (including 1099s if appropriate).

_____ P. Receive supporting papers from Company.

II. ON OR AFTER REDEMPTION DATE

_____ A. Receive funds necessary to cover redemption (including principal, interest, and premium).

_____ B. Notify all stock exchanges on which securities are listed that sufficient funds were deposited.

_____ C. Instruct Opns. Div. to prepare appropriate accounting prior to execution of satisfaction papers.

_____ D. Review Pending file and dispose of any open items.

_____ E. Determine action to be taken with respect to any demands or notices of other Indenture trustees or claimants served upon Bank claiming a lien upon collateral or other property subject to Indenture at time of satisfaction.

_____ F. Consider notifying other Indenture trustees.

_____ G. Determine if obligor wishes to have executed a formal satisfaction and, if necessary, review drafts of supporting documents and form of satisfaction. Determine whether we need to get approval of satisfaction document from our counsel.

_____ H. Execute and deliver satisfaction (after accounting is completed). Consider necessity for obtaining County Clerk's certificates on Notarial Acknowledgment.

_____ I. Consider obtaining written approval of counsel, if counsel is used.

_____ J. Determine fee and prepare memo to fee unit. Review all unpaid bills.

_____ K. Deliver letter covering satisfaction (if requested) and final bill.

_____ L. Prepare Appointment/Termination form.

_____M. Determine from Company and dispose of the following items (also check for any special instructions on file).

    _____ 1. Cash on hand
    _____ 2. Collateral held
    _____ 3. Insurance Policies on file
    _____ 4. Unissued obligations
    _____ 5. Cancelled obligations
    _____ 6. Supplies of executed and/or conformed copies of Indenture, etc.
    _____ 7. Recorded counterparts of Indenture and other instruments
    _____ 8. Stamped original of Indenture

_____ N. Prepare, delete, or note following office records (if only one issue being redeemed under open-end Indenture, only 2 and 9 are applicable):

   _____ 1. State of Incorporation file
   _____ 2. Mortgage file
   _____ 3. Parent-subsidiary files
   _____ 4. Affiliates file
   _____ 5. Authorities file
   _____ 6. Obligors Information Return file
   _____ 7. Have Opns. Div. Instruction Sheets marked "REDEEMED"
   _____ 8. Individual Trustee file
   _____ 9. Tickler register control list
   _____ 10. Obligor's Address Book
   _____ 11. Close cash and/or security accounts

_____ O. Memo to Opns. Div. to remove issue from registered interest list.

_____ P. Prepare instructions to mail by Certified Mail a follow-up notice not later than 60 days after Redemption Date. Prepare an Affidavit of Mailing.

_____ Q. Publish a third notice one year after Redemption Date for all holders of outstanding bearer zero-coupon securities. Prepare an Affidavit of Mailing.

_____ R. At the request of the Company, arrange for a third or special mailing or publication of a follow-up notice. Prepare an Affidavit of Mailing.

_____ S. Ascertain provision of Indenture relating to return of undisbursed funds to Company after a definite period of time. Prepare appropriate Pending card.

_____ T. Document papers.

_____ U. Prepare documents for disposition in accordance with Disposition Guide.

Dated: _____ Prepared: _____ Approved: _____

EXHIBIT 10
Partial Redemption Procedure Guide

OBLIGOR: _____

ISSUE: _____ CUSIP NO. _____

REDEMPTION AMT.: _____ REDEMPTION DATE: _____

PREMIUM (if any): _____ RECEIVE FUNDS BY: _____

INTEREST (if any): _____ BOOKS CLOSE DATE: _____

REDEMPTION PRICE: _____

BOOKS OPEN:
TOTAL FUNDS   (Date of Notice: Publication Date)
REQUIRED: _____ Mail Date: _____

1. Under NYSE Rule 217, securities selected for redemption will not be good delivery after the date called numbers become available (Publication/Mail Date). Notice should be dated the date books open and be mailed on that date.

2. Bonds with stops (and not previously replaced) can be called.

3. Previously reissued portions of called but unpresented bonds should not be called again if efforts to contact holders prove futile (i.e., registered letter is returned by postal authorities as undeliverable).

Enter the following symbols in the column at left to indicate action taken with respect to each requirement:

$\sqrt{}$ = Completed   P = Pending   Ø = Not applicable
                              (Pending card prepared)

I. ONE MONTH PRIOR TO BOOKS CLOSE DATE

_____ A. Advise Opns. Div. of date and principal amount of redemption. Confirm issue is in proof.

_____ B. Verify that sufficient inventory of certificates will be on hand on Redemption Date.

_____ C. Draft notice and consider letter of transmittal and return envelope. Submit to counsel and Company if first call. (Be sure Notice contains CUSIP Number and language on tax information regarding backup withholding).

_____ D. Verify sufficient envelopes will be on hand.

II. TWO WEEKS PRIOR TO BOOKS CLOSE DATE

_____ A. Confirm with Company principal amount to be redeemed; and if securities are held in Company name, whether such are to be included in the call.

_____ B. If OID issue, receive from Company revised OID figures. Notify Opns. Div. and send copy to IRS.

_____ C. Send instructions to Operations Division indicating:

Company and issue (including CUSIP)
Principal amount outstanding
Principal amount to be redeemed
Books close date—Books open date
Call Unit size ($1,000, $100 etc.)
Date by when material must be received

_____ D. If listed on NY Stock Exchange (or other exchange), send letter (at least 10 days prior to books closing) giving amount of call and closing and opening dates for books to Reorganization Section of Depository Trust Co., Moody's, S&P, NASD, Financial Information, Inc., and Kenny Information System.

_____ E. Send request to Opns. Div. to open a special redemption account.

III. ON DAY AFTER BOOKS CLOSE DATE

_____ A. Verify that Opns. Div. has closed the books and that no transfers will be processed. Obtain the last certificate number of each denomination used and the number of last transfer sheet used.

$1,000: _____ $5,000: _____ $10,000: _____

Blanks: _____ Other: _____ Sheet #: _____

_____ B. Make preliminary arrangements with printer and obtain proof of text of notice, Letter of Transmittal, and any other enclosures. (Include number disclaimer, CUSIP number, and tax information as to back-up withholding.)

_____ C. If notice of redemption is required to be published, prepare instruction to advertising agent as to required newspapers and insertion dates.

IV. UPON RECEIPT OF MATERIAL FROM OPNS. DIV.

_____ A. Verify total principal amount called and compare with redemption figure. Make any necessary adjustments to called certificate list and called security holder list.

_____ B. Verify that no transfers have been processed. (See III A.)

_____ C. If the issue is CEDE-FAST:

    _____ 1. Check the call program to determine the CEDE-FAST balance called.

    _____ 2. Instruct Opns. Div to issue next certificate to:

        CEDE & CO.—FAST
        55 Water Street, New York, NY 10041

    in the amount of the balance that was called and to debit the CEDE-FAST total balance by this amount.

    _____ 3. Remove the Call Stop from the CEDE-FAST balance called and place a Call Stop on the new certificate.

    _____ 4. Add this new certificate to the Redemption Notice.

    _____ 5. Notify DTC in writing on Publication/Mail Date of the debit to their total CEDE-FAST balance for this issue and of the new certificate issued in its place. In addition, ask them to provide an "SCL" instructing us what to do with the certificate (i.e., deliver to them or hold until Redemption Date.)

_____ D. Insert certificate numbers on Notice and send to printer.

_____ E. Opns. Div. to receive draft of Notice to check bond numbers and verify that total principal amount called equals total principal amount printed on Notice.

_____ F. Proofread text of Notice, Letter of Transmittal and clear Notice with printer.

_____ G. Determine quantities of Notice, Letter of Transmittal and enclosures, if any, to be ordered.

_____ H. Affix labels for called certificate holders to Letters of Transmittal and stuff envelopes. Verify that number of Notices mailed equals the number of holders affected.

_____ I. Prepare and distribute Redemption Instruction sheets.

(Note: if OID issue, OID amount must appear on Redemption Instructions for backup withholding).

_____ J. Maintain year-to-date payments if accrued interest is to be paid.

_____ K. Copies of Redemption Notices and, if applicable, Letters of Transmittal (quantities vary with size of call) will be delivered by printer for distribution as follows:

      _____ 1. To Opns. Div.

      _____ 2. NYSE (if listed security)

      _____ 3. NASD, Moody's, Standard & Poor's, Financial Information Inc., and Kenny Information System. For municipal issues: *The Daily Bond Buyer* and *Redemption Digest*.

      _____ 4. The Company

      _____ 5. Any Co-Agents

_____ L. All Redemption Notices should be sent to Depository Trust Company, Philadelphia Depository Trust Company and Midwest Securities Trust Company via fax transmission on the Mail or Publication Date. Follow up immediately for the signed receipt from each to be returned via fax. A hard copy should also be sent, same day, via overnight courier (at DTC's expense) to:

Depository Trust Company
711 Stewart Avenue, Garden City, NY 11530
Attn.: Call Notification Dept.

_____ M. Send mailing instructions to Opns. Div. Include request for Affidavits of Selection and Mailing, if necessary.

_____ N. Make arrangement for funds with any Co-Agents (including 1099s, if appropriate).

_____ O. Consider source of funds and upon receipt advise Opns. Div.

_____ P. Prepare special memo for billing purposes.

_____ Q. Prepare instructions to Opns, Div., to mail by Certified Mail a follow-up notice no later than 60 days after Redemption Date. Include request for Affidavit of Mailing.

_____ R. Set up pending cards to publish a third notice one year after the Redemption Date for all holders of outstanding bearer zero-coupon securities. Include request to get Affidavit of Publication.

Dated: _____ Completed: _____ Approved: _____

EXHIBIT 11
Final Principal Accounting Statement

COMPANY: Global Electric Company
INDENTURE: Dated as of November 1, 1968

ISSUE: 6% S/F Debentures due November 1, 1993
PURPOSE: Redemption of all outstanding debentures as of November 1, 1976 and
                satisfaction of indenture

Principal amount issued under Indenture	$60,000,000.
Principal amount retired	20,975,000.
Principal amount outstanding	$39,025,000.

CASH ACCOUNTS	Principal	Premium
Cash held in Sinking Fund A/C #G-7	$ 25,000.	0.
Cash to be deposited in Redemption A/C #G-8	39,000,000.	0.
	$39,025,000.	

TOTAL PRINCIPAL AMOUNT OF SECURITIES AUTHENTICATED AND ISSUED	$117,950,000.

TOTAL PRINCIPAL AMOUNT OF SECURITIES
AUTHENTICATED, ISSUED, AND CANCELLED

A/C Conversion	0.
A/C Correction, Split and Transfer	$ 36,500,000.
A/C Exchange of coupon securities for fully registered	18,500,000.
A/C Exchange of fully registered securities for coupon	2,150,000.
A/C Mutilation	15,000.
A/C Reissuance of uncalled portion	750,000.
A/C Retirement for Sinking Fund	20,975,000.
A/C Temporary securities exchanged for permanent	0.
Total principal amount authenticated, issued, and canceled	$ 78,890,000.

DISPOSITION OF CANCELED SECURITIES

Principal amount of securities canceled and destroyed per destruction certificates on file	$ 45,672,000.
Principal amount of securities canceled and awaiting destruction	33,218,000.
Total principal amount canceled or destroyed	$ 78,890,000

Principal amount of securities authenticated and issued covered by Bonds of Indemnity	$ 35,000.

EXHIBIT 12
Final Interest Accounting Statement

Final Interest Accounting Statement
Company: Global Electric Company
Issue: 6% Debentures due November 1, 1993

INTEREST RATE	TOTAL INTEREST DUE	REGISTERED INTEREST PAID	COUPON DESTRUCTION CERTIFICATES ON FILE		COUPONS PAID AGAINST BOND OF INDEMNITY	CANCELED COUPONS ON HAND	BALANCE OUTSTANDING
			A/C payment	A/C surrender by company			
5/1/69	$1,800,000	$540,000	$1,252,200	$ 7,800	0	$ 0	$ 0
11/1/69	1,800,000	740,000	1,046,710	13,200	0	60	30
5/1/70	1,710,000	713,000	996,880	0	0	30	90
11/1/70	1,710,000	713,000	991,030	5,760	$ 30	30	150
5/1/71	1,620,000	686,000	933,820	0	30	0	150
11/1/71	1,620,000	686,000	933,670	0	30	90	210
5/1/72	1,530,000	659,000	870,670	0	30	60	240
11/1/72	1,530,000	662,900	866,860	0	0	0	240
5/1/73	1,440,000	645,720	780,360	13,500	0	150	270
11/1/73	1,440,000	645,720	775,830	18,000	0	210	240
5/1/74	1,350,000	718,510	624,950	6,000	0	210	330
11/1/74	1,350,000	818,510	515,980	15,000	0	210	300
5/1/75	1,260,000	888,990	0	0	0	370,530	480
11/1/75	1,260,000	888,990	0	0	0	370,380	630
5/1/76	1,170,000	961,930	0	0	0	206,900	1,170
Totals:	$22,590,000	$10,968,270	$10,588,960	$79,260	$120	$948,860	$4,530

Form of accounting for interest obligations. The balance outstanding represents matured coupons unpresented and should equal funds in the hands of the paying agent. If held by an agent other than the trustee, such funds should be paid over to the trustee prior to satisfaction.

EXHIBIT 13
Document Disposition Guide

Category A   Destroy immediately.
Category B   Destroy 10 years after satisfaction.
Category C   Hold indefinitely.

ITEM	*DISPOSITION CATEGORY*
1. Original counterpart of instrument of satisfaction together with all documents relating thereto, including final accounting.	1. C
2. Stamped original of indenture.	2. Return to company, otherwise A. But if only executed counterpart available, treat as provided in item 3 below.
3. One executed counterpart of indenture and other collateral instruments.	3. C.
4. Extra recorded, executed, or conformed counterparts of indenture and other collateral instruments (e.g., lease, assignment).	4. Return to company, otherwise A.
5. Policies of insurance.	5. Return to company, otherwise, A.
6. Insurance (other than policies).	6. A
7. Bond issue papers.	7. C
8. Drafts of bond issue papers.	8. A
9. Corporate documents.	9. A
10. Obligor's instructions	10.
a) those primarily concerning the mechanics of administration.	a) A
b) those of interpretive importance.	b) B
11. Certificates (except destruction).	11. B
12. Destruction certificates.	12. C
13. Recording (opinion and other data).	13. A
14. Releases and condemnations.	14. B
15. Litigation (other than condemnations).	15. C
16. Trustee's reports	16. A

17.	SEC documents (including T-1 and T-2).	17.	A
18.	Financial statements (including 10K SEC reports).	18.	A
19.	Funds documents (including debt service, insurance proceeds, released property, and condemnation awards).	19.	B
20.	Withdrawals	20.	B
21.	Originals of all bonds of indemnity or assumptions of liabilities of others with respect to any indenture securities or other obligations.	21.	C
22.	Any document relating to an obligation or undertaking beyond maturity of indenture securities.	22.	C
23.	General material.	23.	C for information essential to establish basic historical continuity of trusteeship. A for all other general matter.
24.	History of trust.	24.	C
25.	Conversion documents.	25.	B
26.	Specimen bond.	26.	C

EXHIBIT 14
Maturity Procedure Guide

OBLIGOR _____

INDENTURE _____

ISSUE _____

_____ CUSIP NO. _____

MATURITY DATE _____ PRINCIPAL AMOUNT OUTSTANDING _____

TRUSTEE'S COUNSEL _____ OBLIGOR'S COUNSEL _____

Enter the following symbols in the column at the left to indicate action taken with respect to each requirement:

√ = Completed   P = Pending   Ø = Not applicable
                       (Pending card prepared)

I. PRIOR TO MATURITY

_____ A. Determine if Company wishes to mail a Notice of Maturity prior to maturity and review draft. (Be sure Notice contains CUSIP Number and language on tax information regarding backup withholding).

_____ B. If Company requests a mailing of Notice *prior* to maturity prepare mailing instructions and send to Opns. Div.

_____ C. Mail copies of notice to:

      _____ 1. Company
      _____ 2. Registered Holders
      _____ 3. Names received from Company
      _____ 4. Names received from Paying Agent
      _____ 5. Names on two-year list
      _____ 6. Co-Agents

_____ D. Determine if Company wishes to publish Notice of Maturity. If yes, prepare instructions to advertising agents on dates of publication, newspapers, affidavits of publication, number of prints required, etc.

_____ E. Send instructions to Opns. Div. to include our regular maturity notice with mailing of final interest check. (If Company mailed its own notice previously, they may request us not to mail our regular notice.)

_____ F. By memo have Opns. Div. open Cash Account for principal payment.

_____ G. Prepare Maturity Instruction sheet and distribute.
(Note: If OID issue, OID amount must appear on Maturity Instructions for backup withholding).

_____ H. Instruct Opns. Div. to prepare an appropriate accounting prior to executing any satisfaction papers.

_____ I. Review Pending file and dispose of any open items.

_____ J. Determine action to be taken with respect to any demands or notices of other indenture trustees or claimants served upon Bank claiming a lien upon collateral or other property subject to above Indenture at time of satisfaction.

_____ K. Consider notifying other Indenture trustees.

_____ L. Obtain affidavit of mailing and, if requested, send to Company.

_____ M. Obtain affidavit of publication and, if requested, send to Company.

_____ N. Verify with Company amount of funds to be deposited at maturity and arrange for proper receipt and disposition.

_____ O. Prepare pending cards to perform the following:

1. Check balance in maturity account two weeks after Maturity Date.
2. Send first follow-up notice two weeks after Maturity Date.
3. Send second follow-up notice three months after Maturity Date.
4. If "Home Office Payment" issue, follow for securities not yet presented two weeks after Maturity Date.

II. UPON MATURITY

_____ A. Obtain requisite funds to cover maturity of bonds (including principal and interest).

_____ B. Notify in writing all stock exchanges on which securities are listed when funds for maturity have been deposited.

_____ C. Determine if Company wishes to have executed a formal satisfaction and, if necessary, review drafts of supporting documents and form of satisfaction.

_____ D. Determine whether we need to get approval for satisfaction from our counsel.

_____ E. Receive supporting documentation and execute and deliver satisfaction (after accounting has been completed). Consider necessity of obtaining County Clerk's certificate on Notarial acknowledgement.

_____ F. Consider fee and prepare memo to Fee unit. Review all unpaid bills.

_____ G. Deliver letter covering satisfaction (if requested) and final bill.

_____ H. Prepare Appointment/Termination Form.

_____ I. Determine from Company and dispose of the following items (also check for any special instructions on file):

    _____ 1. Cash on hand
    _____ 2. Collateral held
    _____ 3. Insurance policies on file
    _____ 4. Unissued obligations
    _____ 5. Canceled obligations
    _____ 6. Supplies of executed and/or conformed copies of Indenture, etc.
    _____ 7. Recorded counterparts of Indenture and other Instruments

_____ J. Prepare, delete, or note following office records (if only one issue is maturing under open-end Indenture, only 7 is applicable):

    _____ 1. State of Incorporation file
    _____ 2. Mortgage file
    _____ 3. Parent-subsidiary files
    _____ 4. Affiliates file
    _____ 5. Authorities file
    _____ 6. Obligor's Information Return file
    _____ 7. Have Opns. Div. Instruction sheets marked "MATURED"
    _____ 8. Individual Trustee file
    _____ 9. Tickler register control list
    _____ 10. Obligor's address book
    _____ 11. Close cash and/or security accounts

_____ K. Memo to Opns. Div. to delete issue from registered interest list.

_____ L. Prepare instructions to Opns. Div. to mail:
1. First follow-up notice—two weeks after Maturity Date.
2. Second follow-up notice—three months after Maturity Date.

NOTE: Holders of $50,000 p.a. or more must, on first follow-up notice only, be mailed by Registered Mail. All others via first class mail.

———— M. At the request of the Company, arrange for third or special mailing or publication of a follow-up notice only if the Company will pay special fee and cost of such mailing or publication.

———— N. Ascertain provisions of Indenture relating to return of undisbursed funds to Company after a definite period of time. Prepare appropriate Pending card.

———— O. Document papers.

———— P. Prepare documents for disposition in accordance with Disposition Guide. (Not applicable if other issues O/S under open-end Indenture.)

Dated: ———————————— Prepared: ———————————— Approved: ————————————

Exhibit 15
Memorandum Certificate of Ownership

Memorandum Certificate of Ownership
for
Central States Housing Authority
6% Bonds due Serially March 1, 1983/2003

Correspondent ————————————

Collection No. ———— Date ————————

I certify that to the best of my knowledge and belief the information entered hereon is correct.

————————————————————
(Signature of owner, trustee, or agent)

————————————————————
(Address of trustee or agent)

————————————————————

————————————————————

Owner of bonds from which accompanying interest coupons were detached:

Name & Address ————————————

————————————————————

————————————————————

Principal amount of
bonds owned $ ————————————
Date interest was due ———— Date pd. ————
Amount of interest $ ————————————

NOTE: *If name and address of bond holder is not known to final collecting agent, please show, in space to left, name and address of correspondent and collection number if any.*

Exhibit 16

GUIDELINES FOR RETENTION AND DISPOSITION OF CANCELLED SECURITIES

Corporate Securities Services Committee
American Bankers Association
1982

	TRANSFERS	
	I FULLY REGISTERED SECURITIES COVERED BY SECURITIES EXCHANGE ACT OF 1934, § 17A (Registered Transfer Agent for Stock or Debt Securities/Registrar for Debt Securities	**II** SECURITIES NOT COVERED BY SECURITIES EXCHANGE ACT OF 1934, §17A (Transfer Agent for Stock or Debt Securities/Registrar for Debt Securities)
A. RETENTION PERIOD FOR CANCELLED SECURITIES	Six years (first 6 months in easily accessible place) along with supporting documents	Six months to one year after cancellation then option 1) or 4).
B. OPTIONS TO RETENTION:		
1. Microfilm	Retain 6 years in lieu of cancelled securities and supporting documents. Need 2 sets, stored apart, indexed. Need reader/printer. If sent to issuer—see option 2) below. After microfilming—see option 4) below.	Only registered securities and supporting documents. Retain microfilm 6 years. Not recommended for bearer securities. After microfilming—see option 4) below.
2. Return to Issuer	If returned during required 6 year period—issuer must agree to retain for balance of period and to give you and SEC access. Either obtain receipt or record contents of shipment. Retain receipt or shipping record 6 years.	Not recommended unless required in governing agreement/indenture, etc. If required, see Transfers—Col. I (B-2). Except SEC access not required.
3. Return to Principal Agent/Trustee	Not recommended—but if required by agreement then refer to option 2) above.	Not recommended—but if required by agreement then refer to option 2) above.
4. Destroy	After 6 years or after option 1) furnish destruction certificate to issuer with description of securities including issuer's name, class of stock or series of bonds, period covered, reference to specific microfilm record or other list identifying by number the securities shipped. Retain duplicate original in authority file for indefinite period.	Six months to one year after cancellation and (if applicable) microfilming. Destruction certificate described under Transfers—Col. I (B-4).
C. REFERENCE	A. SEC Rule 17Ad-6 and 7. B. Also refer to applicable Federal/State laws, bylaws of issuer and for debt securities refer to agency agreement or indenture.	Refer to applicable Federal/State laws, bylaws of issuer, governing agreement/indenture.

MATURITY/REDEMPTION/PURCHASE		CONVERSION/EXCHANGE
I DEBT SECURITIES AND COUPONS(Principal, Co-Paying Agent/Trustee)	II STOCK (Liquidating Agent, Tender Agent, Paying Agent, Redemption Agent, Depository Agent)	DEBT SECURITIES (Registrar, Conversion Agent) STOCK (Conversion Agent, Exchange Agent, Warrant Agent)
Principal Agent: Six months after maturity/redemption/purchase date. Then option 2) or 4) depending on your agreement. Co-Agent: One month after maturity/redemption/purchase date, then option 2) or 3) or 4)	Six months to one year after payment—option 1) or 2) or 3) or 4)	Six months to one year after cancellation then option 1) or 2) or 3) or 4).
Registered: Microfilm with supporting documents. Retain microfilm 6 years. After microfilming [see option 4). Bearer: Not recommended.	Microfilm cancelled securities and supporting documents. Retain microfilm 6 years [see Transfers—Col. I (B-1).] After microfilming, destroy securities (see option 4) below.]	Only registered securities and supporting documents. Retain microfilm 6 years. Not recommended for bearer securities. Then option 4) below.
Within a reasonable time after each maturity. Either obtain receipt or record contents of shipment. Retain receipt or shipping record 6 years.	Six months to one year after payment. Either obtain receipt or record contents of shipment. Retain receipt or shipping record 6 years.	Not recommended unless required in governing instrument. If required see Transfers—Col. I (B-2). SEC access not required.
Not recommended—but if required by agreement then refer to option 2) above.	Six months to one year after payment. Either obtain receipt or record contents of shipment. Retain receipt or shipping record 6 years.	Not recommended unless required by agreement. If required refer to Transfers—Col. I (B-2).
Six months after cancellation and (if applicable) microfilming. Furnish one destruction certificate to issuer, retain duplicate original in authority file for indefinite period. Destruction certificate must contain the following information. 1. Stock or debt securities: Show issuer's name, series, serial numbers, principal amount, total. 2. Coupons: show the same information included above (option: sole paying agent may omit coupon serial numbers.)	Refer to Maturity/Redemption/Purchase—Col. I (B-4)	Six months to one year after cancellation and (if applicable) microfilming. Furnish destruction certificate described under Transfers—Col. I (B-4)
See Transfers—Col. II (C)	See Transfers—Col. II (C).	See Transfers—Col. II (C).

SECURITIES AND EXCHANGE COMMISSION
REGULATION § 240.17Ad-6(c), 7(d), (f).

RULE 17Ad-6(c):

Every registered transfer agent which, under the terms of its agency, maintains securityholder records for an issue shall, with respect to such issue, retain (1) each cancelled registered bond, debenture, share, warrant or right, other registered evidence of indebetedness, or other certificate of ownership and (2) all accompanying documentation, except legal papers returned to the presentor.

RULE 17Ad-7(d):

The records required by Rule 17Ad-6(c) shall be maintained for a period of not less than six years, the first six months in an easily accessible place.

RULE 17Ad-7(f):

The records required to be maintained pursuant to Rule 17Ad-6 may be produced or reproduced on microfilm and be preserved in that form for the time required by Rule 17Ad-7. If such microfilm substitution for hard copy is made by a registered transfer agent, it shall:

(1) At all times have available for examination by the Commission and the appropriate regulatory agency for such transfer agent, facilities for immediate, easily readable projection of the microfilm and for producing easily readable facsimile enlargements;

(2) Arrange the records and index and file the firms in such a manner as to permit the immediate location of any particular record;

(3) Be ready at all times to provide, and immediately provide, any facsimile enlargement which the Commission and the appropriate regulatory agency by their examiners or other representatives may request; and

(4) For the period for which the microfilmed records are required to be maintained, store separately from the original microfilm records a copy of the microfilm records.

EXHIBIT 17
TIA/Indenture Cross References

Reference is made to the following provisions of the Trust Indenture Act of 1939, as amended, which established certain duties and responsibilities of the Company and the Trustee which are not set forth in this Indenture:

Section	Subject	Section	Subject
310(b)	Disqualification of Trustee for conflicting interest	315(b)	Notice of default from Trustee to Securityholders
311	Preferential collection of claims of Trustee as creditor of Company	315(c)	Duties of Trustee in case of default
312(a)	Periodic filing of information by Company with Trustee	315(d)	Provisions relating to responsibility of Trustee
312(b)	Access of Securityholders to information	315(e)	Assessment of costs against litigating Securityholders in certain circumstances
313(a)	Annual report of Trustee to Securityholders	316(a)	Directions and waivers by Securityholders in certain circumstances
313(b)	Additional reports of Trustee to Securityholders	316(b)	Prohibition of impairment of right of Securityholders to payment
314(a)	Reports of Company, including annual compliance certificate	316(c)	Right of Company to set record date for certain purposes
314(c)	Evidence of compliance with conditions precedent	317(a)	Special powers of Trustee
315(a)	Duties of Trustee prior to default	318(a)	Provisions of Act to control in case of conflict

Exhibit 18
Training Guidelines for Administrators

SUBJECT MATTER	REFERENCE MATERIAL
A. DURING FIRST MONTH	
1. *Orientation* Position profile, Training Program outline, Competency expectations, Performance standards, Appraisal system, and Corporate Trust Orientation	Handbook, Training Guidelines
2. Knowledge of debt and equity securities, differences between secured and unsecured and short-, medium-, and long-term maturities.	CTAM Book
3. *Issuers of Debt Securities* Corporations, Governments, States, State authorities, State agencies, and Municipalities	CTAM Book
4. Role of Investment Bankers and Underwriters	CTAM Book
5. Development of the Trustee concept. Fiduciary Responsibilities defined.	CTAM Book
6. Functions and Responsibilities of a Corporate Trustee	CTAM Book
7. Securities Act of 1933 Securities Exchange Act of 1934 Trust Indenture Act of 1939, as amended	CTAM Book Securities Laws, Handbook
8. *The Trust Indenture* As a Mortgage, Trust, Contract	CTAM Book, An Indenture
9. Public vs. Private Debt Issues	CTAM Book
10. *Functions of Administration*	
a. Trustee Functions Corporate Trustee under trust indentures, Construction Fund Trustee, Bond Fund Trustee, Owner Trustee, and Pledge Agreement	CTAM Book
b. Agency Registrar, Authenticating Agent, Fiscal Agent, Paying Agent—Corporate and Municipal, Exchange Agent, Conversion Agent, Destruction Agent, Escrow Agent, Tender Agent, and Depository	CTAM Book
11. Co-Agency Duties and Responsibilities	CTAM Book
12. Tickler system—Use and Purpose	Handbook
13. Document Files, Correspondence Files, and Retention of Records	Handbook
14. Organization and structure of Bank, Fiduciary Department, Corporate Trust Function	Handbook

15. Use of Telephone, Fax, Office Machines, and Computer   Handbook
    Terminals including Electionic Mail

16. Introduction to Corporate Trust Marketing Function   Tours and
                                                                related
                                                                materials

17. Introduction to Corporate Trust Operations Function   Tours and
                                                                related
                                                                materials

B. DURING FIRST THREE MONTHS

1. Receipt of Interest and Principal   Handbook

2. *Preparation of Debit and Credit Tickets and Advices*   Handbook
   Preparation and knowledge of offsets, Check collection,
   Mailing advices, Use of Clearance Accounts, Transfer of
   funds—money transfer, and Clearing House vs. Federal
   Funds

3. *Private Placements*   CTAM Book,
   HOP Agreements, Use and preparation of amortization   Handbook
   schedules, Pro-rata redemptions. Computation of interest,
   Instructions to Operations.

4. *Corporate Trust Records*   Handbook
   Document files, Use of correspondence file and contact
   file, Use of pending cards, Subsidiary Administration files,
   Trustee Records, Cash and securities ledgers: Opening and
   closing accounts and Termination of accounts

5. Understanding and Use of Procedure Book   Procedure
                                                                Book

6. *Internal Instructions*   Handbook
   Preparation of Operating instructions, Address book, Mailing instructions, and Instructions for lists and labels.

7. *Discussion of:*   CTAM Book,
   Securities Act of 1933, Securities Exchange Act of 1934,   Handbook,
   Trust Indenture Act of 1939, and Articles 8/9 of Uniform   Securities Laws
   Commercial Code.

8. *Usual Provisions of a Typical Indenture*   CTAM Book
   (Composite picture of the scope of a typical Indenture)

C. DURING FIRST SIX MONTHS

1. *Letter and Memo Writing*   Handbook
   Confirmations and Certifications, Presidential letters,
   Bondholder inquiries, and Cables-tested vs. untested.

2. *Review and Execution of Releases*   CTAM Book
   Indenture provisions, Receipt of proceeds, Substitution of
   property, Prepayment of debt securities, and Withdrawals—additions and betterments.

3. *Investments*   Handbook
   Policy & functional areas involved, Understanding of var-
   ious types of securities, Order instructions, Time limits,
   Follow-up of transaction, Maturities, Reinvestments, and
   Remittances—interest and principal

4. *Trustee Reports*   CTAM Book,
   Annual TIA conflict check and Trustee's Annual Report.   Handbook

5. *Preparation of Instructions for Agency Appointments*   Handbook
   Corporate and Municipal agency appointments; corporate
   and municipal issue calls, redemptions, and maturities

6. *Model Indentures*   CTAM Book,
   Model provisions and Simplified Indenture   ABF Model
                                                                          F/R Debenture
                                                                          Indenture,
                                                                          Commentaries,
                                                                          Simplified
                                                                          Indenture

7. *Operations Orientation Tour*   Handbook

8. *Introduction to Corporate Trust's Management Philosophy*   Handbook
   and Style
   Planning process (and cycle), Leading activities including
   group participation, Organizing work flow/structure, and
   Controlling activities and programs

9. *Discussion of Appraisal Program and Salary*   Handbook
   Administration

D. BETWEEN SIX MONTHS AND ONE YEAR

   1. Relationships with other Banking/Operations Divisions

   2. Detailed discussion of Indenture provisions, Issuance, Dat-   CTAM Book,
      ing and interest accrual, Insurance, Maintenance, Finan-   Commentaries
      cials, Recording, Sinking Fund including: Additions and
      Betterments, Cash—Partial Redemptions, and Credit; De-
      fault, Conversion, Concerning the Trustee, and Remedies
      of Trustee and Bondholders

   3. Indenture Reading and Understanding   CTAM Book,
                                                                          Commentaries

   4. Credit Enhancements including Letters of Credit and Bond   CTAM Book
      Insurance

   5. *Closing Functions as Trustee for Noncomplex Public Issues*   CTAM Book,
      Time schedule, Ordering of certificates, Review of docu-   Handbook
      ments, Preparation of supporting documents, Deposit of
      proceeds and collateral, Documenting of closing papers,
      and Preparation of trustee records

6. Basic understanding of complex financings (e.g., structured transactions)   CTAM Book

7. Preparation of Ticklers   Handbook

8. Preparation of Form T-1   CTAM Book, Handbook

9. Filing of Recorded Counterparts   CTAM Book, Handbook

10. *Sinking Funds and Redemptions*
Total, partial, and forced conversion   CTAM Book, Handbook

11. *Satisfactions*
Accountings, Disposition of documents, Agency accounts, and Payment of bond maturities   CTAM Book, Handbook

12. *Review of Certificates, Opinions, and Financial Statements*
Checking indenture provisions, Checking signatures, and Sign off   CTAM Book, Handbook

13. Consents and Waivers   CTAM Book, Handbook

14. Understanding replacement of lost, stolen, and mutilated securities   CTAM Book, Handbook

15. Name Change of Obligor   CTAM Book, Handbook

16. Resignations   CTAM Book, Handbook

17. Organizing work and using available reference resources.

18. Setting Priorities

19. Following up on pending matters

E. BETWEEN ONE AND TWO YEARS

1. Introduction to Financial Planning and Control Programs

2. "Reading" and ability to give comments on New Indentures and Supplements, Private Placement Agreements, Other Financing Documents   CTAM Book, Model Indentures, Commentaries, Other Indentures

3. *Closing functions as Trustee or Owner Trustee for complex financings*
Time schedules, Ordering of certificates, Review of documents, Preparation of supporting documents, Deposit of proceeds and collateral, Documenting closing papers, and Preparation of records   Handbook

4. Merger of Obligor	CTAM Book, Handbook
5. Successor Trusteeships and Indemnifications	CTAM Book, Handbook
6. Understanding of Fee Schedules and Billing Policies and Procedures	
7. Introduction to Default and Bankruptcy Administration	CTAM Book

Reference Material Key

CTAM Book	Landau, *Corporate Trust Administration and Management*
ABF Model	American Bar Foundation, *Model Fully Registered Debenture Indenture*
Commentaries	American Bar Foundation, *Commentaries on Model Indentures*
Handbook	*Corporate Trust Administrator's Handbook*

EXHIBIT 19
Minimum Competencies—Administrators

Administrator	Senior Administrator
1. Reviews new noncomplex indentures, agreements, and other basic documents for further review with account officer.	Reviews new complex indentures, agreements, and other basic documents for proper form and substance for review with account officer; understanding is sufficient to explain comments to our counsel.
2. Reviews all documents and certificates delivered in connection with the issuance of securities with the account officer and assists the account officer on all closing details.	Reviews all documents and certificates delivered in connection with the issuance of securities and handles all closing details with guidance from the account officer.
3. Completes review of all financial statements, certificates, and opinions for account officer.	Completes review and approval of all financial statements, certificates, and opinions.
4. Working knowledge of Model Indenture provisions and mechanics and of least complicated negotiated provisions.	Understands Model Indenture provisions and mechanics and has good working knowledge of most negotiated provisions.
5. Handles details and followup with guidance relative to: a) receipt & disbursement of cash b) sinking funds	Handles details and followup with guidance relative to: a)–g) SAME h) consents & waivers

c) releases
d) investments
e) withdrawals
f) satisfactions
g) preparation of trustee reports

i) name change of obligor
j) resignations
k) mergers

6. Prepares letters, memoranda, and internal instructions for account officer's approval and signature.

Prepares letters, memoranda, and internal instructions for own approval and signature or account officer's based on internal guidelines.

7. Exercises good judgment on what should be referred to account officer, offering optional solutions.

Exercises sound judgment when solving problems and when referring items to account officer. If referred to officer, exercises sound judgment in recommending the appropriate solution.

8. With account officer's guidance, sets priorities and organizes own work in an effective manner.

Sets priorities and organizes own work in efficient and effective manner.

9. Good understanding of Trustee records maintained.

Complete understanding of Trustee records maintained.

10. Handles work without constant supervision on fundamental tasks.

Handles all day-to-day work with only minimal guidance from account officer.

11. Dependent on account officer for guidance. Followup complete.

Dependence on account officer for guidance after problem and possible solutions presented. Followup complete.

12. Recognizes an apparent problem. Presents complete information to account officer.

Recognizes an apparent problem and determines the real issue. Presents complete information to account officer and presents most viable solution to account officer.

13. Originates and suggests to account officer new ideas to promote better safeguards and greater efficiency.

Originates new ideas to promote better safeguards and greater efficiency.

14. Applies appropriate level of job knowledge when solving problems and working under pressure.

SAME

15. Familiarity with the purpose and general applicability of the Trust Indenture Act of 1939, the Securities Act of 1933, and the Securities Exchange Act of 1934.

Familiarity with the purpose and specific application of the conflict and disclosure provisions of the Trust Indenture Act. Understands purpose and applicability of other relevant federal and state laws and regulations.

16. General understanding of debt and equity securities and the markets in which they trade; total understanding of the

Good understanding of debt and equity securities and the markets in which they trade; total understanding of the role played and role played and the function of the Trustee, obligor, and the investment banker.

17. Basic knowledge of Bank and Administration policies as they relate to account administration.

18. N.A.

19. N.A.

20. Basically familiar with Operations functions and key personnel of Operations.

21. Basic knowledge of the organization structure of the Bank, the Trust Dept., and Corporate Trust function.

22. General knowledge of other divisions and department functions in Bank as they relate to the position.

23. With account officer, cultivate relations with customers, counsel, and investment bankers.

24. Complies with position performance standards.

the function of the Trustee, obligor, and the investment banker.

Specific knowledge of Bank and Administration policies as they relate to account administration.

Generally familiar with Administration planning and control programs.

Basically familiar with all fee policies and procedures.

Complete knowledge of Operations functions and key personnel of Operations.

SAME, plus knowledge of other interfacing divisions.

SAME, but greater specific knowledge and understanding.

With guidance from account officer, cultivate relations with customers, counsel, and investment bankers to put the Bank in favorable position to market additional services.

SAME

EXHIBIT 20
Minimum Competencies—Account Officers

Account Officer	*Senior Account Officer*
1. Satisfactorily reviews new indentures, fiscal agency and authenticating agency agreements, etc. and identifies provisions missing or needing revision; gives comments with minimal assistance from Administration Manager.	Throughly reviews new indentures, fiscal agency and authenticating agency agreements, etc. and identifies provisions missing or needing revision and can draft substitute language; gives comments without assistance from Administration Manager.
2. Satisfactorily negotiates basic indenture provisions of the indenture or other agreements.	Effective negotiator in all areas of responsibility.
3. Understands basic debt financing methods.	Understands complex debt-financing methods.

4. Well qualified to administer trust or agency accounts and solve routine account problems.

Fully qualified to administer trust or agency accounts and solve complex account problems.

5. Handles routine accounts with minimal assistance from Administration Manager.

Handles complex, troublesome accounts and defaulted accounts with minimal assistance from Administration Manager.

6. Working knowledge of Trust Indenture Act and the purpose and significant provisions of the Securities Act and the Securities Exchange Act. Familiar with relevant UCC negotiable instrument and security interest provisions.

Fully understands Trust Indenture Act and is able to interpret provisions of the Act in order to make decisions; understands the purpose and relevant provisions of the Securities Act, the Securities Exchange Act. Understands relevant provisions of the Federal Bankruptcy Code and UCC.

7. Writes satisfactory letters and memos; oral communication satisfactory on a one-to-one basis.

Effective use of oral and written communication skills; can conduct training seminars.

8. Recommends appropriate business decisions involving risk.

Within limits of authority, makes appropriate business decisions involving risk.

9. Identifies need for action concerning defaulted and financially troubled accounts.

Ability to make sound judgments with supportable recommendations on defaulted and financially troubled accounts.

10. Qualified to exercise limited independent action as the primary official account contact.

Within limits of authority exercises complete independent action as the primary official account contact.

11. Has basic knowledge of operations and marketing activities and functions of interfacing divisions.

Has extensive knowledge of operations and marketing activities; greater depth of knowledge of interfacing divisions including fiduciary. Maintains knowledge of bank structure and organization.

12. Familiar with Administration planning and control functions.

Good understanding of Administration planning and control activities.

13. Is thoroughly familiar with fee structure and schedules.

Recommends appropriate fees to Administration Manager.

14. Controls work in process; is supervised by Administration Manager.

Controls own work in process effectively.

15. Training skills being developed.

Well qualified to train, counsel, and evaluate administrators and develop account officers.

16. Not an experienced supervisor.

Has been trained in professional management skills; capable of supervising two or more subordinates.

17. Limited contribution to Administration's marketing program.

Is responsible for participation in all sales and marketing activities.

18. Basic familiarity with ongoing developments in CT industry.

Good understanding of changes taking place in the CT and securities industries and trends within commercial banking functions.

19. Ability to perform needs analysis and establish specific objectives.

Establishes and consistently accomplishes in a timely manner difficult specific objectives and special projects.

20. Sets priorities and organizes own work to ensure consistent, timely performance results.

SAME, plus that of assigned administrators.

21. Performance standards for own work are consistently met.

Performance standards for own work and that of assigned administrators are consistently followed.

22. Has been designated as a CERTIFIED CORPORATE TRUST SPECIALIST by the Institute of Certified Bankers.

SAME

Exhibit 21
Administrator Appraisal Document

NAME _____ GRADE _____ S.S. No. _____

DATE ENTERED POSITION _____ MANAGER'S NAME_____

DATE OF LAST APPRAISAL _____DATE OF CURRENT APPRAISAL ____

A) SIGNIFICANCE FACTOR

Each measurable/observable task/work activity/responsibility (Section II) and general performance item (Section III) shall be assigned a significance factor rating based upon its importance (i.e., impact and effect) to the accomplishment of the position's overall objective.

4 = vital to accomplishing the position's objective
3 = important to accomplishing the position's objective
2 = necessary to accomplishing the position's objective
1 = supplementary to accomplishing the position's objective

B) PERFORMANCE RATING (*)

Each task/work activity/responsibility (Section II) and general performance item (Section III) shall be rated based upon measured/observed performance during the evaluation period.

5 = Excellent: The quantity of the work produced is significantly greater than the standard/average, and the quality of the work produced requires no revision and/or rework.

4 = Above Standard: The quantity of the work produced is greater than the standard/average: and the quality of the work produced requires minimal revision and/or rework.

3 = Standard: The quantity of the work produced is equal to the standard/average, and the quality of the work produced requires a reasonable (acceptable) amount of revision and/or rework.

2 = Below Standard: The quantity of the work produced is less than the standard/average, and the quality of the work produced requires a more than reasonable amount of revision and/or rework.

1 = Unsatisfactory: The quantity of the work performed is significantly less than the standard/average, and the quality of the work produced requires substantial revision and/or rework.

(*) Every Performance Rating of "5" or "1" must be fully explained, using relevant examples, in Sections IV or V, respectively.

SECTION I PERFORMANCE AGAINST OBJECTIVES

OBJECTIVE	RESULTS
1.	1.
2.	2.
3.	3.

SECTION II TECHNICAL PERFORMANCE

Performance	Significance Factor (A)	Performance Rating (B)	Point Value (C) $(A \times B = C)$
1. Reviews new Indentures and/or other Agreements for review with account officer.	4		
2. Writes letters and memos.	3		
3. Prepares Trustee Reports.	3		
4. Handles details relative to closings and other meetings.	3		
5. Prepares Form T-1.	3		
6. Reviews financial statements.	3		
7. Assists account officer in review of documents delivered in connection with the issuance of securities.	3		

8. Processes releases.   2

9. Processes substitutions.   2

10. Processes withdrawals.   2

11. Processes receipt and dis-
    bursement of funds in-
    cluding preparation of
    tickets.   4

12. Prepares internal operat-
    ing instructions.   4

13. Processes investments.   4

14. Prepares ticklers.   4

15. Processes sinking funds
    and redemptions.   4

16. Reviews certificates and
    opinions.   4

17. Files recorded counter-
    parts.   1

18. Completes satisfactions.   1

19. Handles consents and
    waivers.   1

20. Effects name change of
    obligor.   1

21. Handles resignations.   1

22. Handles mergers of obli-
    gor.   1

23. Handles appointment as
    successor trustee/agent.   1

24. Knowledge of provisions
    of Indentures and/or other
    Agreements.   4

25. General knowledge of ba-
    sic and complex types of
    security transactions.   4

26. General knowledge of
    Corporate Trust records.   3

27. Knowledge of fiduciary
    responsibilities.   3

28. Knowledge of agency re-
    sponsibilities.   3

29. General knowledge of
    functions of Operations.   3

30. Knowledge of Trust In-
    denture Act of 1939, and
    Securities Acts.   3

31. Knowledge of Corpora-
    tion Trust organization and
    structure.   2

32. General knowledge of
    Corporate Trust Policy and
    Procedure Books.   1

33. Knowledge of replace-
    ment of lost, stolen, and
    mutilated securities.   1

34. Knowledge of organiza-
    tion structure of Bank.   1

35. Knowledge of the role
    played by investment
    bankers.   1

TOTALS	(A)	xxx	(C)
	TOTAL POINT VALUE (C)	TOTAL SUM OF SIGNIFICANCE FACTORS (A)	OVERALL RATING (C ÷ A)

OVERALL RATING _____ × WEIGHT 60% = _____ (D)

SECTION III   GENERAL PERFORMANCE FACTORS

Performance	Significance Factor (A)	Performance Rating (B)	Point Value (C) (A × B = C)
1. Dependability Days Absent: _____ Days Late: _____	4		
2. Interpersonal Skills (ability to deal effectively with others).	4		
3. Oral Communication Skills (ability to express information orally in a clear and effective manner).	3		

4. Written Communication Skills (ability to express information in writing in a clear and effective manner).   3

5. Time Usage (ability to optimize the use of the time available).   3

6. Performance Under Pressure (ability to maintain effective performance under demands of time, workload, and resource constraint).   3

7. Creativity and Imagination (ability to effectively apply independent judgment and resourcefulness in performing required tasks).   2

8. Flexibility and Adaptability (ability to modify behavior and approaches in dealing with different situations).   3

9. Organizing and Planning Skills (ability to establish courses of action for self to accomplish established objectives).   2

10. Perception and Analytical Skills (ability to identify and comprehend the critical elements of a situation and to effectively evaluate factors essential to problem solving).   4

11. Decisiveness (ability to establish a sound course of action and support it when challenged).   2

12. Team Participation (ability to serve as a team

member sharing informa-
tion, ideas, and resources
to support the work group/
unit).   3

13. Initiative (willingness to
    undertake new assign-
    ments and/or responsibili-
    ties as is necessary).   3

14. Reads and Understands
    Complex Material.   4

15. Performs Arithmetic
    Computations Accurately.   4

16. Accuracy of Work.   4

17. Complies with Perfor-
    mance Standards.   4

18. Follows up, with Guid-
    ance from Account Offi-
    cer.   3

19. Recommends Solutions to
    Problems.   3

20. Handles Day-to-Day Work
    Without Constant Super-
    vision on Fundamental
    Tasks.   3

21. Drive (ambition; desire to
    achieve).   2

22. Generates New Ideas.   2

23. Cultivates Relations with
    Customers, with Account
    Officers.   1

TOTALS	(A)	xxx	(C)
	TOTAL POINT VALUE (C)	TOTAL SUM OF SIGNIFICANCE FACTORS (A)	OVERALL RATING (C ÷ A)

OVERALL RATING _____ × WEIGHT 40% = _____ (E)

SECTIONS II AND III OVERALL RATING

Technical Performance Rating (D)   = _____

General Performance Rating (E)   = _____

Composite Rating (D & E)   = _____

Excellent Performance = 4.5–5.0
Above Standard   = 3.6–4.4
Standard   = 2.5–3.5
Below Standard   = 1.6–2.4
Unsatisfactory   = 1.0–1.5

SECTION IV   NOTEWORTHY STRONG AREAS

_____

_____

_____

SECTION V   AREAS REQUIRING IMPROVEMENT

_____

_____

_____

SECTION VI   DEVELOPMENT PLAN

Knowledge/Skill Area   *Action Steps (and Dates)*

1. _____   1. _____

   _____   _____

2. _____   2. _____

   _____   _____

3. _____   3. _____

   _____   _____

SECTION VIII   COMMENT AND SIGNATURES

Manager's Summary Comment

_____

_____

_____

Employee's Comment

_____

_____

_____

Signatures

_____

_____

_____

Manager _____ Date _____

Employee _____ Date _____

Manager's Manager _____ Date _____

THE TRUST INDENTURE ACT OF 1939
AS AMENDED BY
THE TRUST INDENTURE REFORM ACT OF 1990

Contents

Sec. 301   Short Title

This subchapter may be cited as the "Trust Indenture Act of 1939."

Sec. 302   Necessity for Regulation

(a) Upon the basis of facts disclosed by the reports of the Securities and Exchange Commission made to the Congress pursuant to section 211 of the Securities Exchange Act of 1934 and otherwise disclosed and ascertained, it is hereby declared that the national public interest and the interest of investors in notes, bonds, debentures, evidences of indebtedness, and certificates of interest or participation therein, which are offered to the public, are adversely affected—

(1) when the obligor fails to provide a trustee to protect and enforce the rights and to represent the interests of such investors, notwithstanding the fact that (A) individual action by such investors for the purpose of protecting and enforcing their rights is rendered impracticable by reason of the disproportionate expense of taking such action, and (B) concerted action by such investors in their common interest through representatives of their own selection is impeded by reason of the wide dispersion of such investors through many States, and by reason of the fact that information as to the names and addresses of such investors generally is not available to such investors;

(2) when the trustee does not have adequate rights and powers, or adequate duties and responsibilities, in connection with matters relating to the protection and enforcement of the rights of such investors; when, notwithstanding the obstacles to concerted action by such investors, and the general and reasonable assumption by such investors that the trustee is under an affirma-

tive duty to take action for the protection and enforcement of their rights, trust indentures (A) generally provide that the trustee shall be under no duty to take any such action, even in the event of default, unless it receives notice of default, demand for action, and indemnity, from the holders of substantial percentages of the securities outstanding thereunder, and (B) generally relieve the trustee from liability even for its own negligent action or failure to act;

(3) when the trustee does not have resources commensurate with its responsibilities, or has any relationship to or connection with the obligor or any underwriter of any securities of the obligor, or holds, beneficially or otherwise, any interest in the obligor or any such underwriter, which relationship, connection, or interest involves a material conflict with the interest of such investors;

(4) when the obligor is not obligated to furnish to the trustee under the indenture and to such investors adequate current information as to its financial condition, and as to the performance of its obligations with respect to the securities outstanding under such indenture; or when the communication of such information to such investors is impeded by the fact that information as to the names and addresses of such investors generally is not available to the trustee and to such investors;

(5) when the indenture contains provisions which are misleading or deceptive, or when full and fair disclosure is not made to prospective investors of the effect of important indenture provisions; or

(6) when, by reason of the fact that trust indentures are commonly prepared by the obligor or underwriter in advance of the public offering of the securities to be issued thereunder, such investors are unable to participate in the preparation thereof, and, by reason of their lack of understanding of the situation, such investor would in any event be unable to procure the correction of the defects enumerated in this subsection.

(b) Practices of the character above enumerated have existed to such an extent that, unless regulated, the public offering of notes, bonds, debentures, evidences of indebtedness, and certificates of interest or participation therein, by the use of means and instruments of transportation and communication in interstate commerce and of the mails, is injurious to the capital markets, to investors, and to the general public; and it is hereby declared to be the policy of this subchapter, in accordance with which policy all the provisions of this subchapter shall be interpreted, to meet the problems and eliminate the practices, enumerated in this section, connected with such public offerings.

Sec. 303   Definitions

When used in this subchapter, unless the context otherwise requires—

(1) Any term defined in section 2 of the Securities Act of 1933 and not otherwise defined in this section shall have the meaning assigned to such term in such section 2.

(2) The terms "sale," "sell," "offer to sell," "offer for sale," and "offer" shall include all transactions included in such terms as provided in paragraph (3) of section 2 of the Securities Act of 1933, except that an offer or sale of a certificate of interest or participation shall be deemed an offer or sale of the security or securities in which such certificate evidences an interest or participation if and only if such certificate gives the holder thereof the right to convert the same into such security or securities.

(3) The term "prospectus" shall have the meaning assigned to such term in paragraph (10) of section 2 of the Securities Act of 1933, except that in the case of securities which are not registered under the Securities Act of 1933, such term shall not include any communication (A) if it is proved that prior to or at the same time with such communication a written statement if any required by section 306 was sent or given to the persons to whom the communication was made, or (B) if such communication states from whom such statement may be obtained (if such statement is required by rules or regulations under paragraphs (1) or (2) of subsection (b) of section 306) and, in addition, does no more than identify the security, state the price thereof, state by whom orders will be executed and contain such other information as the Commission, by rules or regulations deemed necessary or appropriate in the public interest or for the protection of investors, and subject to such terms and conditions as may be prescribed therein, may permit.

(4) The term "underwriter" means any person who has purchased from an issuer with a view to, or offers or sells for an issuer in connection with, the distribution of any security, or participates or has a direct or indirect participation in any such undertaking, or participates or has a participation in the direct or indirect underwriting of any such undertaking; but such term shall not include a person whose interest is limited to a commission from an underwriter or dealer not in excess of the usual and customary distributors' or sellers' commission.

(5) The term "director" means any director of a corporation, or any individual performing similar functions with respect to any organization whether incorporated or unincorporated.

(6) The term "executive officer" means the president, every vice president, every trust officer, the cashier, the secretary, and the treasurer of a corpora-

tion, and any individual customarily performing similar functions with respect to any organization whether incorporated or unincorporated, but shall not include the chairman of the board of directors.

(7) The term "indenture" means any mortgage, deed of trust, trust or other indenture, or similar instrument or agreement (including any supplement or amendment to any of the foregoing), under which securities are outstanding or are to be issued, whether or not any property, real or personal, is, or is to be, pledged, mortgaged, assigned, or conveyed thereunder.

(8) The term "application" or "application for qualification" means the application provided for in section 305 or section 307 and includes any amendment thereto and any report, document, or memorandum accompanying such application or incorporated therein by reference.

(9) The term "indenture to be qualified" means (A) the indenture under which there has been or is to be issued a security in respect of which a particular registration statement has been filed, or (B) the indenture in respect of which a particular application has been filed.

(10) The term "indenture trustee" means each trustee under the indenture to be qualified, and each successor trustee.

(11) The term "indenture security" means any security issued or issuable under the indenture to be qualified.

(12) The term "obligor," when used with respect to any such indenture security, means every person (including a guarantor) who is liable thereon, and, if such security is a certificate of interest or participation, such term means also every person (including a guarantor) who is liable upon the security or securities in which such certificate evidences an interest or participation; but such terms shall not include the trustee under an indenture under which certificates of interest or participation, equipment trust certificates, or like securities are outstanding.

(13) The term "paying agent," when used with respect to any such indenture security, means any person authorized by an obligor therein (A) to pay the principal of or interest on such security on behalf of such obligor, or (B) if such security is a certificate of interest or participation, equipment trust certificate, or like security, to make such payment on behalf of the trustee.

(14) The term "State" means any State of the United States.

(15) The term "Commission" means the Securities and Exchange Commission.

(16) The term "voting security" means any security presently entitling the owner or holder thereof to vote in the direction or management of the affairs of a person, or any security issued under or pursuant to any trust, agreement,

or arrangement whereby a trustee or trustees or agent or agents for the owner or holder of such security are presently entitled to vote in the direction or management of the affairs of a person; and a specified percentage of the voting securities of a person means such amount of the outstanding voting securities of such person as entitles the holder or holders thereof to cast such specified percentage of the aggregate votes which the holders of all the outstanding voting securities of such person are entitled to cast in the direction or management of the affairs of such person.

(17) The terms "Securities Act of 1933," "Securities Exchange Act of 1934," and "Public Utility Holding Company Act of 1935" shall be deemed to refer, respectively, to such Acts, as amended, whether amended prior to or after August 3, 1939.

(18) The term "Bankruptcy Act" means the Bankruptcy Act or Title 11.

Sec. 304   Exempted Securities and Transactions

(a) The provisions of this subchapter shall not apply to any of the following securities:

(1) any security other than (A) a note, bond, debenture, or evidence of indebtedness, whether or not secured, or (B) a certificate of interest or participation in any such note, bond, debenture, or evidence of indebtedness, or (C) a temporary certificate for, or guarantee of, any such note, bond, debenture, evidence of indebtedness, or certificate;

(2) any certificate of interest or participation in two or more securities having substantially different rights and privileges, or a temporary certificate for any such certificate.

(3) [left blank]

(4) (A) any security exempted from the provisions of the Securities Act of 1933, by paragraphs (2) to (8), or (11) of subsection 3(a) thereof;

(B) any security exempted from the provisions of the Securities Act of 1933, as amended, by paragraph (2) of subsection 3(a) thereof, as amended by section 401 of the Employment Security Amendments of 1970;

(5) any security issued under a mortgage indenture as to which a contract of insurance under the National Housing Act is in effect; and any such security shall be deemed to be exempt from the provisions of the Securities Act of 1933 to the same extent as though such security were specifically enumerated in section 3(a)(2) of such Act;

(6) any note, bond, debenture, or evidence of indebtedness issued or guaranteed by a foreign government or by a subdivision, department, municipality, agency, or instrumentality thereof;

(7) any guarantee of any security which is exempted by this subsection;

(8) any security which has been or is to be issued otherwise than under an indenture, but this exemption shall not be applied within a period of twelve consecutive months to an aggregate principal amount of securities of the same issuer greater than the figure stated in section 3(b) of the Securities Act of 1933 limiting exemptions thereunder, or such lesser amount as the Commission may establish by its rules and regulations;

(9) any security which has been or is to be issued under an indenture which limits the aggregate principal amount of securities at any time outstanding thereunder to $10,000,000, or such lesser amount as the Commission may establish by its rules and regulations, but this exemption shall not be applied within a period of thirty-six consecutive months to more than $10,000,000 aggregate principal amount of securities of the same issuer, or such lesser amount as the Commission may establish by its rules and regulations; or

(10) any security issued under a mortgage or trust deed indenture as to which a contract of insurance under title XI of the National Housing Act is in effect; and any such security shall be deemed to be exempt from the provisions of the Securities Act of 1933 to the same extent as though such security were specifically enumerated in section 3(a)(2), as amended, of the Securities Act of 1933.

In computing the aggregate principal amount of securities to which the exemptions provided by paragraphs (8) and (9) of this subsection may be applied, securities to which the provisions of sections 305 and 306 would not have applied, irrespective of the provisions of those paragraphs, shall be disregarded.

(b) The provisions of sections 305 and 306 shall not apply (1) to any of the transactions exempted from the provisions of section 5 of the Securities Act of 1933 by section 4 thereof or (2) to any transaction which would be so exempted but for the last sentence of paragraph (11) of section 2 of such Act.

(c) The Commission shall, on application by the issuer and after opportunity for hearing thereon, by order exempt from any one or more provisions of this subchapter any security issued or proposed to be issued under any indenture under which, at the time such application is filed, securities referred to in paragraph (3) of subsection (a) of this section are outstanding or on January 1, 1959, such securities were outstanding, if and to the extent that the Commission finds that compliance with such provision or provisions, through the execution of a supplemental indenture or otherwise—

(1) would require, by reason of the provisions of such indenture, or the provisions of any other indenture or agreement made prior to August 3, 1939, or the provisions of any applicable law, the consent of the holders of securities outstanding under any such indenture or agreement; or

(2) would impose an undue burden on this issuer, having due regard to the public interest and the interests of investors.

(d) The Commission may, by rules or regulations upon its own motion, or by order on application by an interested person, exempt conditionally or unconditionally any person, registration statement, indenture, security or transaction, or any class or classes of persons, registration statements, indentures, securities, or transactions, from any one or more of the provisions of this title, if and to the extent that such exemption is necessary or appropriate in the public interest and consistent with the protection of investors and the purposes fairly intended by this title. The Commission shall by rules and regulations determine the procedures under which an exemption under this subsection shall be granted, and may, in its sole discretion, decline to entertain any application for an order of exemption under this subsection.

(e) The Commission may from time to time by its rules and regulations, and subject to such terms and conditions as may be prescribed herein, add to the securities exempted as provided in this section any class of securities issued by a small business investment company under the Small Business Investment Act of 1958 if it finds, having regard to the purposes of that Act, that the enforcement of this subchapter with respect to such securities is not necessary in the public interest and for the protection of investors.

Sec. 305   **Securities Required to Be Registered Under Securities Act**

(a) Subject to the provisions of section 304, a registration statement relating to a security shall include the following information and documents, as though such inclusion were required by the provisions of section 7 of the Securities Act of 1933—

(1) such information and documents as the Commission may by rules and regulations prescribe in order to enable the Commission to determine whether any person designated to act as trustee under the indenture under which such security has been or is to be issued is eligible to act as such under subsection (a) of section 310; and

(2) an analysis of any provisions of such indenture with respect to (A) the definition of what shall constitute a default under such indenture, and the withholding of notice to the indenture security holders of any such default, (B) the authentication and delivery of the indenture securities and the application of the proceeds thereof, (C) the release or the release and substitution of any property subject to the lien of the indenture, (D) the satisfaction and discharge of the indenture, and (E) the evidence required to be furnished by

the obligor upon the indenture securities to the trustee as to compliance with the conditions and covenants provided for in such indenture.

The information and documents required by paragraph (1) of this subsection with respect to the person designated to act as indenture trustee shall be contained in a separate part of such registration statement, which part shall be signed by such person. Such part of the registration statement shall be deemed to be a document filed pursuant to this subchapter, and the provisions of sections 11, 12, 17, and 24 of the Securities Act of 1933 shall not apply to statements therein or omissions therefrom.

(b) (1) Except as may be permitted by paragraph (2) of this subsection, the Commission shall issue an order prior to the effective date of registration refusing to permit such a registration statement to be come effective, if it finds that—

(A) the security to which such registration statement relates has not been or is not to be issued under an indenture; or

(B) any person designated as trustee under such indenture is not eligible to act as such under subsection (a) of section 310;

but no such order shall be issued except after notice and opportunity for hearing within the periods and in the manner required with respect to refusal orders pursuant to section 8(b) of the Securities Act of 1933. If and when the Commission deems that the objections on which such order was based have been met, the Commission shall enter an order rescinding such refusal order, and the registration shall become effective at the time provided in section 8(a) of the Securities Act of 1933, or upon the date of such rescission, whichever shall be the later.

(2) In the case of securities registered under the Securities Act of 1933, which securities are eligible to be issued, offered, or sold on a delayed basis by or on behalf of the registrant, the Commission shall not be required to issue an order pursuant to paragraph (1) of subsection (b) of section 305 for failure to designate a trustee eligible to act under subsection (a) of section 310 if, in accordance with such rules and regulations as may be prescribed by the Commission, the issuer of such securities files an application for the purpose of determining such trustee's eligibility under subsection (a) of section 310. The Commission shall issue an order prior to the effective date of such application refusing to permit the application to become effective, if it finds that any person designated as trustee under such indenture is not eligible to act as such under subsection (a) of section 310, but no order shall be issued except after notice and opportunity for hearing within the periods and in the manner required with respect to refusal orders pursuant to section 8(b) of the Securities Act of 1933. If after notice and opportunity for hearing the Commission issues

an order under this provision, the obligor shall within 5 calendar days appoint a trustee meeting the requirements of subsection (a) of section 310. No such appointment shall be effective and such refusal order shall not be rescinded by the Commission until a person eligible to act as trustee under subsection (a) of section 310 has been appointed. If no order is issued, an application filed pursuant to this paragraph shall be effective the tenth day after filing thereof or such earlier date as the Commission may determine, having due regard to the adequacy of information provided therein, the public interest, and the protection of investors.

(c) A prospectus relating to any such security shall include to the extent the Commission may prescribe by rules and regulations as necessary and appropriate in the public interest or for the protection of investors, as though such inclusion were required by section 10 of the Securities Act of 1933, a written statement containing the analysis set forth in the registration statement, of any indenture provisions with respect to the matters specified in paragraph (2) of subsection (a) of this section, together with a supplementary analysis, prepared by the Commission, of such provisions and of the effect thereof, if, in the opinion of the Commission, the inclusion of such supplementary analysis is necessary or appropriate in the public interest or for the protection of investors, and the Commission so declares by order after notice and, if demanded by the issuer, opportunity for hearing thereon. Such order shall be entered prior to the effective date of registration, except that if opportunity for hearing thereon is demanded by the issuer such order shall be entered within a reasonable time after such opportunity for hearing.

(d) The provisions of sections 11, 12, 17, and 24 of the Securities Act of 1933, and the provisions of sections 323 and 325, shall not apply to statements in or omissions from any analysis required under the provisions of this section or sections 306 or 307 of this title.

Sec. 306   Securities Not Registered Under Securities Act

(a) In the case of any security which is not registered under the Securities Act of 1933 and to which this subsection is applicable notwithstanding the provisions of section 304, unless such security has been or is to be issued under an indenture and an application for qualification is effective as to such indenture, it shall be unlawful for any person, directly or indirectly—

(1) to make use of any means or instruments of transportation or communication in interstate commerce or of the mails to sell such security through the use or medium of any prospectus or otherwise; or

(2) to carry or cause to be carried through the mails or in interstate com-

merce, by any means or instruments of transportation, any such security for the purpose of sale or for delivery after sale.

(b) In the case of any security which is not registered under the Securities Act of 1933, but which has been or is to be issued under an indenture as to which an application for qualification is effective, it shall be unlawful for any person, directly or indirectly—

(1) to make use of any means or instruments of transportation or communication in interstate commerce or of the mails to carry or transmit any prospectus relating to any such security, unless such prospectus, to the extent the Commission may prescribe by rules and regulations as necessary and appropriate in the public interest or for the protection of investors, includes or is accompanied by a written statement that contains the information specified in subsection (c) of section 305; or

(2) to carry or to cause to be carried through the mails or in interstate commerce any such security for the purpose of sale or for delivery after sale, unless, to the extent the Commission may prescribe by rules and regulations as necessary or appropriate in the public interest or for the protection of investors, accompanied or preceded by a written statement that contains the information specified in subsection (c) of section 305.

(c) It shall be unlawful for any person, directly or indirectly, to make use of any means or instruments of transportation or communication in interstate commerce or of the mails to offer to sell through the use or medium of any prospectus or otherwise any security which is not registered under the Securities Act of 1933 and to which this subsection is applicable notwithstanding the provisions of section 304, unless such security has been or is to be issued under an indenture and an application for qualification has been filed as to such indenture, or while the application is the subject of a refusal order or stop order or (prior to qualification) any public proceeding or examination under section 307(c).

Sec. 307   Qualification of Indentures Covering Securities Not Required to Be Registered

(a) In the case of any security which is not required to be registered under the Securities Act of 1933 and to which subsection (a) of section 306 is applicable notwithstanding the provisions of section 304, an application for qualification of the indenture under which such security has been or is to be issued shall be filed with the Commission by the issuer of such security. Each such application shall be in such form, and shall be signed in such manner, as the Commission may by rules and regulations prescribe as necessary or appropriate in the public interest or for the protection of investors. Each such application shall include the information and documents required by subsection (a) of section 305. The information and documents required by paragraph (1) of such subsection with respect to the person designated to act as indenture trustee shall be contained in a separate part of such application, which part shall be signed by such person. Each such application shall also include such of the other information and documents which would be required to be filed in order to register such indenture security under the Securities Act of 1933 as the Commission may by rules and regulations prescribe as necessary or appropriate in the public interest or for the protection of investors. An application may be withdrawn by the applicant at any time prior to the effective date thereof. Subject to the provisions of section 321, the information and documents contained in or filed with any application shall be made available to the public under such regulations as the Commission may prescribe, and copies thereof, photostatic or otherwise, shall be furnished to every applicant therefor at such reasonable charge as the Commission may prescribe.

(b) The filing with the Commission of an application, or of an amendment to an application, shall be deemed to have taken place upon the receipt thereof by the Commission, but, in the case of an application, only if it is accompanied or preceded by payment to the Commission of a filing fee in the amount of $100, such payment to be made in cash or by United States postal money order or certified or bank check, or in such other medium of payment as the Commission may authorize by rule and regulation.

(c) The provisions of section 8 of the Securities Act of 1933 and the provisions of subsection (b) of section 305 shall apply with respect to every such application, as though such application were a registration statement filed pursuant to the provisions of the Securities Act of 1933.

Sec. 308	Integration of Procedure with Securities Act and Other Acts

(a) The Commission, by such rules and regulations or orders as it deems necessary or appropriate in the public interest or for the protection of investors, shall authorize the filing of any information or documents required to be filed with the Commission under this subchapter, or under the Securities Act of 1933, the Securities Exchange Act of 1934, or the Public Utility Holding Company Act of 1935, by incorporating by reference any information or documents on file with the Commission under this subchapter or under any such Act.

(b) The Commission, by such rules and regulations or orders as it deems necessary or appropriate in the public interest or for the protection of investors, shall provide for the consolidation of applications, reports, and proceedings under this subchapter with registration statements, applications, reports, and proceedings under the Securities Act of 1933, the Securities Exchange Act of 1934, or the Public Utility Holding Company Act of 1935.

Sec. 309   Effective Time of Qualification

(a) The indenture under which a security has been or is to be issued shall be deemed to have been qualified under this subchapter—

(1) when registration becomes effective as to such security; or

(2) when an application for the qualification of such indenture becomes effective, pursuant to section 307.

(b) After qualification has become effective as to the indenture under which a security has been or is to be issued, no stop order shall be issued pursuant to section 8(d) of the Securities Act 1933, suspending the effectiveness of the registration statement relating to such security or of the application for qualification of such indenture, except on one or more of the grounds specified in section 8 of the Securities Act of 1933, or the failure of the issuer to file an application as provided for by section 305(b)(2).

(c) The making, amendment, or rescission of a rule, regulation, or order under the provisions of this subchapter (except to the extent authorized by subsection (a) of section 314 with respect to rules and regulations prescribed pursuant to such subsection) shall not affect the qualification, form, or interpretation of any indenture as to which qualification became effective prior to the making, amendment, or rescission of such rule, regulation, or order.

(d) No trustee under an indenture which has been qualified under this subchapter shall be subject to any liability because of any failure of such indenture to comply with any of the provisions of this subchapter, or any rule, regulation, or order thereunder.

(e) Nothing in this subchapter shall be construed as empowering the Commission to conduct an investigation or other proceeding for the purpose of determining whether the provisions of an indenture which has been qualified under this subchapter are being complied with, or to enforce such provisions.

Sec. 310   Eligibility and Disqualification of Trustee

(a) (1) There shall at all times be one or more trustees under every indenture qualified or to be qualified pursuant to this title, at least one of whom shall at all times be a corporation organized and doing business under the laws of the United States or of any State or Territory or of the District of Columbia or a corporation or other person permitted to act as trustee by the Commission (referred to in this subchapter as the institutional trustee), which (A) is authorized under such laws to exercise corporate trust powers, and (B) is subject to supervision or examination by Federal, State, Territorial, or District of Columbia authority. The Commission may, pursuant to such rules and regulations as it may prescribe, or by order on application, permit a corporation or other person organized and doing business under the laws of a foreign government to act as sole trustee under an indenture qualified or to be qualified pursuant to this title, if such corporation or other person (i) is authorized under such laws to exercise corporate trust powers, and (ii) is subject to supervision or examination by authority of such foreign government or a political subdivision thereof substantially equivalent to supervision or examination applicable to United States institutional trustees. In prescribing such rules and regulation or making such order, the Commission shall consider whether under such laws, a United States institutional trustee is eligible to act as sole trustee under an indenture relating to securities sold within the jurisdiction of such foreign government.

(2) Such institution shall have at all times a combined capital and surplus of a specified minimum amount, which shall not be less than $150,000. If such institutional trustee publishes reports of condition at least annually, pursuant to law or to the requirements of said supervising or examining authority, the indenture may provide that, for the purposes of this paragraph, the combined capital and surplus of such trustee shall be deemed to be its combined capital and surplus as set forth in its most recent report of condition so published.

(3) If the indenture to be qualified requires or permits the appointment of one or more co-trustees in addition to such institutional trustee, the rights, powers, duties, and obligations conferred or imposed upon the trustees or any of them shall be conferred or imposed upon and exercised or performed by such institutional trustee, or such institutional trustee and such co-trustees jointly, except to the extent that under any law of any jurisdiction in which any particular act or acts are to be performed, such institutional trustee shall be incompetent or unqualified to perform such act or acts, in which event such rights, powers, duties, and obligations shall be exercised and performed by such co-trustees.

(4) In the case of certificates of interest or participation, the indenture trustee or trustees shall have the legal power to exercise all of the rights, powers, and privileges of a holder of the security or securities in which such certificates evidence an interest or participation.

(5) No obligor upon the indenture securities or person directly or indirectly controlling, controlled by, or under common control with such obligor shall serve as trustee upon such indenture securities.

(b) If any indenture trustee has or shall acquire any conflicting interest as hereinafter defined—

(i) then, within 90 days after ascertaining that it has such conflicting interest, and if the default (as defined in the next sentence) to which such conflicting interest relates has not been cured or duly waived or otherwise eliminated before the end of such 90–day period, such trustee shall either eliminate such conflicting interest or, except as otherwise provided below in this subsection, resign, and the obligor upon the indenture securities shall take prompt steps to have a successor appointed in the manner provided in the indenture;

(ii) in the event that such trustee shall fail to comply with the provisions of clause (i) of this subsection, such trustee shall, within 10 days after the expiration of such 90–day period, transmit notice of such failure to the indenture security holders in the manner and to the extent provided in subsection (c) of section 313; and

(iii) subject to the provisions of subsection (e) of section 315, unless such trustee's duty to resign is stayed as provided below in this subsection, any security holder who has been a bona fide holder of indenture securities for at least six months may, on behalf of himself and all others similarly situated, petition any court of competent jurisdiction for the removal of such trustee, and the appointment of a successor, if such trustee fails, after written request thereof by such holder to comply with the provisions of clause (i) of this subsection.

For the purposes of this subsection, an indenture trustee shall be deemed to have a conflicting interest if the indenture securities are in default (as such term is defined in such indenture, but exclusive of any period of grace or requirement of notice) and—

(1) such trustee is trustee under another indenture under which any other securities, or certificates of interest or participation in any other securities, of an obligor upon the indenture securities are outstanding or is trustee for more than one outstanding series of securities, as hereafter defined, under a single indenture of an obligor, unless—

(A) the indenture securities are collateral trust notes under which the only collateral consists of securities issued under such other indenture,

(B) such other indenture is a collateral trust indenture under which the only collateral consists of indenture securities, or

(C) such obligor has no substantial unmortgaged assets and is engaged primarily in the business of owning, or of owning and developing and/or operating, real estate, and the indenture to be qualified and such other indenture are secured by wholly separate and distinct parcels of real estate:

Provided, That the indenture to be qualified shall automatically be deemed (unless it is expressly provided therein that such provision is excluded) to contain a provision excluding from the operation of this paragraph other series under such indenture, and any other indenture or indentures under which other securities, or certificates of interest or participation in other securities, of such an obligor are outstanding, if—

(i) the indenture to be qualified and any such other indenture or indentures (and all series of securities issuable thereunder) are wholly unsecured and rank equally, and such other indenture or indentures (and such series) are specifically described in the indenture to be qualified or are thereafter qualified under this title, unless the Commission shall have found and declared by order pursuant to subsection (b) of section 305 or subsection (c) of section 307 that differences exist between the provisions of the indenture (or such series) to be qualified and the provisions of such other indenture or indentures (or such series) which are so likely to involve a material conflict of interest as to make it necessary in the public interest or for the protection of investors to disqualify such trustee from acting as such under one of such indentures, or

(ii) the issuer shall have sustained the burden of proving, on application to the Commission and after opportunity for hearing thereon, that trusteeship under the indenture to be qualified and such other indenture or under more than one outstanding series under a single indenture is not so likely to involve a material conflict of interest as to make it necessary in the public interest or for the protection of investors to disqualify such trustee from acting as such under one of such indentures or with respect to such series;

(2) such trustee or any of its directors or executive officers is an underwriter for an obligor upon the indenture securities;

(3) such trustee directly or indirectly controls or is directly or indirectly controlled by or is under direct or indirect common control with an underwriter for an obligor upon the indenture securities;

(4) such trustee or any of its directors or executive officers is a director, officer, partner, employee, appointee, or representative of an obligor upon the indenture securities, or of an underwriter (other than the trustee itself) for such an obligor who is currently engaged in the business of underwriting, except that—

(A) one individual may be a director and/or an executive officer of the trustee and a director and/or an executive officer of such obligor, but may not be at the same time an executive officer of both the trustee and of such obligor,

(B) if and so long as the number of directors of the trustee in office is more than nine, one additional individual may be a director and/or an executive officer of the trustee and a director of such obligor, and

(C) such trustee may be designated by any such obligor or by any underwriter for any such obligor, to act in the capacity of transfer agent, registrar, custodian, paying agent, fiscal agent, escrow agent, or depositary, or in any other similar capacity, or, subject to the provisions of paragraph (1) of this subsection, to act as trustee, whether under an indenture or otherwise;

(5) 10 per centum or more of the voting securities of such trustee is beneficially owned either by an obligor upon the indenture securities or by any director, partner or executive officer thereof, or 20 per centum or more of such voting securities is beneficially owned, collectively by any two or more of such persons; or 10 per centum or more of the voting securities of such trustee is beneficially owned either by an underwriter for any such obligor or by any director, partner, or executive officer thereof, or is beneficially owned, collectively, by any two or more such persons;

(6) such trustee is the beneficial owner of, or holds as collateral security for an obligation which is in default as hereinafter defined—

(A) 5 per centum or more of the voting securities, or 10 per centum or more of any other class of security, of an obligor upon the indenture securities, not including indenture securities and securities issued under any other indenture under which such trustee is also trustee, or

(B) 10 per centum or more of any class of security of an underwriter for any such obligor;

(7) such trustee is the beneficial owner of, or holds as collateral security for an obligation which is in default as hereinafter defined, 5 per centum or more of the voting securities of any person who, to the knowledge of the trustee, owns 10 per centum or more of the voting securities of, or controls directly or indirectly or is under direct or indirect common control with, an obligor upon the indenture securities;

(8) such trustee is the beneficial owner of, or holds as collateral security for an obligation which is in default as hereinafter defined, 10 per centum or more of any class of security of any person who, to the knowledge of the trustee, owns 50 per centum or more of the voting securities of an obligor upon the indenture securities;

(9) such trustee owns, on the date of default upon the indenture securities (as such term is defined in such indenture but exclusive of any period of grace or requirement of notice) or any anniversary of such default while such

default upon the indenture securities remains outstanding, in the capacity of executor, administrator, testamentary or inter vivos trustee, guardian, committee or conservator, or in any other similar capacity, an aggregate of 25 per centum or more of the voting securities, or of any class of security, of any person, the beneficial ownership of a specified percentage of which would have constituted a conflicting interest under paragraph (6), (7), or (8) of this subsection. As to any such securities of which the indenture trustee acquired ownership through becoming executor, administrator or testamentary trustee of an estate which include them, the provisions of the preceding sentence shall not apply for a period of not more than 2 years from the date of such acquisition, to the extent that such securities included in such estate do not exceed 25 per centum of such voting securities or 25 per centum of any such class of security. Promptly after the dates of any such default upon the indenture securities and annually in each succeeding year that the indenture securities remain in default the trustee shall make a check of its holding of such securities in any of the above-mentioned capacities as of such dates. If the obligor upon the indenture securities fails to make payment in full of principal or interest under such indenture when and as the same becomes due and payable, and such failure continues for 30 days thereafter, the trustee shall make a prompt check of its holdings of such securities in any of the above-mentioned capacities as of the date of the expiration of such 30–day period, and after such date, notwithstanding the foregoing provisions of this paragraph, all such securities so held by the trustee, with sole or joint control over such securities vested in it, shall be considered as though beneficially owned by such trustee, for the purposes of paragraphs (6), (7), and (8) of this subsection; or

(10) except under the circumstances described in paragraphs (1), (3), (4), (5) or (6) of section 311(b) of this title, the trustee shall be or shall become a creditor of the obligor.

For purposes of paragraph (1) of this subsection, and of section 316(a) of this title, the term ''series of securities'' or ''series'' means a series, class or group of securities issuable under an indenture pursuant to whose terms holders of one such series may vote to direct the indenture trustee, or otherwise take action pursuant to a vote of such holders, separately from holders of another such series: *Provided,* That ''series of securities'' or ''series'' shall not include any series of securities issuable under an indenture if all such series rank equally and are wholly unsecured.

The specification of percentages in paragraphs (5) to (9), inclusive, of this subsection shall not be construed as indicating that the ownership of such percentages of the securities of a person is or is not necessary or sufficient to constitute direct or indirect control for the purposes of paragraph (3) or (7) of this subsection.

For purposes of paragraphs (6), (7), (8), and (9) of this subsection—

(A) the terms "security" and "securities" shall include only such securities as are generally known as corporate securities, but shall not include any note or other evidence of indebtedness issued to evidence an obligation to repay moneys lent to a person by one or more banks, trust companies, or banking firms, or any certificate of interest or participation in any such note or evidence of indebtedness;

(B) an obligation shall be deemed to be in default when a default in payment of principal shall have continued for thirty days or more, and shall not have been cured; and

(C) the indenture trustee shall not be deemed the owner or holder of (i) any security which it holds as collateral security (as trustee or otherwise) for any obligation which is not in default as above defined, or (ii) any security which it holds as collateral security under the indenture to be qualified, irrespective of any default thereunder, or (iii) any security which it holds as agent for collection, or as custodian, escrow agent or depositary, or in any similar representative capacity.

For the purposes of this subsection, the term "underwriter" when used with reference to an obligor upon the indenture securities means every person who, within one year prior to the time as of which the determination is made, was an underwriter of any security of such obligor outstanding at the time of the determination.

Except is the case of a default in the payment of the principal of or interest on any indenture security, or in the payment of any sinking or purchase fund installment, the indenture trustee shall not be required to resign as provided by this subsection if such trustee shall have sustained the burden of proving, on application to the Commission and after opportunity for hearing thereon, that—

(i) the default under the indenture may be cured or waived during a reasonable period and under the procedures described in such application, and

(ii) a stay of the trustee's duty to resign will not be inconsistent with the interests of holders of the indenture securities. The filing of such an application shall automatically stay the performance of the duty to resign until the Commission orders otherwise.

Any resignation of an indenture trustee shall become effective only upon the appointment of a successor trustee and such successor's acceptance of such an appointment.

(c) The Public Utility Holding Company Act of 1935 shall not be held to establish or authorize the establishment of any standards regarding the eligibility and qualifications of any trustee or prospective trustee under an indenture to be qualified under this subchapter, or regarding the provisions to be included in any such indenture with respect to the eligibility and qualifications of the trustee thereunder, other than those established by the provisions of this section.

Sec. 311 Preferential Collection of Claims Against Obligor

(a) Subject to the provisions of subsection (b) of this section, if the indenture trustee shall be, or shall become, a creditor, directly or indirectly, secured or unsecured, of an obligor upon the indenture securities, within three months prior to a default as defined in the last paragraph of this subsection, or subsequent to such a default, then, unless and until such default shall be cured, such trustee shall set apart and hold in a special account for the benefit of the trustee individually and the indenture security holders—

(1) an amount equal to any and all reductions in the amount due and owing upon any claim as such creditor in respect of principal or interest, effected after the beginning of such three months' period and valid as against such obligor and its other creditors, except any such reduction resulting from the receipt or disposition of any property described in paragraph (2) of this subsection, or from the exercise of any right of setoff which the trustee could have exercised if a petition in bankruptcy had been filed by or against such obligor upon the date of such default; and

(2) all property received in respect of any claims as such creditor, either as security therefor, or in satisfaction or composition thereof, or otherwise, after the beginning of such three months' period, or an amount equal to the proceeds of any such property, if disposed of, subject, however, to the rights, if any, of such obligor and its other creditors in such property or such proceeds.

Nothing herein contained shall affect the right of the indenture trustee—

(A) to retain for its own account (i) payments made on account of any such claim by any person (other than such obligor) who is liable thereon, and (ii) the proceeds of the bona fide sale of any such claim by the trustee to a third person, and (iii) distributions made in cash, securities, or other property in respect of claims filed against such obligor in bankruptcy or receivership or in proceedings for reorganization pursuant to the Bankruptcy Act or applicable State law;

(B) to realize, for its own account, upon any property held by it as security for any such claim, if such property was so held prior to the beginning of such three months' period;

(C) to realize, for its own account, but only to the extent of the claim hereinafter mentioned, upon any property held by it as security for any such claim, if such claim was created after the beginning of such three months' period and such property was received as security therefor simultaneously with the creation thereof, and if the trustee shall sustain the burden of proving that at the time such property was so received the trustee had no reasonable cause to believe that a default as defined in the last paragraph of this subsection would occur within three months; or

(D) to receive payment on any claim referred to in paragraph (B) or (C) of this subsection, against the release of any property held as security for such claim as provided in said paragraph (B) or (C), as the case may be, to the extent of the fair value of such property.

For the purposes of paragraphs (B), (C), and (D) of this subsection, property substituted after the beginning of such three months' period for property held as security at the time of such substitution shall, to the extent of the fair value of the property released, have the same status as the property released, and, to the extent that any claim referred to in any of such paragraphs is created in renewal of or in substitution for or for the purpose of repaying or refunding any preexisting claim of the indenture trustee as such creditor, such claim shall have the same status as such preexisting claim.

If the trustee shall be required to account, the funds and property held in such special account and the proceeds thereof shall be apportioned between the trustee and the indenture security holders in such manner that the trustee and the indenture security holders realize, as a result of payments from such special account and payments of dividends on claims filed against such obligor in bankruptcy or receivership or in proceedings for reorganization pursuant to the Bankruptcy Act or applicable State law, the same percentage of their respective claims, figured before crediting to the claim of the trustee anything on account of the receipt by it from such obligor of the funds and property in such special account and before crediting to the respective claims of the trustee and the indenture security holders dividends on claims filed against such obligor in bankruptcy or receivership or in proceedings for reorganization pursuant to the Bankruptcy Act or applicable State law, but after crediting thereon receipts on account of the indebtedness represented by their respective claims from all sources other than from such dividends and from the funds and property so held in such special account. As used in this paragraph, with respect to any claim, the term "dividends" shall include any distribution with respect to such claim, in bankruptcy or receivership or in proceedings for reorganization pursuant to the Bankruptcy Act or applicable State law, whether such distribution is made in cash, securities, or other property, but shall not include any such distribution with respect to the secured portion, if any, of such claim. The court in which such bankruptcy, receivership, or proceedings for reorganization is pending shall have jurisdiction (i) to apportion between the indenture trustee and the indenture security holders, in accordance with the provisions of this paragraph, the funds and property held in such special account and the proceeds thereof, or (ii) in lieu of such apportionment, in whole or in part, to give to the provisions of this paragraph due consideration in determining the fairness of the distributions to be made to the indenture trustee and the indenture security holders with respect to their respective claims, in which event it shall not be necessary to liquidate or to appraise the value of any securities or other property held in such special account or as security for any such claim, or to make a specific allocation of such distributions as between the secured and unsecured portions of such claims, or otherwise to apply the provisions of this paragraph as a mathematical formula.

Any indenture trustee who has resigned or been removed after the beginning of such three months' period shall be subject to the provisions of this subsection as though such resignation or removal had not occurred. Any indenture trustee who has resigned or been removed prior the beginning of such three months' period shall be subject to the provisions of this subsection if and only if the following conditions exist—

(i) the receipt of property or reduction of claim which would have given rise to the obligation to account, if such indenture trustee had continued as trustee, occurred after the beginning of such three months' period; and

(ii) such receipt of property or reduction of claim occurred within three months after such resignation or removal.

As used in this subsection, the term "default" means any failure to make payment in full of principal or interest, when and as the same becomes due and payable, under any indenture which has been qualified under this subchapter, and under which the indenture trustee is trustee and the person of whom the indenture trustee is directly or indirectly a creditor is an obligor; and the term "indenture security holder" means all holders of securities outstanding under any such indenture under which any such default exists.

In any case commenced under the Bankruptcy Act of July 1, 1898, or any amendment thereto enacted prior to November 6, 1978, all references to periods of three months shall be deemed to be references to periods of four months.

(b) The indenture to be qualified shall automatically be deemed (unless it is expressly provided therein that any such provision is excluded) to contain provisions excluding from the operation of subsection (a) of this section a creditor relationship arising from—

(1) the ownership or acquisition of securities issued under any indenture, or any security or securities having a maturity of one year or more at the time of acquisition by the indenture trustee;

(2) advances authorized by a receivership or bankruptcy court of competent jurisdiction, or by the indenture, for the purpose of preserving the

property subject to the lien of the indenture or of discharging tax liens or other prior liens or encumbrances on the trust estate, if notice of such advance and of the circumstances surrounding the making thereof is given to the indenture security holders, at the time and in the manner provided in the indenture;

(3) disbursements made in the ordinary course of business in the capacity of trustee under an indenture, transfer agent, registrar, custodian, paying agent, fiscal agent or depositary, or other similar capacity;

(4) an indebtedness created as a result of services rendered or premises rented; or an indebtedness created as a result of goods or securities sold in a cash transaction as defined in the indenture;

(5) the ownership of stock or of other securities of a corporation organized under the provisions of section 25(a) of the Federal Reserve Act, as amended, which is directly or indirectly a creditor of an obligor upon the indenture securities; or

(6) the acquisition, ownership, acceptance, or negotiation of any drafts, bills of exchange, acceptances, or obligations which fall within the classification of self-liquidating paper as defined in the indenture.

(c) In the exercise by the Commission of any jurisdiction under the Public Utility Holding Company Act of 1935 regarding the issue or sale, by any registered holding company or a subsidiary company thereof, of any security of such issuer or seller or of any other company to a person which is trustee under an indenture or indentures of such issuer or seller or other company, or of a subsidiary or associate company or affiliate of such issuer or seller or other company (whether or not such indenture or indentures are qualified or to be qualified under this subchapter), the fact that such trustee will thereby become a creditor, directly or indirectly, of any of the foregoing shall not constitute a ground for the Commission taking adverse action with respect to any application or declaration, or limiting the scope of any rule or regulation which would otherwise permit such transaction to take effect; but in any case in which such trustee is trustee under an indenture of the company of which it will thereby become a creditor, or of any subsidiary company thereof, this subsection shall not prevent the Commission from requiring (if such requirement would be authorized under the provisions of the Public Utility Holding Company Act of 1935) that such trustee, as such, shall effectively and irrevocably agree in writing, for the benefit of the holders from time to time of the securities from time to time outstanding under such indenture, to be bound by the provisions of this section, subsection (c) of section 315, and, in case of default (as such term is defined in such indenture), subsection (d) of section 315, as fully as though such provisions were included in such indenture. For the purposes of this subsection the terms "registered holding company," "subsidiary company," "associate company," and "affiliate" shall have the respective meanings assigned to such terms in section 2(a) of the Public Utility Holding Company Act of 1935.

Sec. 312   Bondholders' Lists

(a) Each obligor upon the indenture securities shall furnish or cause to be furnished to the institutional trustee thereunder at stated intervals of not more than six months, and at such other times as such trustee may request in writing, all information in the possession or control of such obligor, or of any of its paying agents, as to the names and addresses of the indenture security holders, and requiring such trustee to preserve, in as current a form as is reasonably practicable, all such information so furnished to it or received by it in the capacity of paying agent.

(b) Within five business days after the receipt by the institutional trustee of a written application by any three or more indenture security holders stating that the applicants desire to communicate with other indenture security holders with respect to their rights under such indenture or under the indenture securities, and accompanied by a copy of the form of proxy or other communication which such applicants propose to transmit, and by reasonable proof that each such applicant has owned an indenture security for a period of at least six months preceding the date of such application, such institutional trustee shall, at its election, either—

(1) afford to such applicants access to all information so furnished to or received by such trustee; or

(2) inform such applicants as to the approximate number of indenture security holders according to the most recent information so furnished to or received by such trustee, and as to the approximate cost of mailing to such indenture security holders the form of proxy or other communication, if any, specified in such application.

If such trustee shall elect not to afford to such applicants access to such information, such trustee shall, upon the written request of such applicants, mail to all such indenture security holders copies of the form of proxy or other communication which is specified in such request, with reasonable promptness after a tender to such trustee of the material to be mailed and of payment, or provision for the payment, of the reasonable expenses of such mailing, unless within five days after such tender, such trustee shall mail to such applicants, and file with the Commission together with a copy of the material to be mailed, a written statement to the effect that, in the opinion of such trustee, such mailing would be contrary to the best interests of the indenture security holders or would be in violation of applicable law. Such written statement shall specify the basis of such opinion. After opportunity for hearing upon the objections specified in the written statement so filed, the Commission may, and if demanded by such trustee or by such applicants shall, enter an order either sustaining one or more of such objections or refusing to sustain any of them. If the Commission shall enter an order refusing to sustain any of such objections, or if, after the entry of an order sustaining one or more of such objections, the Commission shall find, after notice and opportunity for hearing, that all objections so sustained have been met, and shall enter an order so declaring, such trustee shall mail copies of such material to all such indenture security holders with reasonable promptness after the entry of such order and the renewal of such tender.

(c) The disclosure of any such information as to the names and addresses of the indenture security holders in accordance with the provisions of this section, regardless of the source from which such information was derived, shall not be deemed to be a violation of any existing law, or of any law hereafter enacted which does not specifically refer to this section, nor shall such trustee be held accountable by reason of mailing any material pursuant to a request made under subsection (b) of this section.

Sec. 313   Reports by Indenture Trustee

(a) The indenture trustee shall transmit to the indenture security holders as hereinafter provided, at stated intervals of not more than 12 months, a brief report with respect to any of the following events which may have occurred within the previous 12 months (but if no such event has occurred within such period no report need be transmitted):

(1) any change to its eligibility and its qualifications under section 310;

(2) the creation of or any material change to a relationship specified in paragraph (1) through (10) of section 310(b);

(3) the character and amount of any advances made by it, as indenture trustee, which remain unpaid on the date of such report, and for the reimbursement of which it claims or may claim a lien or charge, prior to that of the indenture securities, on the trust estate or on property or funds held or collected by it as such trustee, if such advances so remaining unpaid aggregate more than one-half of 1 per centum of the principal amount of the indenture securities outstanding on such date;

(4)* any change to the amount, interest rate, and maturity date of all other indebtedness owing to it in its individual capacity, on the date of such

*See footnote 6, chapter 12, *supra.*

report, by the obligor upon the indenture securities, with a brief description of any property held as collateral security therefor, except an indebtedness based upon a creditor relationship arising in any manner described in paragraphs (2), (3), (4), or (6) of subsection (b) of section 311;

(5) any change to the property and funds physically in its possession as indenture trustee on the date of such report;

(6) any release, or release and substitution, of property subject to the lien of the indenture (and the consideration therefor, if any) which it has not previously reported;

(7) any additional issue of indenture securities which it has not previously reported; and

(8) any action taken by it in the performance of its duties under the indenture which it has not previously reported and which in its opinion materially affects the indenture securities or the trust estate, except action in respect of a default, notice of which has been or is to be withheld by it in accordance with an indenture provision authorized by subsection (b) of section 315.

(b) The indenture trustee shall transmit to the indenture security holders as hereinafter provided, within the times hereinafter specified, a brief report with respect to—

(1) the release, or release and substitution, of property subject to the lien of the indenture (and the consideration therefor, if any) unless the fair value of such property, as set forth in the certificate or opinion required by paragraph (1) of subsection (d) of section 314, is less than 10 per centum of the principal amount of indenture securities outstanding at the time of such release, or such release and substitution, such report to be so transmitted within 90 days after such time; and

(2) the character and amount of any advances made by it as such since the date of the last report transmitted pursuant to the provisions of subsection (a) of this section (or if no such report has yet been so transmitted, since the date of execution of the indenture), for the reimbursement of which it claims or may claim a lien or charge, prior to that of the indenture securities, on the trust estate or on property or funds held or collected by it as such trustee, and which it has not previously reported pursuant to this paragraph, if such advances remaining unpaid at any time aggregate more than 10 per centum of the principal amount of indenture securities outstanding at such time, such report to be so transmitted within 90 days after such time.

(c) Reports pursuant to this section shall be transmitted by mail—

(1) to all registered holders of indenture securities, as the names and

addresses of such holders appear upon the registration books of the obligor upon the indenture securities;

(2) to such holders of indenture securities as have, within the two years preceding such transmission, filed their names and addresses with the indenture trustee for that purpose; and

(3) except in the case of reports pursuant to subsection (b) of this section, to all holders of indenture securities whose names and addresses have been furnished to or received by the indenture trustee pursuant to section 312.

(d) A copy of each such report shall, at the time of such transmission to indenture security holders, be filed with each stock exchange upon which the indenture securities are listed, and also with the Commission.

Sec. 314   Reports by Obligor; Evidence of Compliance with Indenture Provisions

(a) Each person who, as set forth in the registration statement or application, is or is to be an obligor upon the indenture securities covered thereby shall—

(1) file with the indenture trustee copies of the annual reports and of the information, documents, and other reports (or copies of such portions of any of the foregoing as the Commission may by rules and regulations prescribe) which such obligor is required to file with the Commission pursuant to section 13 or 15(d) of the Securities Exchange Act of 1934; or, if the obligor is not required to file information, documents, or reports pursuant to either of such sections, then to file with the indenture trustee and the Commission, in accordance with rules and regulations prescribed by the Commission, such of the supplementary and periodic information, documents, and reports which may be required pursuant to section 13 of the Securities Exchange Act of 1934, in respect of a security listed and registered on a national securities exchange as may be prescribed in such rules and regulations;

(2) file with the indenture trustee and the Commission, in accordance with rules and regulations prescribed by the Commission, such additional information, documents, and reports with respect to compliance by such obligor with the conditions and covenants provided for in the indenture, as may be required by such rules and regulations, including, in the case of annual reports, if required by such rules and regulations, certificates of opinions of independent public accountants, conforming to the requirements of subsection (e) of this section, as to compliance with conditions or covenants, compliance with which is subject to verification by accountants, but

no such certificate or opinion shall be required as to any matter specified in clauses (A), (B), or (C) of paragraph (3) of subsection (c) of this section;

(3) transmit to the holders of the indenture securities upon which such person is an obligor, in the manner and to the extent provided in subsection (c) of section 313, such summaries of any information, documents, and reports required to be filed by such obligor pursuant to the provisions of paragraph (1) or (2) of this subsection as may be required by rules and regulations prescribed by the Commission; and

(4) furnish to the indenture trustee, not less often than annually, a brief certificate from the principal executive officer, principal financial officer or principal accounting officer as to his or her knowledge of such obligor's compliance with all conditions and covenants under the indenture. For purposes of this paragraph, such compliance shall be determined without regard to any period of grace or requirement of notice provided under the indenture.

The rules and regulations prescribed under this subsection shall be such as are necessary or appropriate in the public interest or for the protection of investors, having due regard to the types of indentures, and the nature of the business of the class of obligors affected thereby, and the amount of indenture securities outstanding under such indentures, and, in the case of any such rules and regulations prescribed after the indentures to which they apply have been qualified under this subchapter, the additional expense, if any, of complying with such rules and regulations. Such rules and regulations may be prescribed either before or after qualification becomes effective as to any such indenture.

(b) If the indenture to be qualified is or is to be secured by the mortgage or pledge of property, the obligor upon the indenture securities shall furnish to the indenture trustee—

(1) promptly after the execution and delivery of the indenture, an opinion of counsel (who may be of counsel for such obligor) either stating that in the opinion of such counsel the indenture has been properly recorded and filed so as to make effective the lien intended to be created thereby, and reciting the details of such action, or stating that in the opinion of such counsel no such action is necessary to make such lien effective; and

(2) at least annually after the execution and delivery of the indenture, an opinion of counsel (who may be of counsel for such obligor) either stating that in the opinion of such counsel such action has been taken with respect to the recording, filing, re-recording, and refiling of the indenture as is necessary to maintain the lien of such indenture, and reciting the details of

such action, or stating that in the opinion of such counsel no such action is necessary to maintain such lien.

(c) The obligor upon the indenture securities shall furnish to the indenture trustee evidence of compliance with the conditions precedent, if any, provided for in the indenture (including any covenants compliance with which constitutes a condition precedent) which relate to the authentication and delivery of the indenture securities, to the release or the release and substitution of property subject to the lien of the indenture, to the satisfaction and discharge of the indenture, or to any other action to be taken by the indenture trustee at the request or upon the application of such obligor. Such evidence shall consist of the following:

(1) certificates or opinions made by officers of such obligor who are specified in the indenture, stating that such conditions precedent have been complied with;

(2) an opinion of counsel (who may be of counsel for such obligor) stating that in his opinion such conditions precedent have been complied with; and

(3) in the case of conditions precedent compliance with which is subject to verification by accountants (such as conditions with respect to the preservation of specified ratios, the amount of net quick assets, negative-pledge clauses, and other similar specific conditions), a certificate or opinion of an accountant, who, in the case of any such conditions precedent to the authentication and delivery of indenture securities, and not otherwise, shall be an independent public accountant selected or approved by the indenture trustee in the exercise of reasonable care, if the aggregate principal amount of such indenture securities and of other indenture securities authenticated and delivered since the commencement of the then current calendar year (other than those with respect to which a certificate or opinion of an accountant is not required, or with respect to which a certificate or opinion of an independent public accountant has previously been furnished) is 10 per centum or more of the aggregate amount of the indenture securities at the time outstanding; but no certificate or opinion need be made by any person other than an officer or employee of such obligor who is specified in the indenture, as to (A) dates or periods not covered by annual reports required to be filed by the obligor, in the case of conditions precedent which depend upon a state of facts as of a date or dates or for a period or periods different from that required to be covered by such annual reports, or (B) the amount and value of property additions, except as provided in paragraph (3) of subsection (d) of this section, or (C) the adequacy of depreciation, maintenance, or repairs.

(d) If the indenture to be qualified is or is to be secured by the mortgage or pledge of property or securities, the obligor upon the indenture securities shall furnish to the indenture trustee a certificate or opinion of an engineer, appraiser, or other expert as to the fair value—

(1) of any property or securities to be released from the lien of the indenture, which certificate or opinion shall state that in the opinion of the person making the same the proposed release will not impair the security under such indenture in contravention of the provisions thereof, and requiring further that such certificate or opinion shall be made by an independent engineer, appraiser, or other expert, if the fair value of such property or securities and of all other property or securities released since the commencement of the then current calendar year, as set forth in the certificates or opinions required by this paragraph, is 10 per centum or more of the aggregate principal amount of the indenture securities at the time outstanding; but such a certificate or opinion of an independent engineer, appraiser, or other expert shall not be required in the case of any release of property or securities, if the fair value thereof as set forth in the certificate or opinion required by this paragraph is less than $25,000 or less than 1 per centum of the aggregate principal amount of the indenture securities at the time outstanding;

(2) to such obligor of any securities (other than indenture securities and securities secured by a lien prior to the lien of the indenture upon property subject to the lien of the indenture), the deposit of which with the trustee is to be made the basis for the authentication and delivery of indenture securities, the withdrawal of cash constituting a part of the trust estate or the release of property or securities subject to the lien of the indenture, and requiring further that if the fair value to such obligor of such securities and of all other such securities made the basis of any such authentication and delivery, withdrawal, or release since the commencement of the then current calendar year, as set forth in the certificates or opinions required by this paragraph, is 10 per centum or more of the aggregate principal amount of the indenture securities at the time outstanding, such certificate or opinion shall be made by an independent engineer, appraiser, or other expert and, in the case of the authentication and delivery of indenture securities, shall cover the fair value to such obligor of all other such securities so deposited since the commencement of the current calendar year as to which a certificate or opinion of an independent engineer, appraiser, or other expert has not previously been furnished; but such a certificate of an independent engineer, appraiser, or other expert shall not be required with respect to any securities so deposited, if the fair value thereof to such obligor as set forth in the certificate or opinion required by this paragraph is less than $25,000 or less

than 1 per centum of the aggregate principal amount of the indenture securities at the time outstanding; and

(3) to such obligor of any property the subjection of which to the lien of the indenture is to be made the basis for the authentication and delivery of indenture securities, the withdrawal of cash constituting a part of the trust estate, or the release of property or securities subject to the lien of the indenture, and requiring further that if

(A) within six months prior to the date of acquisition thereof by such obligor, such property has been used or operated, by a person or persons other than such obligor, in a business similar to that in which it has been or is to be used or operate by such obligor, and

(B) the fair value to such obligor of such property as set forth in such certificate or opinion is not less than $25,000 and not less than 1 per centum of the aggregate principal amount of the indenture securities at the time outstanding,

such certificate or opinion shall be made by an independent engineer, appraiser, or other expert and, in the case of the authentication and delivery of indenture securities, shall cover the fair value to the obligor of any property so used or operated which has been so subjected to the lien of the indenture since the commencement of the then current calendar year, and as to which a certificate or opinion of an independent engineer, appraiser, or other expert has not previously been furnished.

The indenture to be qualified shall automatically be deemed (unless it is expressly provided therein that any such provision is excluded) to provide that any such certificate or opinion may be made by an officer or employee of the obligor upon the indenture securities who is duly authorized to make such certificate or opinion by the obligor from time to time, except in cases in which this subsection requires that such certificate or opinion be made by an independent person. In such cases, such certificate or opinion shall be made by an independent engineer, appraiser, or other expert selected or approved by the indenture trustee in the exercise of reasonable care.

(e) Each certificate or opinion with respect to compliance with a condition or covenant provided for in the indenture (other than certificates provided pursuant to subsection (a)(4) of this section) shall include (1) a statement that the person making such certificate or opinion has read such covenant or condition; (2) a brief statement as to the nature and scope of the examination or investigation upon which the statements or opinions contained in such certificate or opinion are based; (3) a statement that, in the opinion of such person, he has made such examination or investigation as is necessary to enable him to express an informed opinion as to whether or not such covenant or condition has been complied with; and (4) a statement as to whether or not, in the opinion of such person, such condition or covenant has been complied with.

(f) Nothing in this section shall be construed either as requiring the inclusion in the indenture to be qualified of provisions that the obligor upon the indenture securities shall furnish to the indenture trustee any other evidence of compliance with the conditions and covenants provided for in the indenture than the evidence specified in this section, or as preventing the inclusion of such provision in such indenture, if the parties so agree.

Sec. 315   Duties and Responsibility of Trustee

(a) The indenture to be qualified shall automatically be deemed (unless it is expressly provided therein that any such provision is excluded) to provide that, prior to default (as such term is defined in such indenture)—

(1) the indenture trustee shall not be liable except for the performance of such duties as are specifically set out in such indenture; and

(2) the indenture trustee may conclusively rely, as to the truth of the statements and the correctness of the opinions expressed therein, in the absence of bad faith on the part of such trustee, upon certificates or opinions conforming to the requirements of the indenture;

but the indenture trustee shall examine the evidence furnished to it pursuant to section 314 to determine whether or not such evidence conforms to the requirements of the indenture.

(b) The indenture trustee shall give to the indenture security holders, in the manner and to the extent provided in subsection (c) of section 313, notice of all defaults known to the trustee, within ninety days after the occurrence thereof: *Provided,* That such indenture shall automatically be deemed (unless it is expressly provided therein that any such provision is excluded) to provide that, except in the case of default in the payment of the principal of or interest on any indenture security, or in the payment of any sinking or purchase fund installment, the trustee shall be protected in withholding such notice if and so long as the board of directors, the executive committee, or a trust committee of directors and/or responsible officers, of the trustee in good faith determine that the withholding of such notice is in the interests of the indenture security holders.

(c) The indenture trustee shall exercise in case of default (as such term is defined in such indenture) such of the rights and powers vested in it by such indenture, and to use the same degree of care and skill in their exercise, as a prudent man would exercise or use under the circumstances in the conduct of his own affairs.

(d) The indenture to be qualified shall not contain any provisions relieving the indenture trustee from liability for its own negligent action, its own negligent failure to act, or its own willful misconduct, except that—

(1) such indenture shall automatically be deemed (unless it is expressly provided therein that any such provision is excluded) to contain the provisions authorized by paragraphs (1) and (2) of subsection (a) of this section;

(2) such indenture shall automatically be deemed (unless it is expressly provided therein that any such provision is excluded) to contain provisions protecting the indenture trustee from liability for any error of judgment made in good faith by a responsible officer or officers of such trustee, unless it shall be proved that such trustee was negligent in ascertaining the pertinent facts; and

(3) such indenture shall automatically be deemed (unless it is expressly provided therein that any such provision is excluded) to contain provisions protecting the indenture trustee with respect to any action taken or omitted to be taken by it in good faith in accordance with the direction of the holders of not less than a majority in principal amount of the indenture securities at the time outstanding (determined as provided in subsection (a) of section 316) relating to the time, method, and place of conducting any proceeding for any remedy available to such trustee, or exercising any trust or power conferred upon such trustee, under such indenture.

(e) The indenture to be qualified shall automatically be deemed (unless it is expressly provided therein that any such provision is excluded) to contain provisions to the effect that all parties thereto, including the indenture security holders, agree that the court may in its discretion require, in any suit for the enforcement of any right or remedy under such indenture, or in any suit against the trustee for any action taken or omitted by it as trustee, the filing by any party litigant in such suit of an undertaking to pay the costs of such suit, and that such court may in its discretion assess reasonable costs, including reasonable attorney's fees, against any party litigant in such suit, having due regard to the merits and good faith of the claims or defenses made by such party litigant: *Provided,* That the provisions of this subsection shall not apply to any suit instituted by such trustee, to any suit instituted by any indenture security holder, or group of indenture security holders, holding in the aggregate more than 10 per centum in principal amount of the indenture securities outstanding, or to any suit instituted by any indenture security holder for the enforcement of the payment of the principal of or interest on any indenture security, on or after the respective due dates expressed in such indenture security.

Sec. 316   Directions and Waivers by Bondholders;
Prohibition of Impairment of Holder's Right to Payment

(a) The indenture to be qualified—

(1) shall automatically be deemed (unless it is expressly provided therein that any such provision is excluded) to contain provisions authorizing the holders of not less than a majority in principal amount of the indenture securities or if expressly specified in such indenture, of any series of securities at the time outstanding (A) to direct the time, method, and place of conducting any proceedings for any remedy available to such trustee, or exercising any trust or power conferred upon such trustee, under such indenture, or (B) on behalf of the holders of all such indenture securities, to consent to the waiver of any past default and its consequences; or

(2) may contain provisions authorizing the holders of not less than 75 per centum in principal amount of the indenture securities or if expressly specified in such indenture, of any series of securities at the time outstanding to consent on behalf of the holders of all such indenture securities to the postponement of any interest payment for a period not exceeding three years from its due date.

For the purposes of this subsection and paragraph (3) of subsection (d) of section 315, in determining whether the holders of the required principal amount of indenture securities have concurred in any such direction or consent, indenture securities owned by any obligor upon the indenture securities, or by any person directly or indirectly controlling or controlled by or under direct or indirect common control with any such obligor, shall be disregarded, except that for the purposes of determining whether the indenture trustee shall be protected in relying on any such direction or consent, only indenture securities which such trustee knows are so owned shall be so disregarded.

(b) Notwithstanding any other provision of the indenture to be qualified, the right of any holder of any indenture security to receive payment of the principal of and interest on such indenture security, on or after the respective due dates expressed in such indenture security, or to institute suit for the enforcement of any such payment on or after such respective dates, shall not be impaired or affected without the consent of such holder, except as to a postponement of an interest payment consented to as provided in paragraph (2) of subsection (a) of this section, and except that such indenture may contain provisions limiting or denying the right of any such holder to institute any such suit, if and to the extent that the institution or prosecution thereof or the entry of judgment therein would, under applicable law, result in the surrender, impairment, waiver, or loss of the lien of such indenture upon any property subject to such lien.

(c) The obligor upon any indenture qualified under this title may set a record date for purposes of determining the identity of indenture security holders entitled to vote or consent to any action by vote or consent authorized or permitted by subsection (a) of this section. Unless the indenture provides otherwise, such record date shall be the later of 30 days prior to the first solicitation of such consent or the date of the most recent list of holders furnished to the trustee pursuant to section 312 of this title prior to such solicitation.

Sec. 317
Special Powers of Trustee; Duties of Paying Agents

(a) The indenture trustee shall be authorized—

(1) in the case of a default in payment of the principal of any indenture security, when and as the same shall become due and payable, or in the case of a default in payment of the interest on any such security, when and as the same shall become due and payable and the continuance of such default for such period as may be prescribed in such indenture, to recover judgment, in its own name and as trustee of an express trust, against the obligor upon the indenture securities for the whole amount of such principal and interest remaining unpaid; and

(2) to file such proofs of claim and other papers or documents as may be necessary or advisable in order to have the claims of such trustee and of the indenture security holders allowed in any judicial proceedings relative to the obligor upon the indenture securities, its creditors, or its property.

(b) Each paying agent shall hold in trust for the benefit of the indenture security holders or the indenture trustee all sums held by such paying agent for the payment of the principal of or interest on the indenture securities, and shall give to such trustee notice of any default by any obligor upon the indenture securities in the making of any such payment.

Sec. 318   Effect of Prescribed Indenture Provisions

(a) If any provision of the indenture to be qualified limits, qualifies, or conflicts with the duties imposed by operation of subsection (c) of this section, the imposed duties shall control.

(b) The indenture to be qualified may contain, in addition to provisions specifically authorized under this subchapter to be included therein, any other provisions the inclusion of which is not in contravention of any provisions of this subchapter.

(c) The provisions of sections 310 to and including 317 that impose duties on any person (including provisions automatically deemed included in an indenture unless the indenture provides that such provisions are excluded) are a part of and govern every qualified indenture, whether or not physically contained therein, shall be deemed retroactively to govern each indenture heretofore qualified, and prospectively to govern each indenture hereafter qualified under this title and shall be deemed retroactively to amend and supersede inconsistent provisions in each such indenture heretofore qualified. The foregoing provisions of this subsection shall not be deemed to effect the inclusion (by retroactive amendment or otherwise) in the text of any indenture heretofore qualified of any of the optional provisions contemplated by section 310(b)(1), 311(b), 314(d), 315(a), 315(b), 315(d), 315(e), or 316(a)(1).

Sec. 319   Rules, Regulations, and Orders

(a) The Commission shall have authority from time to time to make, issue, amend and rescind such rules and regulations and such orders as it may deem necessary or appropriate in the public interest or for the protection of investors to carry out the provisions of this subchapter, including rules and regulations defining accounting, technical, and trade terms used in this subchapter. Among other things, the Commission shall have authority, (1) by rules and regulations, to prescribe for the purposes of section 310(b) the method (to be fixed in indentures to be qualified under this subchapter) of calculating percentages of voting securities and other securities; (2) by rules and regulations, to prescribe the definitions of the terms "cash transaction" and "self-liquidating paper" which shall be included in indentures to be qualified under this subchapter, which definitions shall include such of the creditor relationships referred to in paragraphs (4) and (6) of subsection (b) of section 311 as to which the Commission determines that the application of subsection (a) of section 311 is not necessary in the public interest or for the protection of investors, having due regard for the purposes of such subsection; and (3) for the purposes of this subchapter, to prescribe the form or forms in which information required in any statement, application, report, or other document filed with the Commission shall be set forth. For the purpose of its rules or regulations the Commission may classify persons, securities, indentures, and other matters within its jurisdiction and prescribe different requirements for different classes of persons, securities, indentures, or matters.

(b) Subject to the provisions of chapter 15 of Title 44 and regulations prescribed under the authority thereof, the rules and regulations of the Commission under this subchapter shall be effective upon publication in the manner which the Commission shall prescribe, or upon such later date as may be provided in such rules and regulations.

(c) No provision of this subchapter imposing any liability shall apply to any act done or omitted in good faith in conformity with any rule, regulation, or order of the Commission, notwithstanding that such rule, regulation, or order may, after such act or omission, be amended or rescinded or be determined by judicial or other authority to be invalid for any reason.

Sec. 320   Hearings by Commission

Hearings may be public and may be held before the Commission, any member or members thereof, or any officer or officers of the Commission designated by it, and appropriate records thereof shall be kept.

Sec. 321   Special Powers of Commission

(a) For the purpose of any investigation or any other proceeding which, in the opinion of the Commission, is necessary and proper for the enforcement of this subchapter, any member of the Commission, or any officer thereof designated by it, is empowered to administer oaths and affirmations, subpena witnesses, compel their attendance, take evidence, and require the production of any books, papers, correspondence, memoranda, contracts, agreements, or other records which the Commission deems relevant or material to the inquiry. Such attendance of witnesses and the production of any such books, papers, correspondence, memoranda, contracts, agreements, or other records may be required from any place in the United States or in any Territory at any designated place of investigation or hearing. In addition, the Commission shall have the powers with respect to investigations and hearings, and with respect to the enforcement of, and offenses and violations under, this subchapter and rules and regulations and orders prescribed under the authority thereof, provided in sections 20 and 22(b),(c) of the Securities Act of 1933.

(b) The Treasury Department, the Comptroller of the Currency, the Board of Governors of the Federal Reserve System, the Federal Reserve Banks, and the Federal Deposit Insurance Corporation are authorized, under such conditions as they may prescribe, to make available to the Commission such reports, records, or other information as they may have available with respect to trustees or prospective trustees under indentures qualified or to be qualified under this subchapter, and to make through their examiners or other employees for the use of the Commission, examinations of such trustees or prospective trustees. Every such trustee or prospective trustee shall, as a condition precedent to qualification of such indenture, consent that reports of examinations by Federal, State, Territorial, or District authorities may be furnished by such authorities to the Commission upon request therefor.

Notwithstanding any provision of this subchapter, no report, record, or other information made available to the Commission under this subsection, no report of an examination made under this subsection for the use of the Commission, no report of an examination made of any trustee or prospective trustee by any Federal, State, Territorial, or District authority having jurisdiction to examine or supervise such trustee, no report made by any such trustee or prospective trustee to any such authority, and no correspondence between any such authority and any such trustee or prospective trustee, shall be divulged or made known or available by the Commission or any member, officer, agent, or employee thereof, to any person other than a member, officer, agent, or employee of the Commission: *Provided,* That the Commission may make available to the Attorney General of the United States, in confidence, any information obtained from such records, reports of examination, other reports, or correspondence, and deemed necessary by the Commission, or requested by him, for the purpose of enabling him to perform his duties under this subchapter.

(c) Any investigation of a prospective trustee, or any proceeding or requirement for the purpose of obtaining information regarding a prospective trustee, under any provision of this subchapter, shall be limited—

(1) to determining whether such prospective trustee is qualified to act as trustee under the provisions of subsection (b) of section 310;

(2) to requiring the inclusion in the registration statement or application of information with respect to the eligibility of such prospective trustee under paragraph (1) of subsection (a) of section 310; and

(3) to requiring the inclusion in the registration statement or application of the most recent published report of condition of such prospective trustee, as described in paragraph (2) of subsection (a) of section 310, or, if the indenture does not contain the provision with respect to combined capital and surplus authorized by the last sentence of paragraph (2) of subsection (a) of section 310, to determining whether such prospective trustee is eligible to act as such under paragraph (2) of subsection (a) of section 310.

(d) The provisions of section 4(b) of the Securities Exchange Act of 1934 shall be applicable with respect to the power of the Commission to appoint and fix the compensation of such officers, attorneys, examiners and other experts, and such other officers and employees, as may be necessary for carrying out its functions under this subchapter.

Sec. 322   Court Review of Orders;
Jurisdiction of Offenses and Suits

(a) Orders of the Commission under this subchapter (including orders pursuant to the provisions of sections 305(b) and 307(c)) shall be subject to review in the same manner, upon the same conditions, and to the same extent, as provided in section 9 of the Securities Act of 1933, with respect to orders of the Commission under such Act.

(b) Jurisdiction of offenses and violations under, and jurisdiction and venue of suits and actions brought to enforce any liability or duty created by, this subchapter, or any rules or regulations or orders prescribed under the authority thereof, shall be as provided in section 22(a) of the Securities Act of 1933.

Sec. 323   Liability for Misleading Statements

(a) Any person who shall make or cause to be made any statement in any application, report, or document filed with the Commission pursuant to any provisions of this subchapter, or any rule, regulation, or order thereunder, which statement was at the time and in the light of the circumstances under which it was made false or misleading with respect to any material fact, or who shall omit to state any material fact required to be stated therein or necessary to make the statements therein not misleading, shall be liable to any person (not knowing that such statement was false or misleading or of such omission) who, in reliance upon such statement or omission shall have purchased or sold a security issued under the indenture to which such application, report, or documents relates, for damages caused by such reliance, unless the person sued shall prove that he acted in good faith and had no knowledge that such statement was false or misleading or of such omission. A person seeking to enforce such liability may sue at law or in equity in any court of competent jurisdiction. In any such suit the court may, in its discretion, require an undertaking for the payment of the costs of such suit and assess reasonable costs, including reasonable attorneys' fees, against either party litigant, having due regard to the merits and good faith of the suit or defense. No action shall be maintained to enforce any liability created under this section unless brought within one year after the discovery of the facts constituting the cause of action and within three years after such cause of action accrued.

(b) The rights and remedies provided by this subchapter shall be in addition to any and all other rights and remedies that may exist under the Securities Act of 1933, or the Securities Exchange Act of 1934, or the Public Utility Holding Company Act of 1935, or otherwise at law or in equity; but no person permitted to maintain a suit for damages under the provisions of this subchapter shall recover, through satisfaction of judgment in one or more actions, a total amount in excess of his actual damages on account of the act complained of.

Sec. 324   Unlawful Representations

It shall be unlawful for any person in offering, selling or issuing any security to represent or imply in any manner whatsoever that any action or failure to act by the Commission in the administration of this subchapter means that the Commission has in any way passed upon the merits of, or given approval to, any trustee, indenture or security, or any transaction or transactions therein, or that any such action or failure to act with regard to any statement or report filed with or examined by the Commission pursuant to this subchapter or any rule, regulation, or order thereunder, has the effect of a finding by the Commission that such statement or report is true and accurate on its face or that it is not false or misleading.

Sec. 325   Penalties

Any person who willfully violates any provision of this subchapter or any rule, regulation, or order thereunder, or any person who willfully, in any application, report, or document filed or required to be filed under the provisions of this subchapter or any rule, regulation, or order thereunder, makes any untrue statement of a material fact or omits to state any material fact required to be stated therein or necessary to make the statements therein not misleading, shall upon conviction be fined not more than $10,000 or imprisoned not more than five years, or both.

Sec. 326   Effect on Existing Law

Except as otherwise expressly provided, nothing in this subchapter shall affect (1) the jurisdiction of the Commission under the Securities Act of 1933, or the Securities Exchange Act of 1934, or the Public Utility Holding Company Act of 1935, over any person, security, or contract, or (2) the rights, obligations, duties, or liabilities of any person under such Acts; nor shall anything in this subchapter affect the jurisdiction of any other commission, board, agency, or officer of the United States or of any State or political subdivision of any State, over any person or security, insofar as such jurisdiction does not conflict with any provision of this subchapter or any rule, regulation, or order thereunder.

Sec. 327   Contrary Stipulations Void

Any condition, stipulation, or provision binding any person to waive compliance with any provision of this subchapter or with any rule, regulation, or order thereunder shall be void.

Sec. 328   Separability of Provisions

If any provision of this subchapter or the application of such provision to any person or circumstance shall be held invalid, the remainder of the subchapter and the application of such provision to persons or circumstances other than those as to which it is held invalid shall not be affected thereby.

Bibliography

ADMINISTRATION—GENERAL

KENNEDY, J. and R. I. LANDAU. *Recent Developments in Debt Financing and Corporate Trust Administration.* 22 THE BUSINESS LAWYER 353 (Jan. 1967).

PARELLA, R. E. and J. E. MILLER. *Modern Trust Forms and Checklists,* vol. 2 chapter 16 (Corporate Trusts). Warren, Gorham & Lamont, Boston (1980).

SKLAR, M. D. *The Corporate Indenture Trustee: Genuine Fiduciary or Mere Stakeholder?* THE BANKING LAW JOURNAL (Jan/Feb 1989).

TOMCZAK, S. L. CORPORATE AND COMMERCIAL FINANCE AGREEMENTS. Mc-Graw-Hill, New York (1984).

Disclosure Guidelines for State and Local Government Securities. GFOA Educational Services Center, 180 N. Michigan Ave., Suite 800, Chicago, IL 60601 (1991).

CONFLICT OF INTEREST

HERMAN and SANFANDA. *The Commercial Bank Trust Department and the Wall.* BOSTON UN. INDUSTRIAL AND COMMERCIAL LAW REVIEW, vol. 14, no. 1 (1972).

OBRZUT, F. R. *The Trust Indenture Act of 1939: The Corporate Trustee as Creditor.* 34 UCLA LAW REVIEW 131 (1976).

BECKER, B. M. *Conflict of Interest, Part I: Corporate Fiduciaries and Trust Beneficiaries.* 116 TRUSTS & ESTATES 111 (1977).

Federal Reserve Policy Statement on the *"Chinese Wall."* 43 FEDERAL REGIS-
TER 12755 (1978).
HERZEL and COLLING. *The Chinese Wall and Conflicts of Interest in Banks.* 34
THE BUSINESS LAWYER 73 (Nov. 1978).

LEGISLATION/REGULATION

Manual of Trust Examination Policies (March 1983). Federal Deposit Insurance
Corporation.
Uniform Commercial Code (Ninth Edition). 1978 Official Text with Comments,
West Publishing Co., 50 W. Kellogg Blvd., St. Paul. MN 55102.
Uniform Unclaimed Property Act (1981). National Conference of Commission-
ers on Uniform State Laws, 676 N. St. Clair Ave., Suite 1700, Chicago, IL
60611.
Bankruptcy Code of 1978. Collier Pamphlet Edition. Part I: Bankruptcy Code,
as Amended (1990/91). Collier Pamphlet Edition, Part 2: Bankruptcy Rules
(1990/91). Matthew Bender, 1275 Broadway, Albany, NY 12204.
Tax Equity and Fiscal Responsibility Act of 1982 (P. L. 97–248). Commerce
Clearing House, 4025 W. Peterson Ave., Chicago, IL 60646.
DUNHAM, WOLCOTT B. and PETER L. BOROWITZ. *The Role of the Indenture
Trustee in Reorganization Cases Under the Bankruptcy Code.* 102 Banking
L. J. 436 (1985).
SHAW, K. D., J. C. SIVON, M. JOHANNES. FIRREA, IMPLEMENTATION, AND
COMPLIANCE, Warren, Gorham & Lamont, Boston (1990).

LITIGATION

JOHNSON, D. *Default Administration of Corporate Trust Indentures: Alterna-
tives to Default, Remedial Provisions, and Judicial Arrangements and Reorganization.* 15 ST. LOUIS U.L.J. 203 (1971).
*Theories of Liability Under Convertible Debenture Redemption Notice Require-
ments.* 44 FORDHAM LAW REVIEW 817 (March 1976).
Defaulted Bonds: Remedies and Related Litigation. Practicing Law Institute.
Real Estate & Practice Course Handbook Series, no. 224 (1982), 810 Sev-
enth Ave., New York, NY 10019.
SPIOTTO, JAMES E. DEFAULTED SECURITIES: THE PRUDENT INDENTURE
TRUSTEE'S GUIDE. American Bankers Association, Washington, D.C.
(1990).

MANAGEMENT

CHANDLER, ALFRED D. STRATEGY AND STRUCTURE: CHAPTERS IN THE HISTORY OF THE INDUSTRIAL ENTERPRISE. MIT Press, Cambridge (1962).

ARGYRIS, CHRIS. INTEGRATING THE INDIVIDUAL AND THE ORGANIZATION. John Wiley, New York (1964).

ALLEN, LOUIS A. THE MANAGEMENT PROFESSION, McGraw-Hill, New York (1964).

BLAKE, ROBERT R. and JANE S. MOULTON. THE MANAGERIAL GRID. Gulf, Houston, (1964).

LIPPITT, GORDON L. ORGANIZATION RENEWAL, Appleton-Century Crofts, New York (1969).

DRUCKER, PETER. MANAGEMENT: TASKS, RESPONSIBILITIES, PRACTICES. Harper & Row, New York (1974).

STEELE, FRITZ. THE OPEN ORGANIZATION. Addison-Wesley, Reading, Mass. (1975).

FOURNIES, F. F. COACHING FOR IMPROVED WORK PERFORMANCE. Van Nostrand Reinhold, New York (1978).

PETERS, THOMAS J. and ROBERT H. WATERMAN, JR. IN SEARCH OF EXCELLENCE. Harper & Row, New York (1982).

TICKY, NOEL M. MANAGING STRATEGIC CHANGE. John Wiley, New York (1983).

KANTER, ROSABETH MOSS. THE CHANGE MASTERS. Simon & Schuster, New York (1983).

PINCHOT III, GIFFORD. INTRAPRENEURING, Harper & Row, New York (1985).

PETERS, TOM and NANCY AUSTIN. A PASSION FOR EXCELLENCE. Random House, New York (1985).

IMAI, MASAAKI. KAIZEN: THE KEY TO JAPAN'S COMPETITIVE SUCCESS. Random House, New York (1986).

PETERS, TOM. THRIVING ON CHAOS, Knopf, New York (1987).

ANDREWS, KENNETH R. THE CONCEPT OF CORPORATE STRATEGY, 3d ed. Irwin, Homewood, Ill. (1987).

ROBERTS, WESS. LEADERSHIP SECRETS OF ATILLA THE HUN. Warner, New York (1989).

MODEL INDENTURES

Commentaries on Model Debenture Indenture Provisions (1965), Model Registered Debenture Indenture Provisions (1967), Mortgage Bond Indenture (1981), Model Simplified Indenture (1983), The American Bar Foundation, 1155 E. 60th St. Chicago, IL 60637.

Sample Indenture for Uncertificated Debt Securities. American Bar Association, Business Law Section, Ad Hoc Committee on Uncertificated Debt Securities (May 1991).

SECURITIES PROCESSING

Securities Processing Digest [periodical]. American Bankers Association, 1120 Connecticut Ave., N.W., Washington, DC 20036.

Mergers—The Bottom Line. Cambridge Report on Corporate Mergers and Corporate Policy, vol. 6, no. 4 (March 10, 1982).

Improving Communications Between Issuers and Beneficial Owners of Nominee Held Securities. Advisory Committee Report (June 1982), Securities and Exchange Commission, Washington, DC 20549.

PETERSEN, J. E. and M. P. BUCKLEY. A GUIDE TO REGISTERED MUNICIPAL SECURITIES. Government Finance Officers Association, 180 N. Michigan Ave., Chicago, 60601 (1983).

WEISS, DAVID M. AFTER THE TRADE IS MADE: PROCESSING SECURITIES TRANSACTIONS. New York Institute of Finance, New York (1986).

RHODES, MARK S. TRANSFER OF STOCK, 6th ed. Bancroft-Whitney, San Francisco (1985). Cumm. Supp (April 1987).

TOROSIAN, M. THE SECURITIES HANDBOOK, MAT Financial Services Corp., Chicago, IL (1988).

GUTTMAN, E. MODERN SECURITIES TRANSFERS, Warren, Gorham & Lamont, Rev. Ed., Boston (1989).

Glossary

Many of these definitions have been derived from CORPORATE TRUST REFER-ENCE MANUAL *(American Bankers Association);* A GUIDE TO REGISTERED MUNICIPAL SECURITIES *(Government Finance Officers Association) and a glossary prepared by the* Cannon Financial Institute.

ACCRUED INTEREST The dollar amount, based on the stated rate or rates of interest, which has accrued from the dated date or other stated date, up to but not including the date of delivery, such interest being paid to the seller by the purchaser, and usually calculated on a 360-day basis.

AD VALOREM TAX A direct tax based on the value of the property. Counties, school districts, and municipalities usually are—and special tax districts may be—authorized by law to levy such taxes on property other than tangible personal property.

ADVANCE REFUNDING A financing structure under which new bonds are issued to repay an outstanding issue prior to its first call date. Generally the proceeds of the new issue are invested in government securities that are held in escrow.

AGENT A party who performs a service for another and charges a fee for that service. In a securities transaction this may be the broker, transfer agent, clearing corporation, paying agent, investment advisor, etc. An agent is *not* a principal (buyer or seller) involved in the transaction.

AGENT FOR SERVICE OF PROCESS An agent appointed by a borrower, pursuant to an agreement to receive legal process in a jurisdiction where the borrower is not physically located.

AMERICAN DEPOSITORY RECEIPT (ADR) A security that represents shares of foreign stock or bonds; a negotiable receipt for foreign securities held by the foreign correspondent bank of an American depository bank.

AMERICAN STOCK EXCHANGE (AMEX) (CURB)   The second largest securities auction market in the United States. Located in New York City, it is the largest market for listed foreign securities.

AMORTIZATION   Repayment of debt by the borrower in a series of installments over a period of time; retirement of debt by a purchase fund or through the operation of a sinking fund.

ARBITRAGE   The simultaneous buying and selling of separate but related currencies, securities, or goods in separate markets (often foreign) in order to profit from the difference in their prices.

ARBITRAGE BONDS   Any bonds the proceeds of which are reasonably expected (at the time of issuance of the bonds) to be used directly or indirectly:
1. to acquire higher yielding investments, or
2. to replace funds which were used directly or indirectly to acquire higher yielding investments.

ASSESSMENT BOND   A type of special-tax municipal bond. Repaid from related taxes, such as real estate or property tax.

ASSETS   The resources and property owned by a corporation, including cash, money due to the corporation, inventories, buildings, machinery, investments, and patents.

ASSETS PLEDGED   Collateral; property, securities, or other valuables that back a bond or note issue or a loan.

ASSIGNMENT   A stock or bond power either separate or printed on the reverse side of a certificate used to designate the name of the transferee.

ASSIGNMENT IN BLANK   Assignment form does not contain the name of the transferee.

ASSIGNMENT SECTION   The space on a stock or bond power, or on the reverse side of the security certificate, used to designate the name of the transferee or the new owner of the security in preparation for transfer.

ATTEST   To authenticate or give proof of, in relation to a document or notice.

ATTORNEY-IN-FACT   An agent acting for the security holder under a power of attorney to effect a transfer.

AUTHENTICATION   A manual certification appearing on a bond or note executed by the trustee (or its agent) under an indenture, or by a fiscal agent under a fiscal agency agreement, under which the bond or note is issued, stating that it is one of the bonds or notes referred to in the relevant indenture or fiscal agency agreement.

AUTHORIZED COMMON STOCK   The total number of common shares the board of directors had voted that the company can issue. The board of directors must vote on any increase in this authorized amount.

AUTHORIZED NEWSPAPER   A newspaper of general circulation in the relevant geographic area printed in the English language and customarily published on each business day whether or not published on Saturdays, Sundays, or holidays.

AUTOMATIC DIVIDEND REINVESTMENT   A plan, offered by the issuer or by a mutual fund, whereby the investor can instruct the other party not to pay such investor's dividends in cash ("suppress" them). Instead, the investor receives additional shares of stock.

BACK-UP WITHHOLDING   Established by the Interest and Dividend Tax Compliance Act of 1983. Requires paying agents to withhold 20 percent of interest, dividend, and principal payments to investors who have not filed an exemption certificate, certified taxpayer identification number, or social security number with the paying agent.

BALANCE SHEET   A financial statement that indicates the dollar value of an entity's assets, liabilities, and capital on a certain date.

BALLOON PAYMENT   A scaled method of bond interest payment (or mortgage payment) that provides for a final payment that is proportionally higher than previous payments.

BANKER'S ACCEPTANCE (BA)   A corporate bank draft (usually for a future delivery of foreign goods) whose payment has been guaranteed and stamped "accepted" by the corporation's bank.

BANS (Bond Anticipation Notes)   Municipal notes maturing in less than one year issued in advance of a new bond issue. Proceeds from bond issue will repay note with interest.

BASIS POINT   A term used in stating bond interest; 100 basis points equal 1 percent.

BEARER FORM   A negotiable security that is not registered in regard to interest or principal. It is presumed in law to be owned by its holder. Title to bearer securities is transferred by delivery.

BENEFICIAL OWNER   The true owner of securities that may be bearer or registered in the name of another, such as a nominee.

BEST EFFORTS   An underwriting method whereby the investment banker sells as much of an issue as possible.

BID   The highest price offered by a potential buyer for a particular security.

BLUE SKY LAWS   A popular name for various state laws enacted to protect the public against securities fraud.

BOND AND COUPON PAYING AGENT   A corporate agent responsible for paying interest and repaying principal to bondholders from funds provided by the issuer.

BOND CERTIFICATE   An interest-bearing debt obligation, under whose terms a borrower contracts, inter alia, to pay the holder a fixed principal amount on a stated future date and normally a series of interest payments during its life. A long-term debt instrument. In this sense, it may also be referred to as a debenture or note.

BOND COUNSEL   An attorney (or firm) retained by the issuer to give a legal opinion that a municipal issuer is authorized to issue proposed securities and has met all legal requirements necessary for issuance and that the interest on the securities will be exempt from federal income tax, and where applicable, from state and local tax.

BONDHOLDERS   Investors who lend money to an enterprise for a stated period of time and receive interest and repayment of principal. Their claims on a corporation's assets take precedence over the claims of preferred and common stockholders.

BOND OPINION   Usually covers the following matters: (1) whether the bonds are valid and binding obligations of the bond issuer; (2) the source of payment or security for the bonds; (3) whether and to what extent interest on the bonds is exempt from federal income tax and from taxes imposed by the state in which the issuer is located.

BOND POWER   An assignment separate from certificate used for bonds.

BOND PURCHASE AGREEMENT   An agreement between an issuer and the underwriter of the bonds, setting forth the terms of the sale, including price, premium or discount, interest rate, the closing conditions, restrictions on liability of the issuer, and any indemnity provisions.

BOND REGISTRAR   A corporate agent responsible for effecting registrations of transfer and maintaining records of registered debt security holders.

BOND RESOLUTION   The document(s) representing action of a municipal issuer authorizing the issuance and sale of securities. Such will also describe the nature of the obligation and the issuer's duties to the bondholders.

BOND TRUSTEE   See "Trustee."

BOOK-ENTRY SETTLEMENT   An accounting method for securities transactions and funds movements, whereby no physical movement of the certificates or funds is necessary. Instead, debits and offsetting credits (and vice versa) are posted to the accounts of the transaction's principals. These parties are usually members of the same securities depository, clearing house, Federal Reserve System, or they maintain special accounts with a common bank or broker.

BROKER A general term meaning either a brokerage firm or an individual stockbroker or registered representative.

BROKER CONFIRMATION A receipt sent to a customer by a broker after trade execution. The "confirm" indicates customer name, broker account number, description of security, quantity, price, dollar amounts, delivery and receiving parties, etc. Also called Trade Confirmation, or Trade Confirm.

BROKER/DEALER A party who effects securities transactions on behalf of its customers, as well as for its own market position. A broker may not buy and sell from its own account; it charges fees for the services performed. A dealer may purchase and resell the securities to its customer, charging a markup for its services. A broker/dealer may serve the customer in either a broker or dealer capacity.

BROKER'S LOAN A loan made to brokers, secured by pledged securities. Brokers use these loans to finance underwriting and inventory or to secure funds for their advances of credit to their customers who maintain margin accounts.

BULLDOG BOND A Sterling-denominated bond marketed in the United Kingdom by a non-British entity.

BULLET ISSUE An issue of securities with no amortization feature in which the principal amount is repaid entirely at the maturity date.

BUSINESS DAY Always specifically defined in the Indenture or Fiscal Agency Agreement but usually means:
  1. In the Euromarkets, when two related markets are open for b5nking business; in the Eurodollar market, a day when both London and New York banks are open for business;
  2. In the U.S. domestic market, any day, excluding Saturdays, Sundays, or legal or statutory holidays, on which business can be conducted.

BUY-IN If the selling party to a securities trade fails to deliver, the buyer may buy the securities through other sources at the market price then prevailing. The defaulting seller is liable for the difference in price. (The buyer must notify the seller of its intentions to buy the securities elsewhere before resorting to the buy-in.)

CALLABLE SECURITY A bond issue, all or part of which may be redeemed under definite conditions before maturity pursuant to indenture provisions.

CALL OPTION A short-term security that gives the owner the right to buy a security at a fixed price until a stated future date.

CALL PROTECTION   The period of time during which the issuer cannot call the security for redemption.

CALL PROVISION   A feature of bonds or preferred stock that allows the issuer to repurchase part or all of an issue before it matures.

CAPITAL   The funds invested in a company on a long-term basis, obtained: by issuing preferred or common stock, by retaining a portion of the company's earnings from date of incorporation, and by long-term borrowing.

CAPITALIZATION   Total amount of the various securities issued by a corporation. Capitalization may include preferred and common stock, bonds, debentures, and surplus.

CAPITALIZED INTEREST   A portion of the proceeds of an issue which will be used to pay interest on the bonds for a specific period of time; usually the period of construction of a project financed by the issue.

CAPITAL STOCK   Generally the same as common stock. Usually used when the corporation does not have preferred stock.

CASH DIVIDEND   Dividends paid in cash to stockholders of record.

CASH FLOW   The cash return generated by revenues or investment securities timed to meet the interest and principal payments of a bond issue.

"CASH" SETTLEMENT   Cash settlement usually takes place on trade date, avoiding the usual five-day settlement delay.

CEDE & CO.   Depository Trust Company's nominee name, used on all registered securities DTC holds in storage.

CEDEL AND EUROCLEAR   The Eurobond Clearing systems, which provide safekeeping, custody, and clearance services for holders of Eurobonds and Yankee bonds.

CERTIFICATE   An instrument that evidences ownership in a corporation or debt of the issuer.

CERTIFICATES OF ACCRUAL ON TREASURY SECURITIES (CATS)   CATS represent ownership in serially maturing interest payments or principal payments on specific underlying U.S. Treasury Notes and Bonds. Each CATS entitles the holder to receive a single payment at its maturity.

CERTIFICATE OF DEPOSIT (CD)   An interest bearing negotiable certificate representing a deposit with a fixed maturity issued by a commercial bank; being traded on a yield basis with interest computed for the actual number of days held on a 360-day year basis.

CHARTER, CORPORATE   The corporation's constitution granted by its state of incorporation, which specifies rules and limitations of ownership, operation, funding, security issuance, etc.

CLASSES OF STOCK   *Common:* Represents the principal ownership of the corporation, the first class to be issued and the last to be retired.

Classified Common Stock: Division of the common stock usually into two classes, class A and class B, to differentiate controlling or voting power.

Preferred: A cross between common stock and a bond. Holders receive dividends before profits are distributed to common stockholders.

Cumulative Preferred: Dividends, if not paid to stockholders, are accumulated and paid at a future date.

Noncumulative Preferred: The stockholder is paid dividends if they are earned, without any cumulative provision.

Participating Preferred: The stockholder will receive a specified dividend and may also be entitled to additional earnings generally available to common stockholders.

Classified Preferred Stock: 4.25 PFD, Class A PFD, Class B PFD, etc. These distinctions usually relate to different rates or voting privileges.

Convertible Preferred: This class carries a provision giving a privilege to the stockholder to convert such stock into common stock.

CLEARING CORPORATION   A clearing organization affiliated with a securities exchange that expedites the clearance and settlement of securities purchased or sold by members of that exchange.

CLEARING HOUSE FUNDS
1. funds used in settlement of equity, corporate, and municipal bond settlement transactions.
2. A term to mean "next day availability" of funds.

CLOSED-END (MORTGAGE) BONDS   A type of security (usually first mortgage bonds) which prohibits any future sale of a junior issue with the same priority of lien on the corporate assets covered by the original indenture.

CLOSED-END (MANAGEMENT) INVESTMENT COMPANY   A company whose primary business is investing its assets in securities of other companies. A closed-end company raises substantially all its funds at the time it is established.

CLOSELY HELD COMPANY   A corporation with a small number of owners, all living within one state at the time its stock is issued. The issue need not be registered with the SEC.

CLOSING   The consummation of the sale of the securities, usually at a meeting, with payment made to the borrower against delivery of the securities.

CLOSING DATE   The date on which a new issue's proceeds are paid to the borrower by the lead-manager against delivery of the securities in temporary or definitive form.

COLLATERAL   Property, securities, or other assets pledged to secure a loan.

COLLATERAL AGENT   A private financial institution, typically a bank and often the trustee, that serves as an agent for the credit enhancement provider. It holds and maintains the collateral which is pledged to the trustee to secure the obligations of the credit enhancer under the credit facility.

COLLATERAL AGREEMENT   The agreement under which a credit enhancement provider will pledge collateral (e.g., cash or readily marketable securities) to a collateral agent to hold as security for the bonds.

COLLATERALIZED MORTGAGE OBLIGATION   A bond with two or more classes of maturities secured by a pool of mortgages or mortgage instruments (e.g., "Ginnie Mae's").

COLLATERAL TRUST BOND   Bonds secured by securities owned by the issuer that are deposited with an indenture trustee.

COMMERCIAL PAPER   A negotiable, unsecured, short-term note issued in bearer form by a large and well-known corporation. Usually sold on a discount basis with a maximum maturity of nine months.

COMMON STOCK   Securities that represent ownership in a corporation; the one type of security that *must* be issued by a corporation.

COMPETITIVE BIDDING   A sealed envelope bidding process employed when various underwriter groups are interested in handling the distribution of a securities issue. The mandate or contract is awarded to one group by the issuer on the basis of the highest price paid, and lowest interest cost.

COMPOUND INTEREST   Interest paid on original capital and on the interest that has been added to the capital. Interest can be compounded daily, weekly, monthly, quarterly, semiannually, or annually.

COMPTROLLER OF THE CURRENCY   An official of the U.S. government, appointed by the President and confirmed by the Senate, who is responsible for the chartering, examining, supervising, and liquidating of all national banks.

CONDUIT FINANCING   Bonds issued by a governmental unit to finance a project to be used primarily by a third party, usually a corporation engaged in private enterprise. The security for such bonds is the credit of the private user rather than the governmental issuer. Generally, such bonds do not constitute obligations of the issuer because the corporate obligor is liable for generating the pledged revenues (e.g., industrial revenue bonds).

CONSTRUCTION FUND   A fund, usually held by the trustee under an indenture, into which proceeds of an issue are deposited for payment of authorized project costs.

CONTINUOUS NET SETTLEMENT   A securities trade settlement option which summarizes multiple transactions into a single net security settlement and a single net money affirmation, wherein the identity of the contra side is lost. The bank and broker settle all security and money transactions with the clearing corporation.

CONVERSION   An indenture provision giving the holder of a bond or note the right to exchange it for other securities of the issuer (usually shares of common stock).

CONVERSION AGENT   A bank designated by the issuer of convertible securities to convert, at the investor's request, debt or equity securities of the issuer into the number of shares of stock specified in the trust indenture or stock offering agreement. The Conversion Agent will requisition the shares of stock from the stock transfer agent and draw a check for any cash fraction thereof upon surrender of the convertible securities.

CONVERSION PRICE   The price at which a corporation's convertible security may be converted into its common stock.

CONVERSION RATIO   The number of common shares that will be issued for each $1,000 bond or preferred share.

CONVERTIBLE DEBENTURES   Securities that may be exchanged for common stock of the same company at a set conversion price stated in the bond indenture.

CONVERTIBLE PREFERRED STOCK   Stock that may be exchanged for common stock of the same company, usually at a fixed ratio or price.

CO-OPS (Banks for Cooperatives)   Banks that make loans to farmers' associations through issuance of bonds. These are not guaranteed by the U.S. government but are secured obligations of the banks that are under governmental supervision.

CORPORATE REORGANIZATION   A major change in capital structure and financial operation of a corporation, often requiring new issues and/or exchanges of securities.

CORPORATE RESOLUTION   A formal document issued by a corporation to make a statement, ratify actions, or grant authority to individuals to act for the corporation on specific matters.

CORPORATE TRUSTEE   A bank or trust company that administers the indenture provisions of a debt issue.

CORPORATION   A body of one or more persons authorized by law to perform specific functions as defined in its charter. The corporation, rather than its shareholders, is solely responsible for its debts.

COUPON   Evidence of a legal obligation to pay a fixed amount of interest on specified dates to the holder, such being normally attached to a bearer bond when issued.

COUPON BOND   A bearer bond with coupons attached. The interest on the bond is collected by detaching and presenting the coupons as they become due.

COVENANT   A provision in an indenture setting forth an undertaking or agreement of the issuer in regard to specific matters. Such may be either affirmative or negative in character.

COVERAGE   The portion of pledged revenues available annually to pay debt service, as compared to the annual debt service requirement. The ratio is one indication of the margin of safety for payment of debt service.

CREDIT ENHANCEMENT   An external credit support of a debt obligation. Included are letters of credit, municipal bond insurance, and third-party guarantees.

CREDIT ENHANCEMENT PROVIDER   Insurance companies, banks, S&Ls, municipal bond sureties, or other private financial institutions that provide additional security for tax-exempt bonds by guaranteeing or insuring the repayment of the bonds.

CURRENT YIELD   Annual interest (or dividends) divided by current market price of a bond (or stock).

CUSIP   (Acronym for Committee on Uniform Securities Identification Procedures). A uniform numbering system widely used to identify specific securities and their issuers. It includes corporate, municipal, state, federal, and some foreign issues. The CUSIP number appears on the certificates and in documents relating to securities processing.

CUSTODIAN   An agent, usually a bank, that safekeeps securities for its customers and performs dividend and interest collection services. It also buys, sells, receives, and delivers securities if so instructed by the customer.

CUSTODY   The service of safekeeping customer assets, including securities, and collecting interest and dividends; also the buying, selling, receiving, and delivering of securities.

DATE OF ASSIGNMENT   The date when the certificate is endorsed.

DATED DATE   The date of a bond issue, printed on each bond, from which interest usually starts to accrue, even though the bonds may actually be delivered at some later date.

DEALER   An individual or firm in the securities business acting as principal rather than as agent. Typically a dealer buys for its own account and sells to a customer from its own inventory.

DEBENTURE   An unsecured debt certificate backed by the general credit of the issuer.

DEBT SERVICE   Payments of interest and principal on total borrowings that must be made by the borrower during the period in which its debt is outstanding.

DEBT SERVICE RESERVE FUND   The fund usually held by the trustee under an indenture established for the payment of debt service on bonds in the event pledged receipts are insufficient.

DEEP DISCOUNT BOND   A bond sold at a substantial discount below its par value bearing interest at a rate significantly below the current interest rates or with no interest at all.

DEFAULT   The failure by the issuer of bonds or notes to comply with one or more of its obligations in the indenture under which the bonds are issued.

DEFEASANCE   A general term reflecting the termination of the rights and interests of bondholders and extinguishment of their lien on any property or collateral pursuant to the terms of an indenture or bond resolution. May also refer to the termination of an issuer's obligations under such contracts upon the refunding of the issue or by provisions for the future payment of interest and repayment of principal.

DELAYED DELIVERY   A partial delivery of new issue securities to the lead manager subsequent to the closing date, pursuant to an agreement.

DELIVERY VS. PAYMENT (DVP)   A physical delivery of securities against payment of the purchase price. Normally, payment is due on scheduled settlement date, even if securities are delayed.

DEMAND OPTION   A right, which may be evidenced by a certificate, given the holder of a debt security to sell it back to the issuer at any time prior to the security's maturity.

DEPOSITORY AGENT   An agent retained by the maker of a tender offer to receive securities forwarded to the agent by the owners, hold the securities, and make payment in cash and/or securities to the owners when so authorized by the maker of the tender offer.

DEPOSITORY TRUST COMPANY (DTC)   The New York depository serving institutional participants such as banks, brokers, insurance companies, and other high-volume securities traders.

DIRECT PAY LETTER OF CREDIT   A letter of credit that covers an amount equal to the principal of and interest on the bonds and that is drawn upon by the trustee on each bond payment date in an amount equal to the full amount of principal, interest, and premium, if any, due in respect of the bonds. Such letter may also provide for reinstatement of the interest component after any drawing thereon in respect of interest unless the issuing bank notifies the trustee to the contrary within a certain period of time after such drawing.

DISCOUNT   The amount by which a security is selling below its par value. In the case of original issuance, this is referred to as the original issuance discount (OID).

DIVIDEND   A proportion of net earnings paid periodically by a corporation to its stockholders as a return on investment.

DIVIDEND, CASH   Cash payments authorized by a corporation's board of directors to be made to stockholders of record, usually quarterly.

DIVIDEND PAYING AGENT   An institution, usually a bank, that disburses declared dividends on behalf of its corporate client and files tax information reports with government authorities. If such agent is not also the transfer agent, the dividend paying agent prepares and mails checks based on a list of holders submitted by the transfer agent. For a stock dividend, the transfer agent issues new certificates.

DIVIDEND, STOCK   Payment of additional shares of common stock by the corporation to the stockholders.

DIVIDEND REINVESTMENT AGENT   An agent of the issuer that will process the automatic reinvestment of a stockholder's dividends in additional company shares.

D.K. (DON'T KNOW)   A D.K. results when the purchaser's clearing house or bank refuses to accept a security delivery simply because it "doesn't know" about it and is not expecting it.

DROP LOCK BOND   A hybrid debt security issued as a floating rate instrument but that becomes a fixed-rate bond when its rate falls below a predetermined trigger rate.

DUE BILL   An assignment or similar instrument given by the seller in a trade to transfer title to dividends, interest, or other rights legally due to the buyer.

DUE DILIGENCE   Investigation conducted by underwriters and their counsel and, in some cases, also by bond counsel and the issuer's counsel to determine whether all material items in connection with the issuer, the issue, and the security for the issue have been accurately disclosed in the Official Statement, and that no material disclosure has been omitted.

DUE DILIGENCE MEETING   A meeting between corporate officers and the underwriting group to:
1. discuss and review detailed information in the registration statement;
2. prepare a final prospectus;
3. negotiate a formal underwriting agreement.

DUPLICATE SECURITY   A security issued as a replacement of a lost or stolen certificate.

DUTCH AUCTION   An auction in which securities are awarded at the price that represents the lowest accepted bid. All bidders pay the lowest bid accepted.

ENDORSEMENT   The signature written on the back of a negotiable instrument (or in an accompanying power) that transfers the instrument to another party. The signer must have the legal right to transfer the instrument if the endorsement is to be valid.

ENDORSEMENT, SPECIAL   An endorsement that designates the party to whom the instrument is to be transferred.

ENDORSEMENT IN BLANK   The signature of an authorized person on the back of a negotiable instrument, or on a separate power, which does not indicate the specific name of the party to whom the instrument is being transferred. Endorsement in blank makes the instrument as transferable as if it were in bearer form.

ENTERPRISE ACTIVITY   A revenue-generating project or business which supplies funds necessary to pay debt service on bonds issued to finance the facility. The debt of such projects is self-liquidating when the projects earn sufficient monies to cover all debt service and other requirements imposed under the bond contract.

EQUIPMENT TRUST BONDS   Bonds secured by machinery and equipment issued pursuant to an equipment trust agreement between the issuer and an indenture trustee.

EQUITY   Value of the stockholders' ownership of the corporation, which equals the difference between the company's total assets and its total liabilities. "Equity" includes preferred stock, common stock, retained earnings, and other surplus reserves. Equity is also called "book net worth" or "total proprietorship."

EQUITY SECURITIES   Securities evidencing ownership of a corporation. Includes preferred and common stock of all types.

ERASURE GUARANTEE   Any irregularity in the assignment guaranteed by the broker or the commercial bank before the registration of transfer is effected.

ESCHEAT   Revision of property to the state when there are no legal heirs or claimants.

ESCROW   An agency providing for the physical holding of cash, securities, or documents until certain conditions called for in an agreement between two parties are met.

ESCROW AGENT   An institution, usually a bank, designated by two or more parties to hold securities, funds, or documents that are to be delivered upon compliance with the conditions contained in the escrow agreement, usually within a specified period of time.

EURODOLLAR BOND   A U.S. dollar-denominated bond marketed wholly outside the United States of America (primarily in Europe). No registration statement is required to be filed with the SEC.

EUROMARKET   General term for the European capital markets that comprise, inter alia, the markets for Eurobonds, Euro FRNs, Euro CDs/FRCDs, and Euro syndicated credits.

EUROPEAN CURRENCY UNIT ("ECU")   A standard basket of European Economic Community member currencies.

EUROSTERLING BOND   A sterling-denominated bond issued in bearer form only, marketed solely outside the United Kingdom and the United States.

EVENTS OF DEFAULT   Specific defaults, whose occurrence and continuance permit the trustee (or a holder of bonds or notes) to exercise the remedies in the indenture under which the bonds or notes are issued.

EXCHANGE AGENT   A bank, usually the bond registrar, designated by an issuer of securities to process the exchange of bonds of an issue for other bonds of the same issue (e.g., registered bonds for bearer and interdenominational exchanges) or to process the exchange of bonds or stock for other securities of the same issuer or of a different company as a result of a merger or acquisition.

EX-DIVIDEND DATE   The date after a dividend has been declared when a security is traded without the dividend. The date is determined by the exchange on which the security is traded and is usually four business days before the record date.

EXTENSION LETTER OF CREDIT   A letter of credit that provides for a single draw in the event of the acceleration of the bonds in an amount equal to all payments made on the bonds during the period of a specified number of days (usually ninety-one) prior to the occurrence of (1) an act of bankruptcy that triggers acceleration or (2) the drawing on the letter of credit if no act of bankruptcy has occurred.

FACE AMOUNT   The par value (i.e., principal or maturity value) of a security appearing on the face of the instrument.

FACSIMILE SIGNATURE   A machine signature as opposed to a manual signature.

FAIL   Failure of the seller to deliver securities to the buyer on settlement date and/or failure of the buyer to accept and pay for the securities. Also called a settlement fail.

FANNIE MAE (Federal National Mortgage Association)   A privately owned company that adds liquidity to the residential mortgage market by buying mortgages from the original lenders, such as savings and loans, banks, and insurance companies. Fannie Mae buys mortgages guaranteed or insured by government agencies, as well as conventional mortgages. To raise funds, it sells debentures, notes, and mortgage-backed certificates to the investing public and occasionally to the U.S. Treasury.

FARM CREDIT ADMINISTRATION   An independent U.S. government agency that provides credit and financial services to farmers, ranchers, and allied businesses. For details, see: Co-Ops (Banks For Cooperatives); FICB (Federal Intermediate Credit Banks); FLB (Federal Land Banks).

FDIC (Federal Deposit Insurance Corporation)   An agency of the U.S. government that insures depositors' accounts at most commercial banks and mutual savings banks.

FEASIBILITY STUDY   A report of the financial practicality of a proposed project and financing thereof that may include estimates of revenue that will be generated and a review of the physical, operating, economic, or engineering aspects of the proposed project.

FEDERAL FUNDS
1. Excess reserve balances of a member bank on deposit at a Federal Reserve Bank. This money may be made available to eligible borrowers on a short-term basis.
2. Funds used for the settlement of money market instruments and U.S. government securities transactions.
3. A term used to mean "same day availability" of funds. Cf. "Clearing House Funds."

FEDERAL RESERVE SYSTEM (FRS)   Known as "the Fed," it is the central banking system as established by the Federal Reserve Act of 1913. It regulates the nation's supply of money, determines the legal reserve requirement of member banks, oversees the Mint, effects transfers of funds, promotes and facilitates the clearance and collection of checks, and examines member banks.

FHA (Federal Housing Administration)   Responsible to HUD, the Department of Housing and Urban Development, it insures residential mortgages, settles claims for defaulted mortgages in cash, and issues registered, transferable debentures that have an unconditional U.S. government guarantee.

FHLB (Federal Home Loan Bank System)   The federal system that supervises all nationally chartered savings and loan associations and mutual savings banks. State-chartered thrift organizations may also be eligible for membership. One purpose of the FHLB is to promote availability of funds for home loans and mortgages.

FHLMC (Federal Home Loan Mortgage Corporation)   See "Freddie Mac."

FICB (Federal Intermediate Credit Banks)   Responsible to Farm Credit Administration, providing short- and medium-term financing to financial institutions that serve the farm credit market. See also "Farm Credit Administration."

FIDUCIARY   An individual or institution responsible for acting for the benefit of another in specified matters or for the holding of something in trust.

FINANCIAL ADVISOR   With respect to a new issue of municipal bonds, a consultant who advises the issuer on matters pertinent to the issue, such as structure, timing, marketing, fairness of pricing, terms, and bond ratings.

FINS (Financial Industry Numbering System)   A numerical code (similar in structure to the CUSIP numbering system) identifying financial institutions such as banks and brokerage firms. Used in security trade documents, depository accounting procedures, etc.

FISCAL AGENT   A person, normally a bank or trust company, authorized to enter into a Fiscal Agency agreement with an issuer of bonds or notes (usually a government entity). The agreement provides for control of the issue and its servicing, but the Fiscal Agent does not have fiduciary responsibilities.

FIXED-INCOME SECURITIES   Interest-bearing securities and preferred stock.

FLB (Federal Land Banks)   Responsible to Farm Credit Administration. FLBs arrange long-term loans to farmers and ranchers, secured by mortgages on farm or ranch properties. FLB bonds are issued to finance these loans. See also "Farm Credit Administration."

FLOAT   A colloquial term meaning the earnings on uninvested balances held by a bank.

FLOATER   Common term used to describe a security with a variable interest rate.

FLOATING RATE   An interest rate that is not a fixed percentage of principal.

The issuer typically "pegs" the future rate it will pay to the future rate of a basic short-term financial instrument (such as a specific U.S. Treasury issue) and pays a small stated percentage above the rate.

FLOWER BOND   A class of Treasury bond no longer being issued, but previous issues will mature through 1998. If the bondholder dies before the bond matures, the heirs may redeem the bond at full face value to pay federal estate taxes.

FmHA (Farmers Home Administration)   Agency of the Department of Agriculture that aids loan programs in rural areas. Its outstanding securities have a U.S. government guarantee.

FNMA (Federal National Mortgage Association)   See "Fannie Mae."

FORWARDING AGENT   An institution, usually a bank, that receives securities during a tender offer and forwards them to the appropriate depository agent daily with an accounting record.

FRACTIONAL RIGHTS   The residual portion of the total rights received by a stockholder in a rights offering that is too small to allow the purchase of a full share.

FRACTIONAL SHARE   A portion of a share of stock.

FREDDIE MAC (Federal Home Loan Mortgage Corporation)   Supplies mortgage credit for residential housing, mostly through Federal Home Loan Banks. (The FHLB system serves thrift institutions much as the Federal Reserve System serves commercial banks.) Freddie Mac issues bonds, debentures, notes, and certificates.

FREEDOM SHARES   Nonmarketable U.S. Treasury savings notes. Not issued after 1970, but many will be outstanding until 1994. Payable on presentation to certain banks, as well as the Bureau of Public Debt. Also known as U.S. Savings Notes.

FULLY GUARANTEED OBLIGATIONS   Obligations of some federal agencies that are fully guaranteed by the U.S. government for both principal and interest.

FULLY REGISTERED BONDS   Bonds that are registered for both principal and interest in a holder's name.

GENERAL OBLIGATION BOND (GO)   Municipal bond issues by any level of government below the U.S. government, which is backed by the full faith, credit, and taxing power of the issuer.

GINNIE MAE (Government National Mortgage Association)   A corporation wholly owned by the U.S. government that buys mortgages from banks and other private lenders and resells them to investors. It issues and guarantees mortgage-backed bonds and pass-through certificates.

GLASS-STEAGALL ACT (Banking Act of 1933)   A federal law that limits the types of business a bank can do and restrains competition among banks.

GLOBAL CERTIFICATE   A single certificate, in either bearer or registered form, representing an entire issue or maturity of an issue of securities. Such certificates are used in registered book-entry systems where issuers are obligated under state law to issue at least one certificate per maturity. For book-entry only bonds, the issuer will deliver the global certificate(s) to the securities depository where they are retained until maturity.

Such certificates may also be used, especially in the Euro market, when definitive bonds are not available at the closing.

GNMA (Government National Mortgage Association)   See "Ginnie Mae."

GOING CONCERN   A company actively conducting a business, as opposed to one that merely holds assets.

GOOD DELIVERY   A term referring to all conditions of a securities delivery that must be met by the seller.

GOVERNMENT NATIONAL MORTGAGE ASSOCIATION (GNMA)   See "Ginnie Mae."

GRANTING CLAUSES   The section of a trust indenture that sets forth the security for the obligations to be issued. It includes a recital of the consideration, a specific grant to the trustee, and a legal description of the real property if it is to be mortgaged.

GUARANTEED BOND   A bond guaranteed for interest and principal by a third party, normally the parent or affiliate of the issuer, but usually larger, better-known, or more creditworthy than the issuer.

GUARANTEED INTEREST CERTIFICATE   Registered negotiable instruments, by means of which the Small Business Administration raises funds for loans to small businesses.

GUARANTEED INVESTMENT CONTRACTS (GICs)   Investment offered by financial service institutions that pays investors a fixed rate of return, usually close to the current yield on high-grade bonds, for a stated term of generally not exceeding ten years.

GUARANTEED MORTGAGE CERTIFICATES   Certificates backed by mortgages and also by a guarantee. FHLMC issues certificates of this type in registered form, backed by conventional residential mortgages.

GUARANTY AGREEMENT   An agreement of a third party, for consideration, to pay debt service on an issue that is the primary obligation of another party or the promise of the primary obligor under a sale and leaseback by a separate agreement to pay debt service on the issue.

HOLDER OF RECORD   The person whose name appears in the records of the corporation.

HOME OFFICE PAYMENT AGREEMENT   An agreement in connection with the private placement of debt securities, whereby in consideration of payments of principal being made to the holder without presentation of such security for notation of payment, the holder agrees that it will, before the disposition thereof, present such securities to the issuer (or its agent) for notation of payment or issuance of new security reflecting the unpaid balance thereof.

HOSPITAL AND HEALTH CARE REVENUE BONDS   Bonds usually secured by a first lien on the revenues of a hospital.

HUD (Department of Housing and Urban Development)   A U.S. department responsible for three groups that circulate funds for construction and major improvement of housing and urban renewal. (See Glossary entries under FHA, Ginnie Mae, and HUD Public Housing Notes and Bonds.)

HUD SECURITIES (Public Housing Notes and Bonds)   Notes and bonds issued by local communities to fund public housing or urban renewal. HUD guarantees approved securities for payment of interest and repayment of principal.

HYPOTHECATION   Pledging of securities as collateral for a loan.

INCOME BOND   Issued only to replace older bond issues on which a corporation has defaulted. Both principal amount and interest rate on the income bonds are greater than on the bonds they replace. Interest is paid only if earned, but unpaid interest accrues, to be paid when and if possible. Also called adjustment bonds.

INDENTURE   A contract between the issuer of bonds or notes and a trustee under which such securities are to be issued setting forth the rights, duties, and obligations of each, as well as the rights of the holders of the securities.

INDUSTRIAL REVENUE BONDS   Issued to support the economic development of a community. Funds raised are used to construct facilities for lease to a corporation whose operations will bring jobs to the community. Repayment is based on the corporation's lease payments.

INTEREST   Amount paid by a borrower to a lender in exchange for the use of the lender's money for a period of time. Interest is paid on debt securities either at regular intervals or when the issue matures.

INTESTATE   A person who dies leaving property but no will. A court in the state where the decedent lived will appoint a personal representative to distribute the property according to the state's law.

ISSUED AND OUTSTANDING   The portion of debt and equity securities authorized for sale by a corporation's board of directors that has been sold by the corporation and is currently owned by the public. Excludes securities that have been repurchased from the public and are either held in the corporation's treasury or have been retired.

ISSUER   A public or private entity that signs an evidence of obligation, such as a note, bond, or stock certificate, in return for which the issuer receives cash, goods, or services.

JOINT TENANCY   Type of ownership by two or more people with right of survivorship. If one dies, the survivor(s) takes full ownership.

JUMBO   General term for a large-denomination certificate.

JUNIOR LIEN   A security that represents a claim on the issuer's income or assets subordinate to the claim of another security.

JUNK BONDS   A generic description of high-yield debt securities typically issued by commercial borrowers to finance leveraged buyouts, generally subordinated to other indebtedness of the borrower.

LEGAL OPINION
1. The statement of counsel that must be obtained by the issuer before a municipal issue can be sold and that is usually printed on the back of each certificate.
2. An opinion rendered to an indenture trustee pursuant to the terms of an indenture or otherwise requested by the trustee.

LEGAL TRANSFER   Transfer of securities registered in the name of decedents, fiduciaries, trusts, corporations, partnerships, clubs, institutions, etc. Transfer of items that are not generally recognized as good delivery items.

LETTER OF CREDIT   A financial instrument issued to a company (or individual) by a bank that substitutes the bank's credit for the company's (or individual's) credit. Frequently used by companies ordering goods from foreign suppliers with which they have no credit relationship.

LETTER OF ERASURE   Letter signed by an authorized person indemnifying the transfer agent and the corporation against liability in effecting a transfer on an erased or altered assignment.

LETTER OF INDEMNITY   Letter signed by an authorized person indemnifying the transfer agent or indenture trustee and the issuer against liability in replacing a lost, stolen, or mutilated certificate.

LETTER OF TRANSMITTAL   A form used in transmitting securities to the depository agent in the case of a tender offer.

LETTERS OF ADMINISTRATION   A certificate issued by a court evidencing the appointment of the administrator of an estate.

LETTERS TESTAMENTARY   A certificate issued by the court evidencing the appointment of the executor of an estate.

"LETTER" STOCK   Also called Restricted Stock. A special issue of common stock a corporation is legally permitted to sell without SEC registration to a small group of investors. The buyer must sign a letter of intent stating that the purchase is for investment purposes and will not be sold. "Letter Bonds" can also be issued.

LEVEL DEBT SERVICE   An arrangement of serial maturities in which the amount of principal maturing increases at approximately the same rate as the amount of interest decreases, resulting in substantially equal annual debt service payments over the life of the bonds.

LEVERAGE LEASE   A financing vehicle involving the acquisition of property by an investor (usually through a trustee) providing a minor portion of the cost thereof (with lenders providing the balance) and the leasing of such property to the lessee. The lender's investment is usually represented by bonds under an indenture.

LIBOR (London Interbank Offered Rate)   Eurodollar deposits between banks. There is a different LIBOR rate for each deposit maturity.

LIEN   A legal interest in specific personal property of a borrower that provides security in the event the borrower defaults on its obligation.

LIMITED OPEN-END INDENTURE   A mortgage arrangement that sets a limit on the principal amount of bonds that may be issued in the future under the same indenture and with the same priority of lien on corporate assets.

LIMITED PURPOSE TRUST COMPANY   Trust companies, state-chartered and regulated, that are permitted to perform specified trust functions.

LIQUIDATION   The complex procedure whereby the assets of a corporation are sold and the net proceeds, after all expenses, are paid to creditors (including bondholders) and shareholders in accordance with the laws and contracts protecting each class of creditor.

LISTED SECURITIES
    1. Specifically, securities traded on the NYSE and the AMEX.
    2. Generally, securities traded on any regional exchange.

LOWER FLOATER   General term for a security with a variable interest rate and also having a tender feature.

MANDATORY REDEMPTION ACCOUNT   A separate fund into which the issuer makes periodic deposits to purchase bonds in the open market or to pay the costs of calling bonds in accordance with the mandatory redemption schedule in the bond contract. Such account is also known as a bond amortization fund.

MARITIME ADMINISTRATION   A U.S. government agency which issues notes, bonds, and other obligations secured by ship mortgages and directly guaranteed by the U.S. government.

MARK-TO-MARKET   The process of valuing a portfolio, a securities position, or a trade by multiplying the number of shares (or principal amount in the case of bonds) by the current market price per share (or per bond).

MARKET MAKER   A dealer that buys and sells specific issues in the over-the-counter market or on stock exchanges.

MARKET ORDER   An order for securities in which the buyer/seller does not specify an exact dollar price but agrees to trade immediately at the best price available in the market at the time.

MARKET VALUE   The current date's value of a security, i.e., the value of the last recorded sale on the present date, the value at market close of the prior business day, or the closing value at the date of the report in which market value is shown, depending on definition.

MASTER SERVICER   The entity specified in the prospectus supplement for a bond issue secured by mortgage loans that will administer and supervise the performance by servicers of their duties and responsibilities under serving agreements in respect of the collateral for the securities.

MATURITY   The date specified in a note, bond, or other evidence of debt on which the debt is due and payable.

MIDWEST CLEARING CORPORATION   Facility capable of handling settlement of transactions by members of Midwest Stock Exchange.

MIDWEST SECURITIES TRUST CO.   Securities depository facility for members of Midwest Stock Exchange.

MINOR   A person under the age at which he or she receives full civil rights.

MINORITY STOCKHOLDERS   A group with common corporate interests but with holdings too small to significantly influence actions of the corporation under regular voting procedures.

MONEY CENTER BANKS   Banks located in a city that is recognized as a major financial center.

MONEY MARKET   The money market does not have a specific location. It is a loose network of parties willing to buy/sell financial securities and credit instruments. The instruments traded are of high-credit quality and are short term, typically ninety days or less. Participants in this market involve banks and other financial institutions, the U.S. Treasury, and other governments, money market fund managers, and numerous specialized dealers.

MOODY'S INVESTORS SERVICE, INC.   A major investment advisory service. Publishes financial manuals that analyze many thousands of corporations that sell securities to the public. Continuously rates the investment quality of debt instruments issued by these corporations and by governments. These bond ratings are announced regularly and greatly influence investors' decisions.

MORAL OBLIGATION FUND   Typically, a state agency–issued security secured by the revenues of the financed project as well as a nonbinding promise by the superior level of government to use state funds to make up any deficiencies in the debt service reserve fund.

MORTGAGE-BACKED BOND   A bond that is a general obligation of the issuer and further secured by a pool of mortgages.

MORTGAGE-BACKED CERTIFICATE   A debt certificate secured by a pool of mortgages. Such certificates issued by Fannie Mae are secured by conventional mortgages and guaranteed for interest and principal.

MORTGAGE BOND   A debt security backed by a legal interest in specified real property of the issuer, pursuant to a trust indenture.

MORTGAGOR   A borrower who offers real property as loan collateral in the event of default.

MUNICIPAL BOND   Issued by a state or local government, or its agencies or authorities, or by a possession or territory of the United States. Such bonds are often called "tax-exempts," for interest paid on most of these issues is exempt from federal income taxes and also from state and local income taxes within the state of origin.

MUNICIPAL BOND INSURANCE   The payment of principal and interest is insured or guaranteed by an insurance carrier group.

MUNICIPAL NOTES   Debt securities issued by municipalities for a period of less than one year. (See also BANs, RANs, and TANs.)

MUNICIPALS   General term for securities issued by a state, local government entity, or agency thereof.

MUNICIPAL SECURITIES RULEMAKING BOARD (MSRB)   An independent, self-regulatory organization established by the Securities Act Amendments of 1975 that has rule-making authority over dealers, dealer banks, and brokers in municipal securities.

NATIONALLY RECOGNIZED MUNICIPAL SECURITIES INFORMATION REPOSITORY (NRMSIR)   Organizations authorized by the MSRB to receive from municipal securities underwriters and others disclosure materials pertaining to such securities and to retain those materials for public access.

NEGATIVE PLEDGE AGREEMENT   Agreement by an issuer or by the entity providing security for an issue not to create any new debt or to pledge or encumber its revenues and/or assets except under specified limitations or conditions.

NEGOTIABLE   The condition of an instrument, the legal interest in which can be transferred by delivery, without need for endorsement. Bearer securities are inherently negotiable, whereas registered securities can be rendered negotiable by the completion of a power of assignment.

NET INTEREST COST (NIC)   A common method of computing the interest expense to the issuer of bonds, which usually serves as the basis of award in a competitive sale. The NIC allows for premium and discount and represents the dollar amount of interest payable over the life of an issue, without taking into account the time value of funds.

"NO ACTION" LETTER   An SEC staff letter stating that the staff has determined not to recommend to the Commission that it take any enforcement or injunctive action against a particular issuer, or other party to a transaction, based on the facts and circumstances set forth in the letter to the staff that requested such a letter.

NO CALL PROVISION   An indenture provision prohibiting the optional redemption of a debt issue before a specified date or its maturity.

NOMINEE   A financial services entity that holds its customers' securities as custodian and/or as investment agent for trust portfolios; a mechanism for simplifying securities deliveries between banks, brokers, institutions, and individuals, as well as simplifying dividend and interest payments by issuers.

NONNEGOTIABLE   The condition of an instrument that requires additional certifications or documents to effect a delivery or transfer.

NO PAR VALUE   A security to which the issuer has not assigned a specific dollar value.

NONREFUNDABLE PROVISION   An indenture provision prohibiting the optional redemption of debt securities for a specified period by using funds borrowed at an interest rate less than that borne by such securities.

NOTICE OF REDEMPTION   A publication of the issuer's intention to call outstanding bonds prior to their stated maturity date, in accordance with the bond contract.

OBLIGOR   Every person who is liable upon a debt security, including a guarantor.

ODD LOT   Any number of shares of stock less than one hundred, except for a few issues.

OFFERING CIRCULAR   Usually prepared by the underwriters of an issue setting forth basic information on the issuer and the issue to be offered in the primary market.

OFFICIAL STATEMENT   A document published by a municipal issuer disclosing material information on a new issue, including purpose of issue, how such will be repaid, and the financial, economic, and social characteristics of the issuing entity.

ONE-AND-THE-SAME GUARANTEE   Certification used in the event that the signature of the security holder differs slightly from the name appearing on the face of the certificate.

OPEN-END MORTGAGE BONDS   Issued under an indenture that allows additional series of bonds to be issued in the future under the same indenture.

OPTION   A right to buy (call) or sell (put) a fixed amount of a given security (usually stock) at a specified price within a limited period of time.

ORIGINAL ISSUE DISCOUNT (OID)   The excess of the stated redemption price at maturity of a security over the issue price. Individual security holders are required by law to report as income a portion of the discount each year until maturity.

OVER-THE-COUNTER (OTC) MARKET   A securities market made up of securities dealers who may or may not be members of national exchanges. The OTC is a nationwide network of broker/dealers that buy and sell securities that are normally not listed on any national exchange.

OVER THE WINDOW   Direct delivery of a security made to the receiving window of a bank, brokerage house, or securities depository.

PAR VALUE   The face value of a share of stock or debt certificate having no relation to its market value.

PASS-THROUGH CERTIFICATES   Securities that represent undivided interests in pools of mortgages. Principal and interest payments from the mortgagors are passed through to certificate holders as received. Because mortgagors may prepay mortgages, the pass-through payments to certificate holders fluctuate.

PAYABLE DATE

1. The date established by a corporation's board of directors for payment of a dividend to the stockholders of record. Usually fifteen to twenty days after record date; or
2. The date fixed in an indenture or bond resolution for the payment of interest or principal.

PAYING AGENT   An institution, normally a bank, authorized by the issuer to pay the principal of (premium if any) and interest on any debt securities on behalf of the issuer.

POINT   One percent of par value. Because bond prices are quoted as a percentage of $1000, a point is worth $10 regardless of the actual denomination of a bond.

POISON DEBT   Issuance by a company of debt securities containing terms and provisions designed to discourage a hostile takeover.

POISON PILL   Rights or warrants granted to stockholders that become exercisable if a raider obtains a specified percentage of the company's shares.

POLLUTION CONTROL BONDS   A type of municipal bond, similar to industrial revenue bonds, whose proceeds are used to fund construction of air and water pollution control facilities.

POWER   A common term for a stock or bond assignment form that, when properly signed and executed, permits record ownership of securities to be transferred from seller to buyer.

PREFERRED STOCK   A hybrid security issue that is a cross between common stock and a bond issue. Holders of preferred stock are entitled to receive dividends (if declared), and liquidation payments (if any) before any profits are distributed to common stockholders. However, preferred shareholders are subordinated to bondholders. (Also called preference stock.)

PREFERRED STOCK, CUMULATIVE   Stock that is entitled to receive at a later date those dividends that accumulate (dividends in arrears) during profitless years. During such years, holders of common stock and regular preferred stock are generally not paid any dividends.

PRELIMINARY OFFICIAL STATEMENT (Red Herring or POS)   A preliminary version of the official statement used by the issuer or underwriters to describe the proposed issue of municipal bonds prior to the determination of an interest rate and offering price. Normally, no offer for acceptance of bonds can occur on the basis of the preliminary official statement, and a legend to that effect appears on the face of the document in red print, which gives the document its nickname—Red Herring.

PREMIUM   The amount a security may sell above its par value. In the case of a new issue of stock or bonds, the premium is the amount the market price rises over the original selling price.

PRICE-EARNINGS RATIO   The price of a share of stock divided by earnings per share for a twelve-month period.

PRIMARY MARKET
1. a term referring to organized national stock exchanges.
2. a term used to define the new issue market as opposed to the secondary market.

PRINCIPAL   The person for whom a broker executes an order or a dealer buying or selling for his/her own account. The term also may refer to the face amount of a bond.

PRINCIPAL TRANSFER AGENT   A corporate agent responsible for original issuance of securities and for registration of transfer of a security from one owner to another.

PRIVATE ACTIVITY BONDS   Bonds issued by a municipality that are not classified as governmental bonds. They are tax-exempt if they constitute qualified bonds as determined by the Tax Reform Act of 1986.

PRIVATE PLACEMENT   The sale (to a limited number of institutional investors) of securities not involving a public offering and exempt from registration under the Securities Act of 1933.

PROJECT NOTES   Municipal notes with maturities ranging from three to twelve months that provide short-term financing for federally assisted public housing and urban renewal projects. HUD may guarantee these notes as to principal and interest.

PROPERTY DIVIDENDS   Dividends in the form of actual property of the issuer, given to shareholders.

PROSPECTUS   Official document that must be given to buyers of new SEC-registered issues. Describes the issuer's products and business and the industries in which it competes, physical facilities, management background, etc., and presents historical financial statements. Describes the issue and intended use of the funds to be received. The SEC neither approves nor disapproves the prospectus, which is an abstract of the lengthy registration statement filed with the SEC.

PROXY   The authority or instrument that permits a shareholder's voting right to be granted to an agent of the shareholder. Proxy may also mean the person empowered to act as agent to vote in place of the shareholder.

"PRUDENT MAN" RULE   A common law standard of conduct, which requires a fiduciary or trustee to deal with the trust estate as if it were such fiduciary's or trustee's *own* property. In effect, a standard of due diligence and care.

PUBLIC HOUSING BOND   Debt securities issued by state or local governments to provide funds for loans made to developers, home buyers, and lending institutions that service home buyers. HUD (Department of Housing and Urban Development) may guarantee some of these bonds.

PUBLICLY HELD COMPANY   A company whose common stock has been registered with the SEC and sold to the general public.

PUBLIC SECURITIES ASSOCIATION   A national trade organization of dealers and dealer banks that underwrite, trade, and sell municipal, U.S. government, and federal agency securities.

PUBLIC UTILITY REVENUE BONDS   Municipal bonds issued to raise funds to create or improve electric, gas, water, and sewer services.

PUT BONDS   Securities issued that give the purchaser (owner) the right to redeem the bond at a fixed price (usually par) on a set date or dates.

PUT OPTION   A right, which may be evidenced by a certificate, given to the holder of a debt security to sell it back to the issuer, at one or more fixed future dates prior to the security's maturity.

RANs (Revenue Anticipation Notes)   Municipal notes maturing in less than one year, issued in expectation of revenue from particular projects.

RATING AGENCY   A private company that rates the creditworthiness of bonds; the three most well known are Moody's Investors Services, Standard & Poor's Corporation, and Fitch Investor's Service, Inc.

RATINGS   Evaluations of the credit quality of bonds and notes usually made by independent rating services. Ratings generally measure the probability of timely repayment of principal of and interest on debt securities.

REBATE CALCULATION   A mathematical calculation to determine if funds held in accounts for tax-free bond issues have earned more than permitted by law (an amount greater than interest paid on the outstanding tax-free bonds.) The calculation must be done annually and the excess segregated and remitted to the Internal Revenue Service every five years.

RECORD DATE
   1. The date set by the directors of the corporation that determines eligibility to receive the current declared dividend.
   2. In the case of bonds, the dates fixed in the indenture that determine eligibility to receive the current interest payment. The standard record dates are: the fifteenth day of the month preceding a payment on the first day of the following month; and the last business day of the month preceding payment on the fifteenth day of the following month.

RED HERRING   Short preliminary form of a prospectus available to potential investors in a new issue before the prospectus is published. Contains company and industry information, financial statements, etc., but does not indicate price per share, which is determined just before the issue is offered for sale. Called a red herring because the front cover bears a legend printed in red announcing that it is not the final official prospectus.

REDEMPTION PROVISIONS   The terms of the indenture giving the issuer the right or requiring the issuer to redeem or call all or a portion of an outstanding bond issue prior to its stated maturity date at a specified price, usually above par. Common types of such provisions include:

Optional Redemption: The issuer has the right to redeem bonds, usually after a stated date and at a premium, but is not required to do so.

Mandatory Redemption: The issuer is required to call outstanding bonds based on a predetermined schedule or as otherwise provided in the indenture. The issuer may also be allowed to make open market purchases or to solicit tenders in lieu of calling bonds.

Extraordinary Optional Redemption: The issuer has the right to call or redeem an issue of bonds upon the occurrence of a certain event, as opposed to redemption at any time during the period specified by the bonds' terms.

Extraordinary Mandatory Redemption: Usually derived from insurance proceeds or condemnation awards from destruction or seizure of property or from unspent bond proceeds; the purpose is to prevent bonds becoming arbitrage bonds.

REFERENCE AGENT   A bank appointed to calculate, notify, and publish the interest rate applicable for each interest period for a floating rate note issued according to a formula contained in the applicable agreement. Also sometimes referred to as Agent Bank.

REFUNDING   Issuance of new debt securities to replace an older issue.

REGISTERED BOND   A bond whose owner's name and address are recorded on the issuer's books.

REGISTERED (BOND) AS TO INTEREST ONLY   A bond in bearer form without coupons, the owner's name and address being recorded on the issuer's books so that interest checks can be sent automatically when due.

REGISTERED (BOND) AS TO PRINCIPAL ONLY   A bond in bearer form with coupons, whose owner's name is inscribed on the certificate and recorded on the issuer's books.

REGISTERED INTEREST   Interest paid to holders of debt securities in fully registered form (normally by check or draft) by the obligor or its paying agent.

REGISTRAR   A bank, normally the trustee or fiscal agent for a debt issue, maintaining the records of bearer certificates registered as to principal only and certificates in fully registered form. The Registrar processes registrations of transfer and exchanges of such securities.

REGISTRATION OF TRANSFER   The process whereby the title of ownership of a security is changed on the corporation's or its agents' books of record.

REGISTRATION STATEMENT   The statement (or document), including any amendment thereto filed with the SEC in connection with the proposed sale of securities to the public.

REINVESTMENT AGENT   A bank, usually the paying agent, designated by the issuer of securities, to reinvest upon the written request of the security holders all or part of the dividends or interest to be paid to such security holders.

REMARKETING AGENT   A bank or investment banking firm that agrees to remarket bonds tendered or "put" by their owners after the initial issuance.

REMEDIES   The legal means available to the trustee under an indenture in the event the issuer fails to comply with its obligations under the covenants in the indenture (subject to stated preconditions of time and actions by the trustee).

REMICS (Real Estate Mortgage Investment Conduits)   Tax-advantaged vehicles created by the Tax Reform Act of 1986 to hold real estate mortgages and issue securities representing interests in those mortgages.

REPO   See "Repurchase Agreement."

REPURCHASE AGREEMENT (Repo)   A contract between a seller and buyer of U.S. government and other securities under which the seller agrees to buy back the securities at a specified price after a stated period of time. In the interim, the seller has the use of the buyer's funds, for which service the seller pays a fee.

RESERVE FUNDS   In revenue bond issues, specific funds earmarked for purposes of securing the payment of debt service (principal and interest), making extraordinary repairs of replacements or covering other areas of risk exposure to bondholders. Reserve funds can either be capitalized from bond proceeds or built up over a period of time from project revenues.

RESOLUTION TRUST CORPORATION (RTC)   Established by the Financial Institutions Reform, Recovery, and Enforcement Act of 1989, the RTC is responsible for the sale and disposition of assets of thrift institutions that were in receivership on November 1, 1989, or that fail after that date until August 9, 1992.

RESTRICTED STOCK   See "Letter stock."

RETIREMENT   See "Redemption."

REVENUE BOND   A state or local government bond on which the interest and principal payments are met from the revenues produced by the project financed by the bond issue. Water, sewer, gas and electrical facilities, roads, and bridges are typical projects.

REVERSE STOCK SPLIT An action by which the issuer replaces outstanding very low-priced stock with a reduced number of shares. A proportionate increase in the market price per share results.

RIGHTS See "Subscription Rights."

ROUND LOT The usual unit of trading in a security or a multiple thereof. A round lot of stock is generally one hundred shares; for bonds, $1,000 par value is typical.

RULE 144 A A regulation of the SEC, under the 33 Act, that exempts from registration the resale of privately placed securities to "qualified" institutional investors, thus creating a viable secondary market for such securities.

RULE 17F-1 A regulation of the SEC, under the 34 Act, dealing with the loss, counterfeiting, and theft of securities (other than U.S. government securities). It established the Securities Information Center (SIC) as a central agency to maintain a file of reported lost or stolen securities and to respond to inquiries related to such.

RULE 10B-5 A regulation of the SEC, under the 34 act, that makes it unlawful for any person to employ any devise, scheme, or artifice to defraud; to make any untrue statement of a material fact; or omit any true statement of a material fact or to omit a material fact necessary in order to make the statements made, in light of the circumstances under which they were made, not misleading; or to engage in any act, practice, or course of business that operates or would operate as a fraud or deceit upon any person, in connection with the purchase or sale of any security.

SALLIE MAE (Student Loan Marketing Association) A privately owned, U.S. government–sponsored corporation founded to help students repay educational loans. Under its warehousing program, Sallie Mae makes large loans to lending institutions that grant loans to students. Under its loan purchase program, it makes direct loans to students.

SAMURAI BOND A Japanese yen-denominated bond marketed in Japan by a non-Japanese entity.

SATISFACTION AND DISCHARGE When an obligor has discharged all its obligations to security holders, trustee, and agents under the terms of an indenture, the trustee will then satisfy the mortgage or lien and release the property to the obligor.

SCRIP AGENT Scrip is a temporary certificate issued to a stockholder that represents fractional shares. Before the scrip expiration date, the stockholder must decide to round up or down to full shares. The scrip agent issues shares or cash as required to the investor upon surrender of scrip.

SECONDARY MARKET
> 1. A term referring to the trading of securities not listed on an organized exchange.
> 2. A term used to describe the trading of securities other than a new issue.

SECURITIES   A general term that includes all instruments representing evidence of ownership or debt, issued by a corporation. It also refers to debt issued by tax-exempt entities. Securities usually refer to stock and bond certificates.

SECURITIES ACT OF 1933 (33 Act)   Statute requiring, among other provisions, the filing of a registration statement before the public sale of certain securities, disclosing substantial information on the issuer and the issue, as well as provisions for furnishing prospectuses upon distribution of such security.

SECURITIES ACTS AMENDMENTS OF 1975   A federal law amending previous securities statutes, designed to provide additional protection for investors. Among other provisions it establishes standards of performance for securities dealers, clearing corporations, depositories, and transfer agents.

SECURITIES AND EXCHANGE ACT OF 1934 (34 Act)   Statute providing for the regulation of securities exchanges and over-the-counter markets, as well as the establishment of the SEC.

SECURITIES AND EXCHANGE COMMISSION (SEC)   An agency created by the Congress to regulate the securities market for the protection of investors.

SECURITIES INDUSTRY ASSOCIATION   A not-for-profit industry organization representing the interests of investment banking and securities brokerage firms.

SELLING SYNDICATE   A group of securities dealers whose members each buy small portions of a new issue from the underwriters, which are then sold to the investing public in the primary market, supplementing the selling efforts of the underwriters.

SERIAL ISSUE   Bonds that mature on a scheduled basis over several years, thereby allowing the issuer to amortize the loan over a period of years. Almost all municipal bonds are serial issues.

SETTLEMENT DATE   The date on which a contract for the purchase or sale of securities is to be completed or settled.

SHELF REGISTRATION   A procedure allowed by the SEC permitting qualified issuers to file a single registration covering its long-term securities' financing plans for a two-year period.

SHELLS   Special envelopes designed to hold bond coupons being presented for payment. Each shell must contain only the coupons from the same bond issue with the same payment date and all owned by one owner. The name, address, and taxpayer identification number of the owner are written on the shell, which is presented to the paying agent for payment.

SIGNATURE GUARANTEE   A guarantee (normally obtained from a commercial bank or securities dealer) of the seller's endorsement, which appears on the stock or bond power accompanying the security being sold. Such guarantee affirms (1) that the person who signed the power is the person in whose name the securities are registered or is authorized to act on behalf of such person and (2) that the signature is genuine.

SINKING FUND   The periodic retirement of portions of a debt issue before the stated maturity of the issue (by repayment or purchase), pursuant to the terms of an indenture.

SLGS (State and Local Government Series)   U.S. government securities issued to municipalities at various interest rates to ensure that issues of tax-free bonds do not violate arbitrage rules. These bonds do not trade in the open market and are carried in book-entry form only at the Federal Reserve Bank.

SLMA (Student Loan Marketing Association)   See "Sallie Mae."

SPECIAL DRAWING RIGHT (SDR)   A composite currency unit designed by the International Monetary Fund based upon a standard basket system of valuation.

SPECIAL TAX BONDS   Municipal bonds backed by the proceeds of a specific related tax, e.g., a highway bond issue secured by gasoline taxes.

SPONSORED ADR   An American Depository Receipt issue "sponsored" by the foreign corporation whose securities the ADR represents; the corporation pays the fees of a securities transaction, such as transfer of dividend fee, cable charge, postage, and insurance.

SPREAD   The difference between the bid and asked price (or yield) in the quotation of a security, or between two security issues of differing maturities; the difference between an underwriter's bid on a bond issue and its resale price to the public; or the difference between what funds cost a bank and the rate at which its lends such funds.

STANDARD & POOR'S   A financial services firm that rates bonds and offers financial publications and computerized information that provide pertinent facts about thousands of issues.

STANDBY LETTER OF CREDIT   A letter of credit that covers an amount equal to the principal of and a portion of the interest on the bonds and that provides for a single draw in the event of the acceleration of the bonds.

STOCK   A general term meaning common and preferred stock and also stock certificates. (See "Classes of Stock.")

STOCK/BOND POWER   See "Power."

STOCK CERTIFICATE   Printed and signed certificate that is evidence of an investor's partial ownership of a corporation.

STOCK DIVIDEND   See "Dividend, stock."

STOCK EXCHANGE   An organized, regulated marketplace where officials of brokerage firms meet physically to buy and sell securities as directed by their customers, the investors.

STOCK LOAN   Stock lent by one institution to another in exchange for an amount of cash equivalent to the market value of the stock.

STOCK POWER   See "Power."

STOCK REGISTRAR   A corporate agent whose principal function is to prevent issuance of more stock than the issuer's board of directors has authorized to be outstanding.

STOCK SPLIT   Division of an outstanding stock issue into a larger number of shares, resulting in a lower market value per share.

STOCKHOLDER   The owner of common or preferred stock of a corporation. Also called "Shareholder."

STOP ORDER   A notification by a holder of a security requesting the obligor, the trustee, or its agent(s) not to effect registration or transfer of such security nor to pay it upon maturity or redemption.

STREET NAME   When a certificate is registered in the name of a bank, brokerage firm, or its nominee, it is said to be in street name. Securities are sometimes registered in this manner to facilitate delivery, collection of dividends and proxies, etc. All securities purchased on margin must be registered in street name.

STRIPPING   Removing interest coupons from bonds, with the intent of selling the coupons separately from the certificates.

SUBORDINATED   Describes a security whose claim on the issuer's assets ranks below that of another class of security.

SUBROGATION   The substitution of one person for another with reference to a lawful claim, demand, or right.

SUBSCRIPTION
1. The procedure of buying securities by exercising rights or warrants.
2. The purchase of part of a bond issue on original issuance by members of the selling syndicate.

SUBSCRIPTION AGENT
1. A bank, acting on behalf of a lead manager, appointed to collect the initial proceeds of a bond issue and pay them at the closing to the borrower.
2. Also acts as transfer agent when a stockholder exercises his/her rights or warrants. See "Subscription Right."

SUBSCRIPTION RIGHT   A right present in some common stock issues that gives the holder of common stock the right to buy a proportionate amount of any new common stock issued by the company ahead of the general public.

SURETY BOND   A bond from a surety company by which the replacement of a lost or stolen security is made possible.

SYNDICATE   A group of underwriters formed to purchase (i.e., underwrite) a new issue of securities from the issuer and offer it for resale to the general public. One member will be designated as lead manager to administer the syndicate's operations.

TAC (Transfer Agent Custodian)   A transfer agent depository service designed to speed the transfer process when new physical certificates must be issued.

TAKE OR PAY CONTRACT   A sales agreement that requires the purchaser to pay the seller whether or not goods or services are available and, if available, whether or not the purchaser uses them.

TAKE OUT   A permanent loan commitment. The proceeds of the permanent loan are used to pay or "take out" the interim construction loan.

TAKEOVER   A merger, or merger offer, that may be resisted by the company to be acquired. See "Tender Offer."

TANs (Tax Anticipation Notes)   The most common type of municipal note, sold in anticipation of tax receipts.

TAX ANTICIPATION BILL   A special class of security, occasionally sold by the U.S. Treasury to corporations. Usually matures one week after a tax date but can be turned in at full value when taxes are paid, thus earning an extra week's interest.

TAX ANTICIPATION NOTES   See "TANs."

TAX EXEMPTS   See "Municipal Bonds."

TAXPAYER IDENTIFICATION NUMBER   The number assigned by the Internal Revenue Service to persons or entities required to file tax returns or pay Social Security tax.

TAX TAILS   A series of short-term taxable bonds added to a tax-exempt bond issue for the purpose of paying cost of issuance expenses not allowed under federal regulation by reason of exceeding 2 percent of bond proceeds.

T-BILLS (Treasury bills)   Securities with a life of one year or less, sold on a discount basis in minimum denomination of $10,000, in book-entry form only.

TENANTS BY THE ENTIRETY   Denotes joint ownership by two persons. Each has full ownership but cannot dispose of the security without permission from the other. Upon the death of one, the survivor becomes the full owner.

TENANTS IN COMMON   Denotes ownership by two or more persons, without right of survivorship. Upon death of one owner, the decedent's share passes to his or her heirs.

TENDER AGENT   Private financial institution, usually a bank, that will serve as agent for the trustee or the remarketing agent to accept bonds that are tendered or "put" under the provisions allowing the bondholders to require the bond issuer to repurchase the bonds at certain times or intervals.

TENDER OFFER
> 1. Offer to buy made to holders of a particular issue by a third party. Detailed offer is made by public announcement in newspapers and by personal letter to each stockholder.
> 2. Offer by a corporation to buy back a portion of its own shares. This is normally done when the corporation has excess cash and when it believes the market price of its stock is unreasonably low. The reduced share count may result in higher future dividends-per-share on the remaining shares.

TERM BOND   A bond whose principal amount is repaid at maturity date of the issue. An issue of term bonds has one maturity date for all bonds in the issue.

TOMBSTONE   An advertisement placed by underwriters announcing the sale of a new issue, reflecting the name of the issuer, description of the issue, interest rate, maturity, and names of the underwriting syndicate.

TRADE DATE   Date on which a securities trade was actually made (executed).

TRANSFER   See "Registration of Transfer."

TRANSFER AGENT   An agent responsible for the registration of transfer of registered securities from one holder to another. (See also "Bond Registrar.")

TRANSFER AGENT CUSTODIAN   See "TAC."

TRANSFEREE   The assignee (new security holder).

TREASURY BILLS   See "T-Bills."

TREASURY BOND   An obligation of the federal government with a maturity ranging from ten to over forty years. Available in registered and book-entry form; bearer form sales were ended January 1, 1983.

TREASURY NOTE   An obligation of the federal government with a maturity of at least one year but not more than ten years. Large-denomination notes are purchased extensively by commercial banks. U.S. government agencies, and pension trust funds.

TREASURY STOCK   Previously issued stock that a corporation has bought back from its stockholders. Not entitled to vote or receive dividends.

TRUST   A relationship in which one person or institution (the trustee) holds legal title to property that the trustee administers for the benefit of the beneficiary. (See also "Fiduciary.")

TRUSTEE   A trust company or bank having trust powers authorized to enter into an indenture with an issuer of debt securities with such to be issued under and in accordance with the provisions of the indenture.

TRUST FUNDS   A term for cash held by a fiduciary under an indenture or other agreement.

TRUST INDENTURE ACT (TIA)   The Trust Indenture Act of 1939 as amended. The Act contains, among other provisions, standards for the eligibility and qualification of trustees for public issues.

TURNAROUND RULES   A set of rules imposed on registered transfer agents by the SEC pursuant to section 17A of the 34 Act.

UNDERWRITER   An entity that purchases a large block of securities at the initial offering. The underwriter acts as a wholesaler between the issuing entity and a syndicate or between the issuing entity and the general investing public.

UNDERWRITING AGREEMENT   The contract between the investment banker and the corporation, containing the final terms, conditions, and prices of the issue.

UNIFORM ACTS   A series of model acts promulgated by the Commissioners on Uniform State Laws designed to standardize state laws governing a particular activity. State legislatures may modify their existing laws or conform new laws to the proposed Uniform Act.

UNIFORM COMMERCIAL CODE (UCC)   Designed to facilitate business and commercial transactions and to establish a uniform set of rules, the Code has been adopted in forty-nine states, the District of Columbia, and the Virgin Islands. Articles 8 (investment securities) and 9 (secured transactions) are of particular importance to transfer agents and bond registrars.

UNISSUED STOCK   Stock that has been authorized by the directors of a corporation but not yet sold.

UNIT INVESTMENT TRUST (Municipal)   A fixed portfolio of municipal bonds sold to investors in fractional, undivided interests, usually in denominations of $1,000. The same bonds are held in the portfolio until they mature or are redeemed.

UNLIMITED (BLANK) DENOMINATION BONDS   Bonds in fully registered form without preprinted dollar denominations appearing thereon. Upon complying with certain conditions, such bonds meet New York Stock Exchange requirements for good delivery.

UNSECURED DEBT   An obligation not backed by the pledge of an issuer's assets. Unsecured bonds are called debentures or notes.

UNSPONSORED ADRs   American Depository Receipts not "sponsored" by the foreign corporation whose securities underlie the ADRs. The investor must pay the fees associated with issuing or canceling the ADR, collecting and paying dividends, etc.

U.S. SAVINGS NOTES   See "Freedom Shares."

VARIABLE RATE SECURITIES   Floating or variable interest rates on either short- or long-term securities whose interest rates are adjusted as often as weekly, monthly, or quarterly. The rate is a function of a market indicator, such as the prime rate, the U.S. Treasury Bill or Bond rate, or a combination of both.

VOTING RIGHT   A legal right of holders of common stock and, in some instances, of holders of preferred stock arising out of their ownership of a corporation.

VOTING TRUST CERTIFICATE (VTC)   A certificate issued by a commercial bank in exchange for common stock deposited under terms of a voting trust. These certificates are comparable to the common stock itself but do not carry voting privileges in the affairs of the underlying corporation.

WARRANT   A certificate, either attached to a debt security or issued separately, that gives the holder the right to purchase a specified amount of another security (either a debt security or common stock) issued by the borrower, for a limited period of time, which may lapse before, on, or after the maturity of the debt security.

WILL   A legal declaration of a person's directions as to how securities and other property owned at the time of death should be distributed after the person's death.

YANKEE BOND   A U.S. dollar–denominated bond marketed publicly in the United States by a non-U.S. corporation or governmental entity. A registration statement for such issue is required to be filed with the SEC.

YIELD TO MATURITY   The discount rate that makes the present value of a bond's cash flow until maturity equal to the bond's market price. Yield to maturity takes into account the total interest payments to be received until maturity, plus the difference between current market price and the par value the investor will receive at maturity; it expresses this total return on capital on an annual basis.

ZERO COUPON   A term applied to debt securities that are offered initially by the issuer without provision for periodic payments of interest, the final payment at maturity covering principal and all interest due for the life of the security.

Index